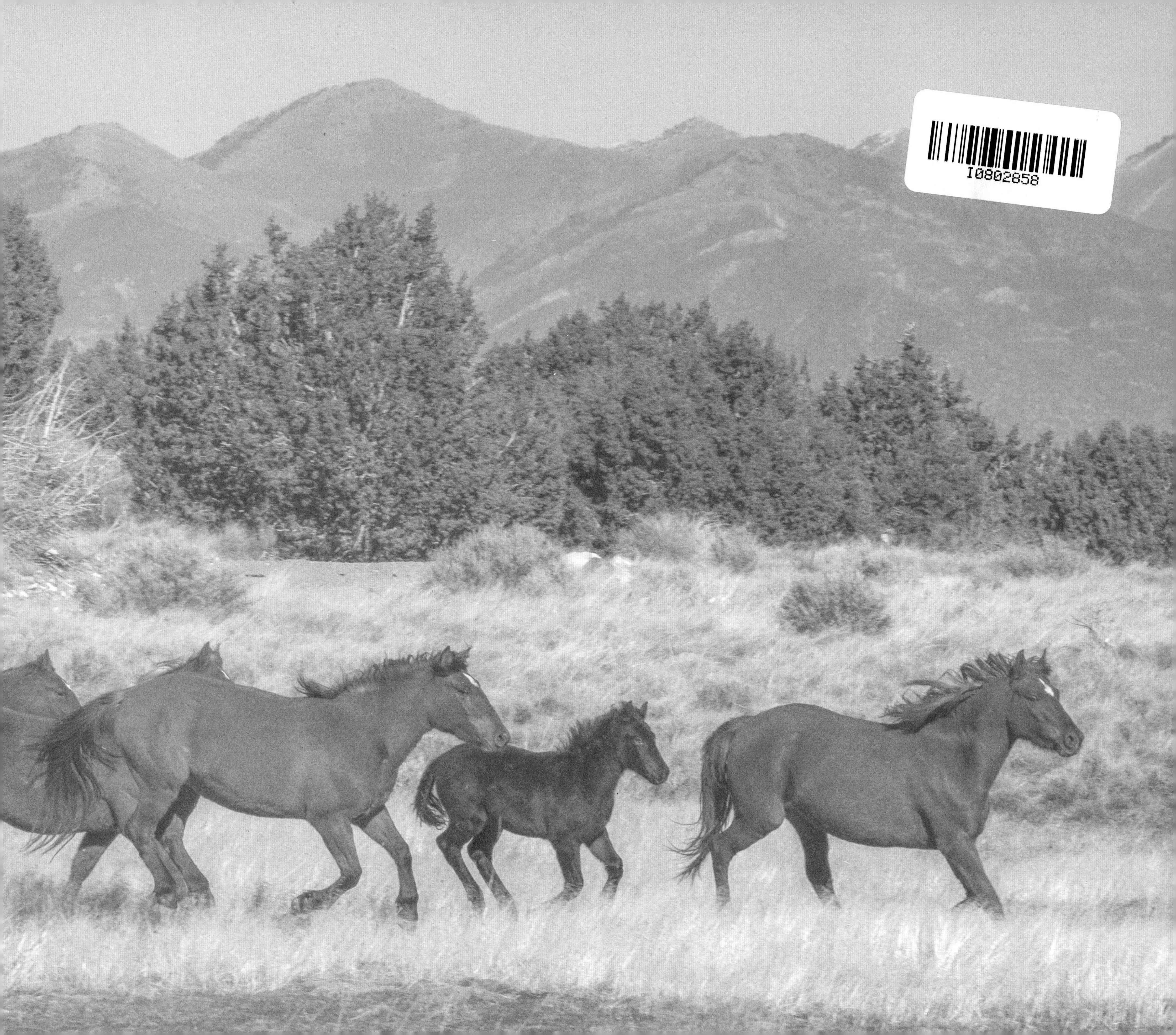

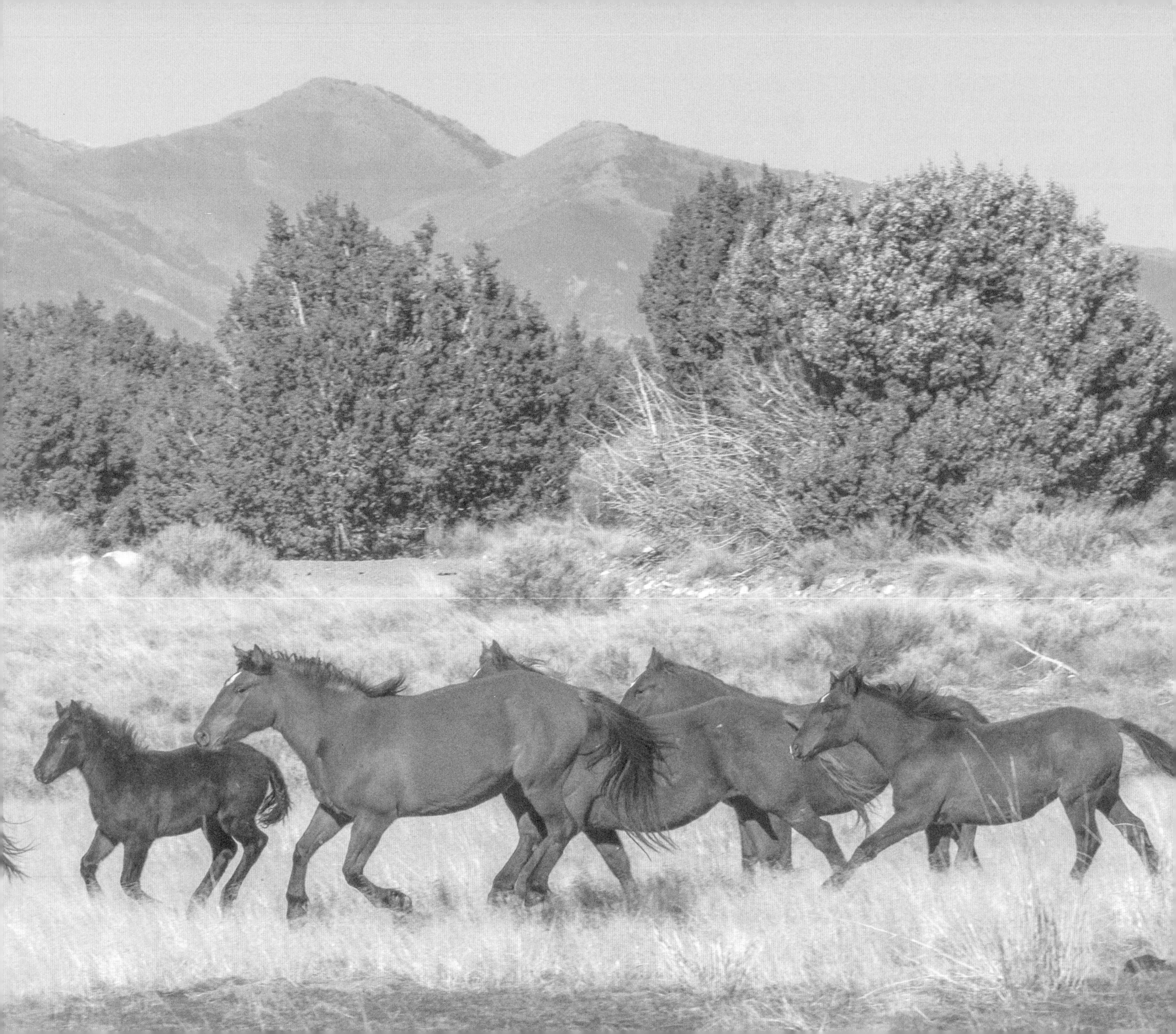

WILD HORSES OF THE WEST

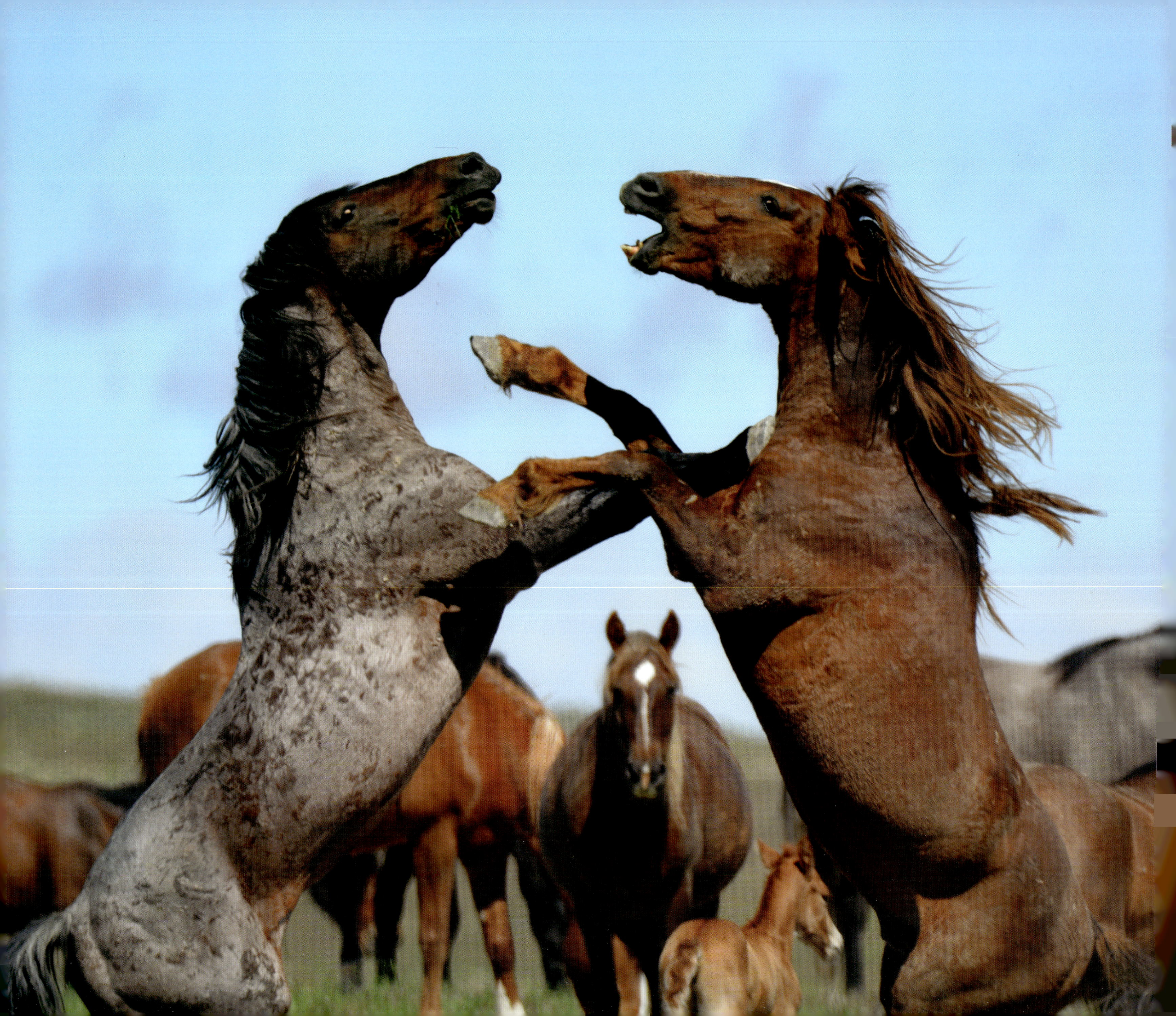

WILD HORSES · OF THE · WEST

JAN DRAKE

GIBBS SMITH
TO ENRICH AND INSPIRE HUMANKIND

Dedicated to Don Cook, Tim Clark, and Peggy Spear for always being willing to go out on adventures to photograph wild horses with me, and to Stella Tavilla for introducing them to me.

First Edition

27 26 25 24 9 8 7 6

Published by
Gibbs Smith
P.O. Box 667
Layton, Utah 84041

1.800.835.4993 orders
www.gibbs-smith.com

Designed by Jeff Wincapaw

Gibbs Smith books are printed on paper produced from sustainable PEFC-certified forest/controlled wood source. Learn more at www.pefc.org.
Printed and bound in China

Library of Congress Control Number: 2020933161
ISBN: 978-1-4236-5530-5

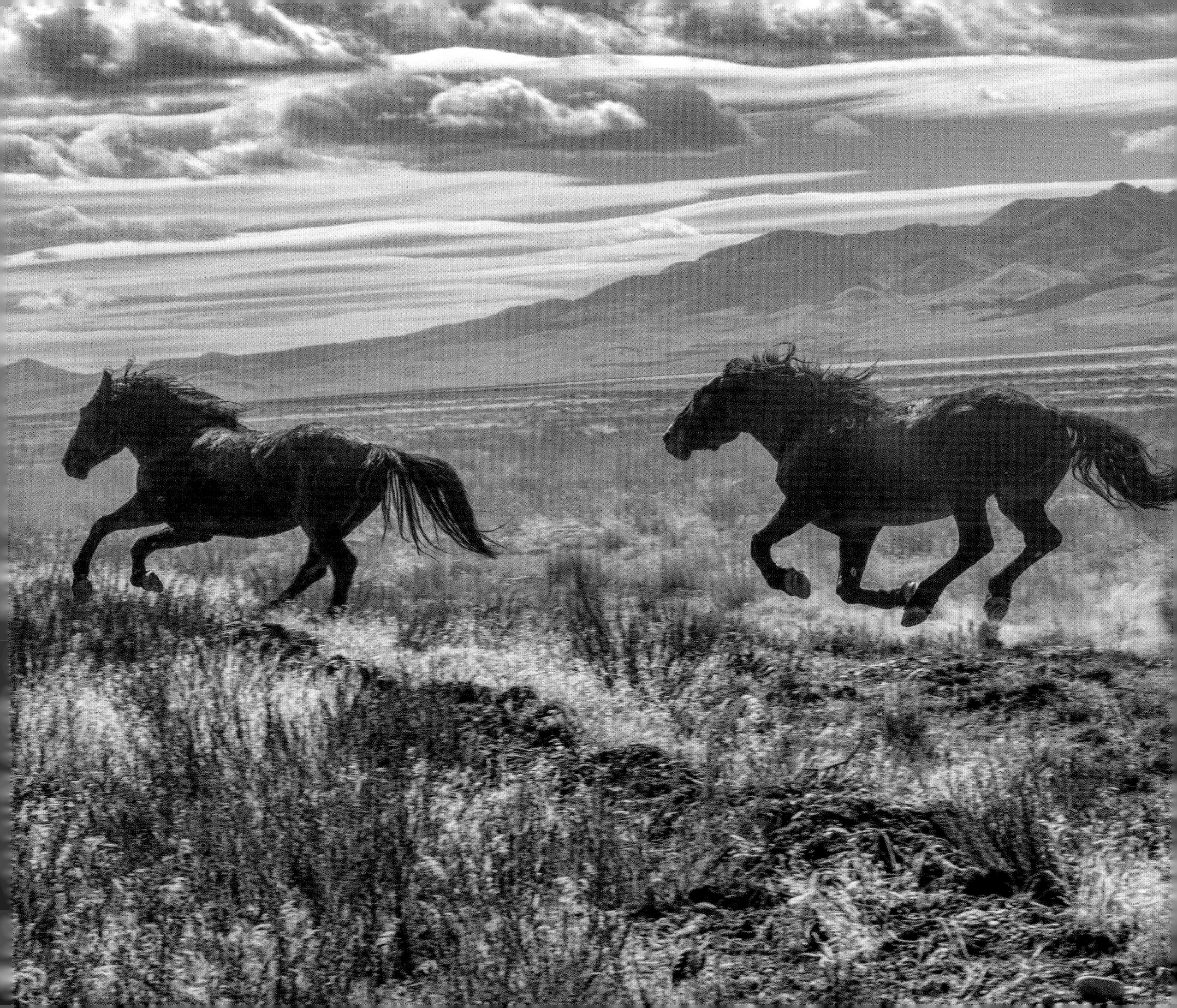

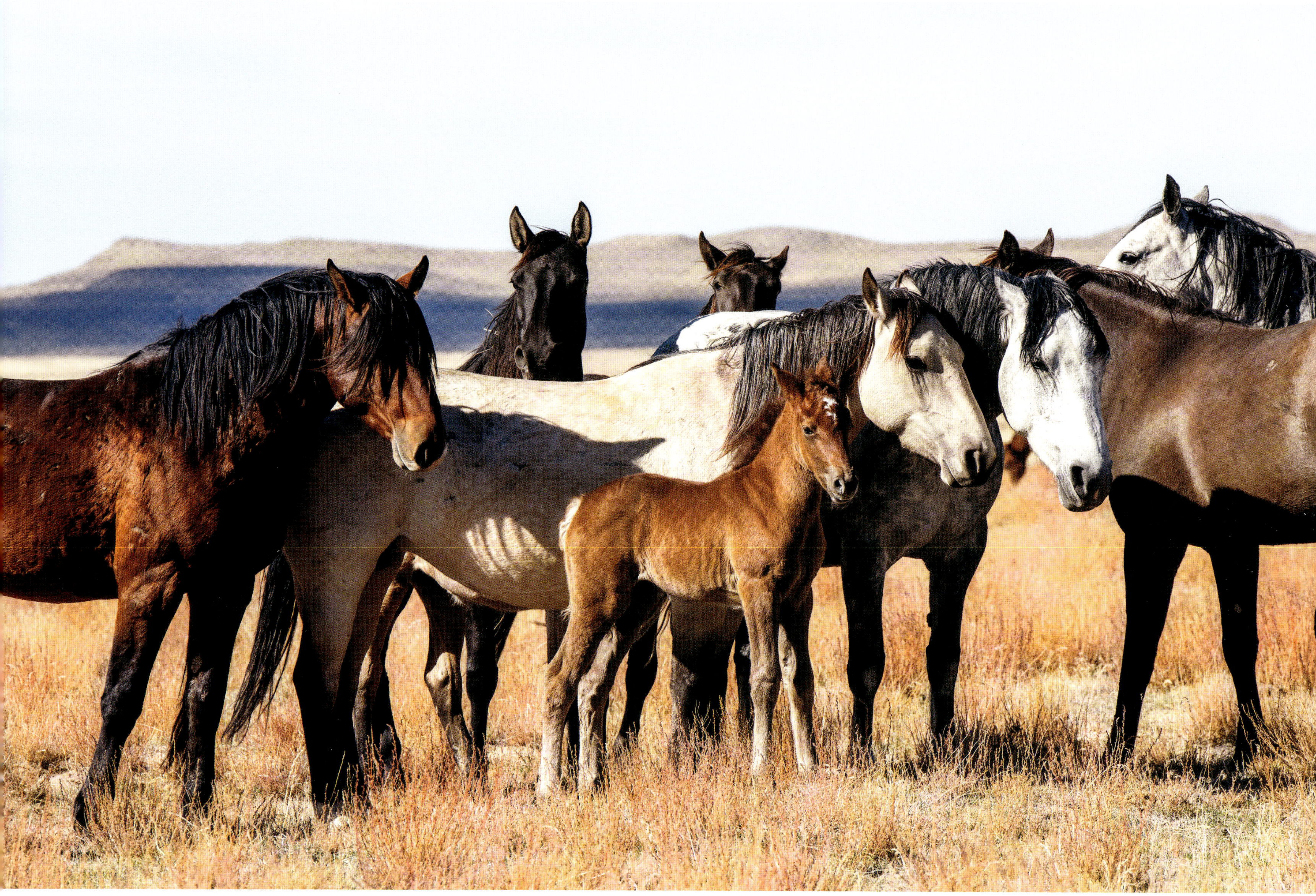

Contents

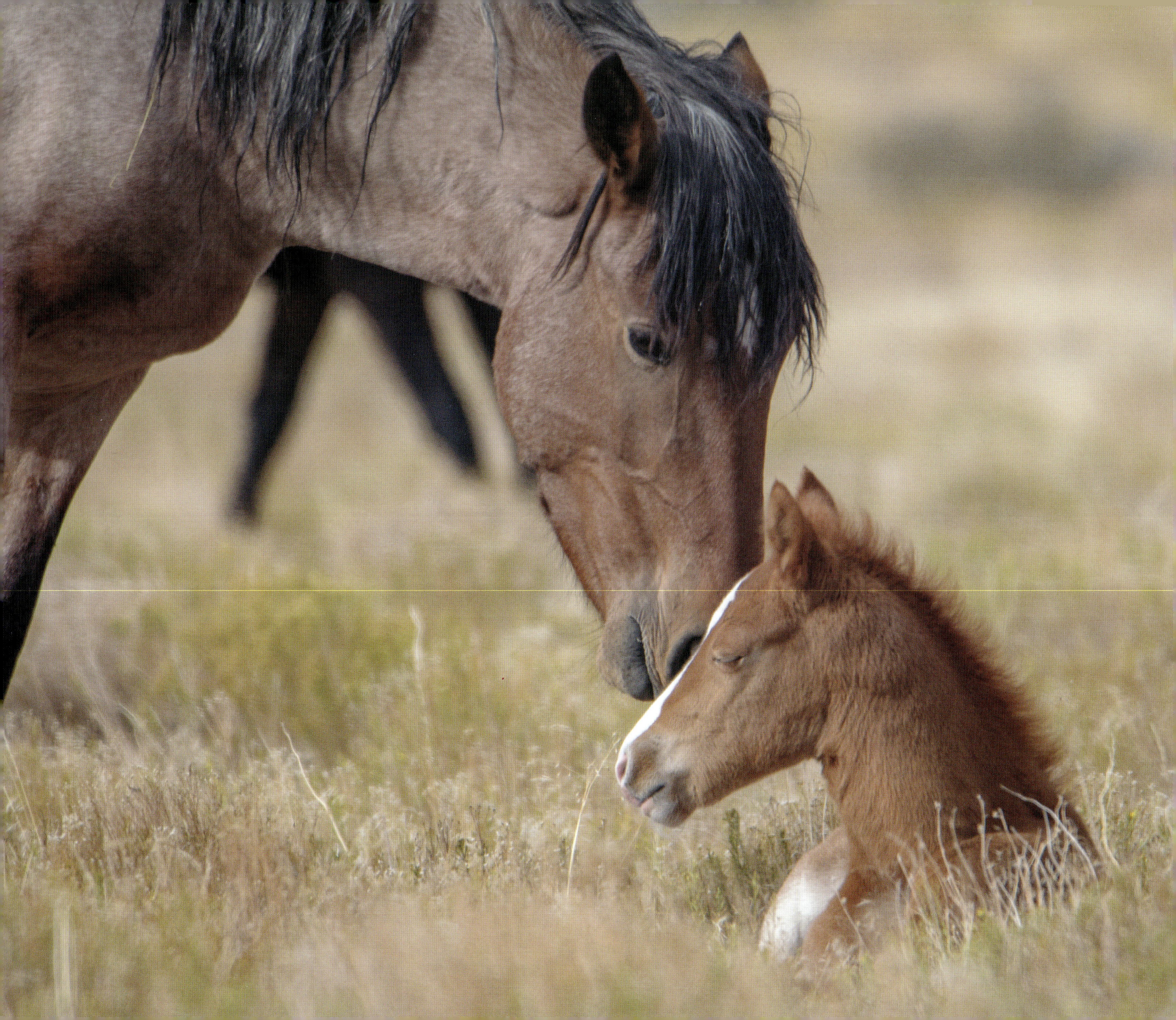

Foreword

I was one of those girls born with the horse gene. As far back as I can remember, I have always loved horses. I grew up on a small farm in northeastern Utah. Once I had my own horse, an Arabian/Quarter gelding, I spent every waking moment of my free time chasing my wild imagination. I explored every crevice and gulch within fifteen miles of my home on horseback.

As time passed and my gelding climbed in age, my husband, Cliff, and I decided we were ready to add another horse to our family. We had the time to commit to another horse's training, but not the money. Thoroughbred horses require registration papers and other expenses. A mustang seemed like the perfect answer. Wild mustangs can be adopted for only $125, and they are hardy animals. They are easily nourished on the basics without extra additives in their feed, and their hard feet are less likely to need shoes.

What Cliff and I learned about mustang adoption intrigued us, so we dug deeper. I became involved in a mustang adoption support organization and was suddenly immersed in all things mustang. Around the same time, I was introduced to a local trainer who had a contract with the Bureau of Land Management to gentle older geldings. I asked him if I could assist him, hoping to learn to gentle my own horse someday. Gentling is the more "natural horsemanship" terminology, as opposed to "breaking" a horse. When gentling, you are working with the horses' natural curiosities and mannerisms, not forcing your will on them. I quickly learned that gentling a wild mustang could be an incredible experience.

Within a few months, Cliff and I made plans to attend a satellite adoption where a trainer was present doing gentling demonstrations. In the span of two hours, he had taken an untouched horse and was sitting on him bareback. Mustangs are a flight or fight prey animal—their instincts tell them, with every cell in their body, to run away from danger. For this mustang to trust a human to make that first contact is remarkable.

A cute little red roan mare with a big blaze face caught my eye as we browsed the facility. I could tell she was dominant, even though she was the smallest in the pen; the other mares were very respectful of her space. Something told me she was the one. She stayed at the back of her pen, but no matter where I was in the building, I always found her looking at me. I don't know if it was her small size or the fact that she wouldn't interact with any other human, but no one else bid on her that day. I ended up taking my little roan mare home and named her Ladybug.

She was feisty and opinionated in the beginning. But we soon reached a balance and understanding and her gentling training progressed. Our training began with a chute that let us touch her but kept us all safe. We did this daily to start, working with her for ten to twenty minutes at a time. Gradually, as Ladybug could tolerate longer sessions, we increased the length. She wasn't comfortable with us touching her face early on, so we settled on her shoulders. We continued with a lot of touching, petting, and massaging until she was comfortable with us touching her anywhere.

I have now had Ladybug for over twenty years. We have done and seen some pretty amazing things. We have ridden in Fort Meade, South Dakota, where Custer was stationed; we've explored the North Rim of the Grand Canyon, the Redwood Forest of Northern California, and the desert landscape of Death Valley. We've trekked into the beautiful red hoodoo formations in Bryce Canyon and the Badlands of North Dakota.

It was an emotional venture, taking an animal who was completely wild, gentling her, and experiencing her become my best friend. There is no experience like it—this is a journey I have wanted to share with others for some time now.

My adoption of Ladybug set me on a course of volunteering for the BLM Wild Horse & Burro program. Cliff and I also founded Intermountain Wild Horse & Burro Advisors, a nonprofit adopter support organization. We mentor through email and phone calls, and we even visit adopters in person to offer new ideas for gentling or just an encouraging word. In our mentoring, we have seen the amazing connections that adopters make with their mustangs. Wild horses are unlike domestic horses—they know how to live without human intervention. When they *choose* to trust a human, it is an unexplainable, heartfelt connection that is amazing to be a part of.

Wild horses of the West deserve to be seen as successful equine partners and legendary icons of the American West. Their spirit encourages us to live free and reach for our dreams. Jan's photographs capture that spirit, bringing it into our homes and making it part of our lives.

—Janet Tipton
Founder, Intermountain Wild Horse & Burro Advisors

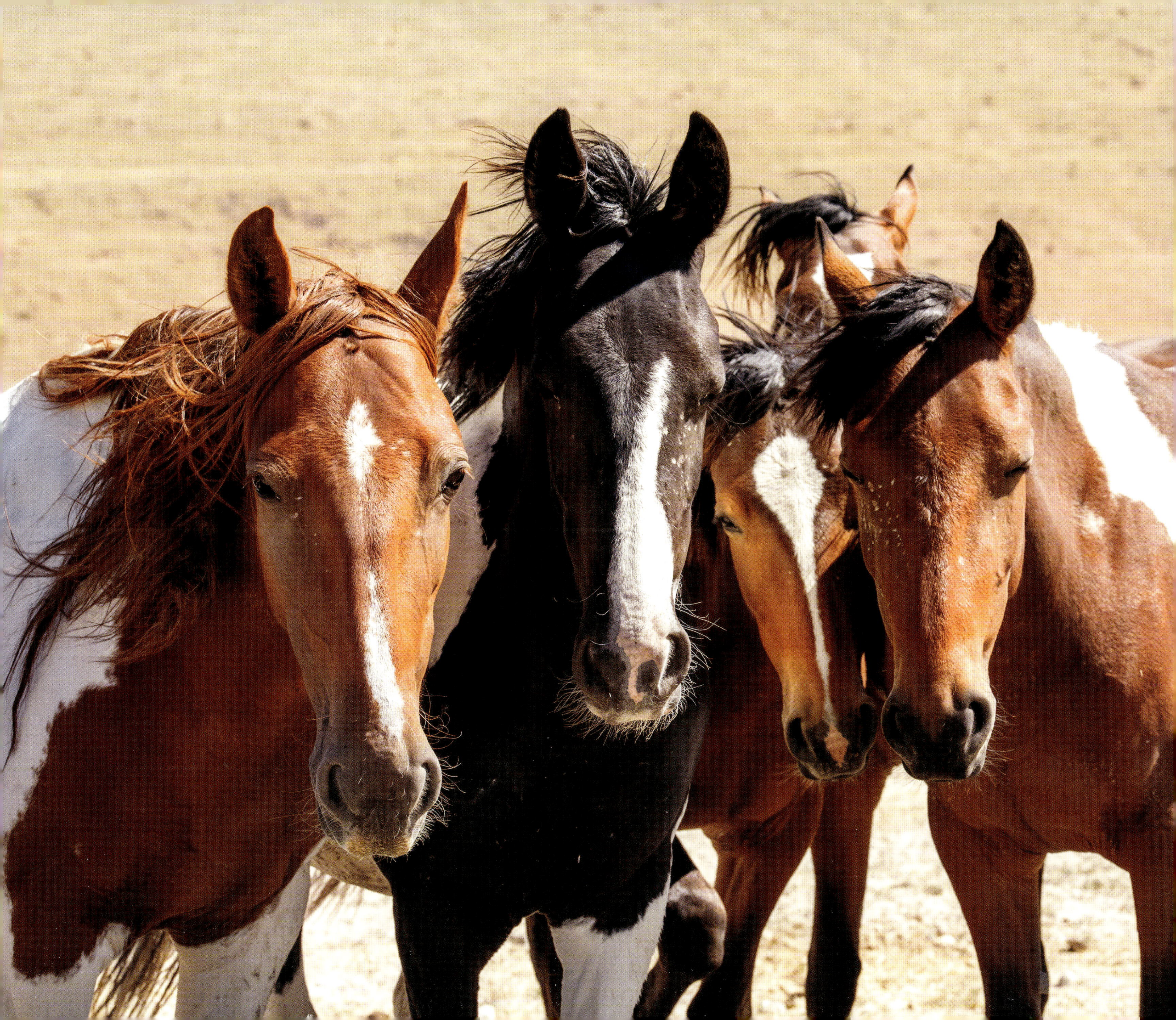

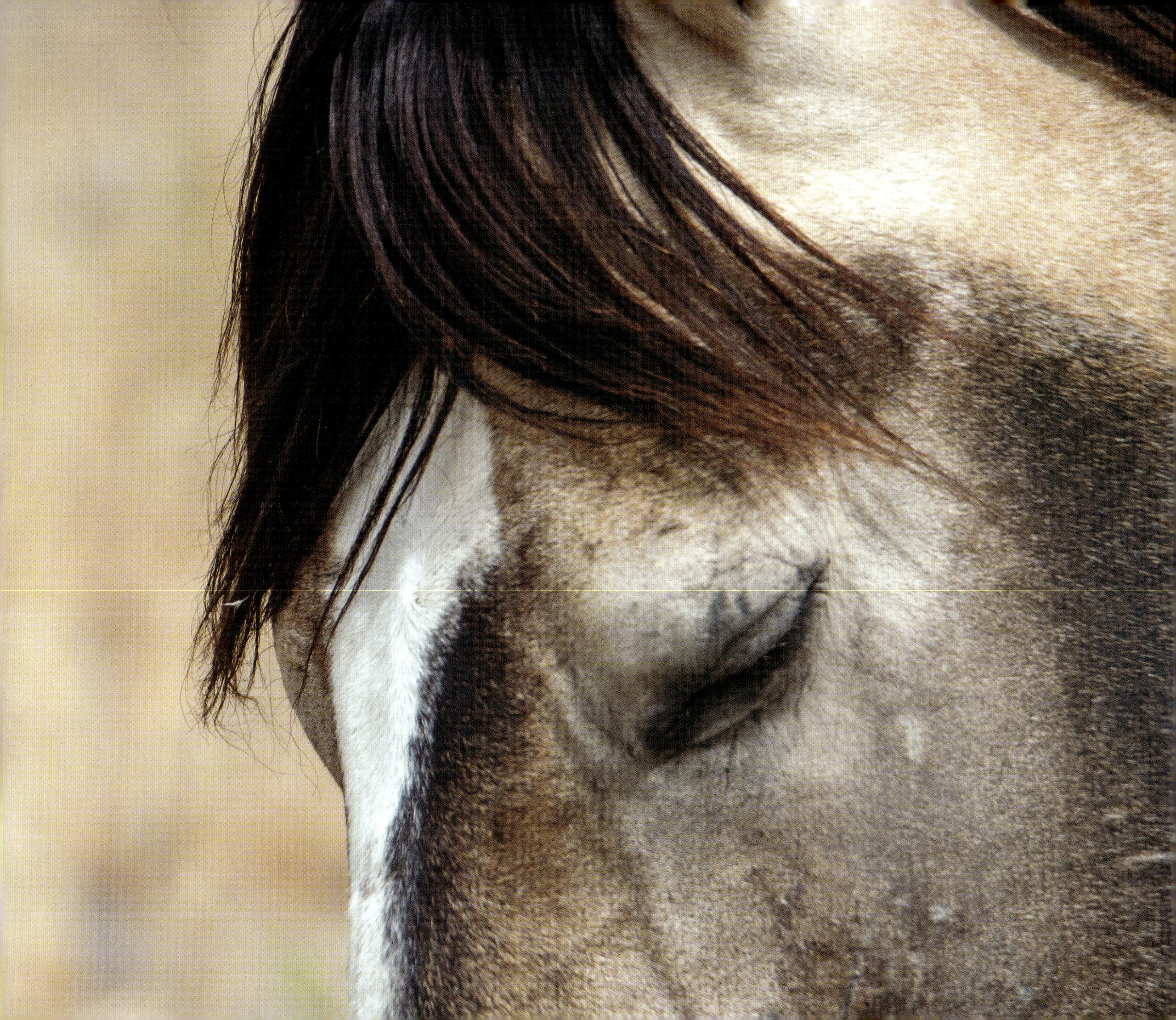

INTRODUCTION

My journey photographing wild horses began on a hot July day in 2006 with a black-and-white pinto band stallion. I ventured out to the desert with a good friend and her niece, hoping to find the herd. None of us had any idea where to start. We found a large waterhole along the road, sat on the hillside a good distance away, and waited. After a couple of hours, we spotted something off in the distance. It wasn't just one band—several bands of wild horses streamed into the waterhole (unlike today, when the bands form a mob). Each band kept its distance, taking their turn at the waterhole then moving to the other side of the waterhole to get a good roll in the dirt. One band stallion caught my eye. He was a black-and-white pinto—rather small for a band stallion, but unwilling to back down from any challenges. I was enraptured.

Horses have been a part of my life since I was a kid. Our first horse was one of the ones you see outside of the local Kmart store—the kind you put a quarter into for a three-minute ride. Our father, a route salesman for a beverage company, purchased one of the full-size horses for us when I was four years old. It was a beautiful black-and-white paint. We spent many enjoyable hours playing on that horse.

After a while, the mechanical horse was not enough—I convinced our father that it was time for the real deal. We ended up with a Shetland pony named Tiny and a big gray Quarter horse named Snowfire. We were city kids, but we would go out to the country to ride the horses on a friend's ranch—these were the happiest days of my childhood.

Horses took a back seat when I got older and busier with school, work, and friends. I traded the horses for a more convenient mode of transportation: my car. That Ford Galaxy 500 soon segued into having multiple Ford Mustangs—which helped define my love for the mustang horse in some crazy way. This was also around the time I picked up photography, a hobby that would serve me into adulthood. Photography became, for me, an outlet that allowed me to create and manipulate photographs into different types of art. I started with film, of course, developing my own pictures, and continued to photograph architecture and wildlife until I moved out west. There, I discovered the mustangs.

I relocated to Utah in 2001, enticed by the mountains, the open land, the recreation—everything the Mountain West boasts of. It was here that I became a volunteer for the equestrian program at the National Ability Center and my story with horses continued.

I started out in the fall of 2001 doing volunteer work, and by summer I was getting involved in the summer camps and taking care of the horses. The time spent at the National Ability Center taught me much about the world of adaptive recreation and the ways that horses help humans. I was intrigued—I wanted to continue in this field. When a paid position for a full-time employee to help manage the horses became available, I threw my hat in the ring—to my surprise, they hired me.

I never thought I'd be working in a therapeutic recreation job or taking care of animals. My goal had been to work in business. It was an interesting learning curve, to say the least. I didn't know a lot about taking care of horses at the time, but there is a lot to be said about on-the-job training. Shortly after accepting the position, a horse of ours went down in the snow and I knew we had to get him to the clinic for medical attention as fast as possible. I had never driven a horse trailer before, but it was just one of those instances when you tackle the situation and let your instincts take over—everything will turn out all right. And that's what I've been doing ever since. It's turned into twenty years of working with horses and the people who love them. I wouldn't trade it for the world.

Horses are empathic—when you're looking into their eyes, whether they're wild or gentled, there's no question that these majestic creatures have soul. While horses may have started out as war steeds and agriculture beasts of burden, their purpose has evolved beyond the utilitarian to the emotional and spiritual. Horses can change lives—not just with their speed or strength, but with the connection they make with people in recreation and therapy.

I've happily kept one foot in each world—the world of the wild mustang and that of the gentled therapy horse—for fourteen years now. It's an incredible privilege to care for these national treasures in a way that honors the horse, the land, and the people with whom horses create such remarkable connections. In order to help keep the wild horses healthy and safe, organizations such as the Wild Horses of America Foundation and Intermountain Wild Horse & Burro Advisors work with the Bureau of Land Management (BLM) to gather, gentle, and adopt out mustangs every year. Without this cooperation, the herds become overpopulated, inbreeding becomes a problem, and food and water become too scarce for the number of horses the land is trying to support. Instead, mustangs (previously domesticated horses who became feral from living on their own for hundreds of years) are humanely gathered and adopted out to families and equestrian programs. I've adopted several wild mustangs to use in our program at the National Ability Center and it's remarkable to witness what these horses can do.

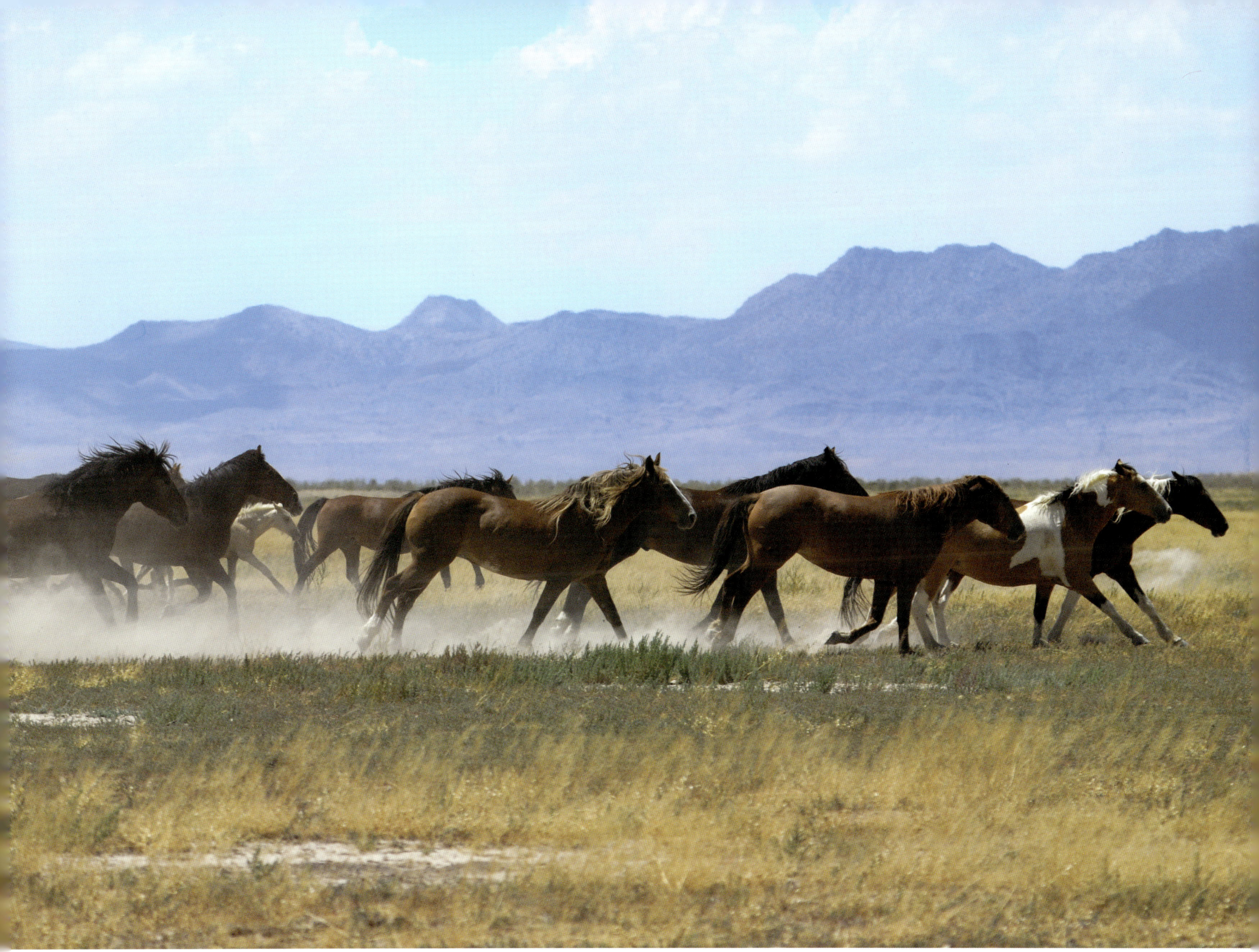

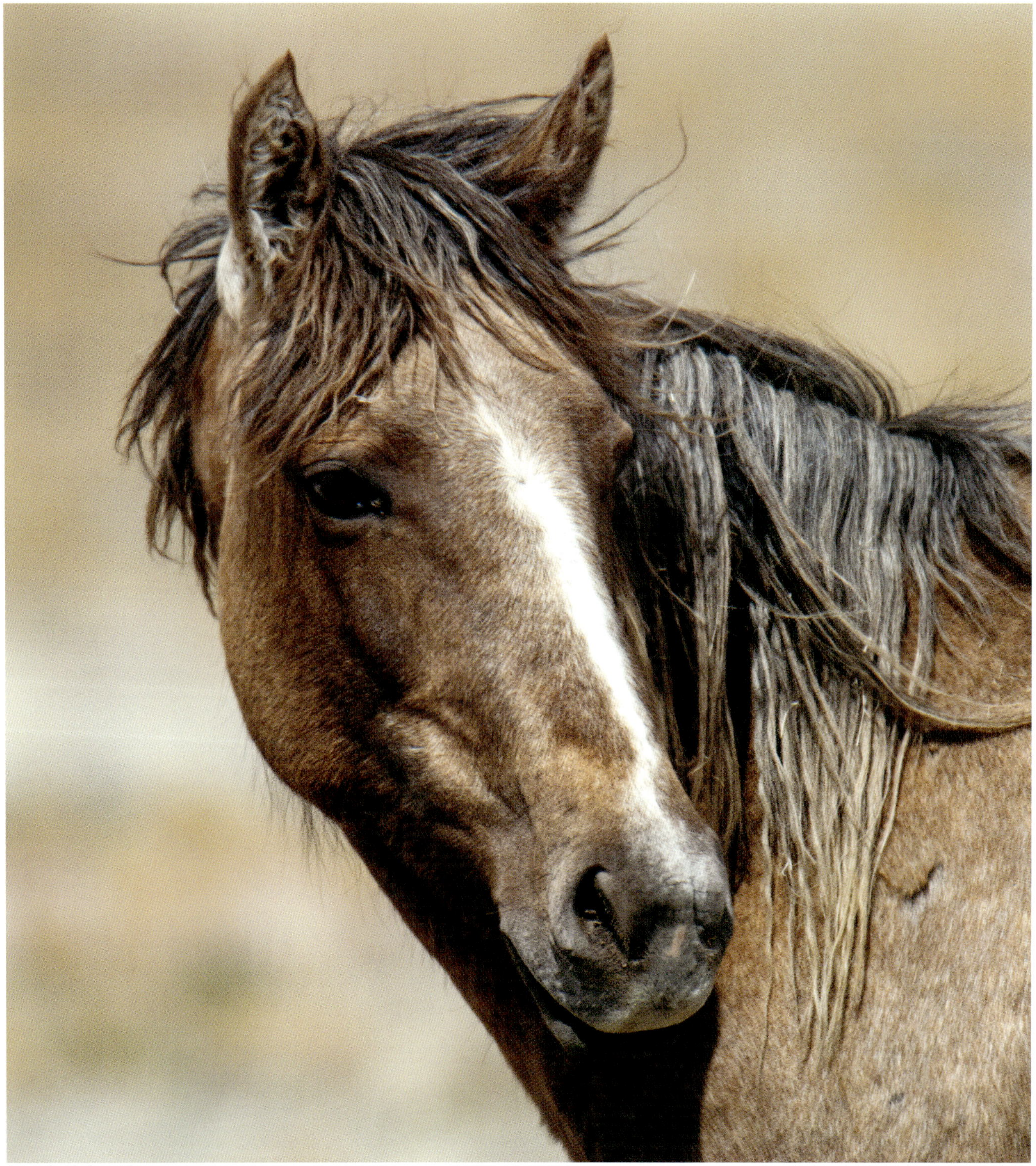

Horses don't have judgment. They accept you for what you are. If you come in pissy and cranky, they're going to be pissy and cranky right back. But with the kids at the National Ability Center—kids who may have a host of physical or cognitive disabilities—the horses' behavior completely changes. They know, "We have to take care of this kid."

I see that all the time in our program. The horses have a sixth sense. They know who's on their back. If a staff member is schooling them, they can be a little ornery. But when a participant is in their saddle, they're so intuitive. Especially with kids on the autism spectrum. A lot of people think of the mustang as a mutt—as not really understood or accepted in the domesticated horse world. They're wild. Kids on the autism spectrum aren't always understood by society, either. When you put the two together, the results are amazing.

As just one example, I adopted two wild horses for our program at the National Ability Center and gentled them. Two young adults on the autism spectrum began working with them in the pen (not riding the horses but teaching them commands and how to accept a saddle). One of them built the confidence to help others at the barn. I once found him comfortably chatting with perfect strangers about horses at a fundraising event. All this from a supposedly nonsocial kid. What the horses do in my line of work is just phenomenal. The horses accept you as you are, and it changes people.

Since that July day in 2006, I've made more than a hundred drives out to see the wild horses. I often bring my camera, but sometimes I go alone, just to enjoy watching them. It's peaceful—no cellular service, not many people around. Wild horses, most of the time, are pretty quiet—they've got their heads down, just grazing the wild landscapes under an open sky. It's cathartic to be in such peaceful surroundings. Season after season, it never gets old.

I had the pleasure of photographing the black-and-white pinto until 2017, when he just disappeared. He was one of the first wild horses to capture my heart and I'll always be grateful to him for leading me toward an enduring love for the wild horses of the West. It is my passion to photograph them, to assist in improving their living conditions alongside the Wild Horses of America Foundation and the BLM, and to welcome gentled mustangs into much-needed therapy programs that prove, time after time, the power horses have to heal and to connect.

—Jan Drake

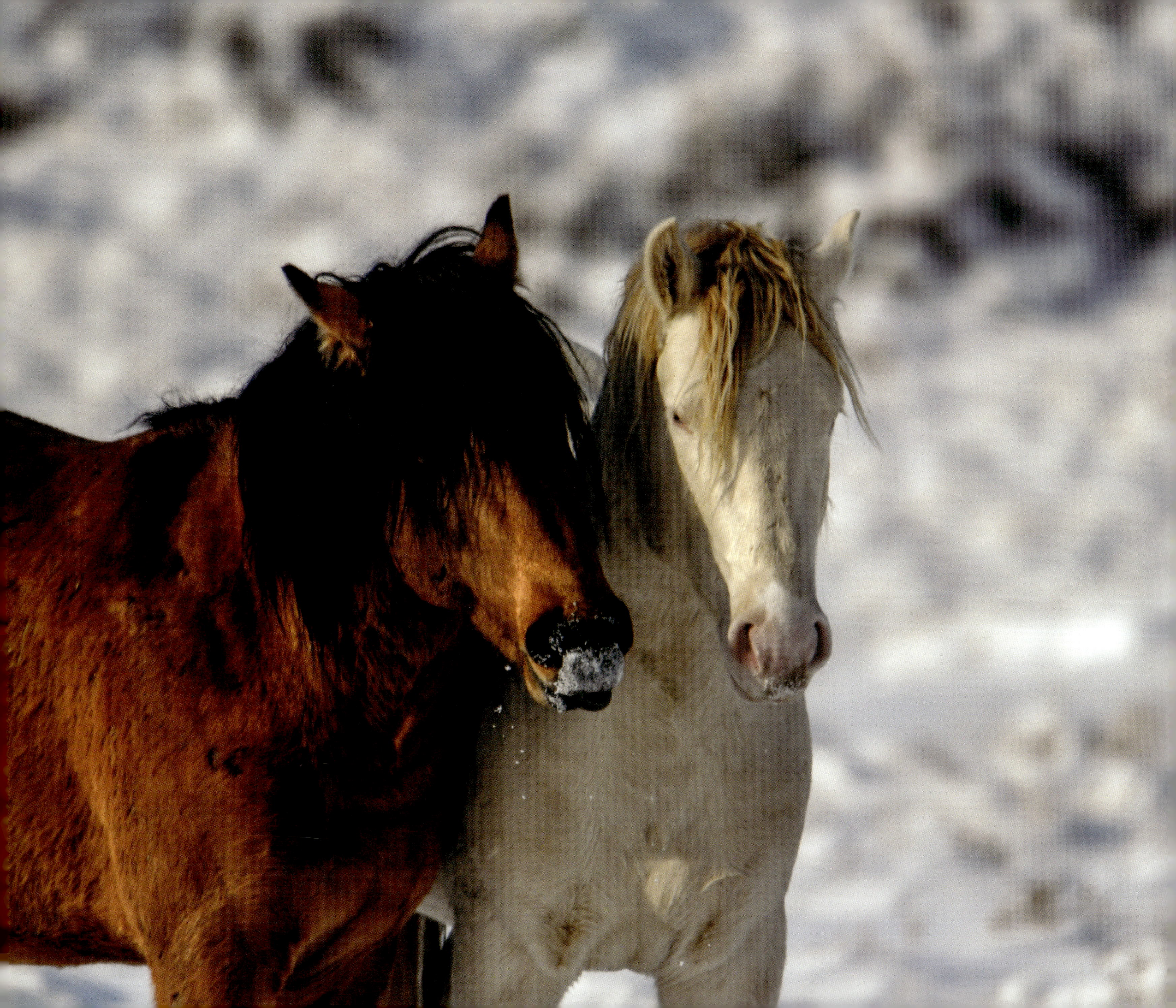

than twenty horses, led by an alpha mare. Older and more experienced, the alpha mare decides when the band moves on for water or food.

While the mare leads the band, the breeding stallion travels at the rear, protecting the mares from threats or other bachelor stallions. Young bachelor stallions in the band may act as lieutenants, keeping other bachelor stallions away, always under the careful watch of the band stallion.

Mares push their offspring colts out of the band around the age of two or three to find a bachelor band to run with. Young mares are either taken by these young bachelor stallions or leave to form separate bands.

For wild horses, these bands become like families, providing social interaction, warmth, and companionship. Wild horses in the band will groom one another, and the mares of the group keep a watchful eye, acting as protectors for even the foals who aren't their own. These herds rely on each other, ensure safety, and form bonds that last years.

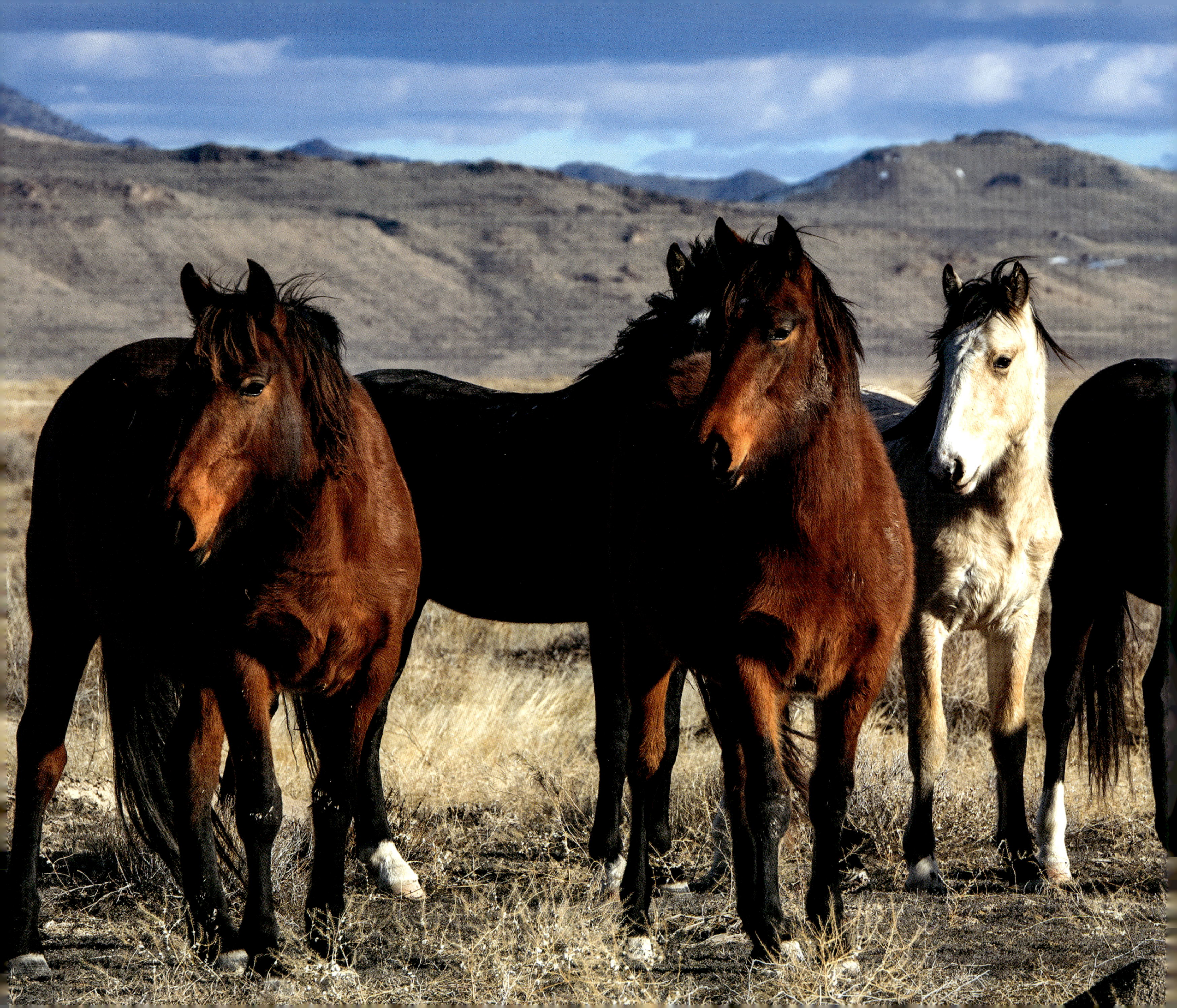

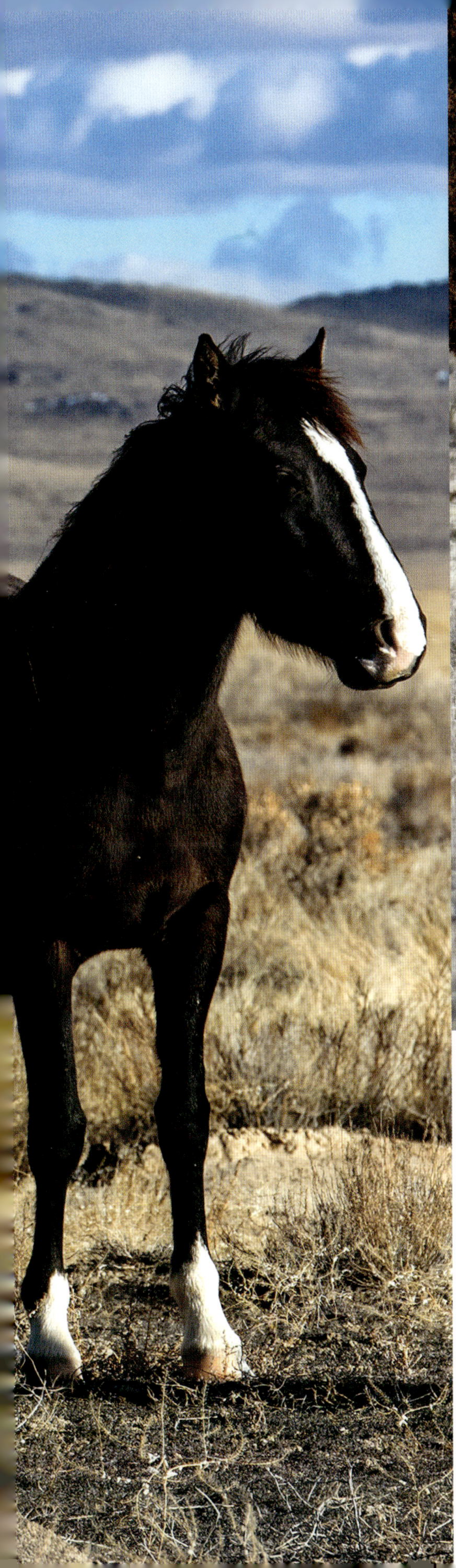

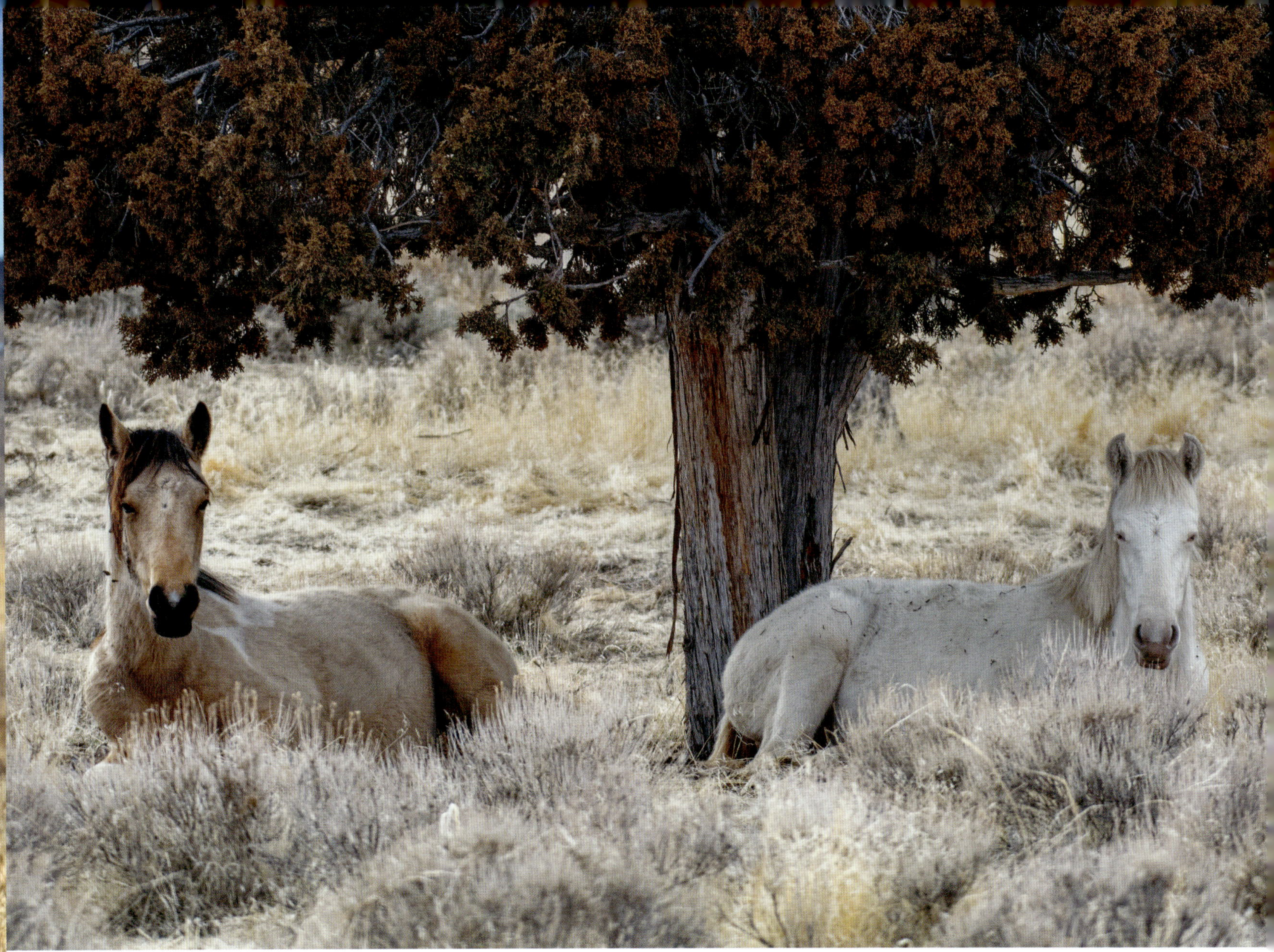

Left: A group of young bachelor stallions curiously watch the range.

Above: Young mares enjoy a nap on a warm winter's day.

Next page: A large family band amongst the many colors of springtime in the desert.

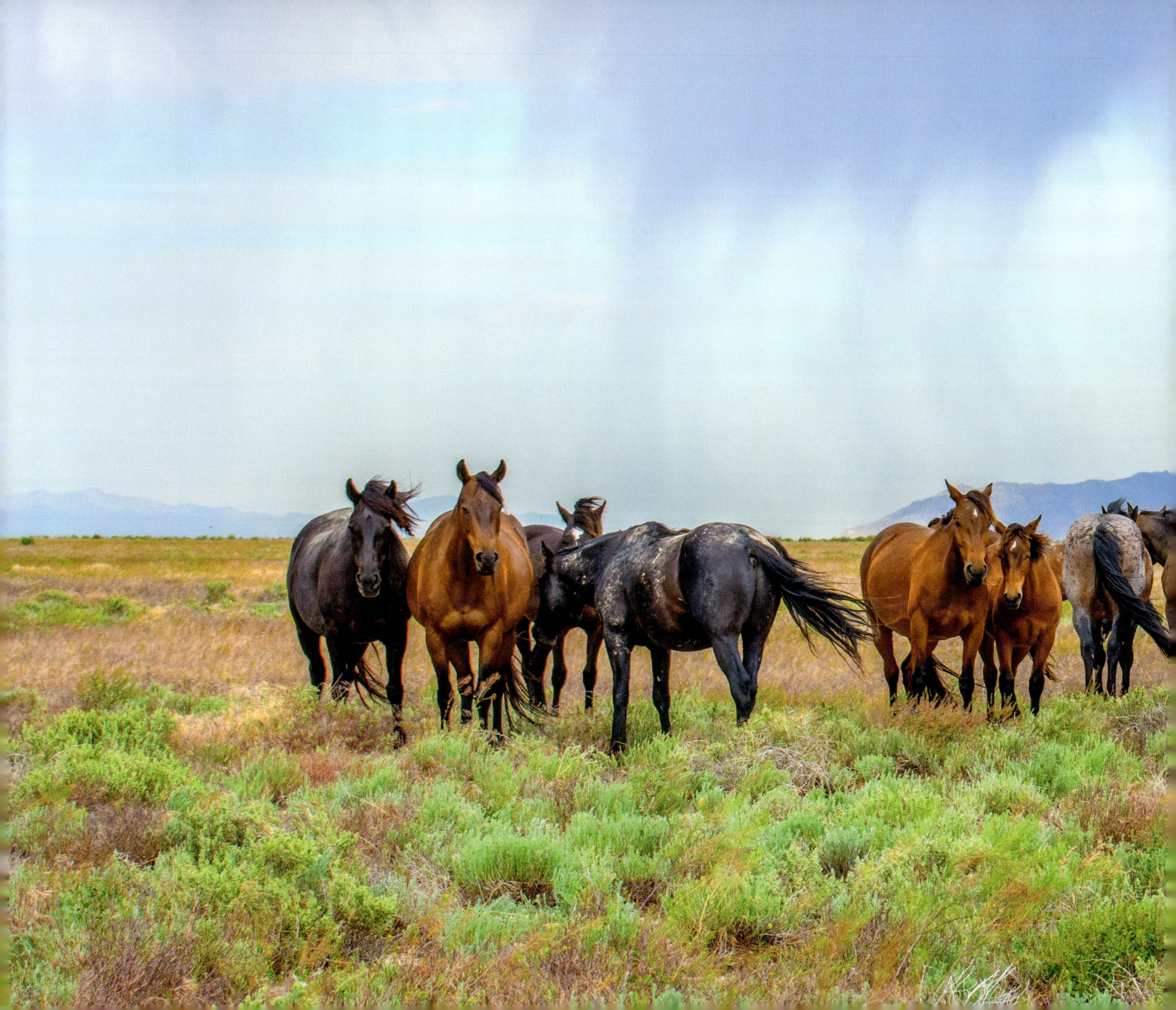

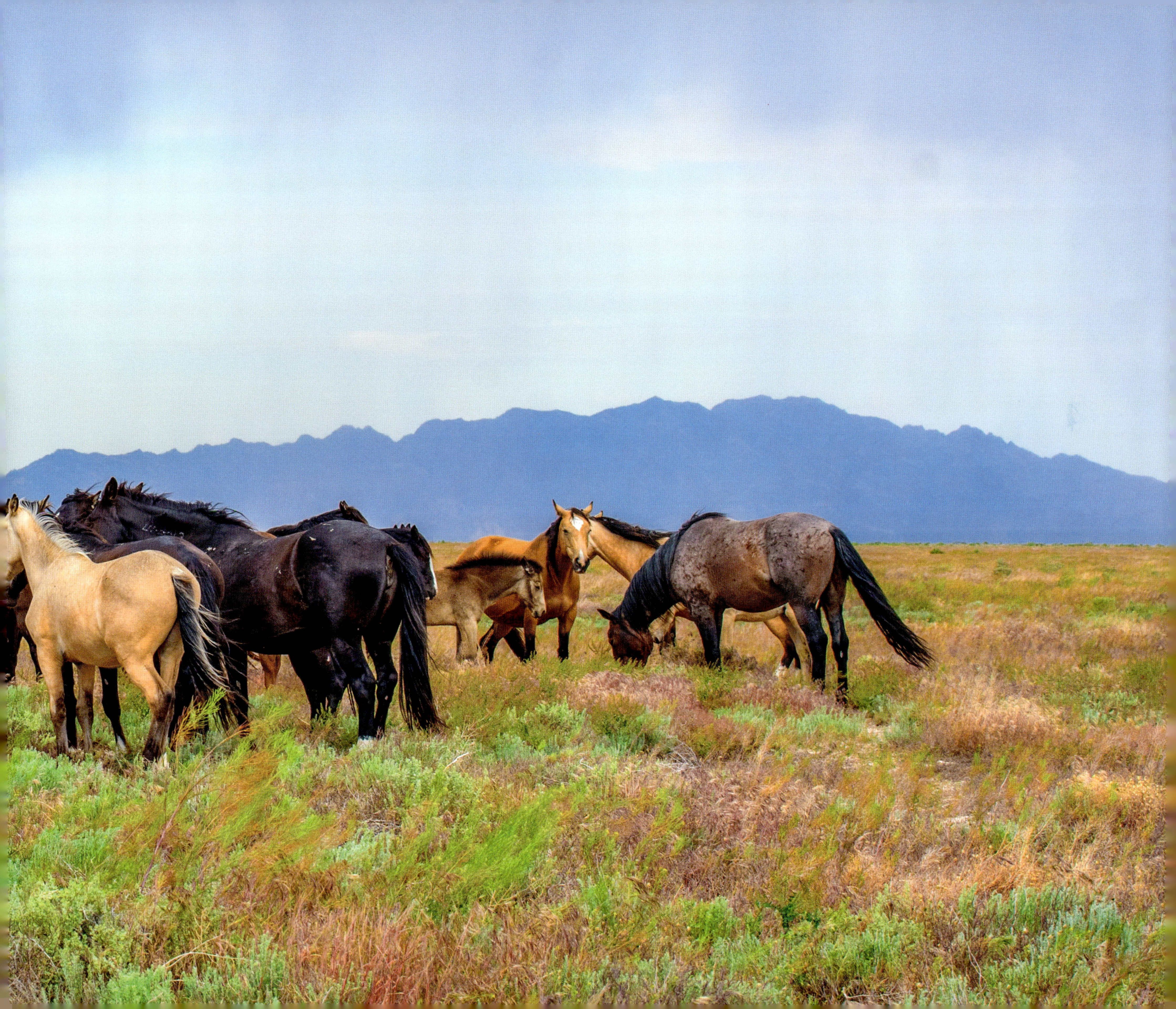

SNAKING

"Snaking" is a behavior used by stallions to herd a band. The stallion lowers his head, pinning his ears back and moving forward, swinging his head side to side. This behavior establishes dominance, allowing the stallion to direct the mares or to herd a mare that has strayed from the band. When the stallion has successfully moved his mares back to where he wants them, the behavior in the herd returns to peaceful grazing.

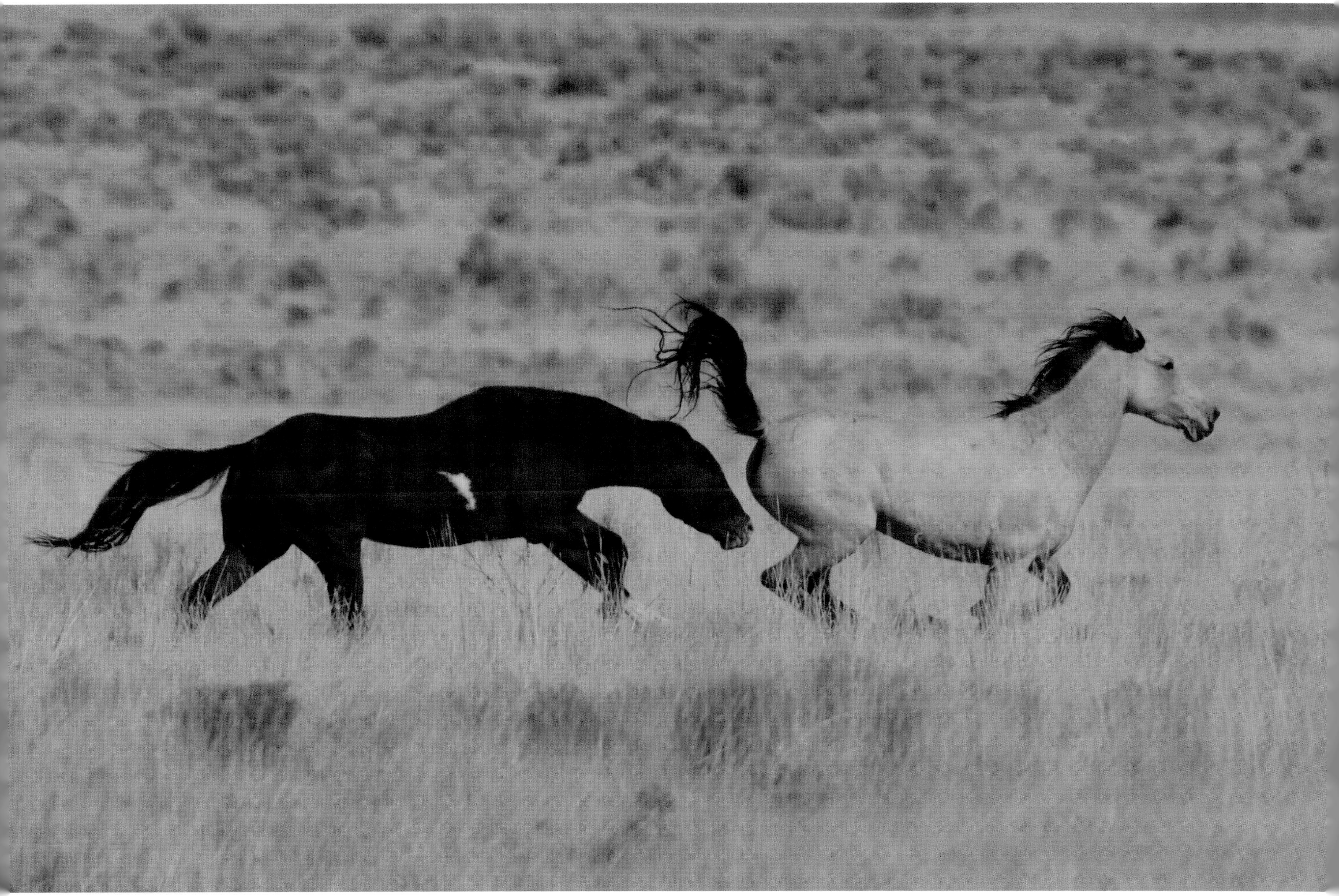

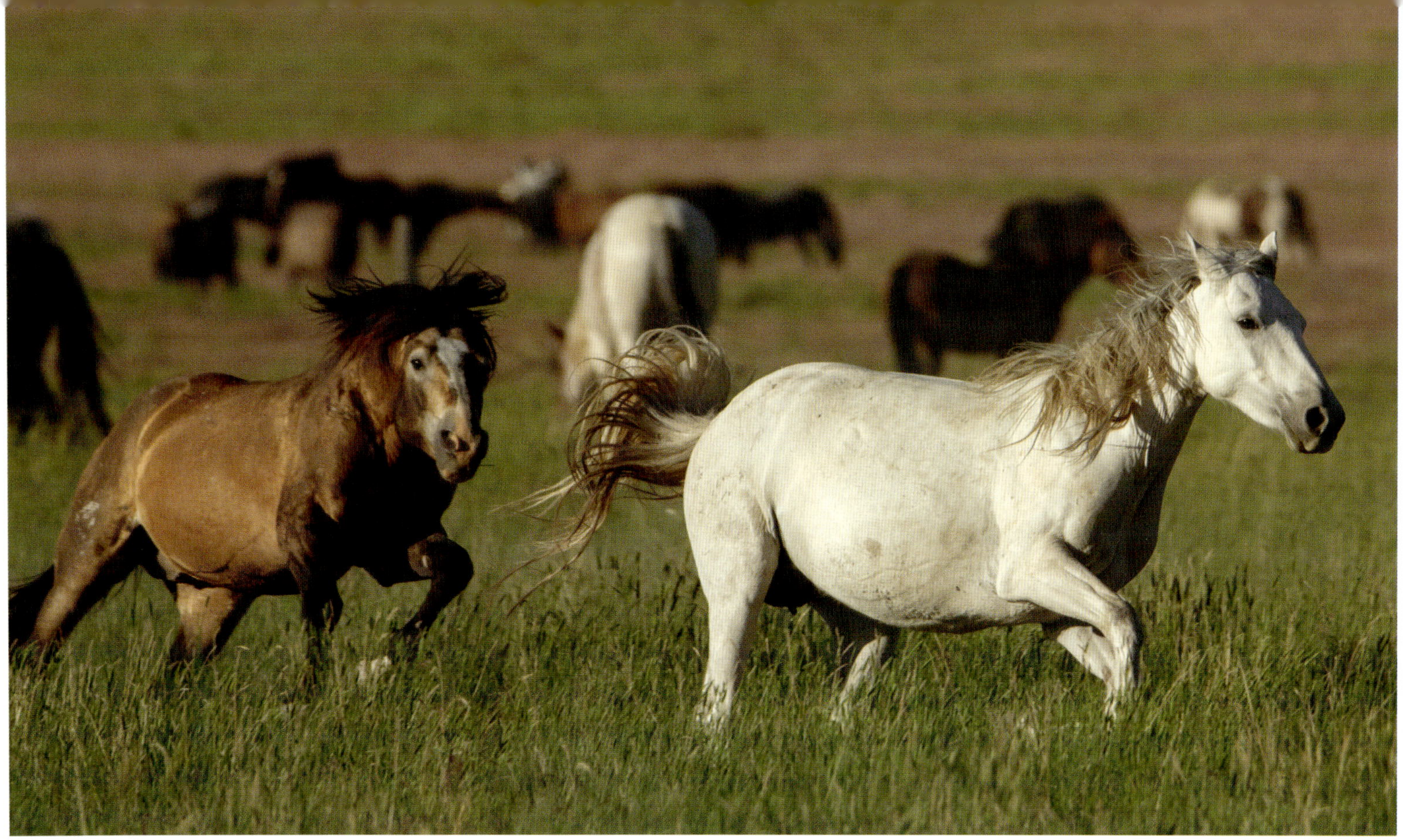

Left: The band stallion, Buck, snakes his mare back to the herd.

Opposite: The pinto mare leads her band while the band stallion moves them away from a would-be challenger.

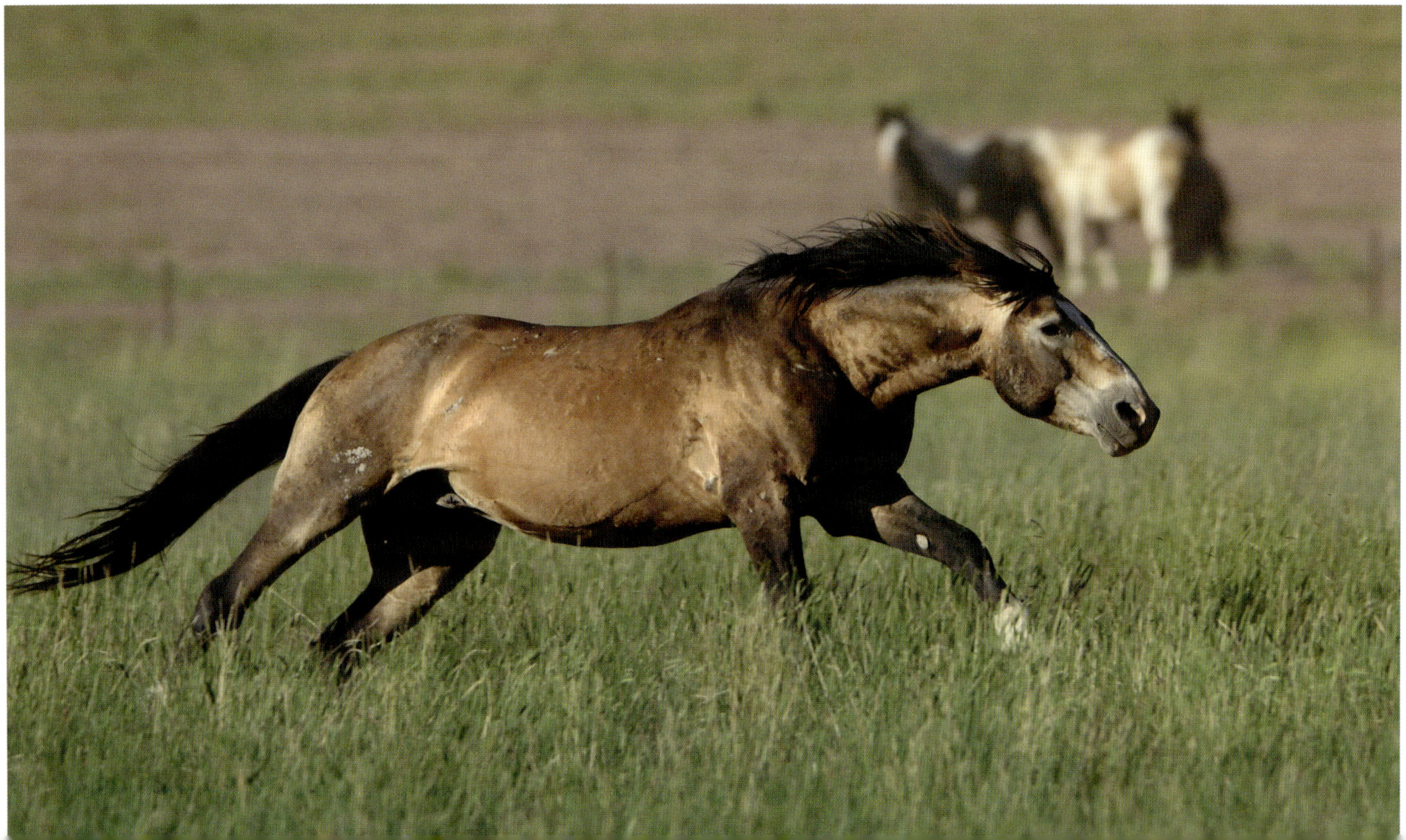

Left: After snaking his mares back to the herd, the band stallion is off to chase away a rival bachelor stallion.

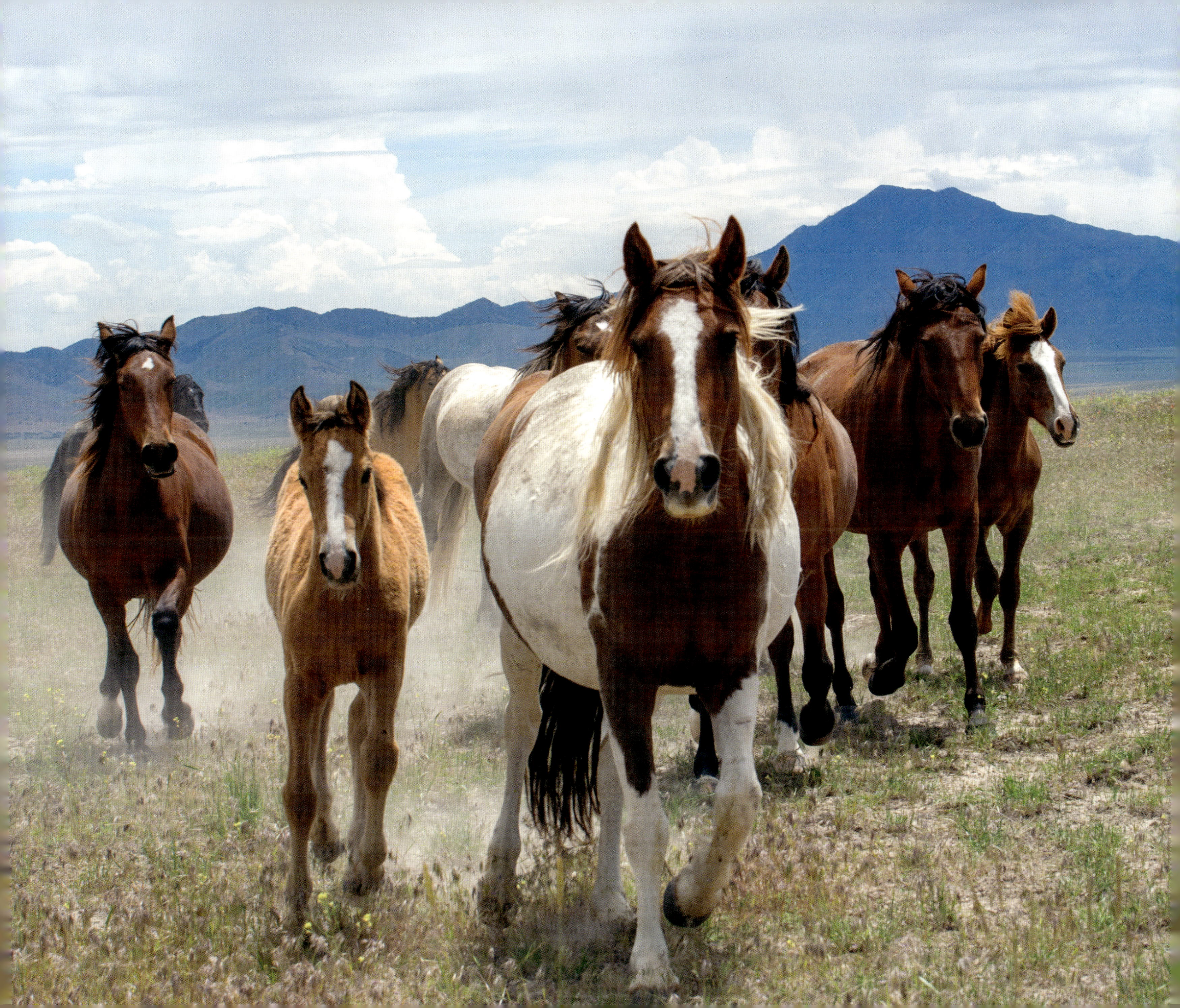

A family band moves across the range. Rush Valley, Utah.

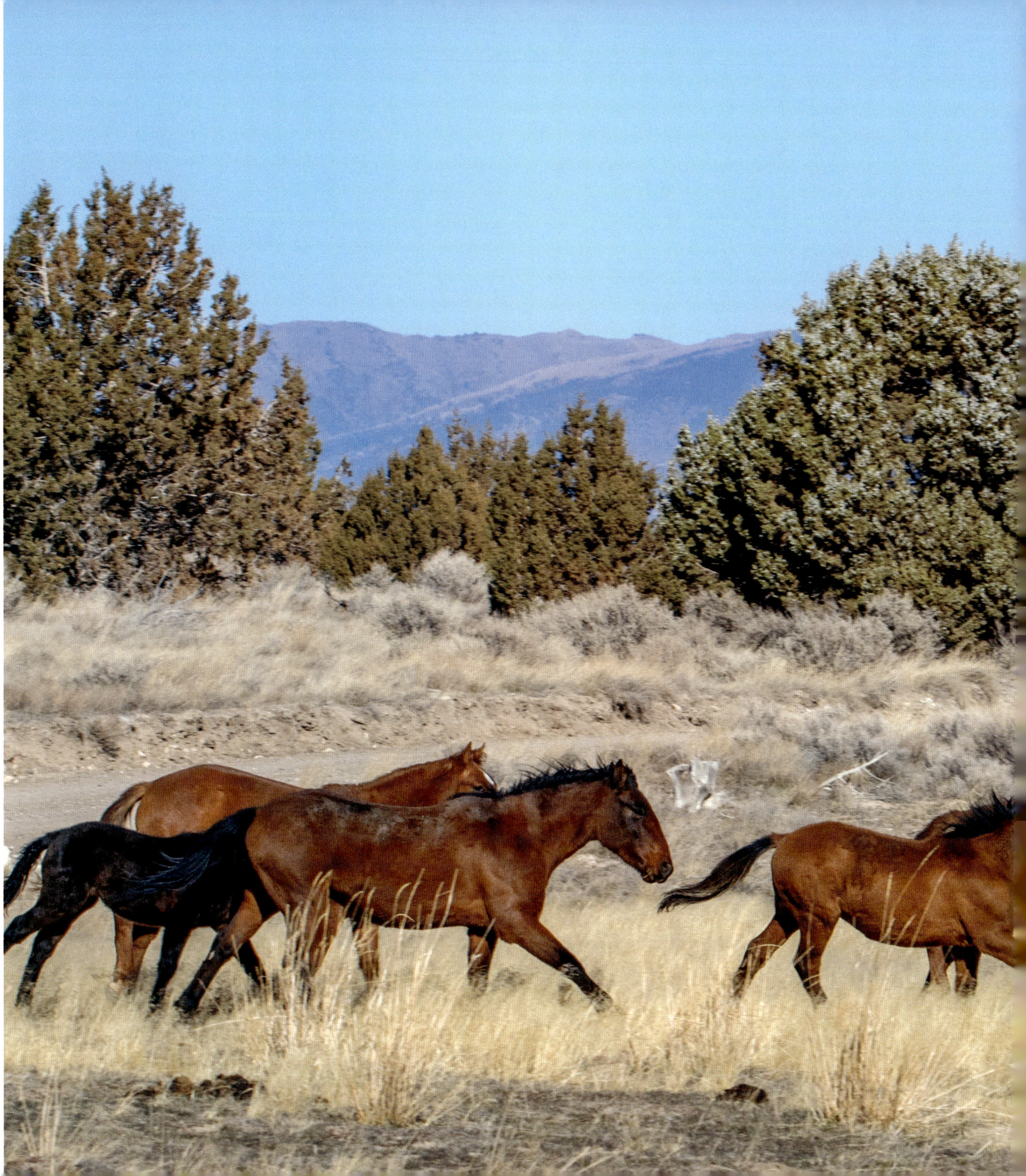

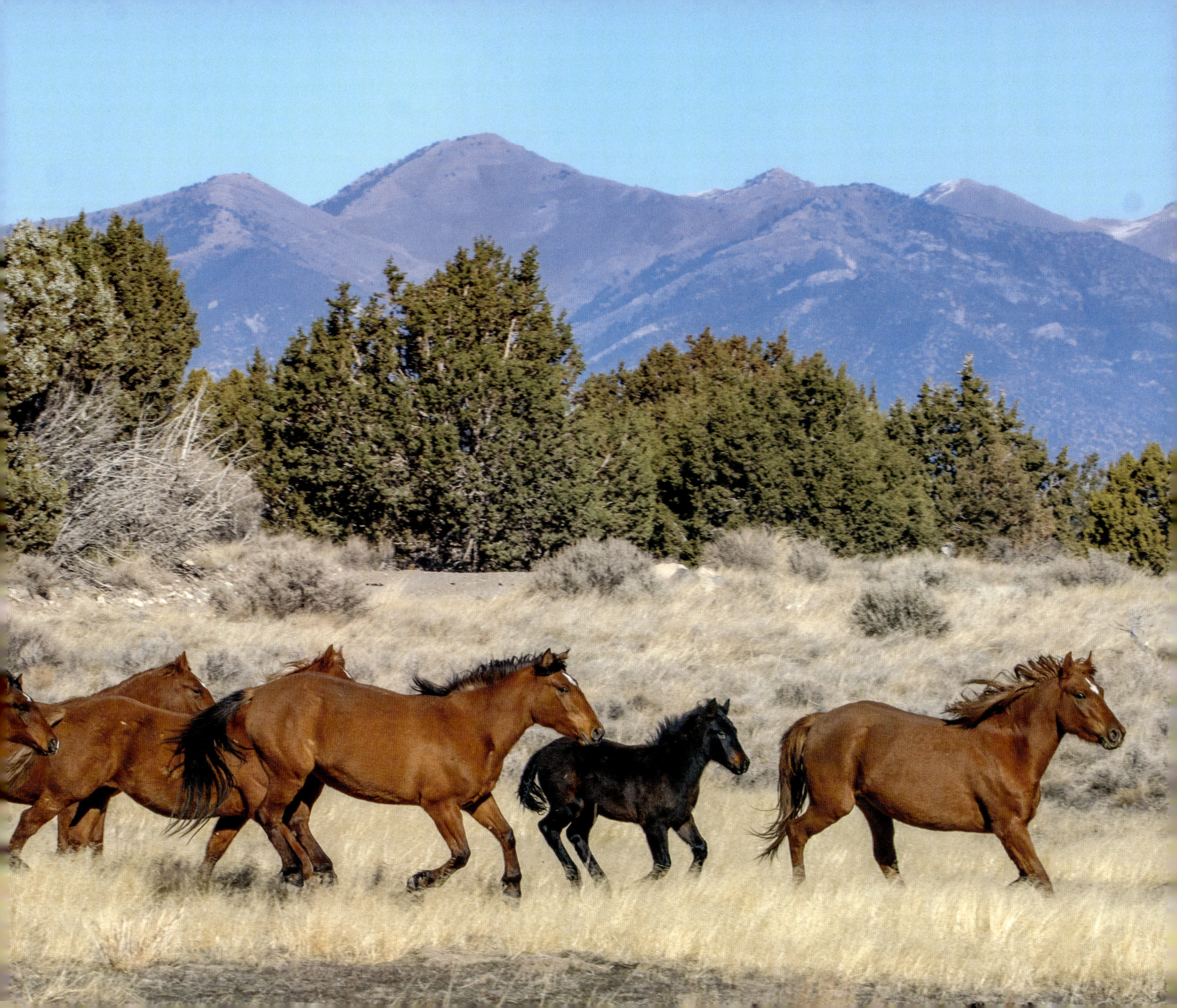

BRANDED MARES

Among the thousands of mares roaming the range are a number of them bearing a brand on their left hip or neck—a brand signaling the growing population of mares who have been given the Porcine Zona Pellucida (PZP) vaccination. With increasing numbers of wild horses on the range today, population growth is becoming a significant concern.

In 2017, the Bureau of Land Management stated that the nearly 27 million acres it manages for wild horses can only sustain about 27,000 animals. With more than 72,000 wild horses estimated, resources and survival have become strained. Statistics show that a wild horse herd can increase 25 percent annually if left untreated.

PZP has been used in wildlife contraception since the late 1980s, but it was around 2005 that the Bureau of Land Management started its birth control program for the Onaqui herd in hopes of slowing down its population growth. The contraceptive is administered through a dart to selected mares on the range. It is safe, reversible, and has an efficacy rate of over 90 percent.

Data has shown that the vaccination has no effects on herd social structure or behavior. In fact, without the strain of giving birth each year, mares given PZP tend to be healthier and have longer lifespans. Reducing the population growth betters the health, space, and resource situation of the horses on the range overall, allowing these herds to thrive.

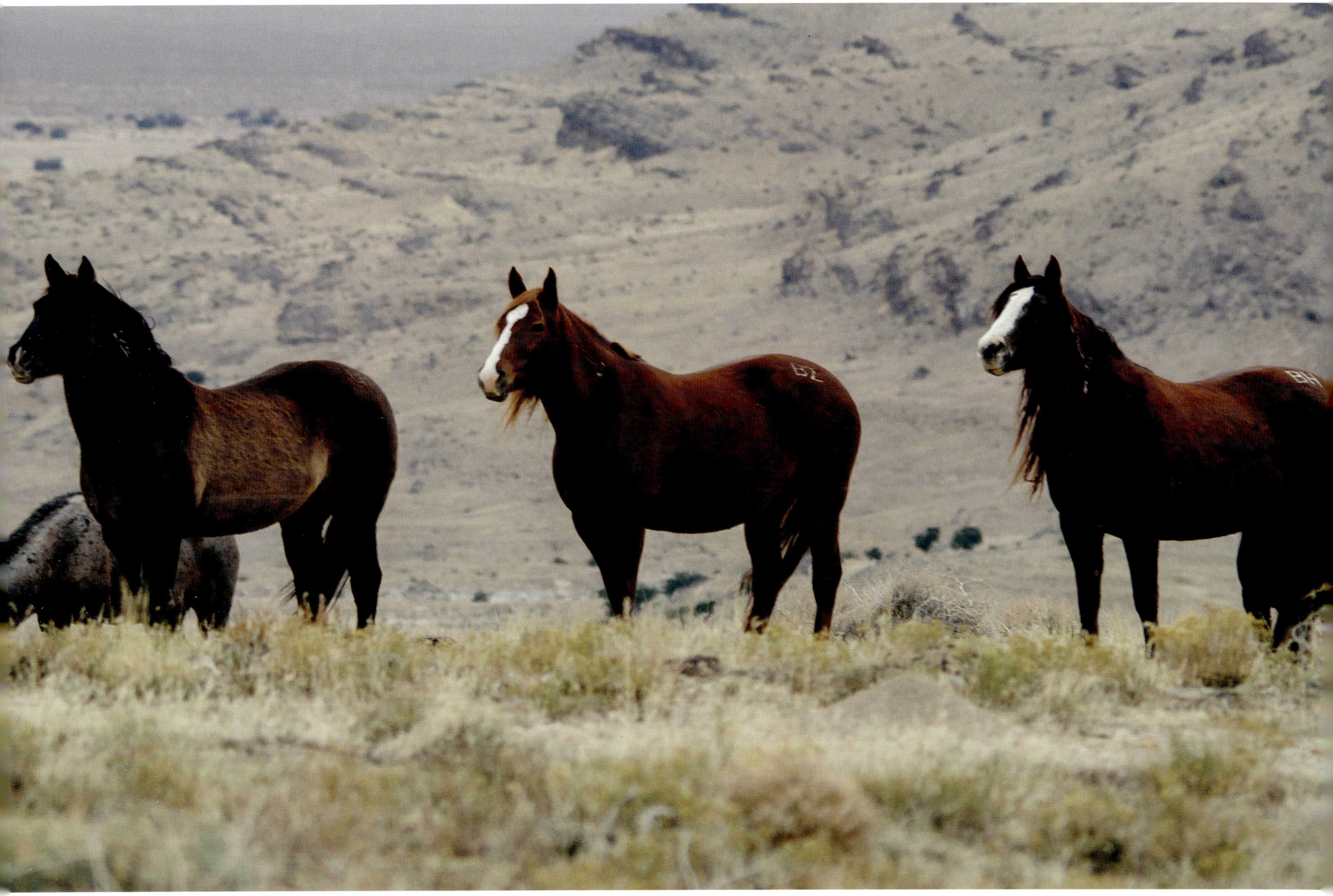

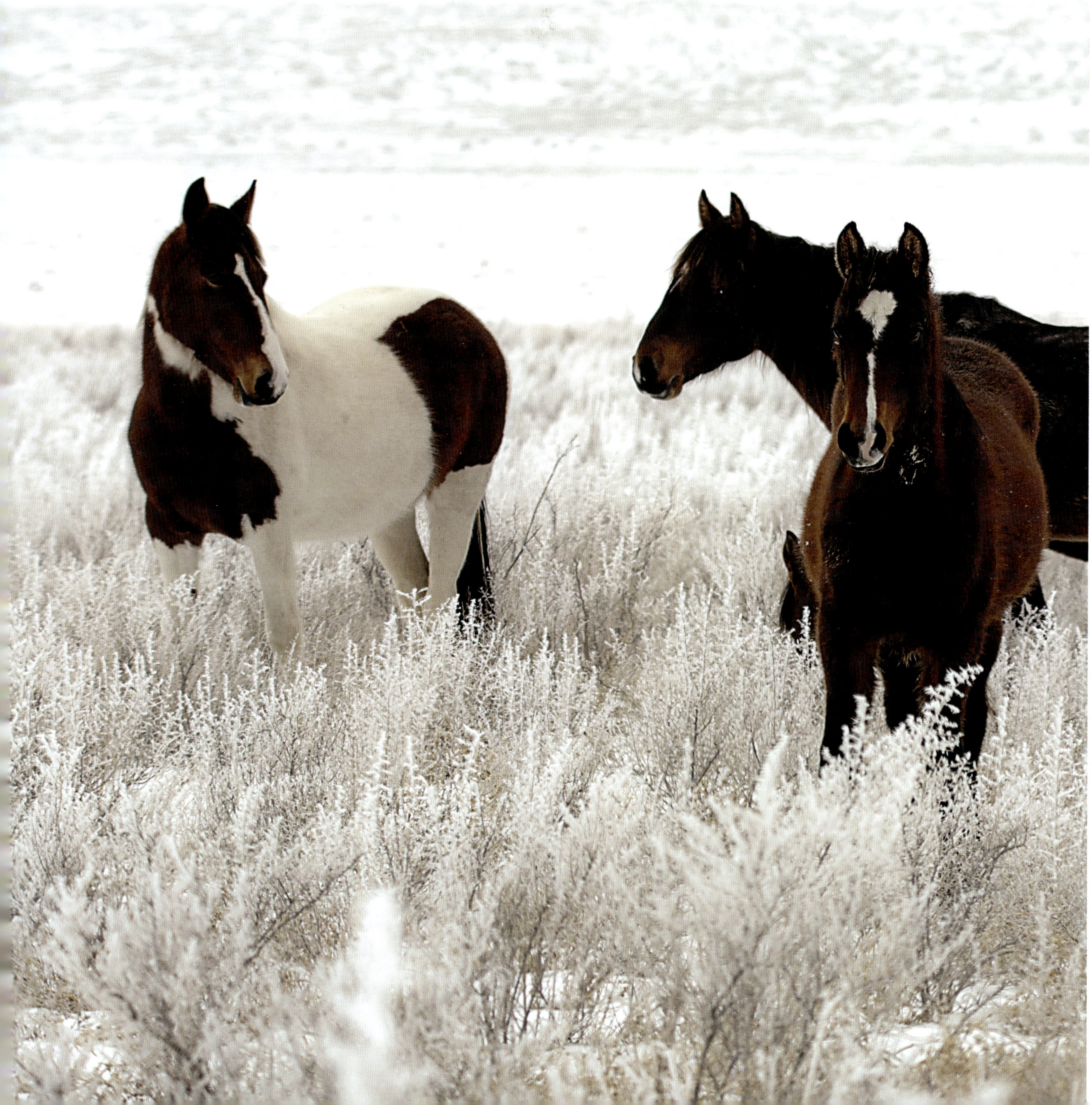

Left: A frigid winter morning covers the desert floor with a heavy coating of frost.

Opposite: Mares move through the fresh snowfall.

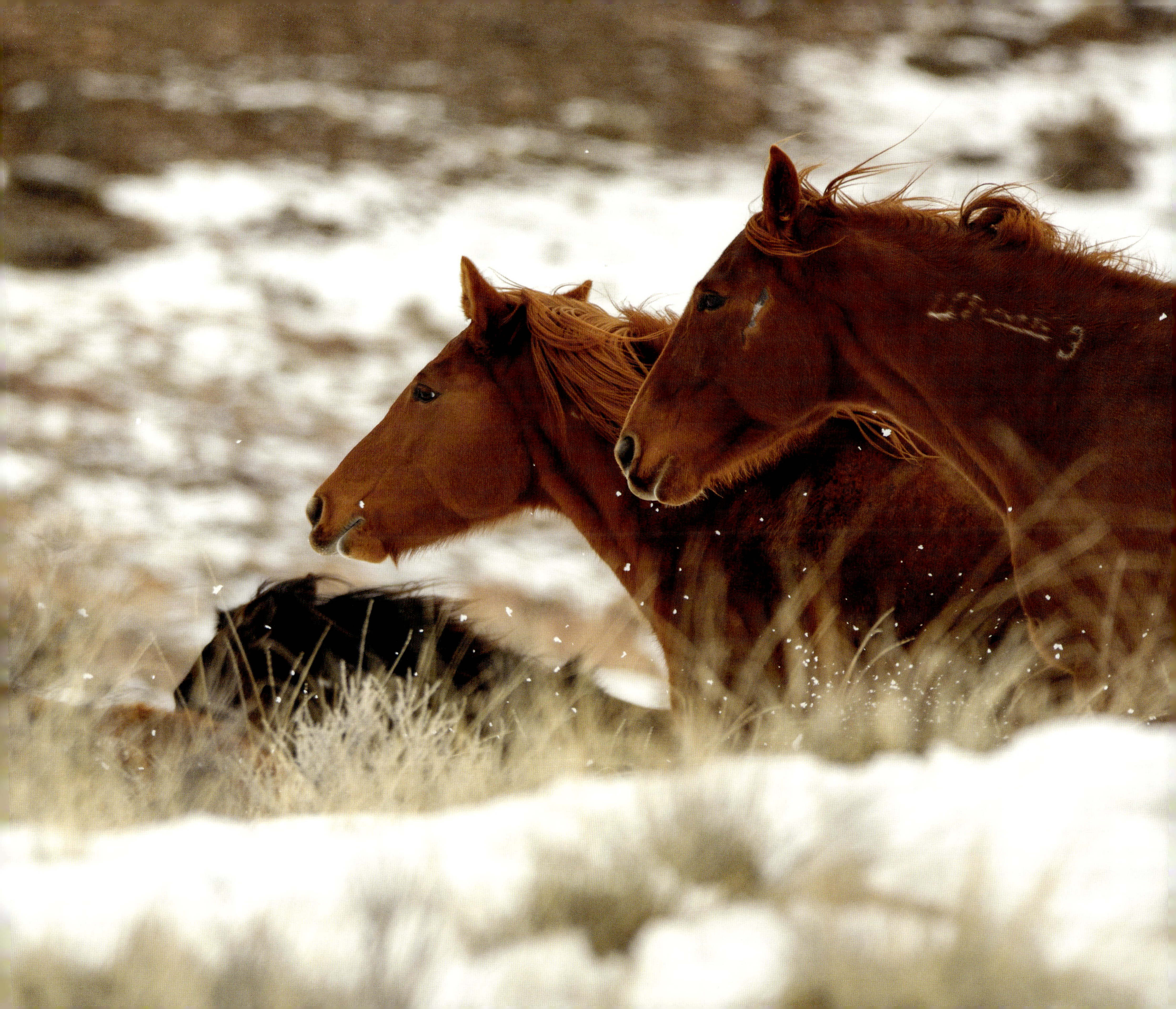

WATERHOLE ETIQUETTE

For wild horses, waterholes are not only necessary for survival; they are a place where herd dynamics play a significant role in behavior. When wild horses approach a waterhole and another band is there, the approaching band will wait until the first band is finished. Once the waterhole is free, the mares and young ones will approach. The band stallion is the first to drink; he and his lieutenant then protect the band. Bachelor stallions will use the waterhole to try to claim young mares for their own, so the band stallion and lieutenant must be vigilant. Once finished, the lead mare will move her band away from the waterhole to continue to graze or move to a different location.

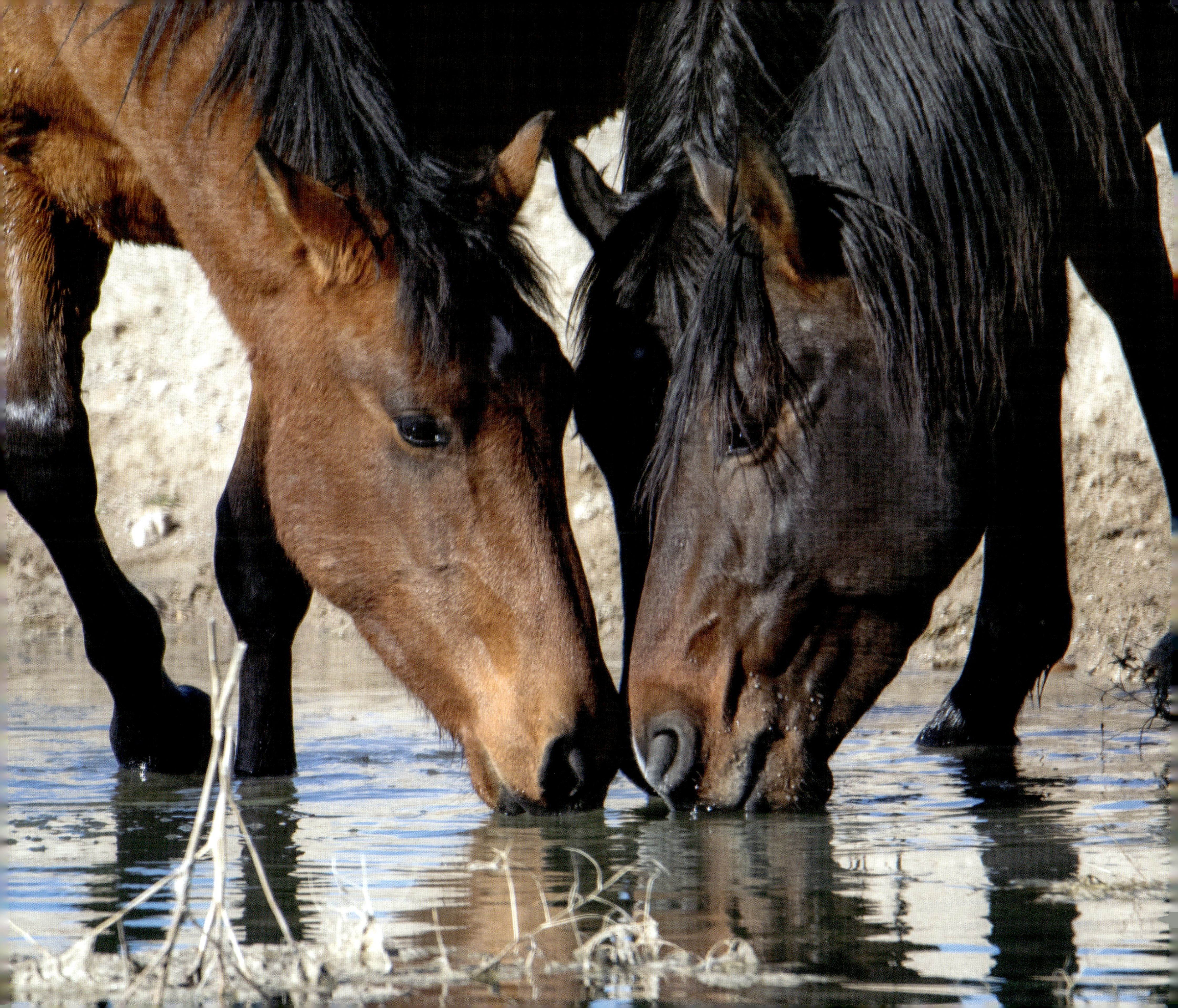

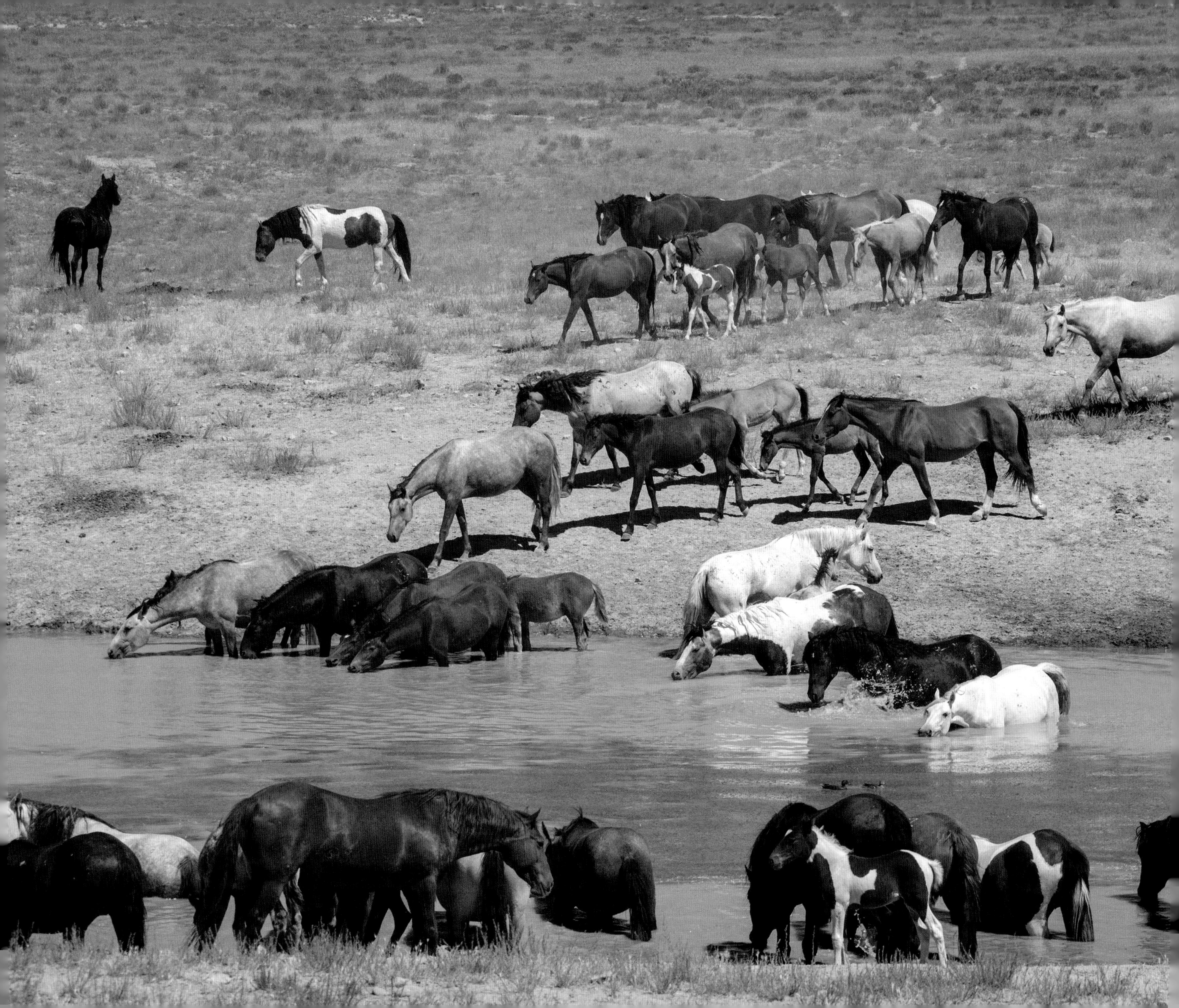

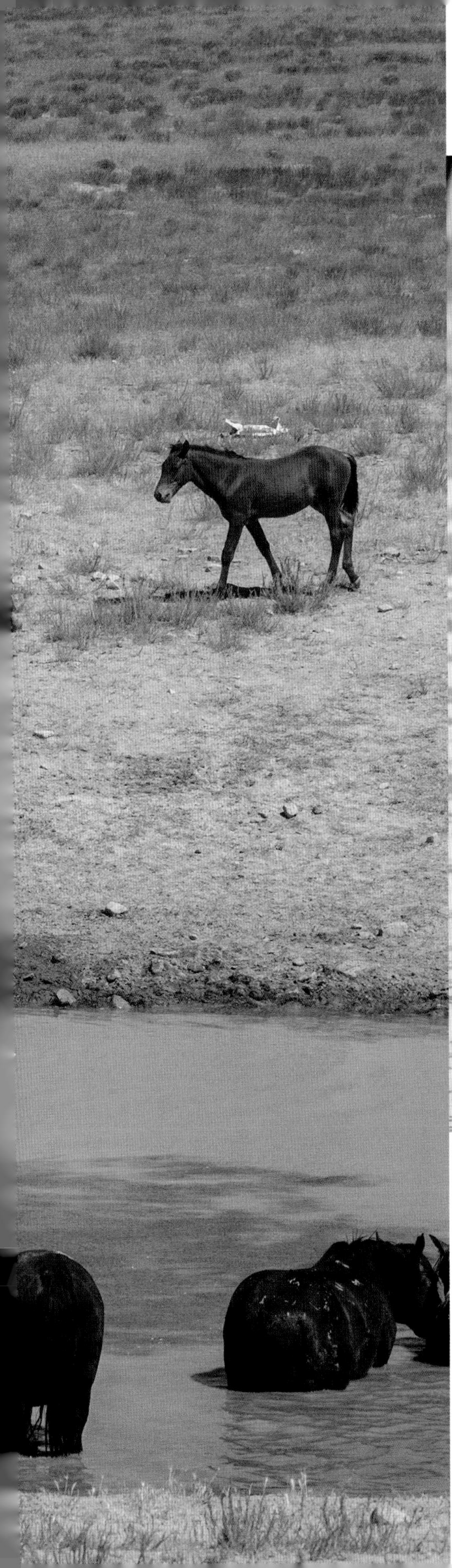

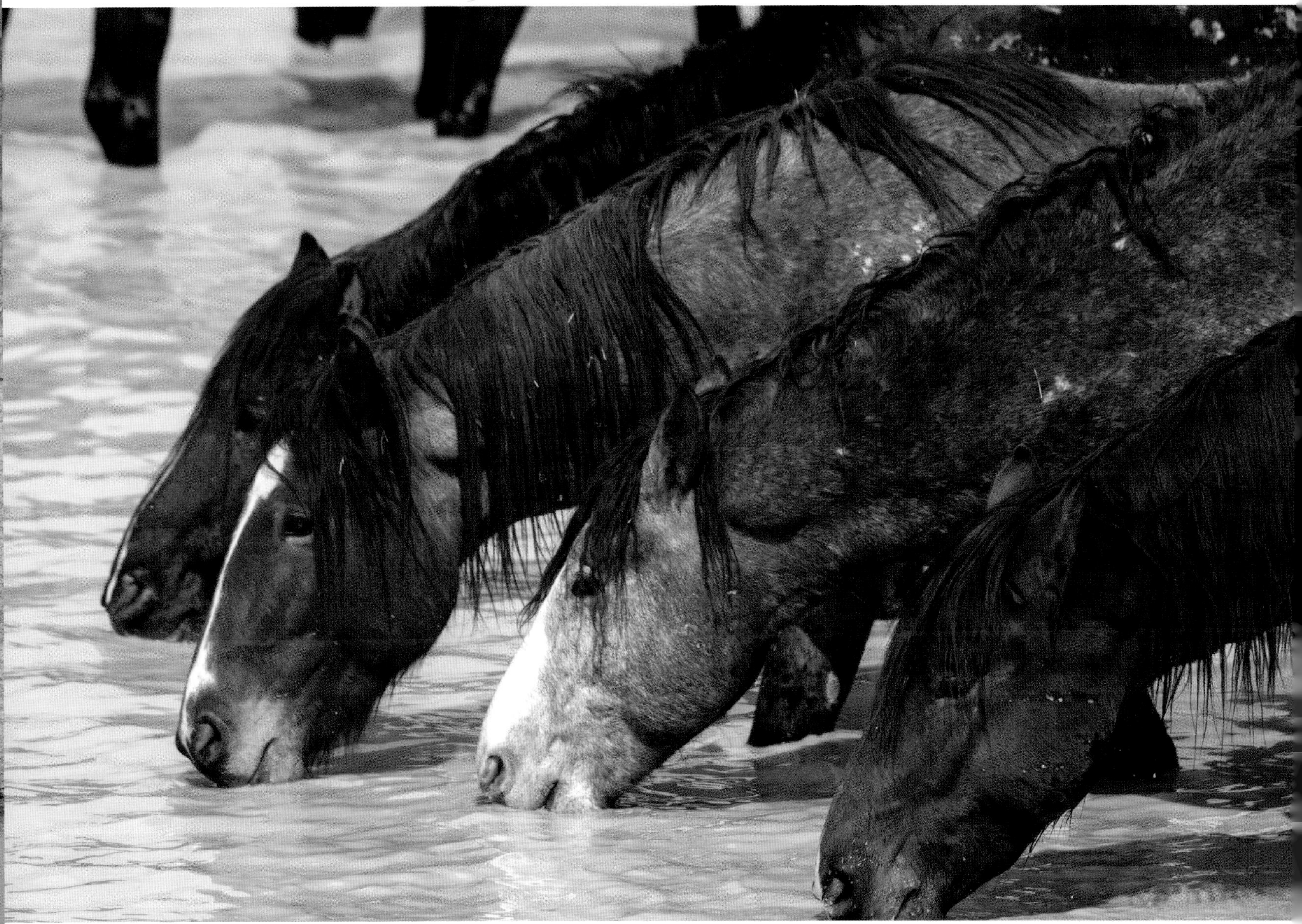

Left: If there is enough water in the ponds, the wild horses will venture in belly deep to get a drink.

Above: A group of mares pause for a drink and to cool off in the water.

Next page: Mares enjoy the waterhole.

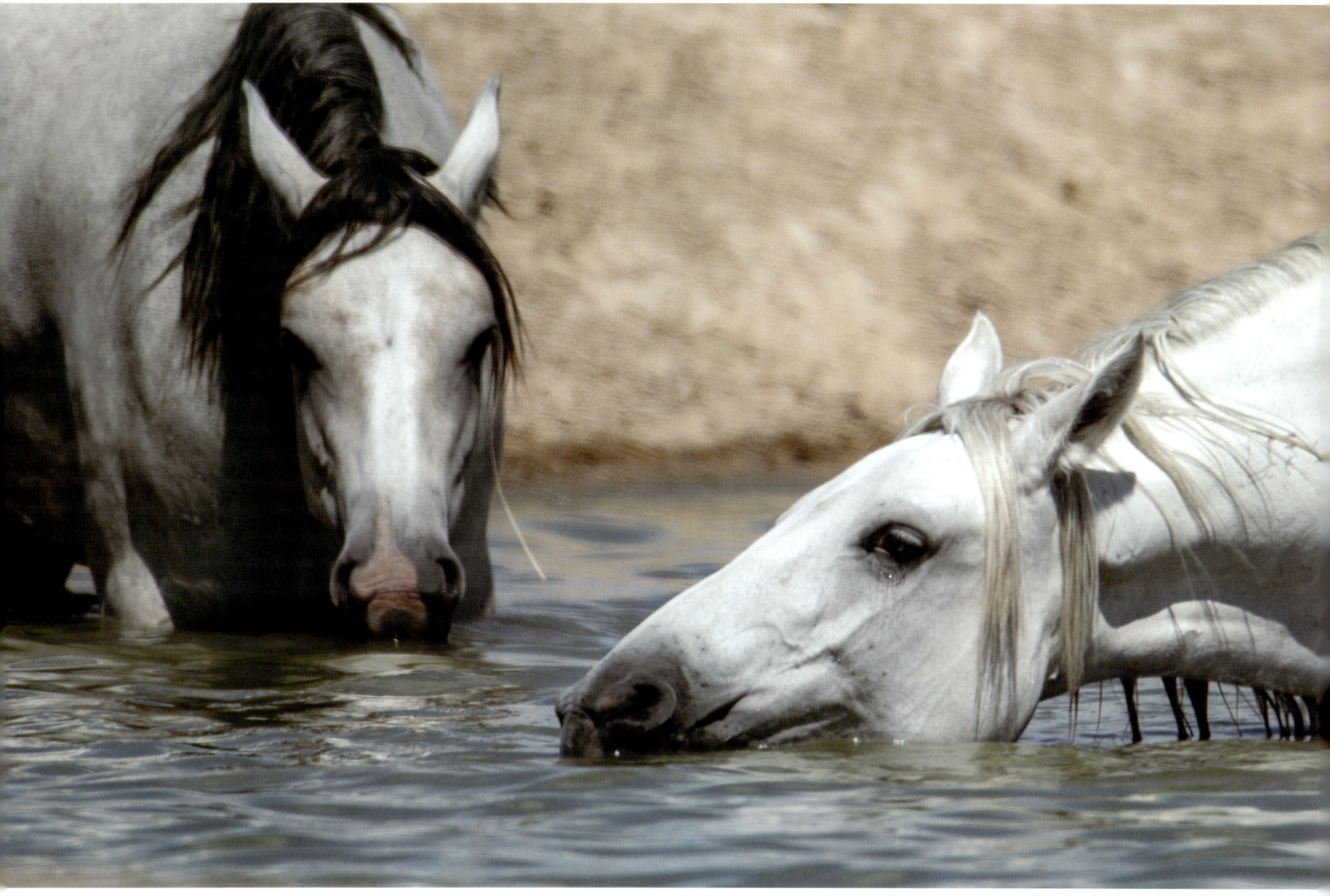

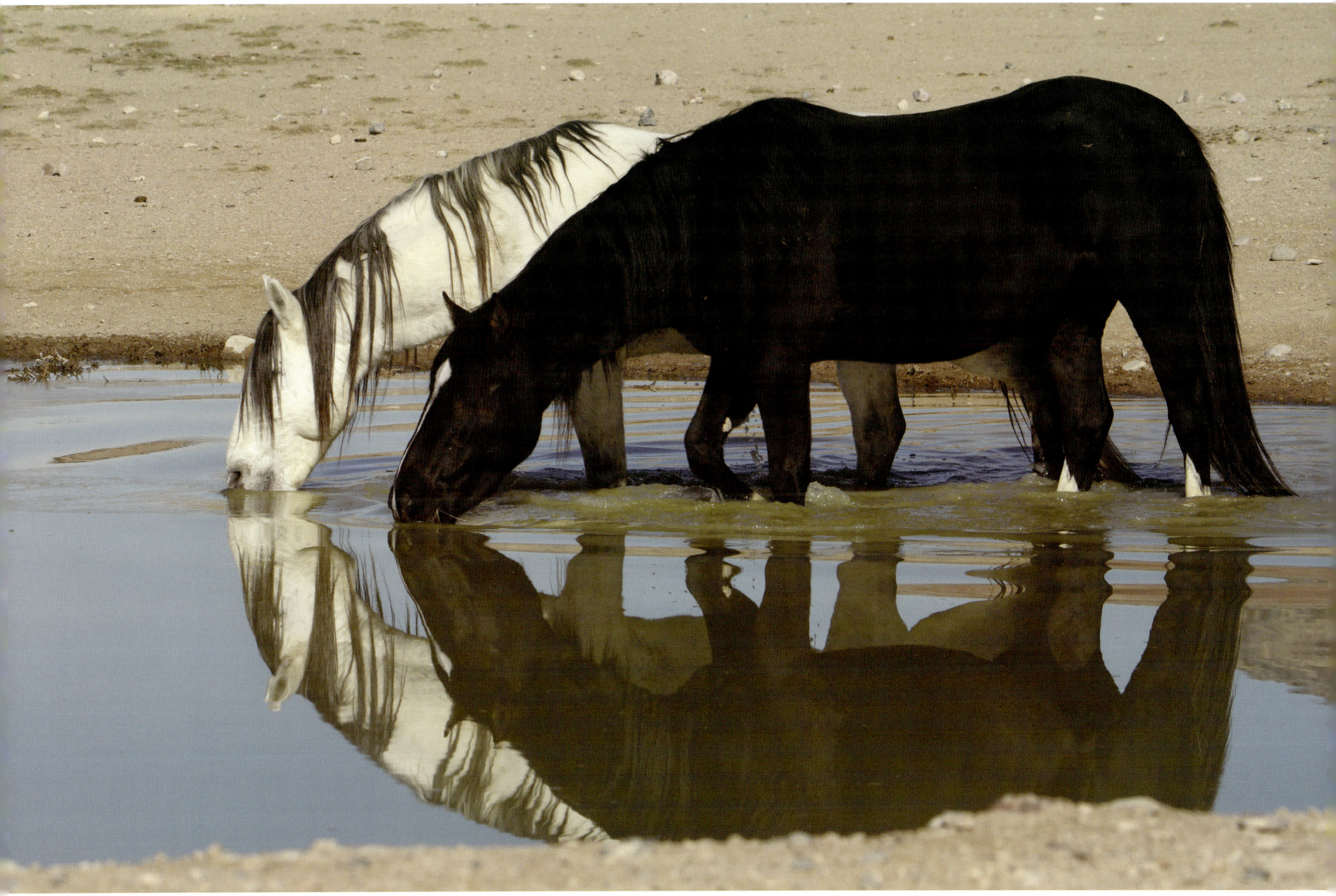

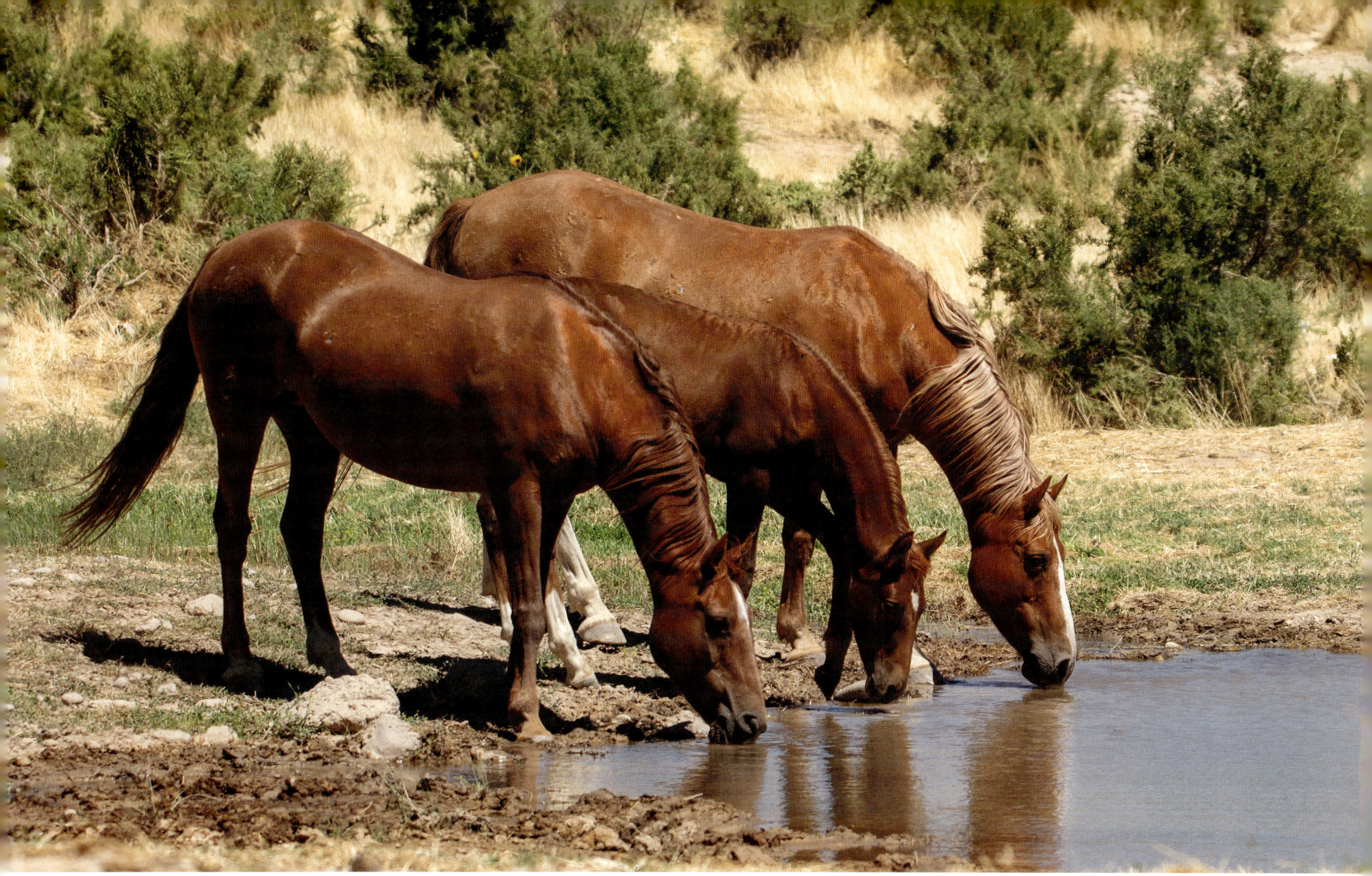

Above: A small band stops for a quick drink at the spring-fed waterhole.

opposite: Several bands congregate together at the mudflat ponds for a rest.

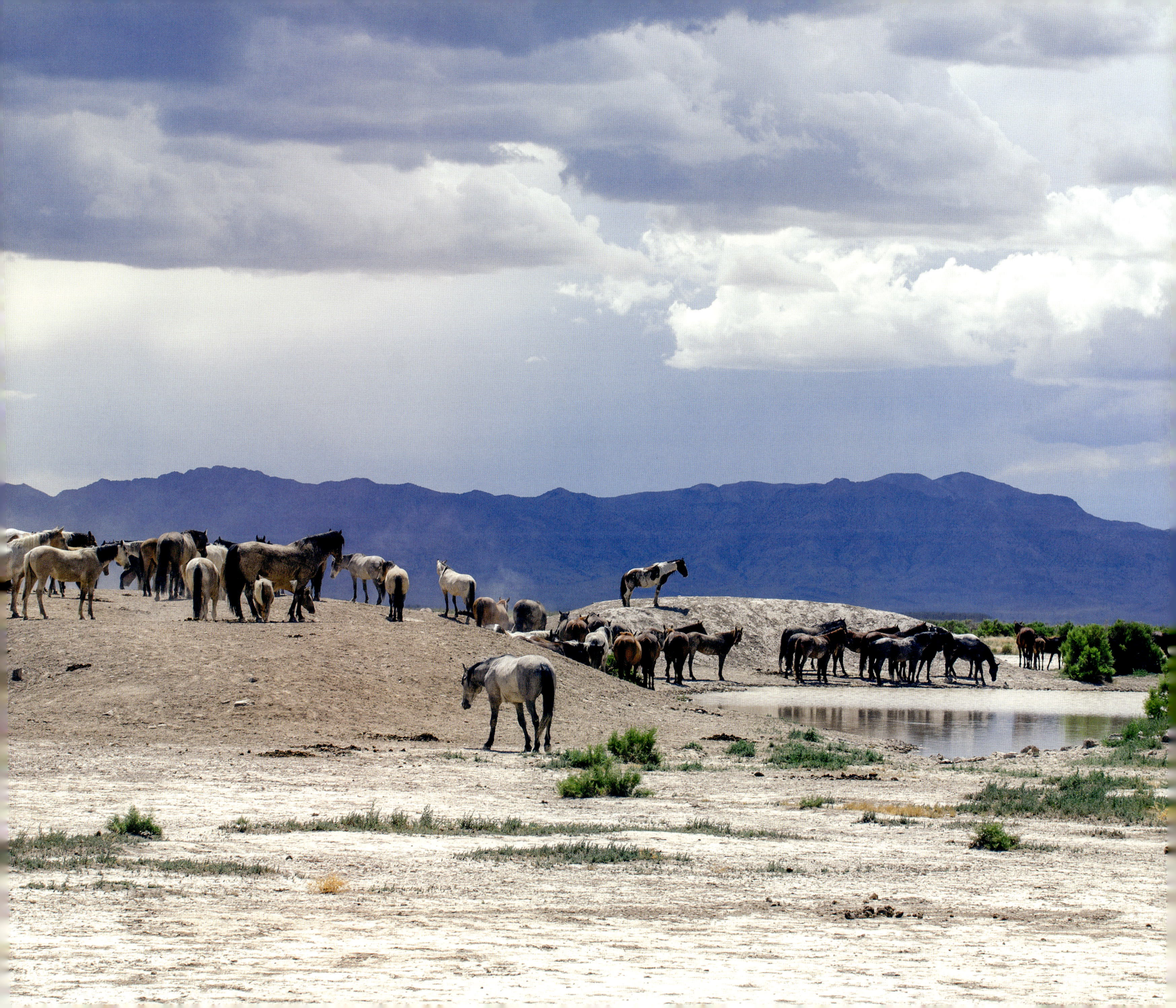

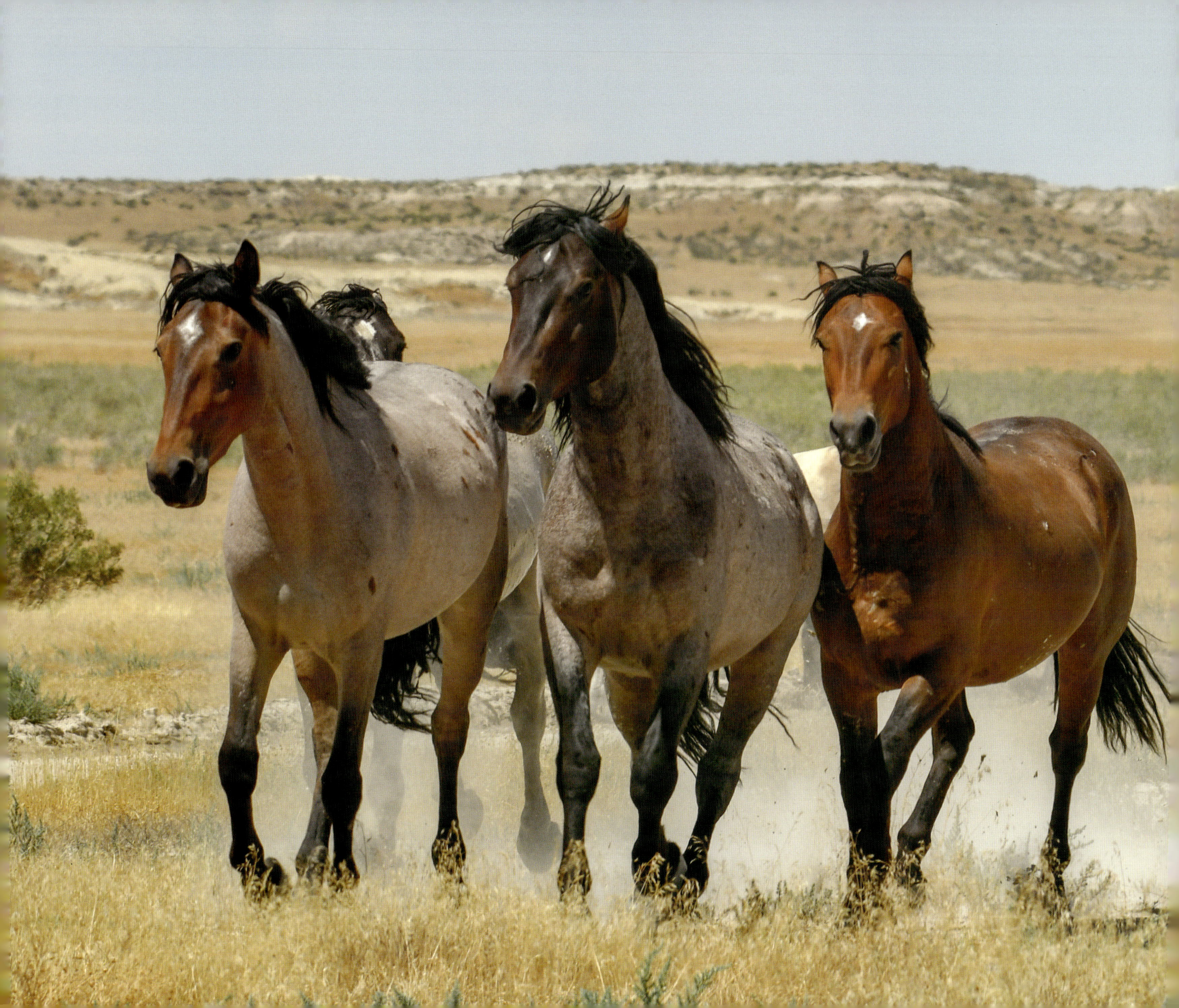

OPPOSITE: A band stallion returns his mares to the rest of the band.

RIGHT: After a quick snow shower, the beauty of these gray mares is even more evident.

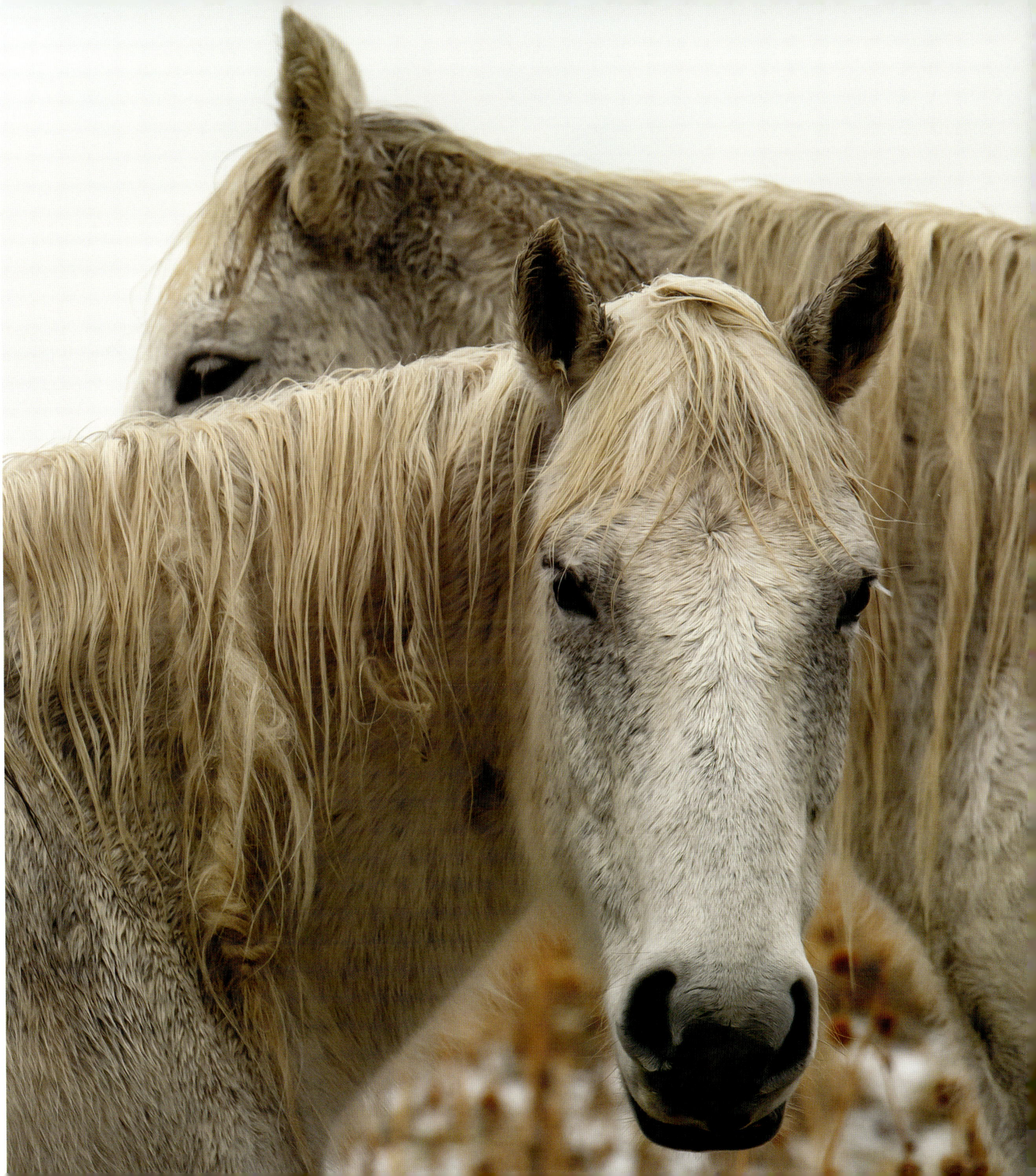

NEXT PAGE LEFT: A family band stops to let the young foal get a drink of its mother's milk.

NEXT PAGE RIGHT: A family band of bay- and sorrel-colored horses halts to see what is out on the range.

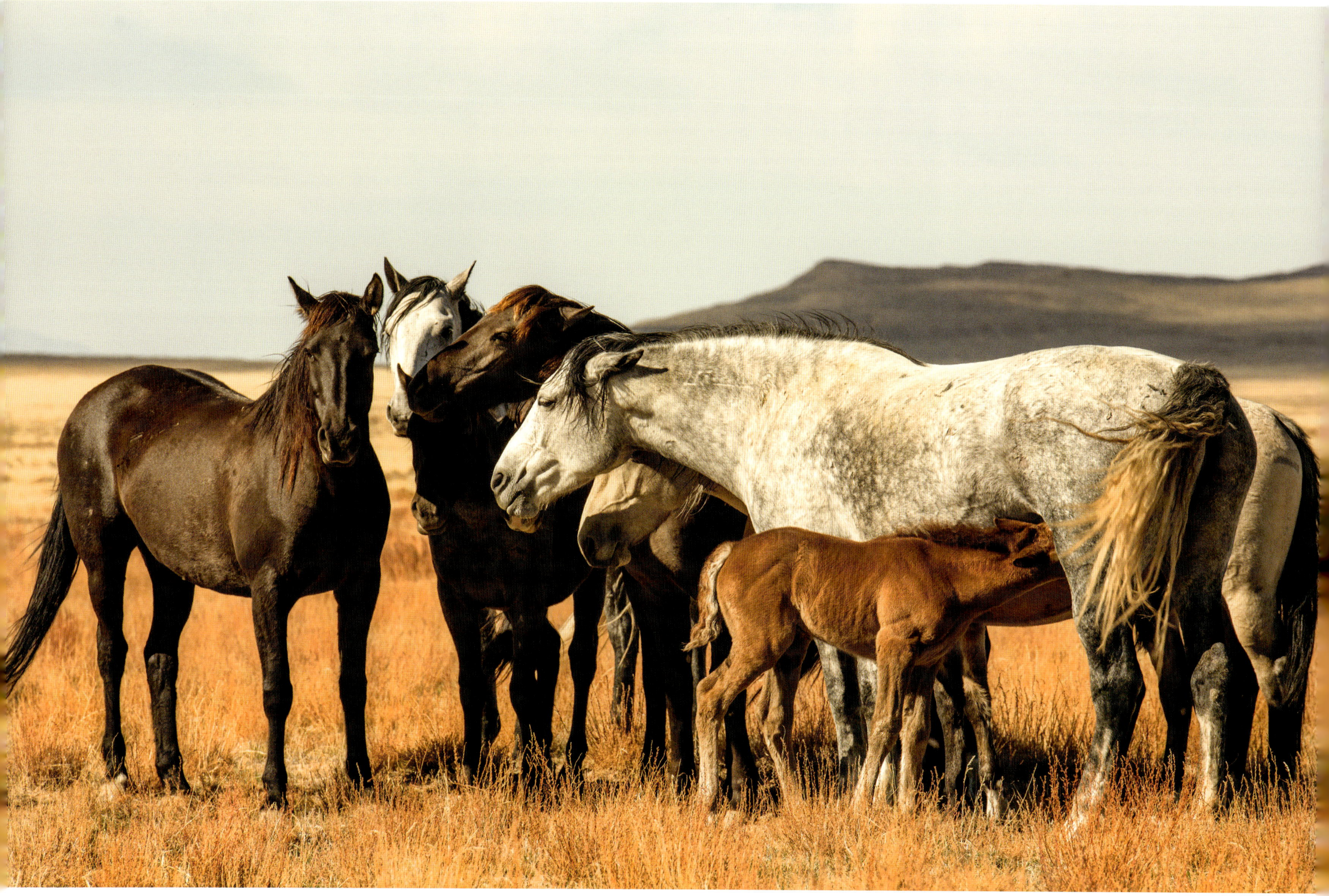

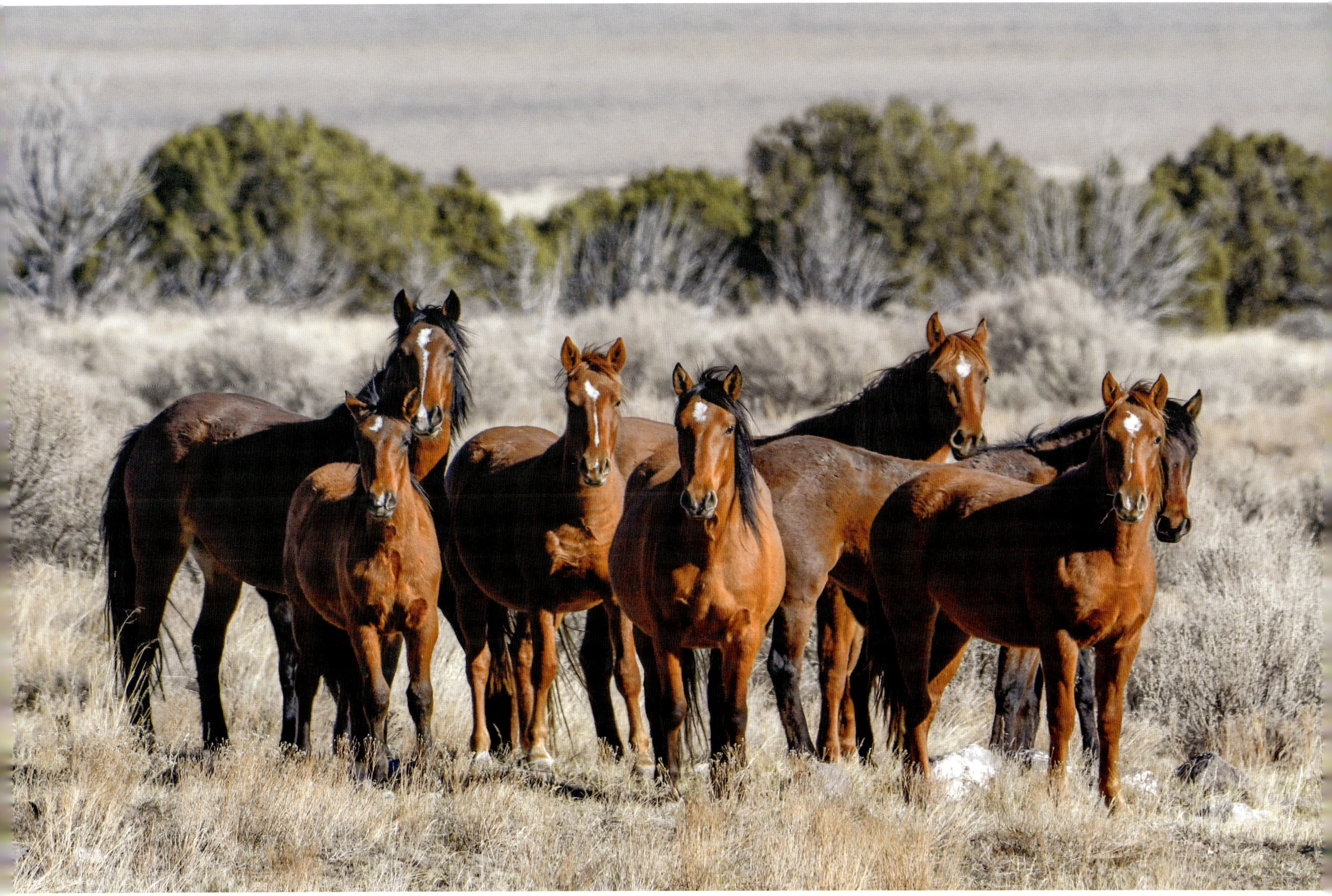

WIND BRAIDS

One of the most magical things on the range are wind braids—braids within the horses' manes that are woven by the wind. They are rare, and while many are small and hard to see, some horses have several within their mane and, if you're lucky, you can catch the few that are quite long. They are also called "elf knots"; myths tell of fairies and magical creatures that visit the horses at night and tie knots in their manes, tying themselves stirrups to ride the horses.

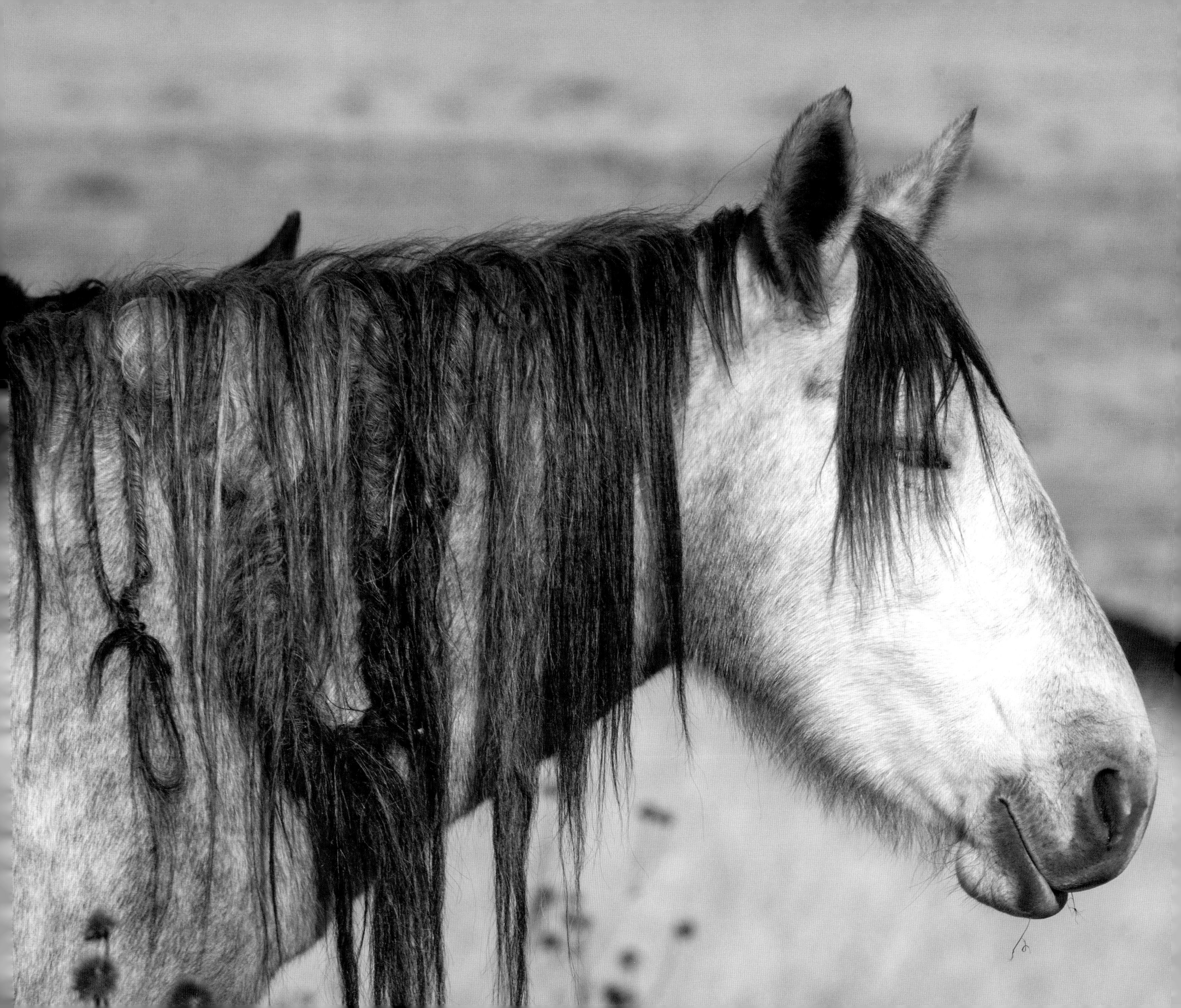

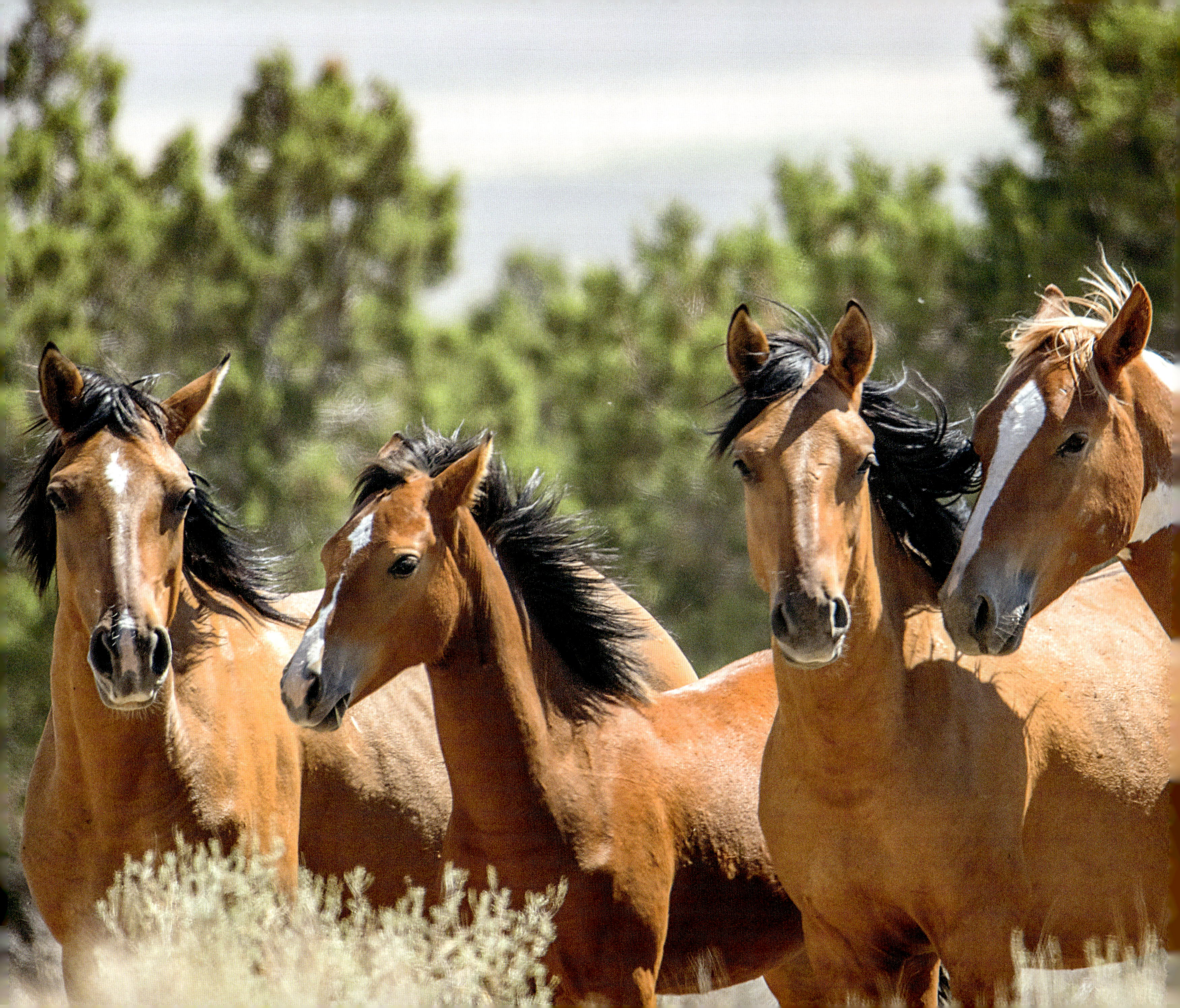

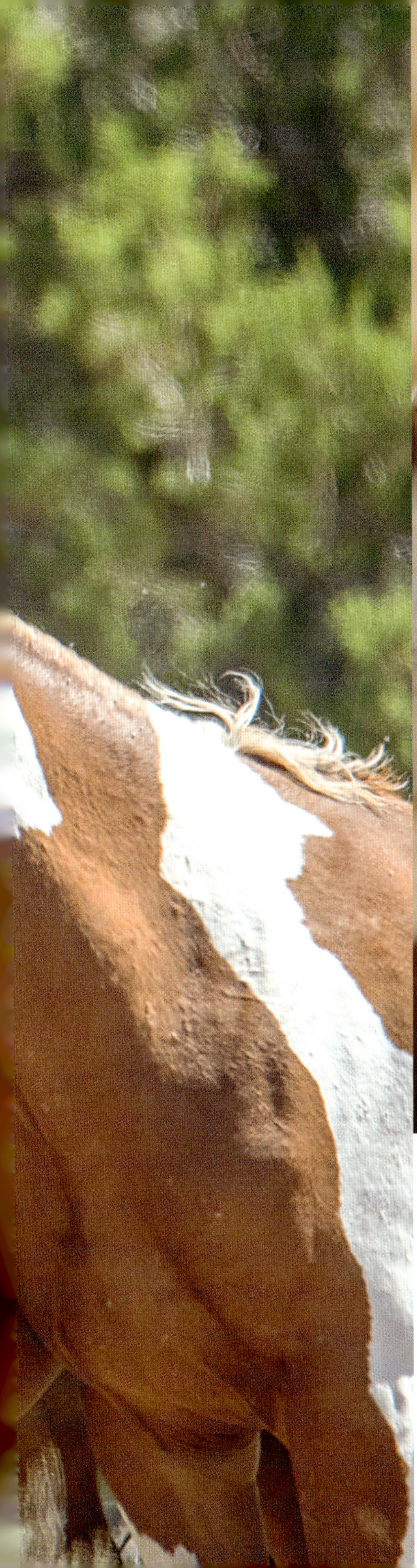

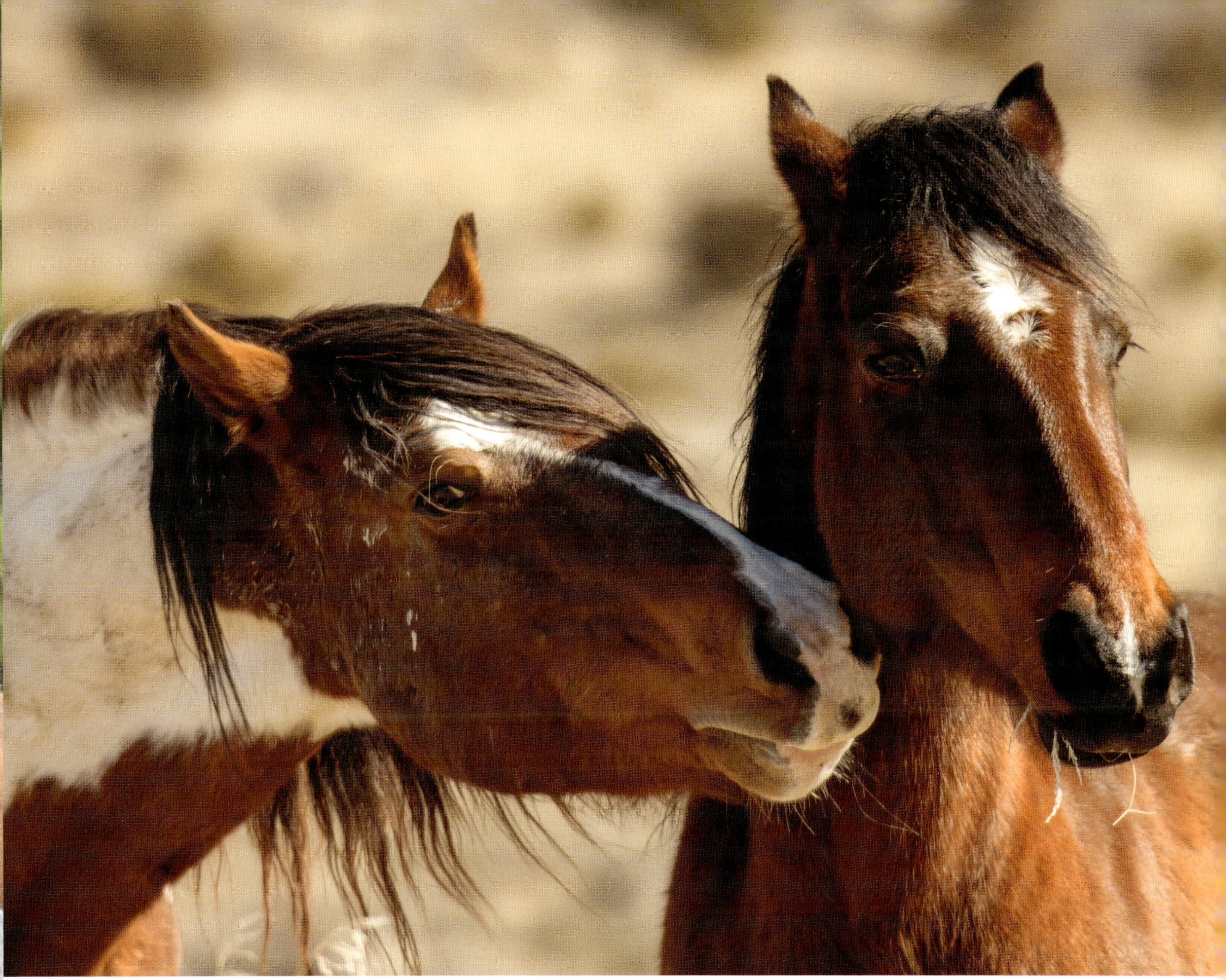

Left: A young pinto stallion with his small group of mares.

Above: A pinto stud courts a young mare, trying to persuade her that he would be a good suitor for her.

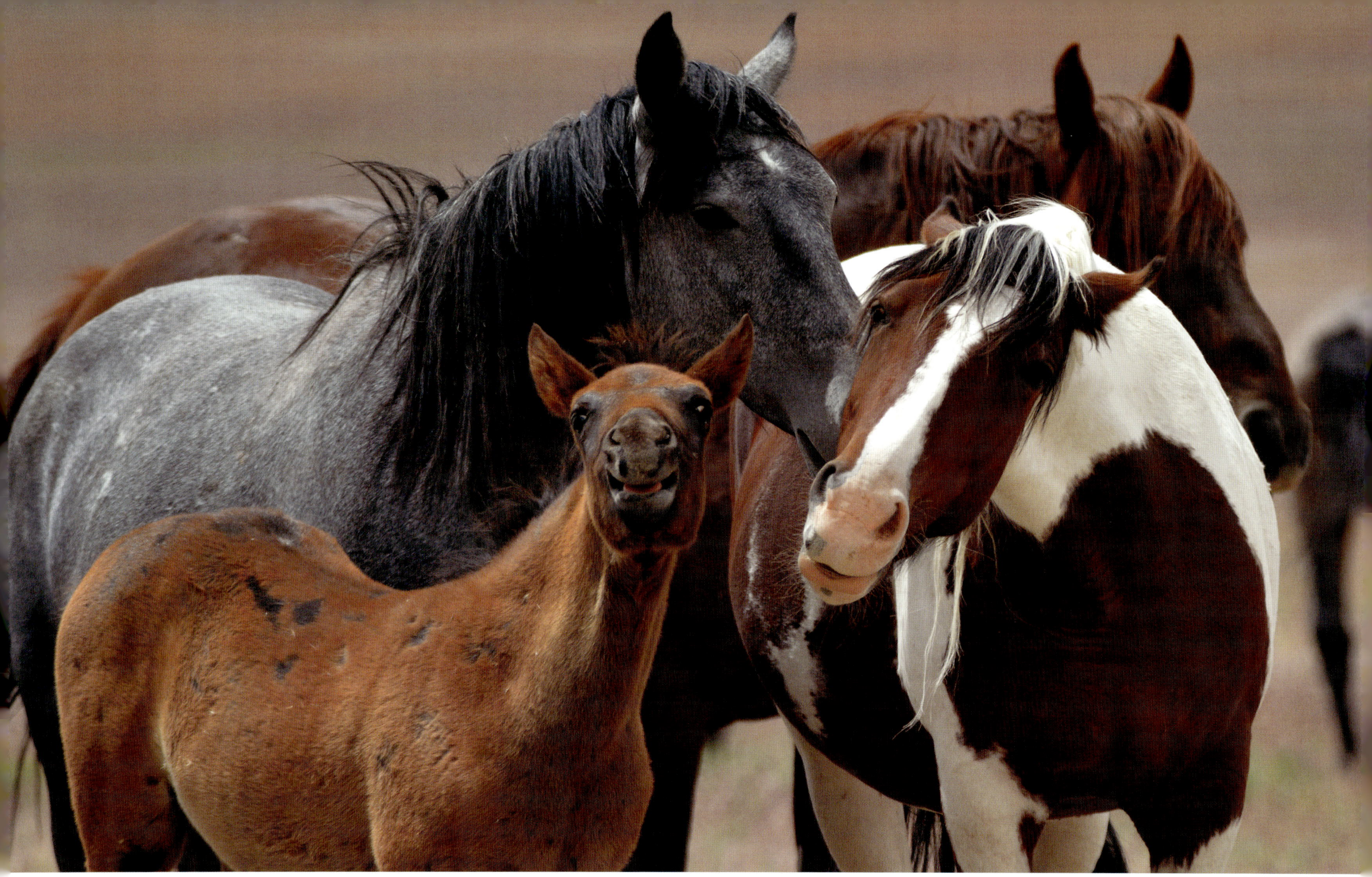

ABOVE: Silly faces are one of the many things young foals do that make them fun to photograph; this time, the older mare joins him.

OPPOSITE: The gray mare leads her band to the waterhole. Horses tend to move single file toward water sources.

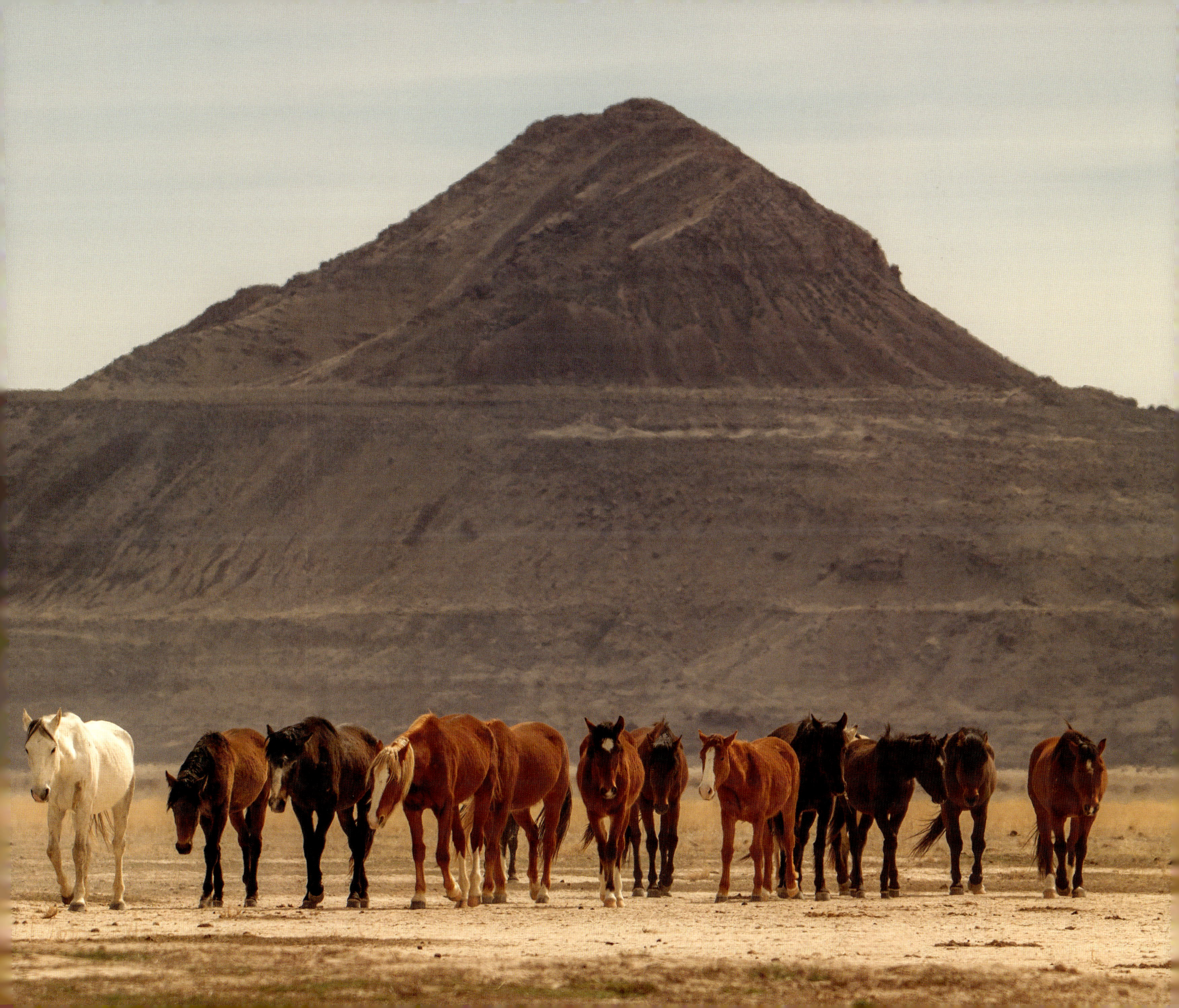

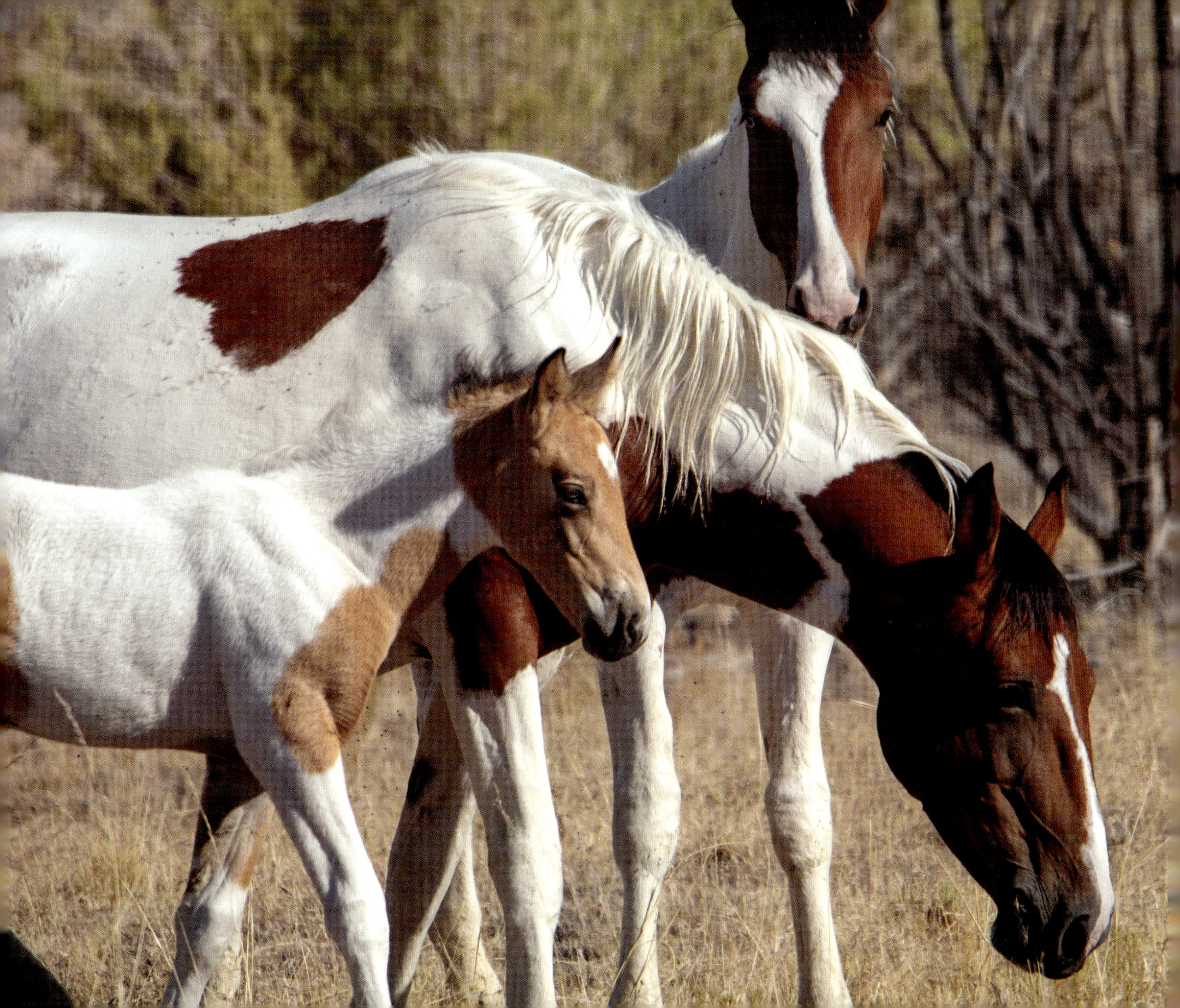

Opposite: Three generations of pintos. Pinto is a color, not a breed of horse; a pinto horse has a coat that consists of large patches of white and any other color.

Right: The beauty of morning's first sunlight reflects on this family band.

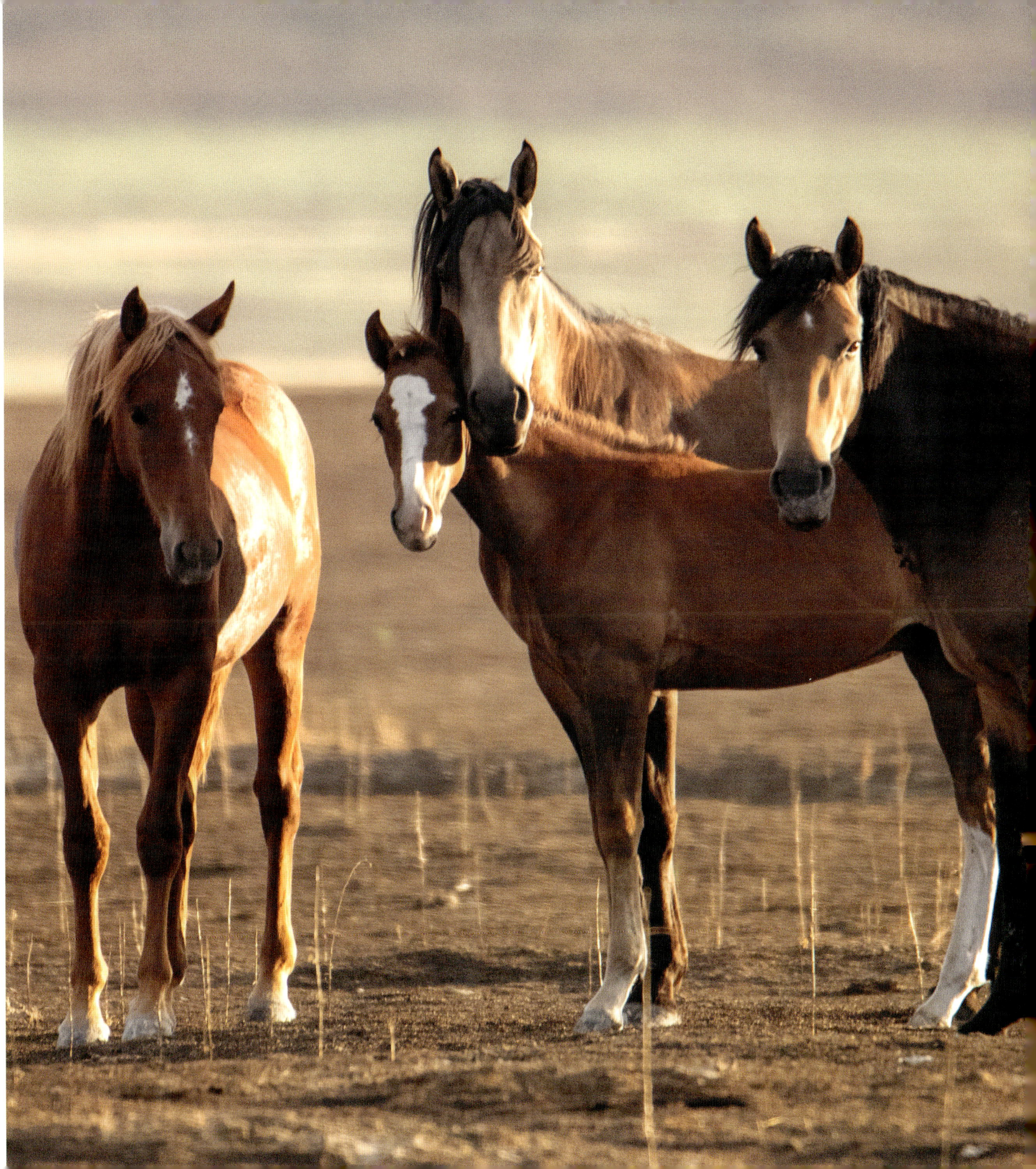

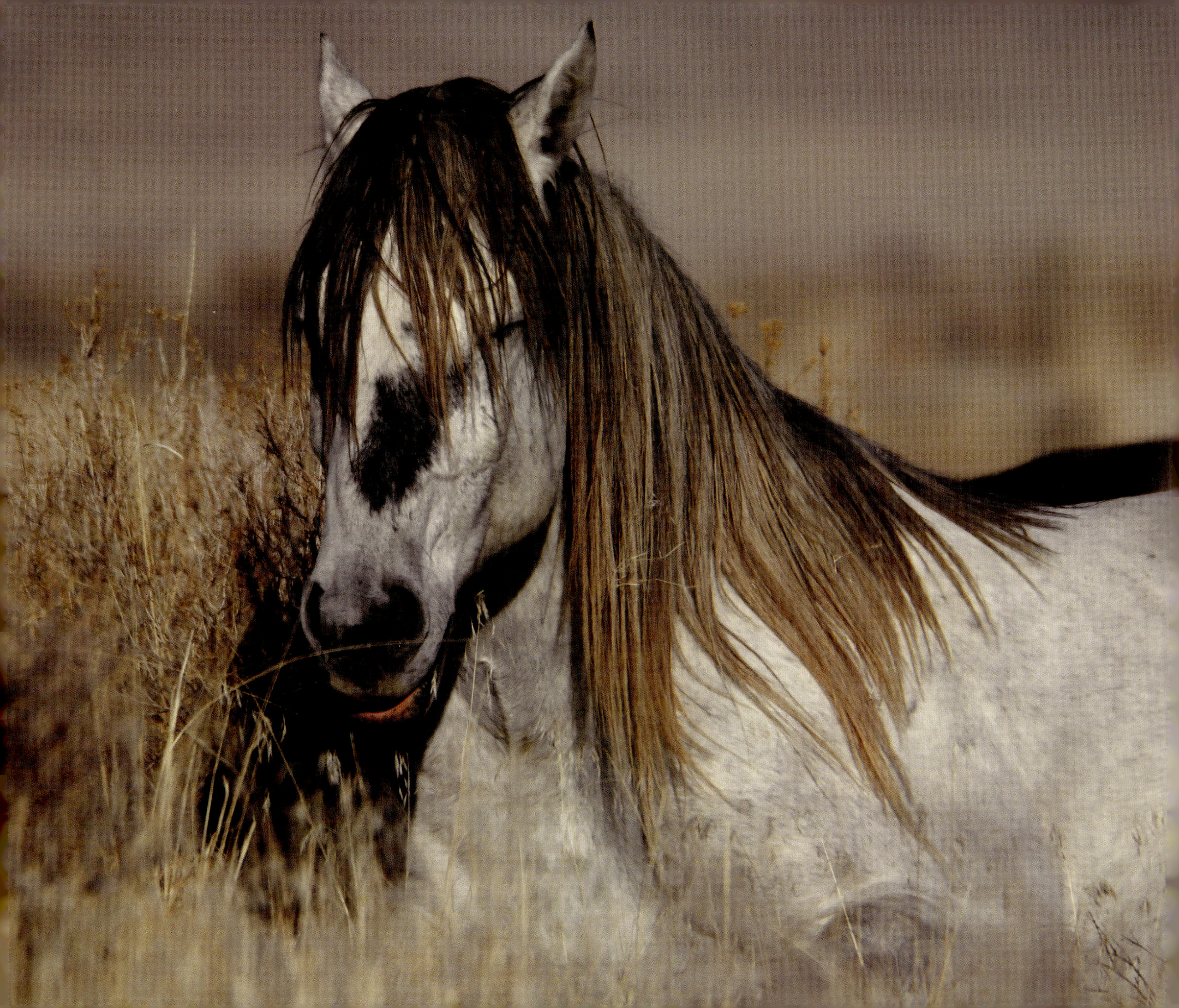

BAND STALLIONS & BACHELORS

♦ ♦ ♦

Within the herds of wild horses are bands: groups of horses consisting of one stallion and a group of mares. These stallions will fight to keep their mares, which are sometimes stolen away for a new band by a younger and stronger stallion. These bloody battles chisel away at the established hierarchy within the herd—stallions often wear the scars of a life that is challenging and brutal.

Young stallions form close-knit bands in their youth, known as bachelor bands, until they become restless and realize they need a band of their own. Bachelor bands, of any age, stay close to the main herd and travel with it.

While older stallions are often the ones who have protected a band over many years, the fighting eventually gets to be too much. The stallions resign themselves to a solitary life or to the company of another older stallion. Those with a keen eye will spot the solitary stallions who have left their herd, keeping their distance from the bands, and showcasing the true spirit of wild horses—endurance, freedom, and survival.

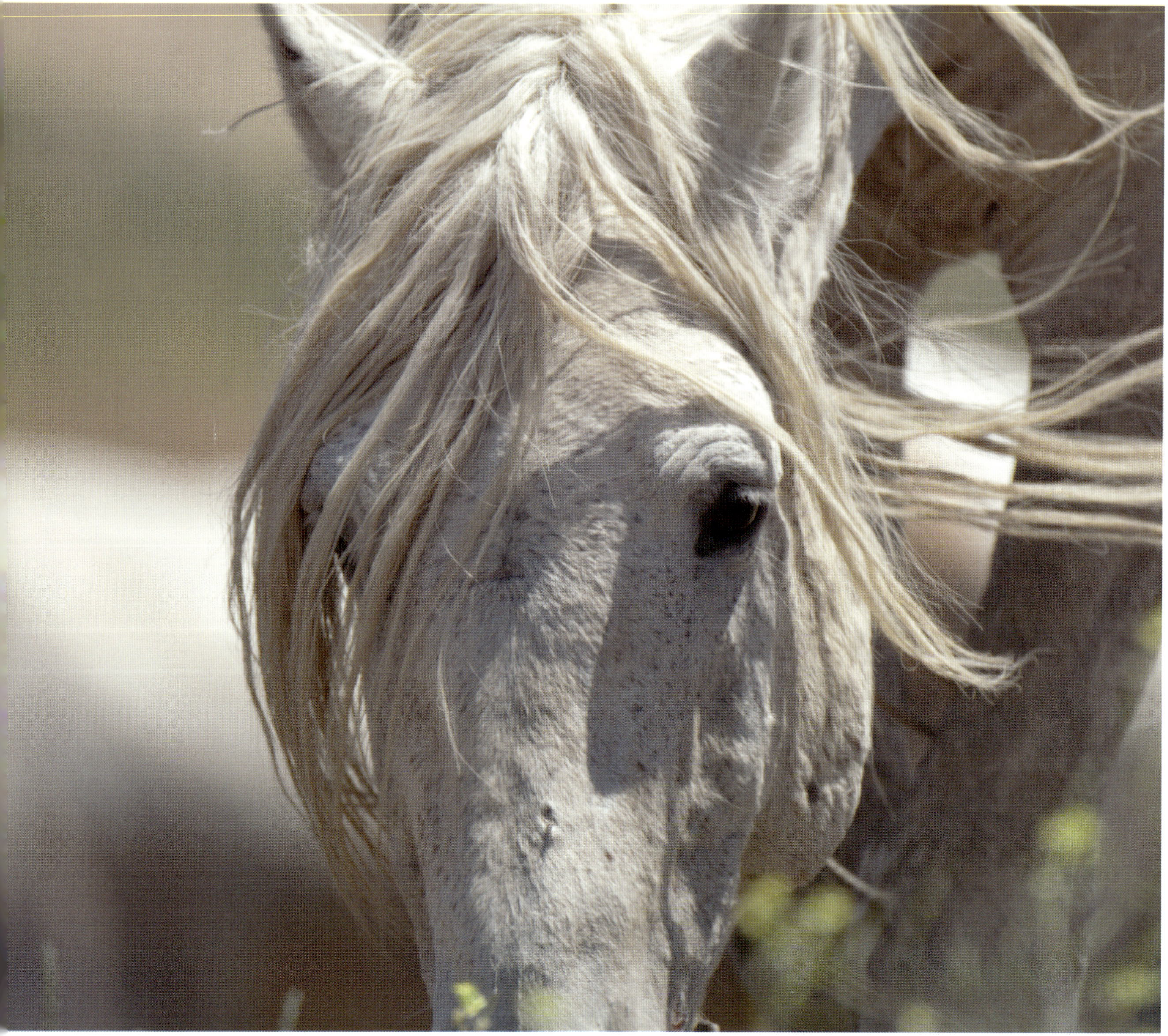

Left: It's been said that one's eyes are the windows to the soul. With the Old Man, I'm sure his soul has many stories to tell.

Opposite: The cremello bachelor stallion, wild and proud.

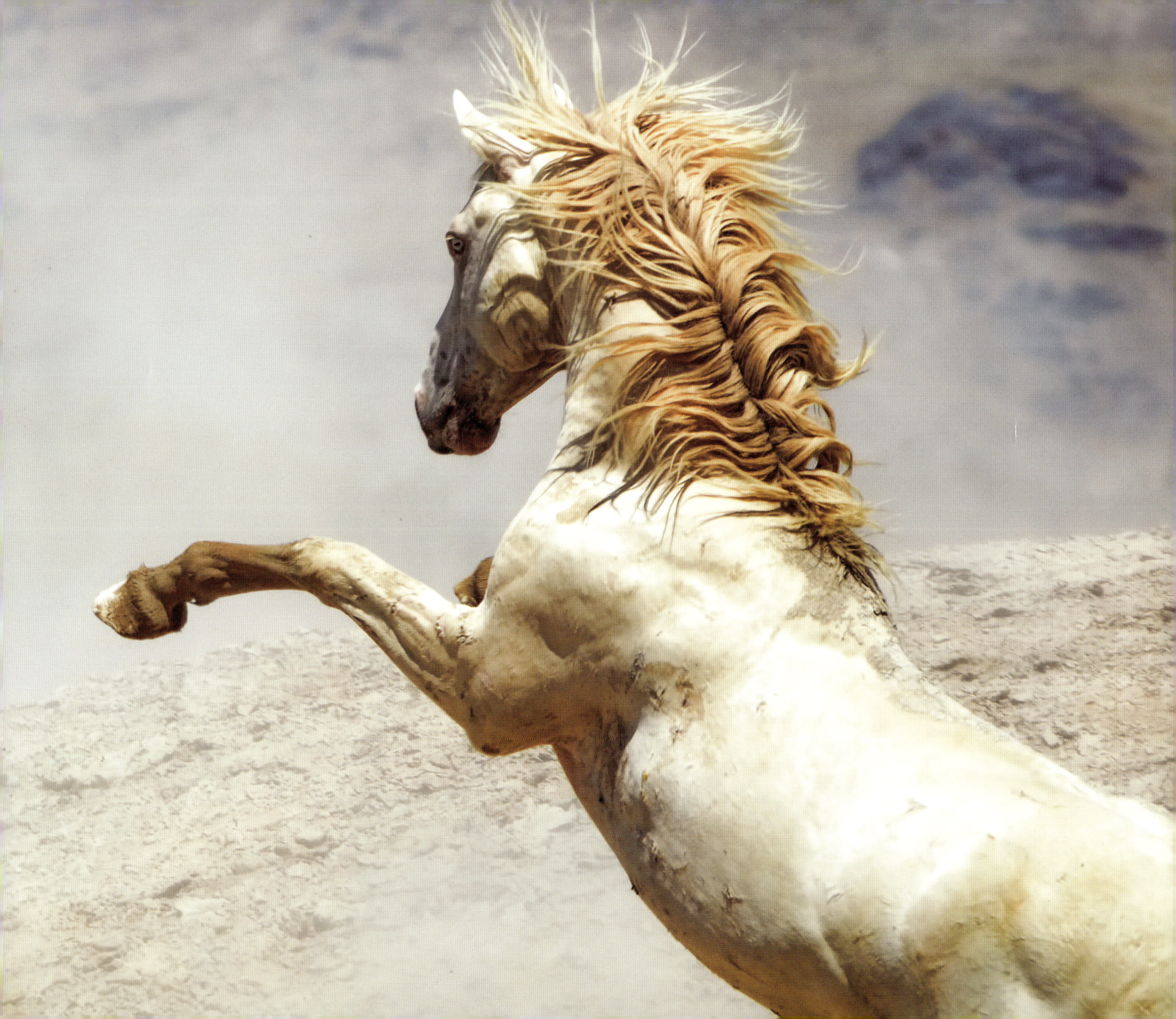

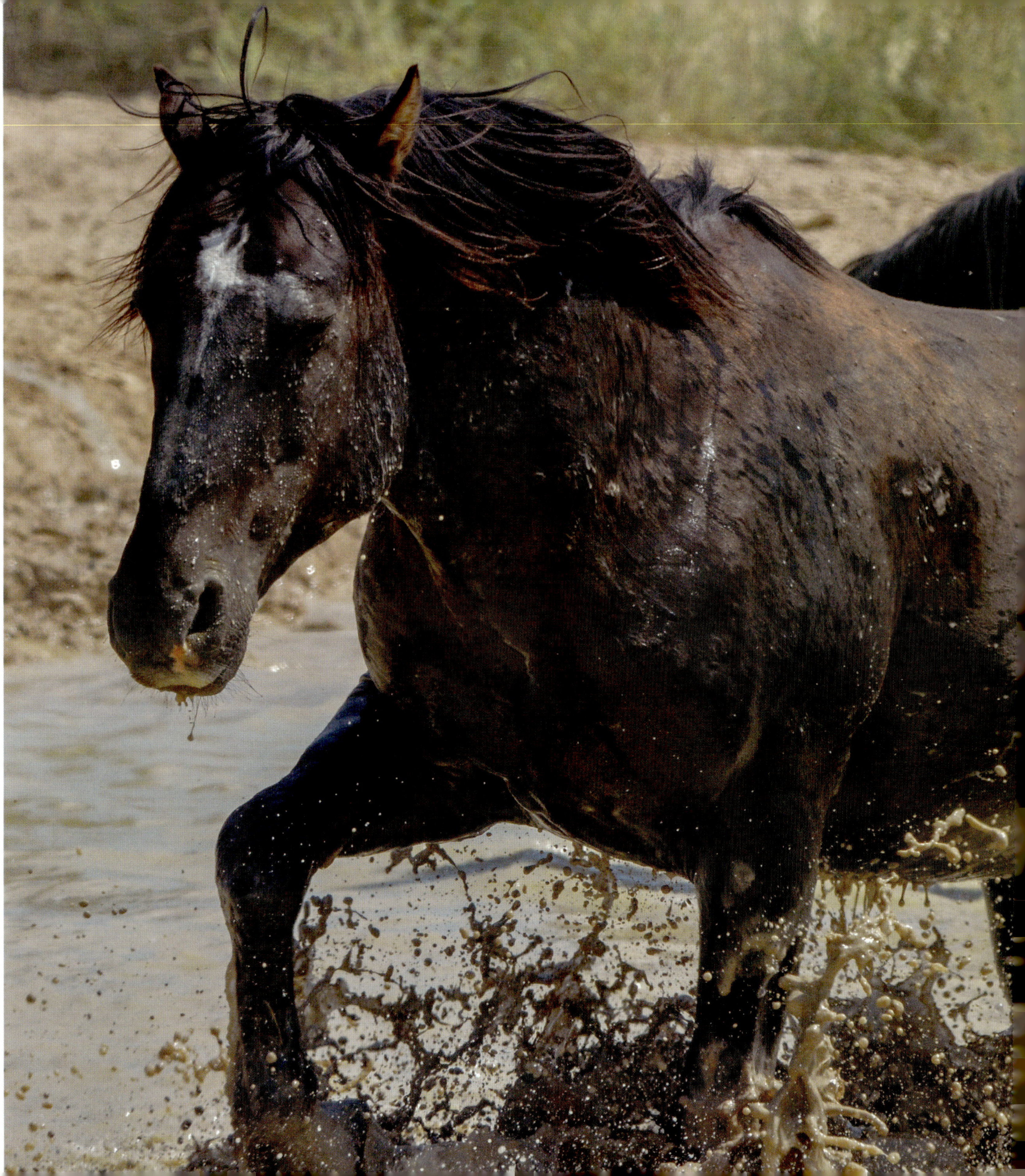

Old Man and the black stallion enjoying what seems to be a synchronized water dance.

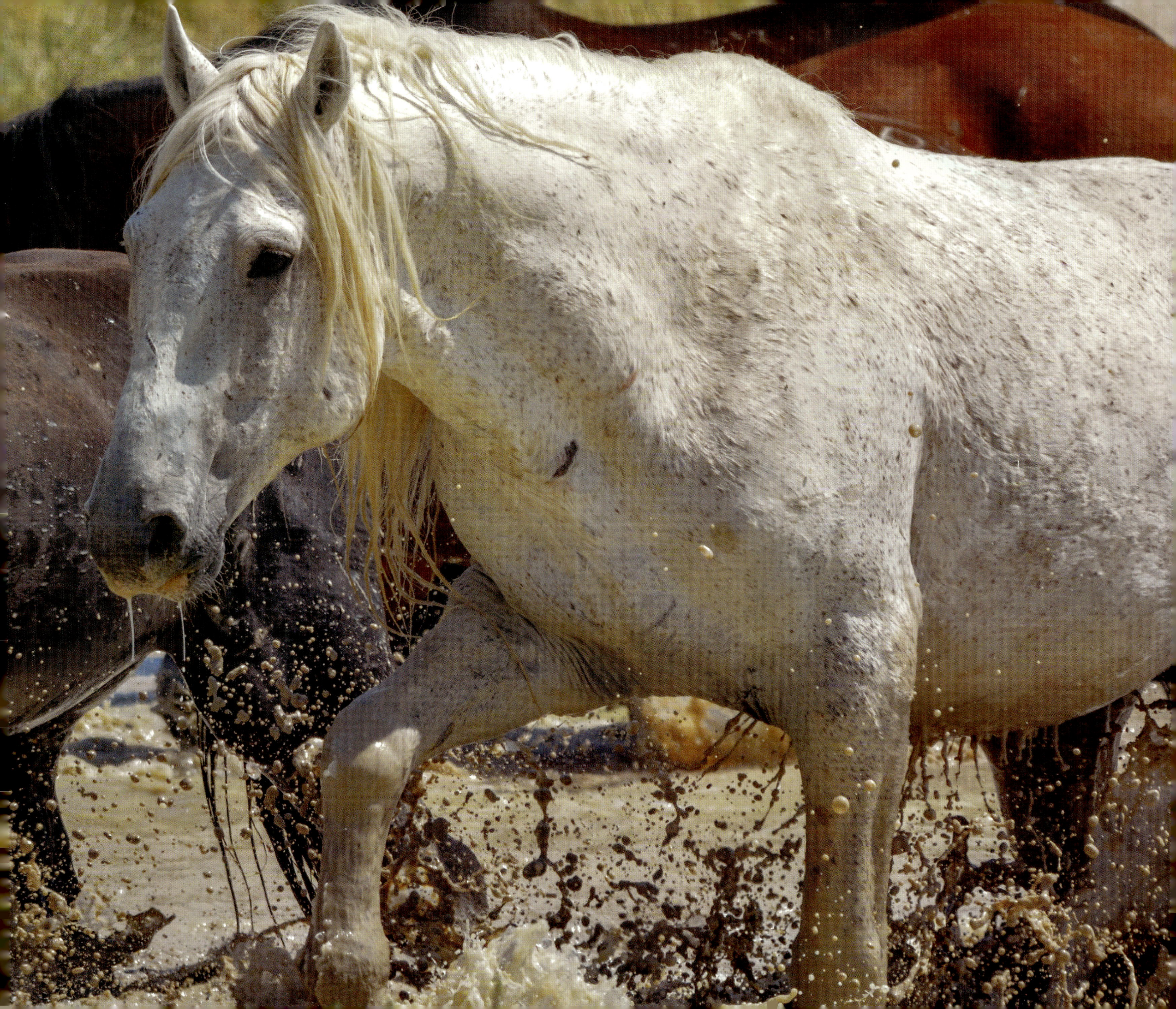

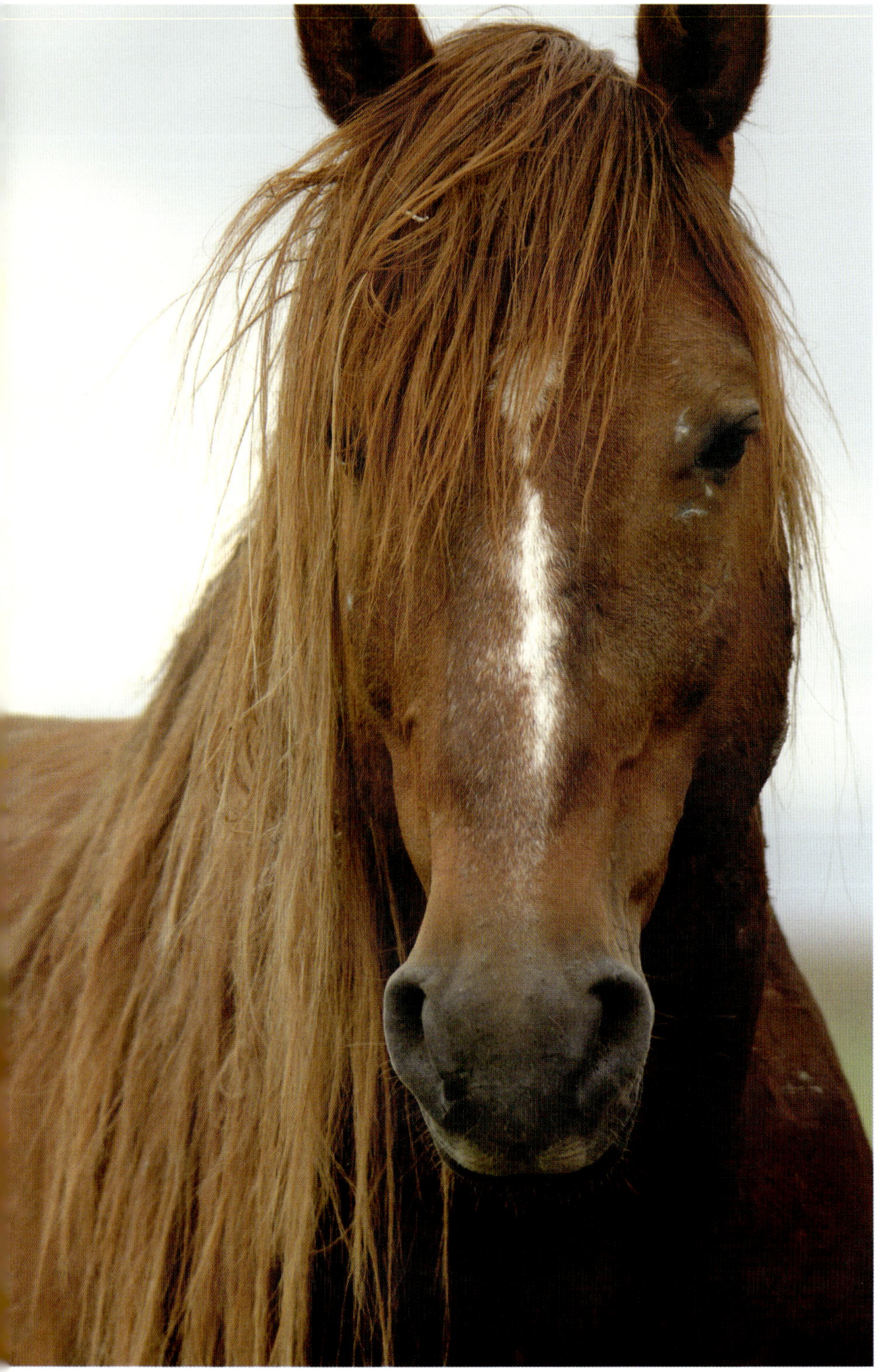

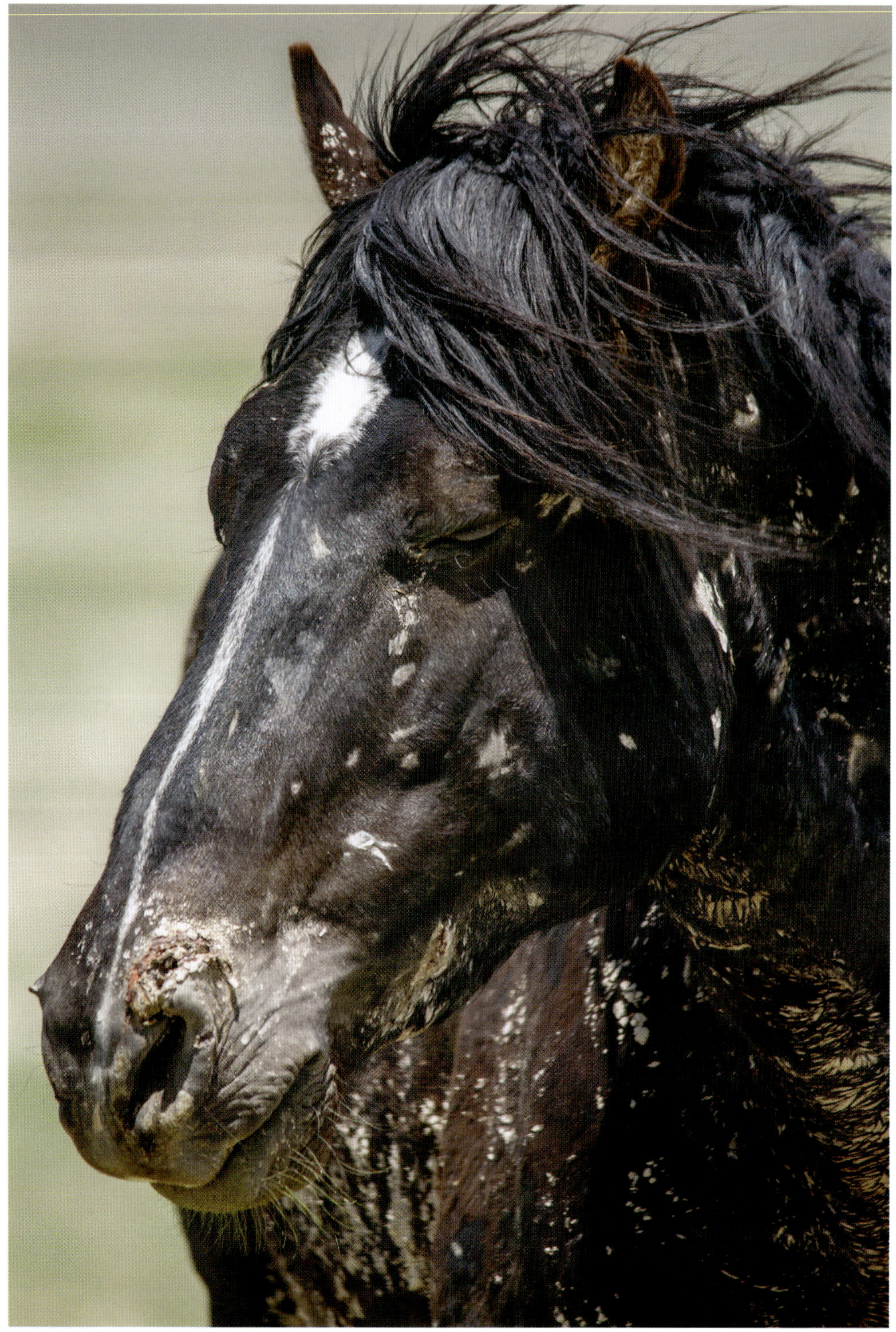

Opposite left: The band stallion they call "Red Lion." His forelock and mane make him seem almost like a rock star.

Opposite right: The black bachelor stallion. His face and body show the scars of the many challenges he has met.

Right: Two stallions in a "yin yang," one of the many posturing moves that precede a fight.

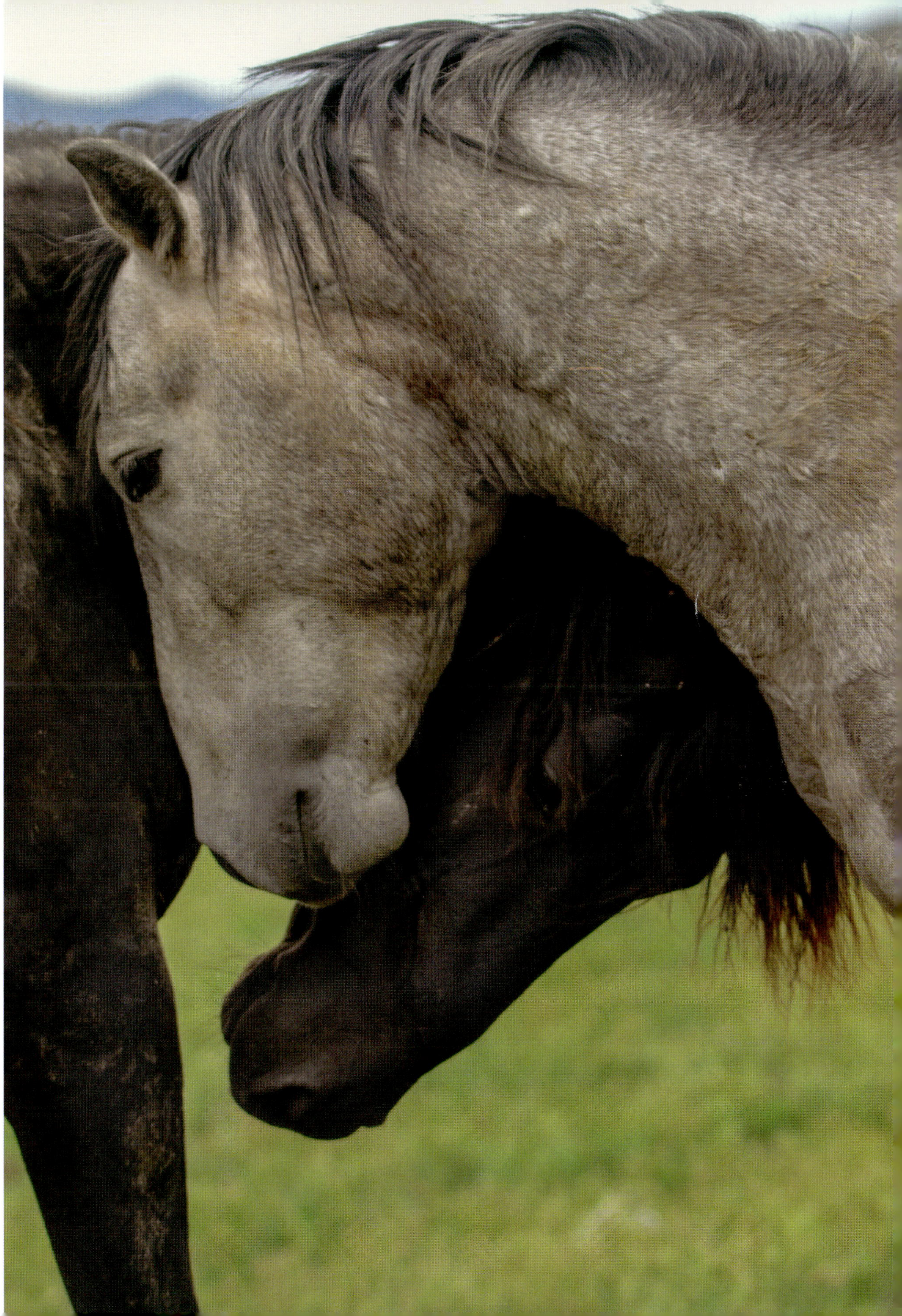

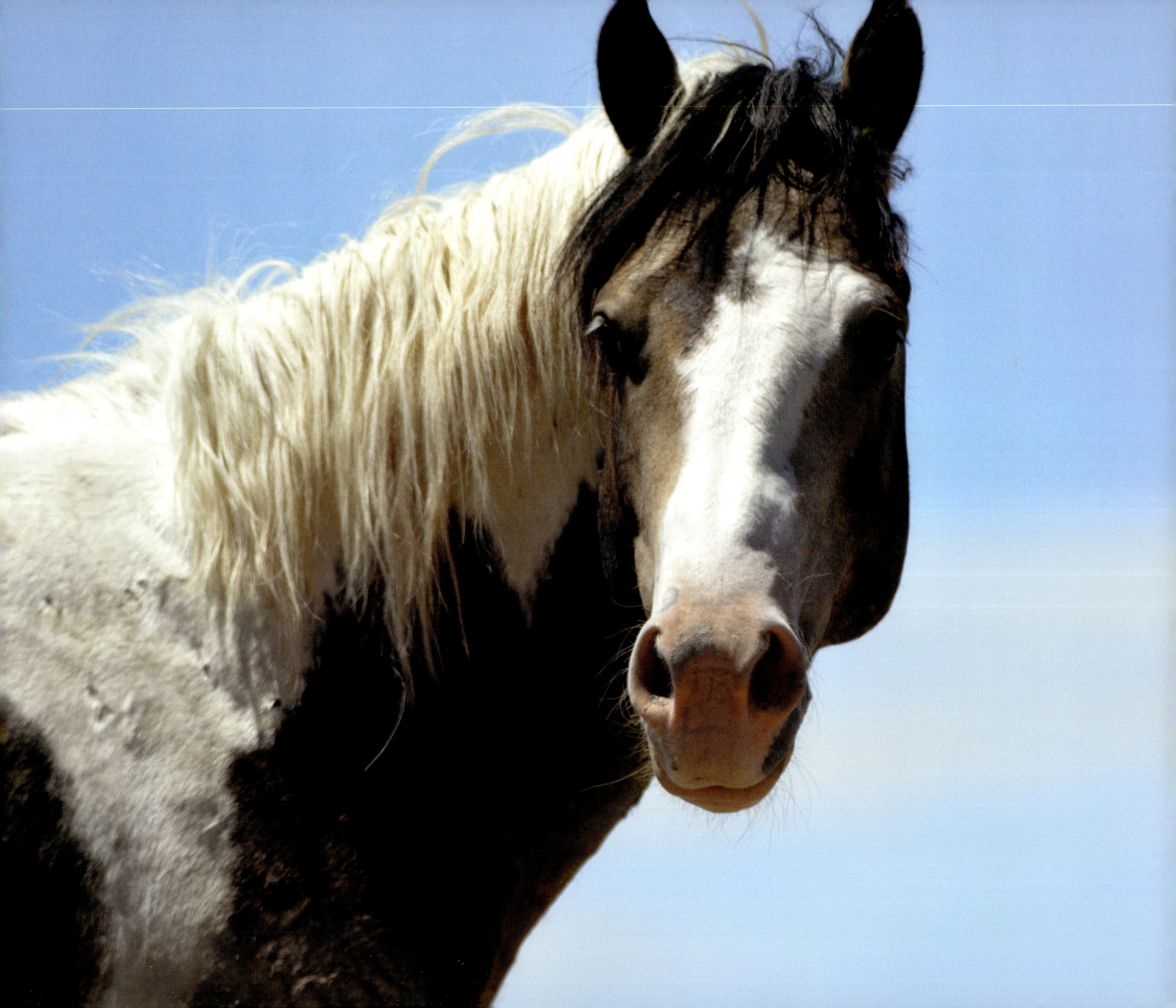

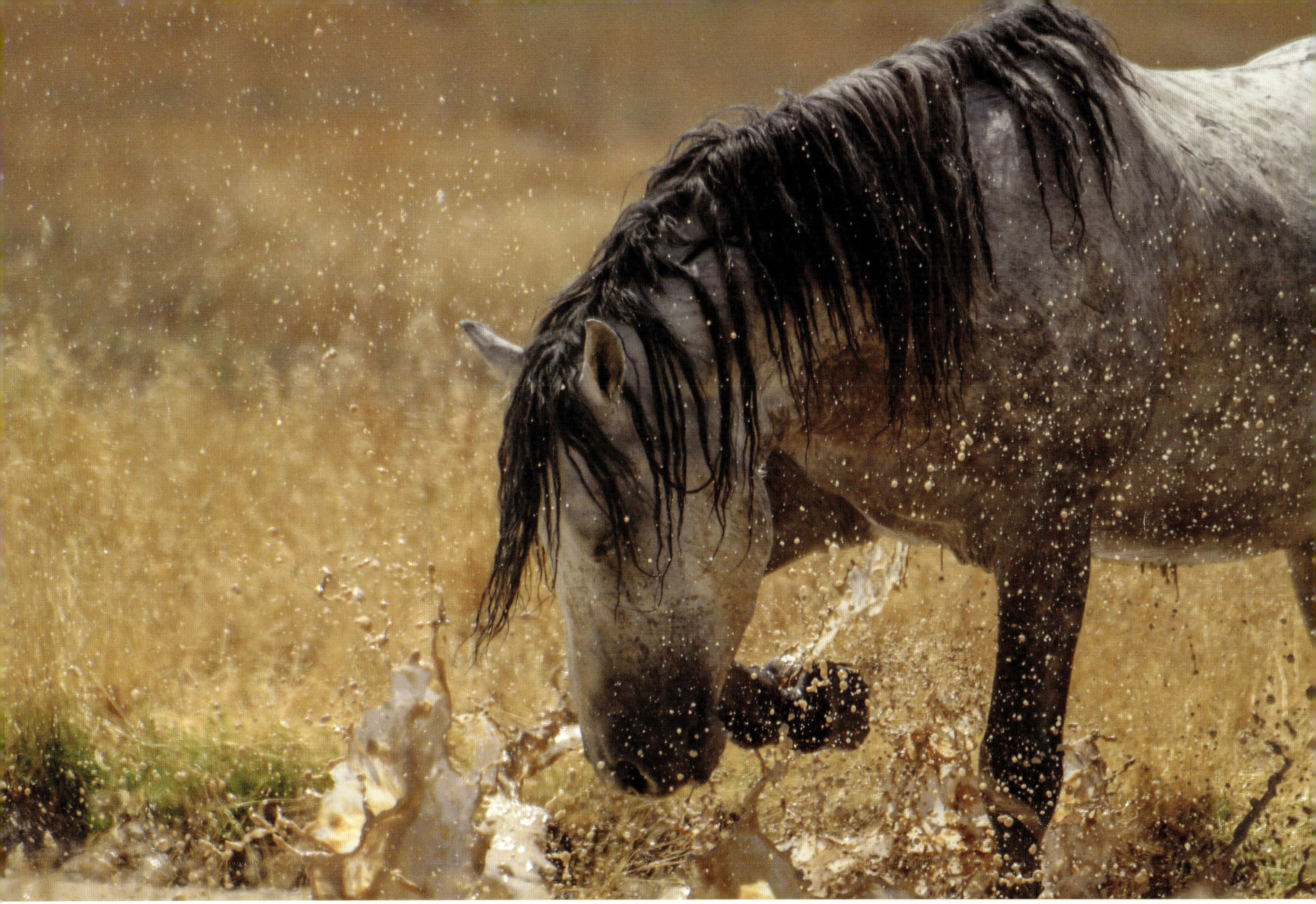

Opposite: A pinto bachelor stallion watches as a band moves across the range.

Above: A stout gray band stallion splashes in the waterhole before getting a drink.

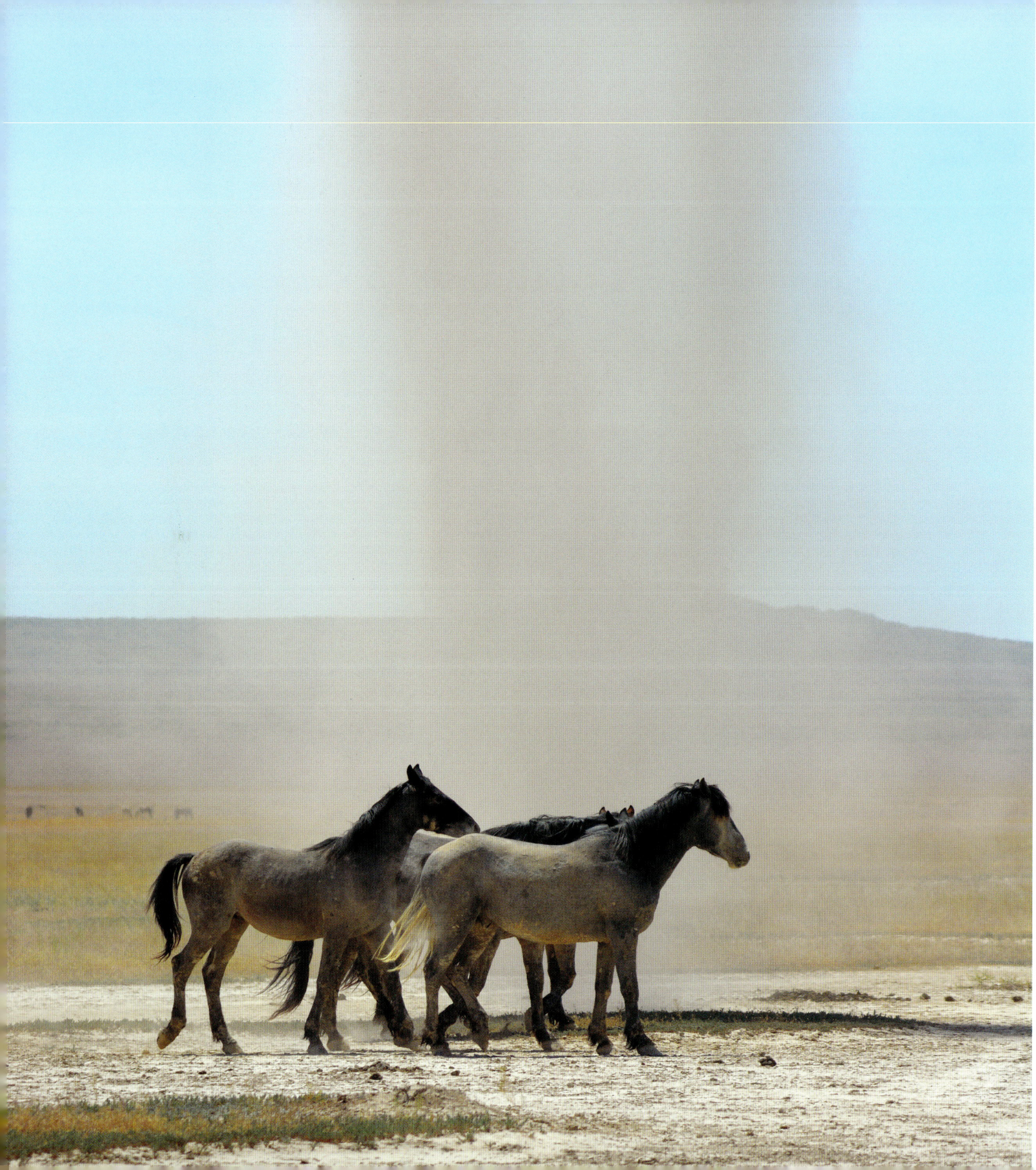

Left: It is a rarity to capture a photo of a perfect dust devil in the desert; to catch one with the wild horses in it is priceless.

Opposite: Many of the gray horses you find in the desert were once black or a dark gray. As they mature their dark coats begin silvering.

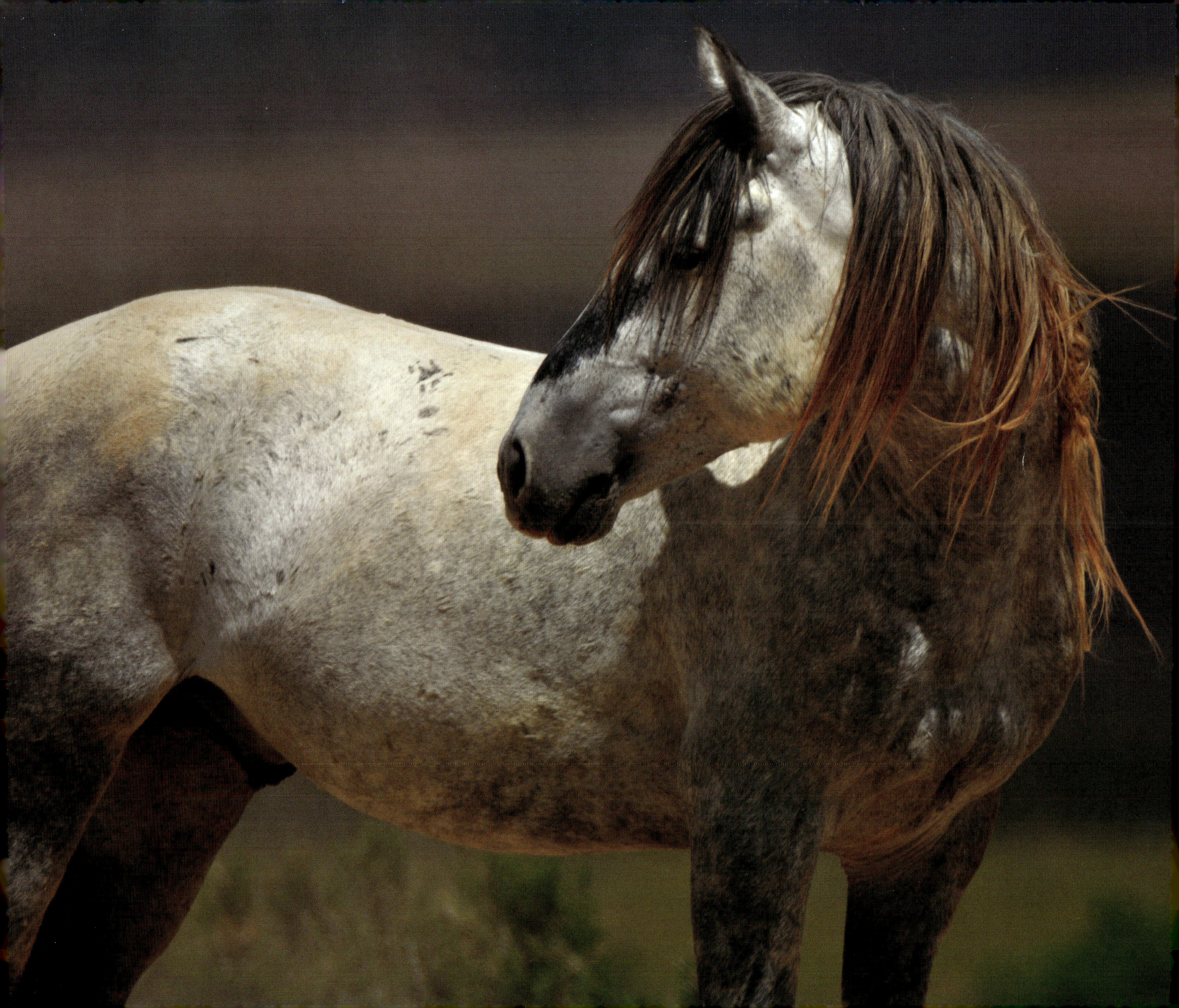

THE CREMELLO BROTHERS

The cremello colts were foaled in the spring of 2012 to separate mares—a buckskin mare and a pinto mare. Immediately inseparable, the colts, who became known as the Cremello Brothers, stayed at each other's side for more than four years.

As young bachelor stallions, they traveled the range together with two others. This small band worked often—mostly unsuccessfully—to steal mares from other bands. Failure did not deter them. Undaunted, they would work together to harass band stallions and their lieutenants in violent challenges that could last up to several minutes.

The Cremello Brothers went their separate ways in the fall of 2016. The larger stallion was able to steal a young mare and foal, only to lose them to their original stallion a few months later. He stayed close to a new band in the following years, eventually taking over the band and leading it.

The smaller cremello stallion disappeared in late 2016, his fate left unknown.

The photographs of them are a record of the bond that earned them their name. They were brothers not by blood, but in everything else: fortitude, strength, and spirit.

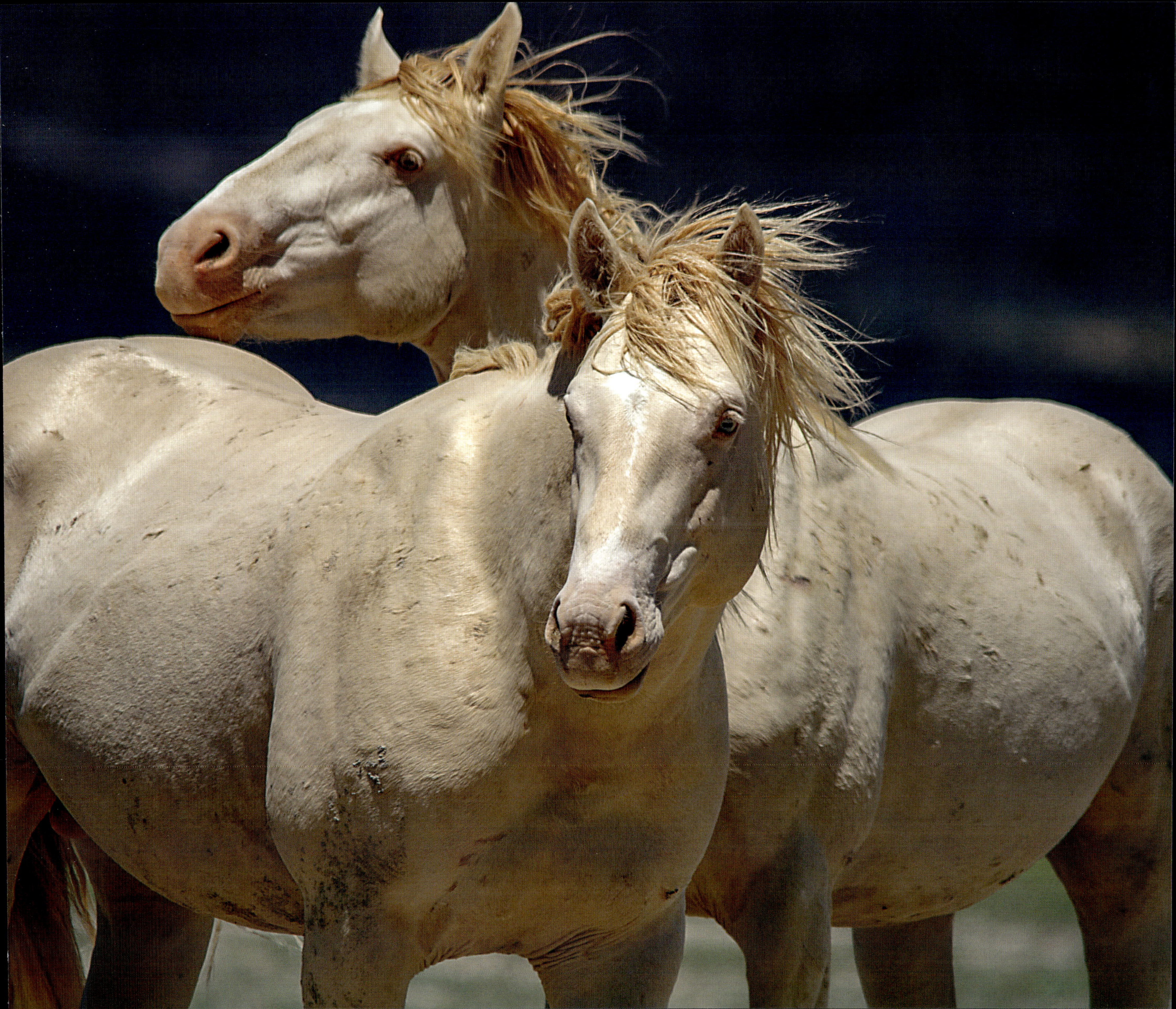

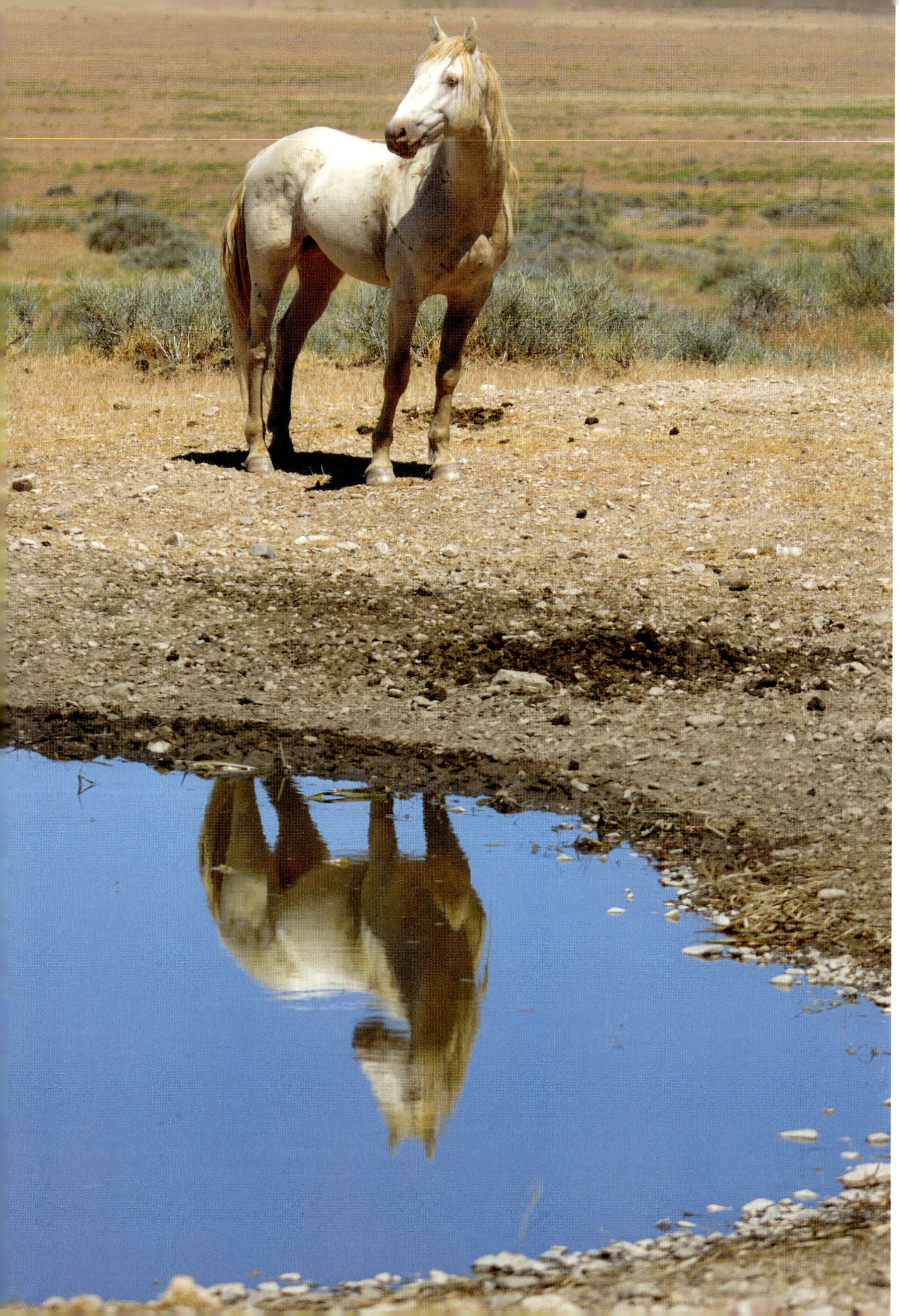

Left: The stillness of the water and the still wind provides the prefect refection of this cremello stallion.

Opposite: The Cremello Brothers on alert. The cremello horse has a cream coat with pink skin and blue or glass-colored eyes. Their manes and tails are white. The cream color can vary from a soft white to a pale gold.

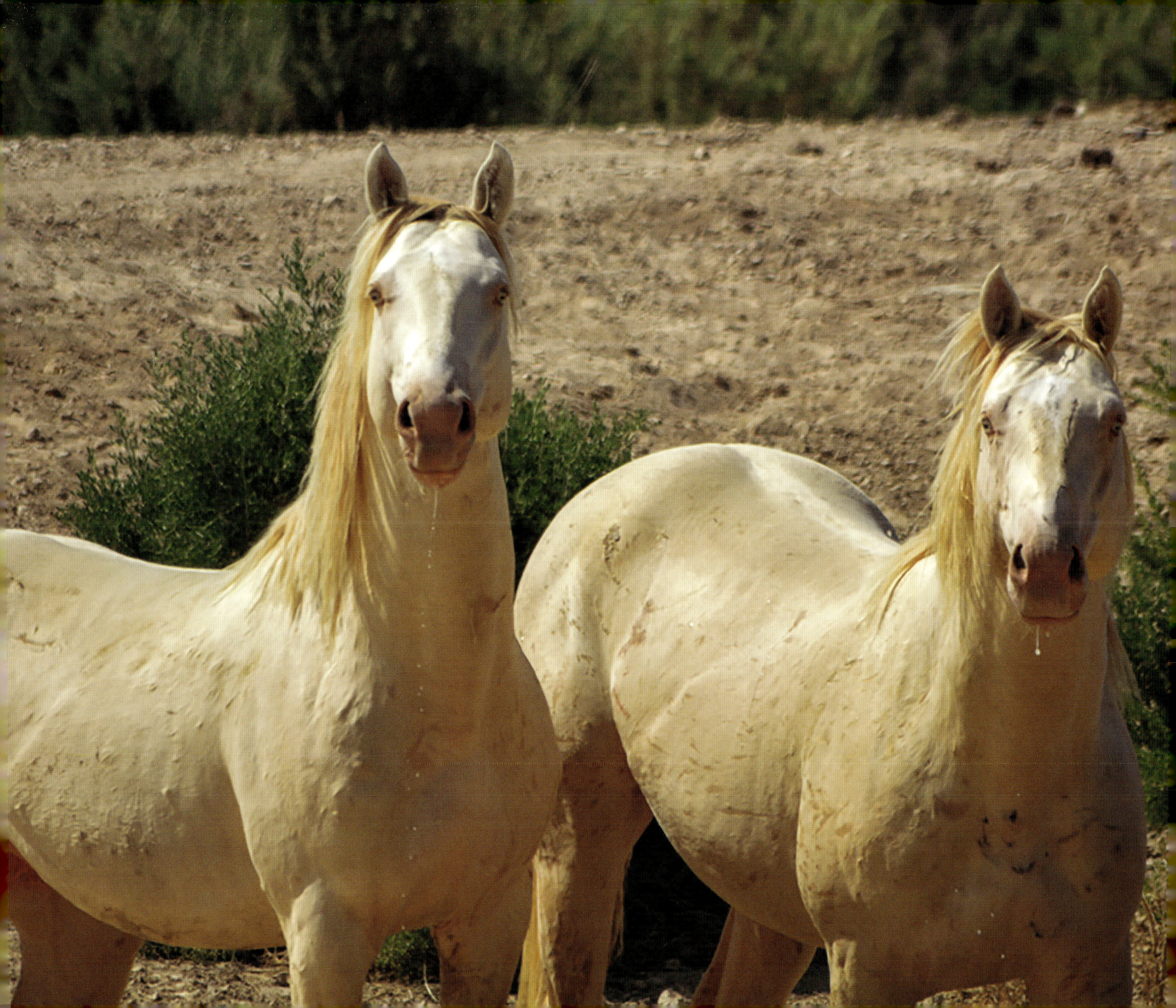

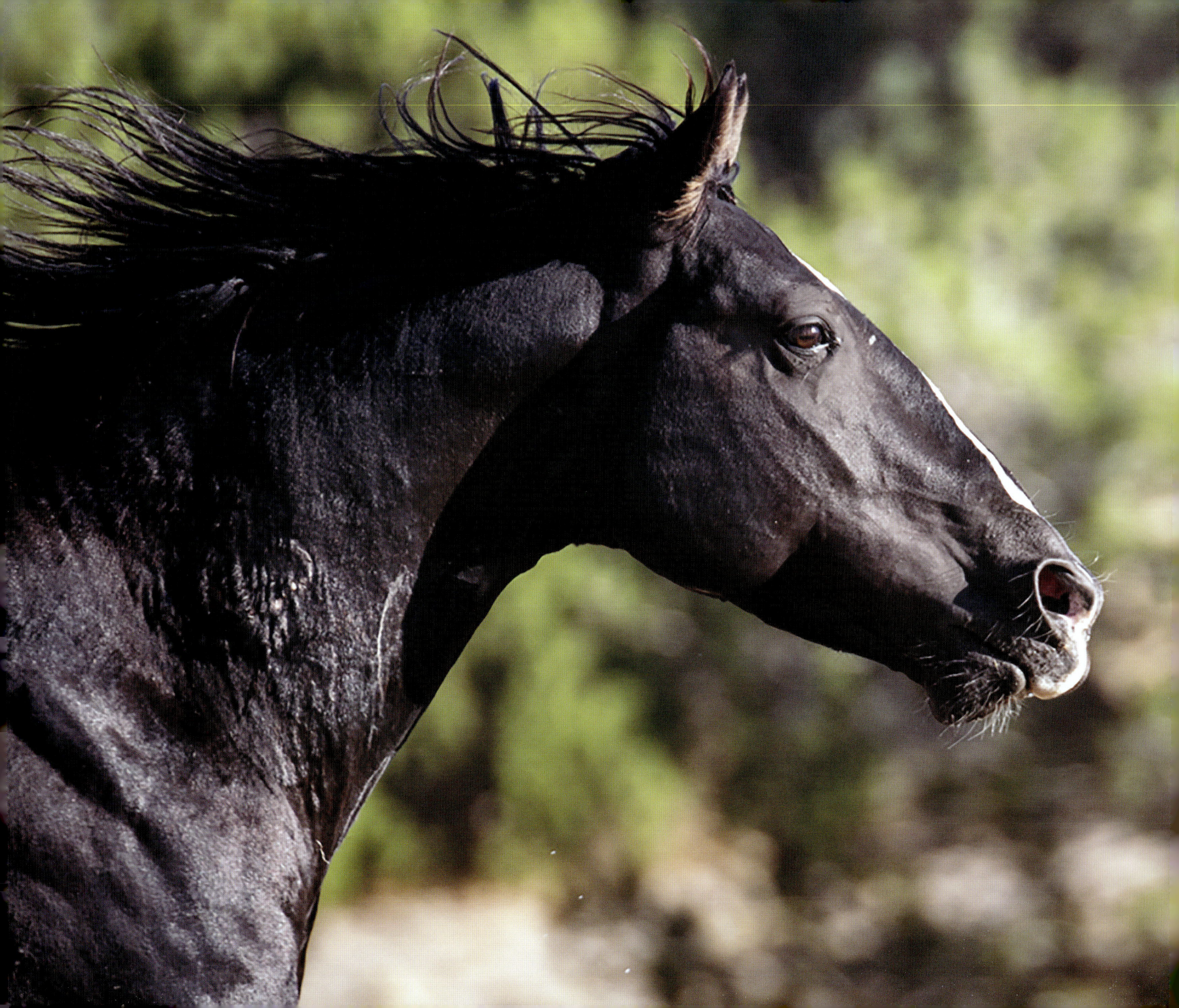

Opposite: A bachelor stallion moves to catch up to his band.

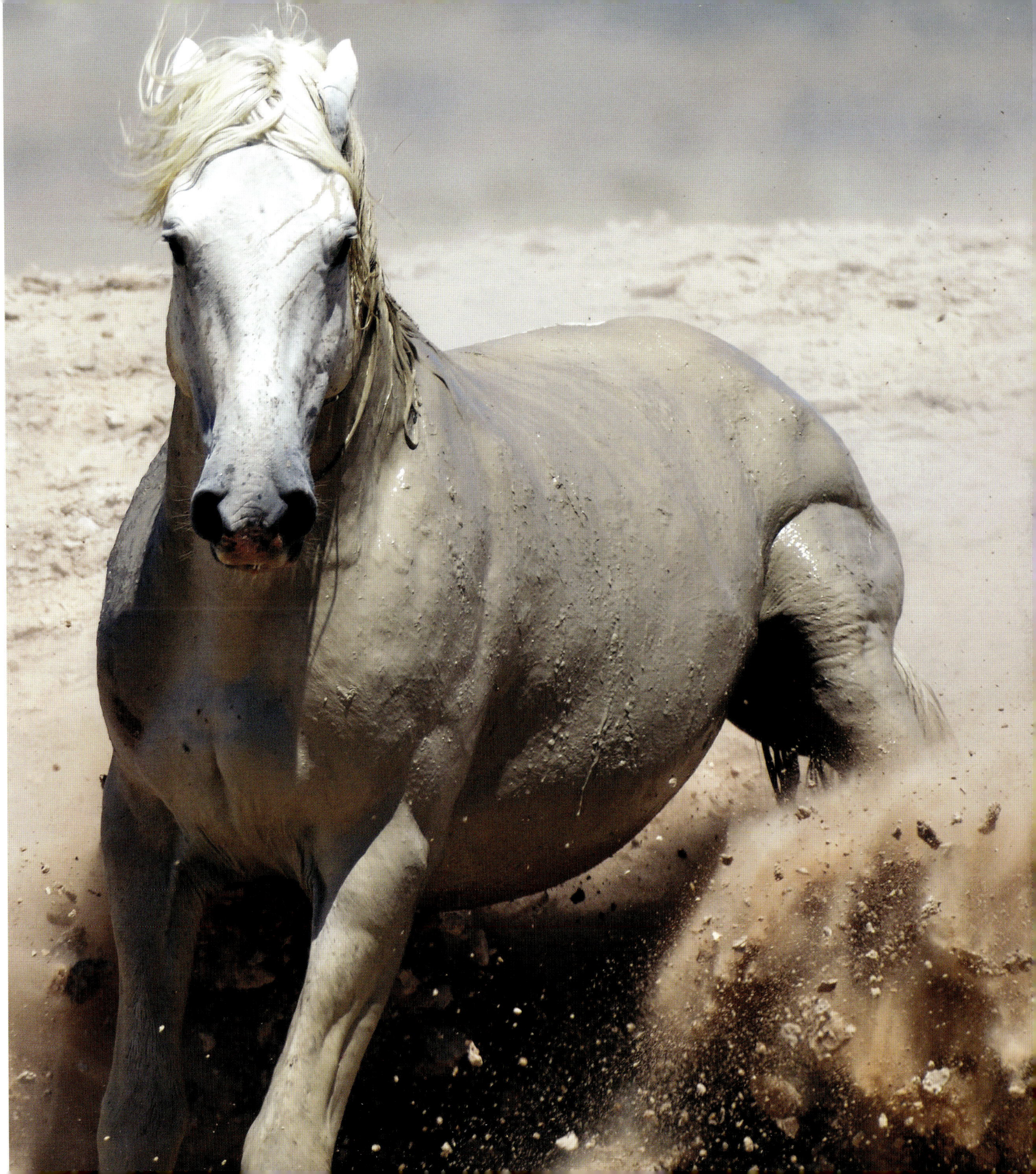

Right: A gray bachelor stallion slides down a sand dune as he pursues his rival.

Next page left: A stallion chase along the ridgeline.

Next page right: A bachelor stallion with a very long wind braid.

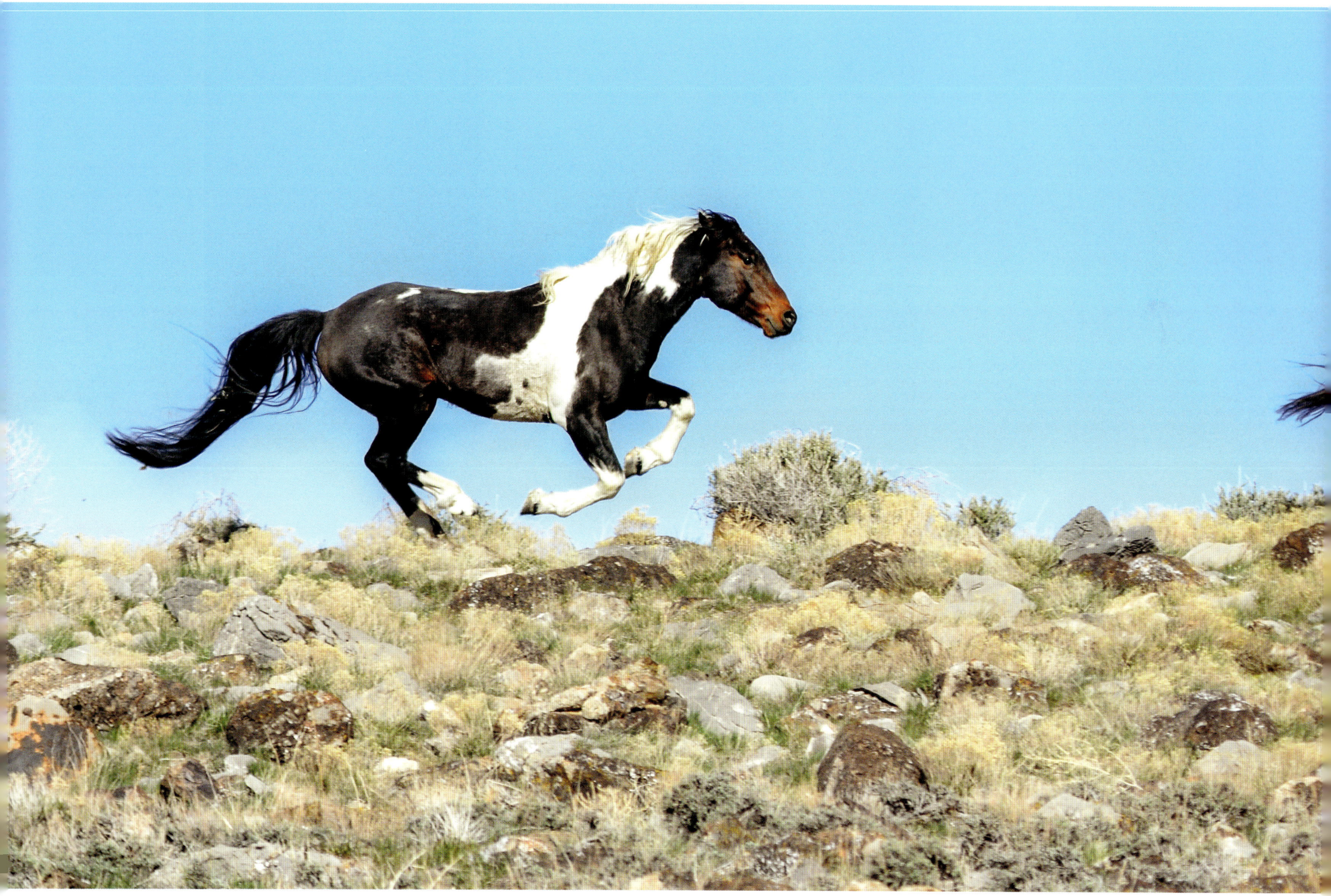

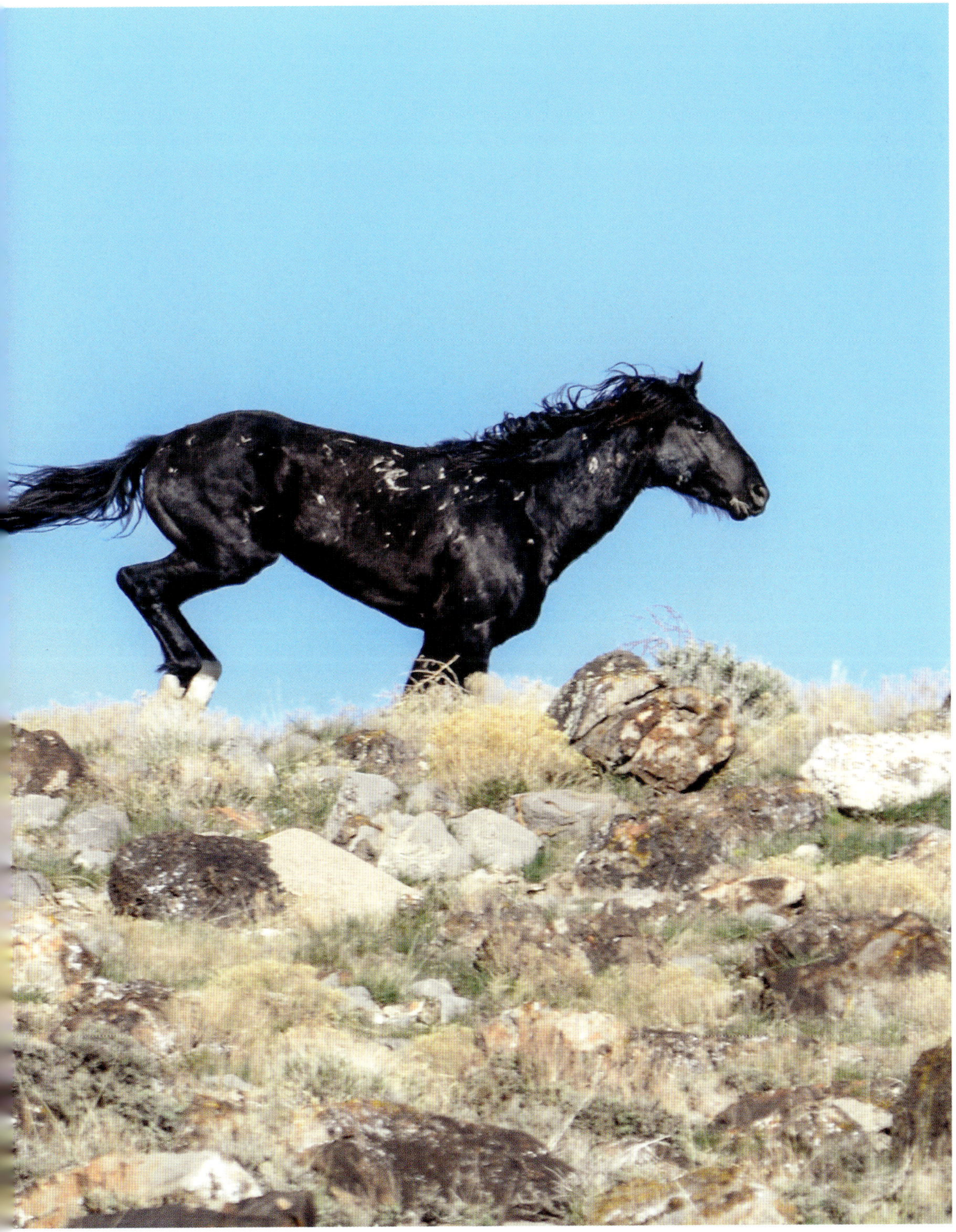

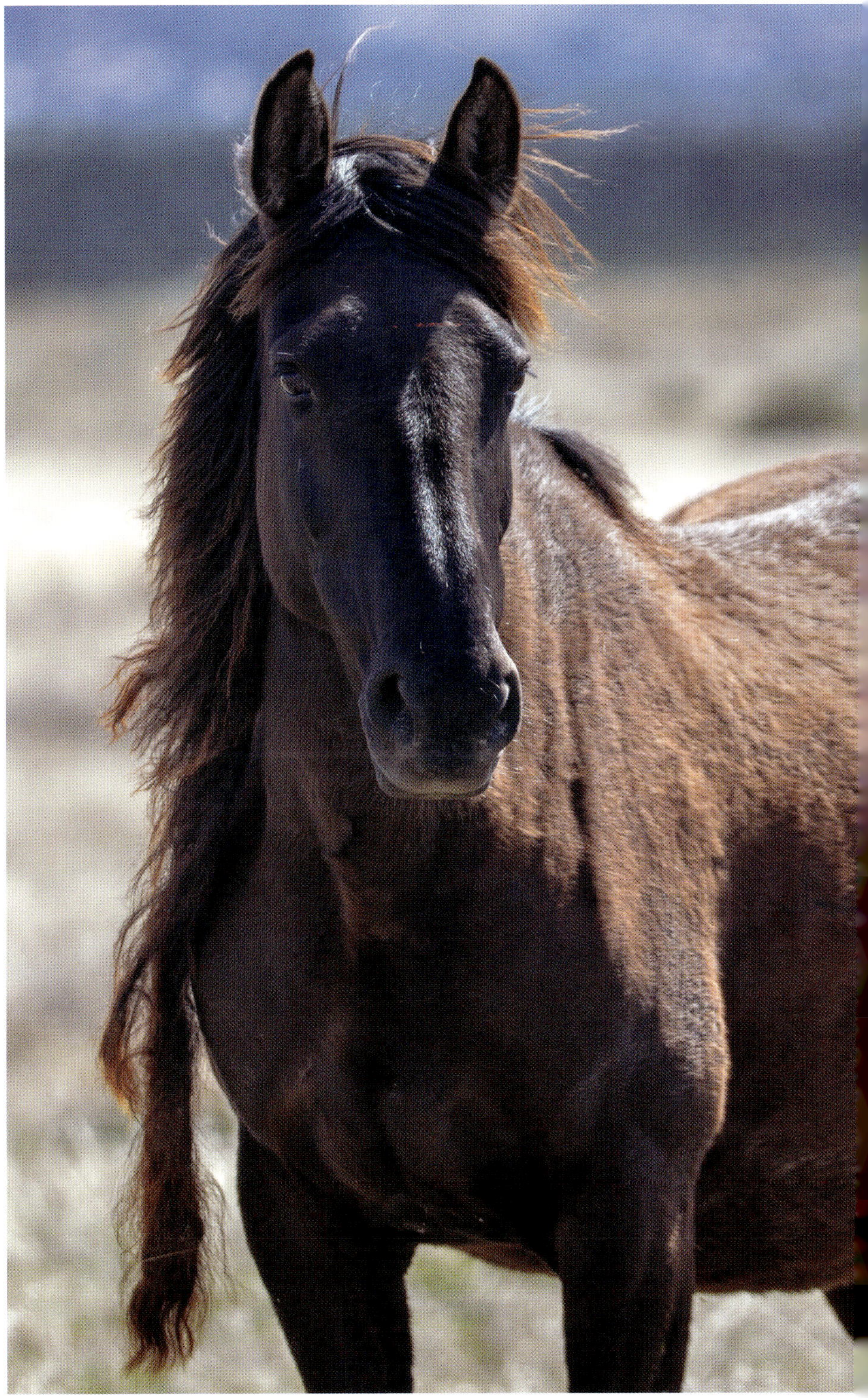

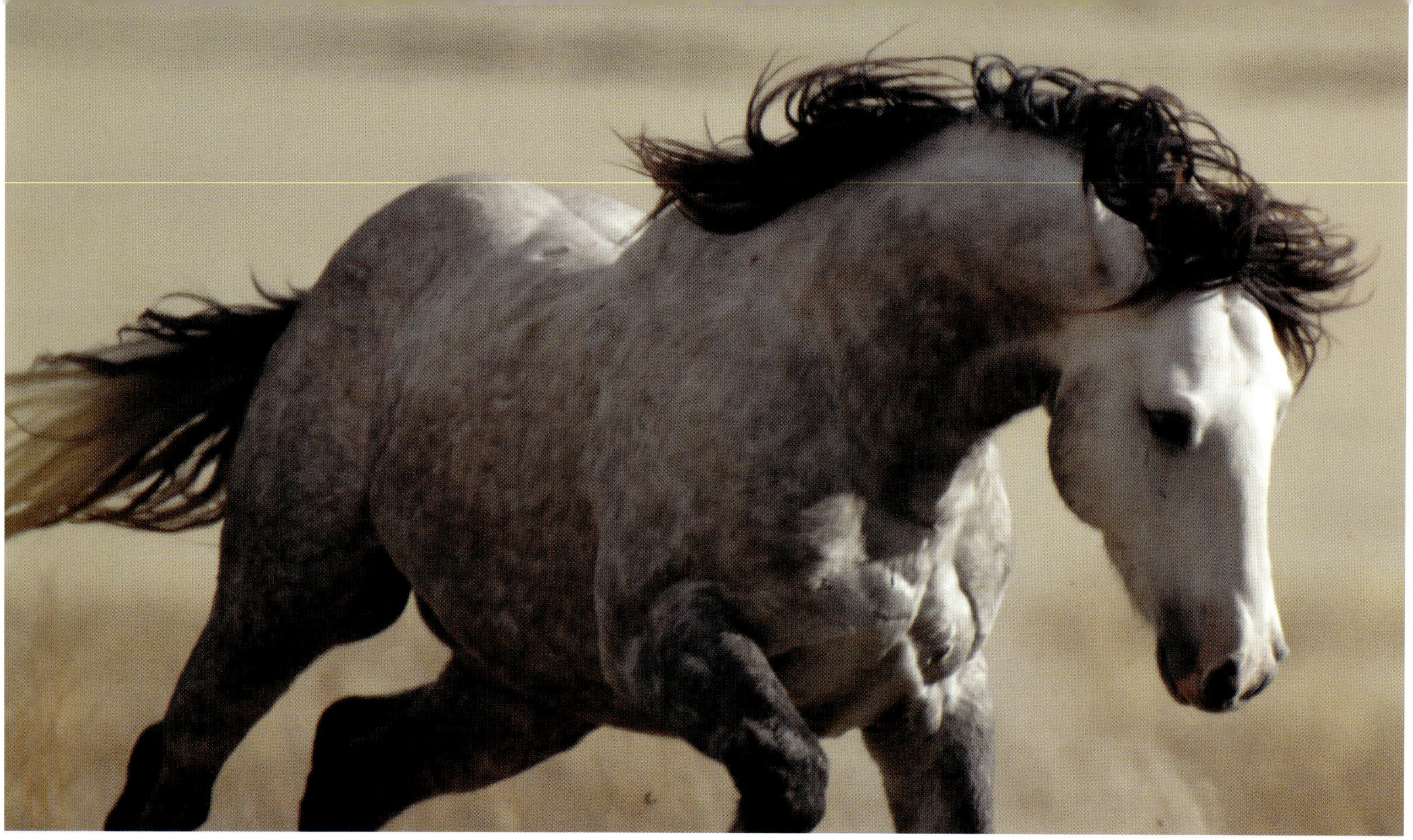

CLOCKWISE, FROM TOP LEFT: The athleticism and power of wild stallions are shown here as a gray stallion chases a rival stallion. The arching of the neck is a form of posturing as stallions battle one another. The outstretched body of the bachelor stallion shows the speed of the chase.

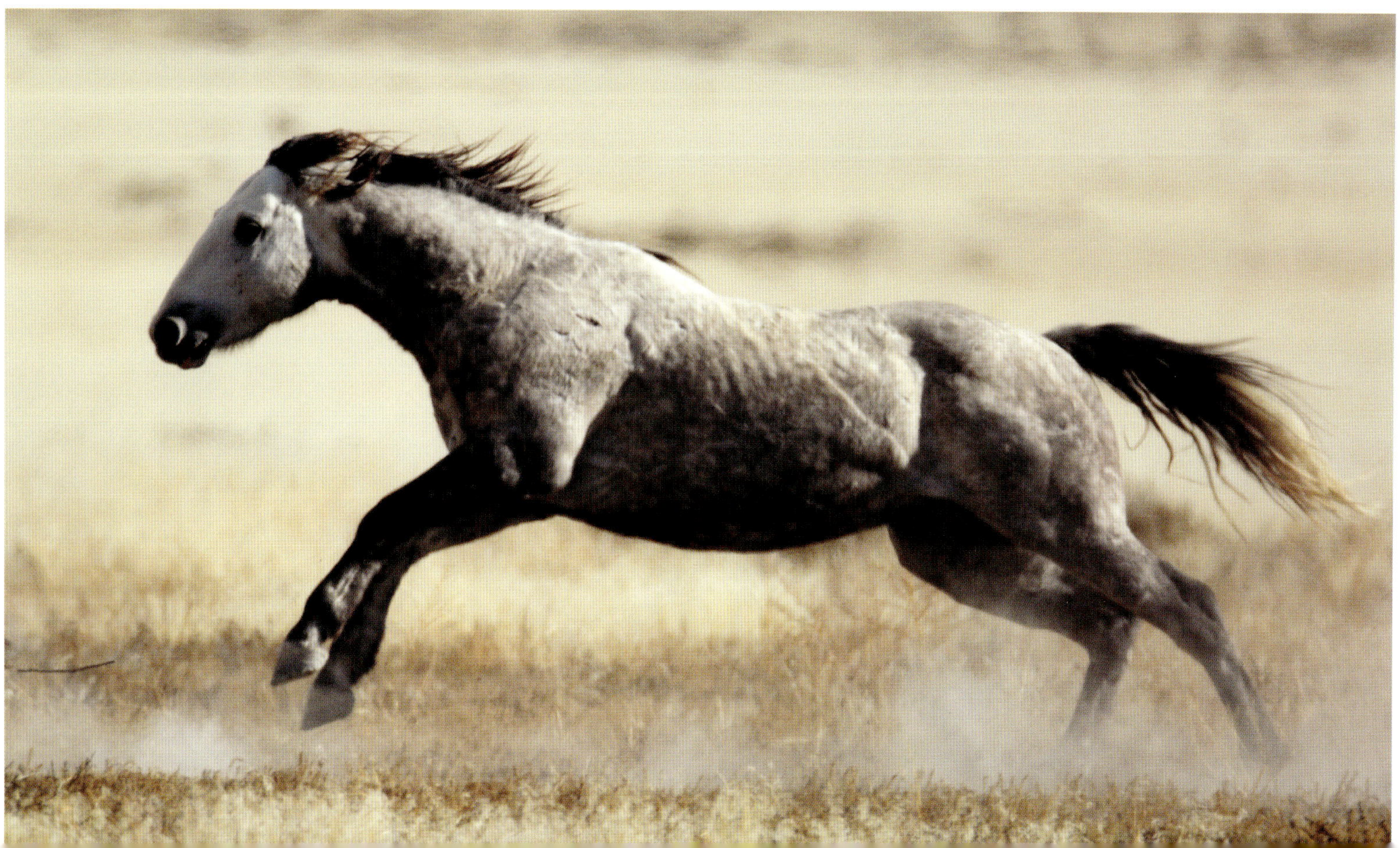

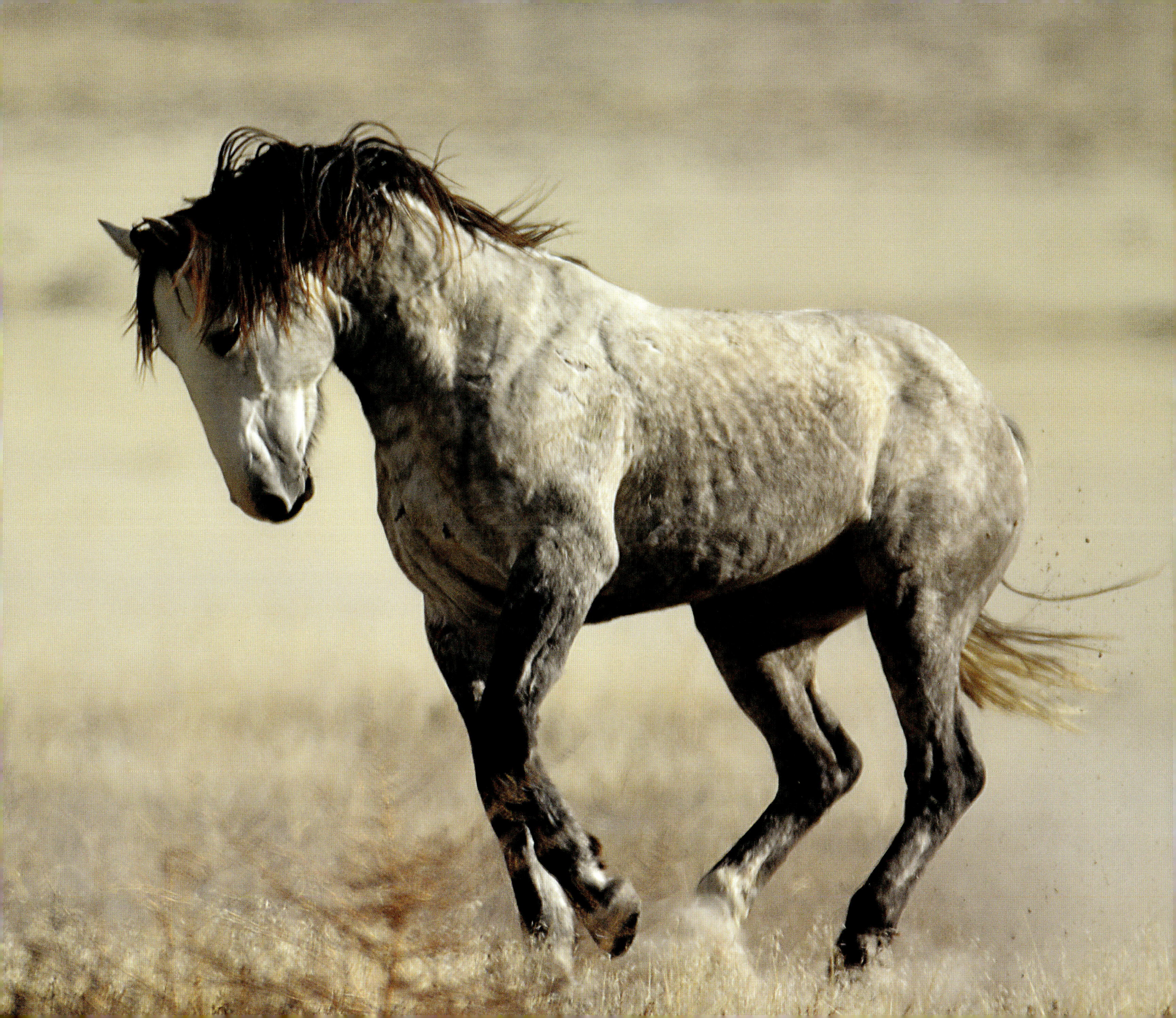

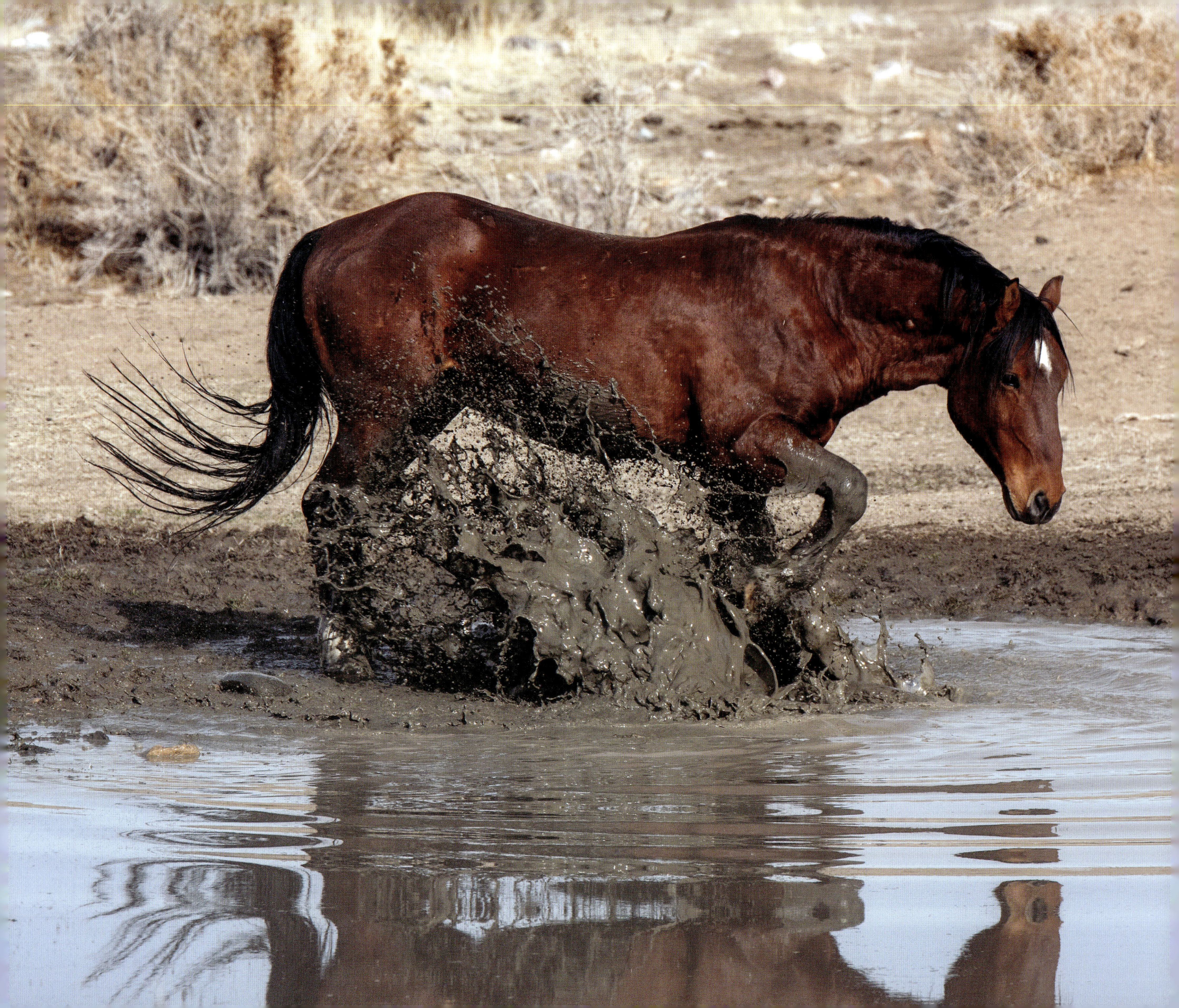

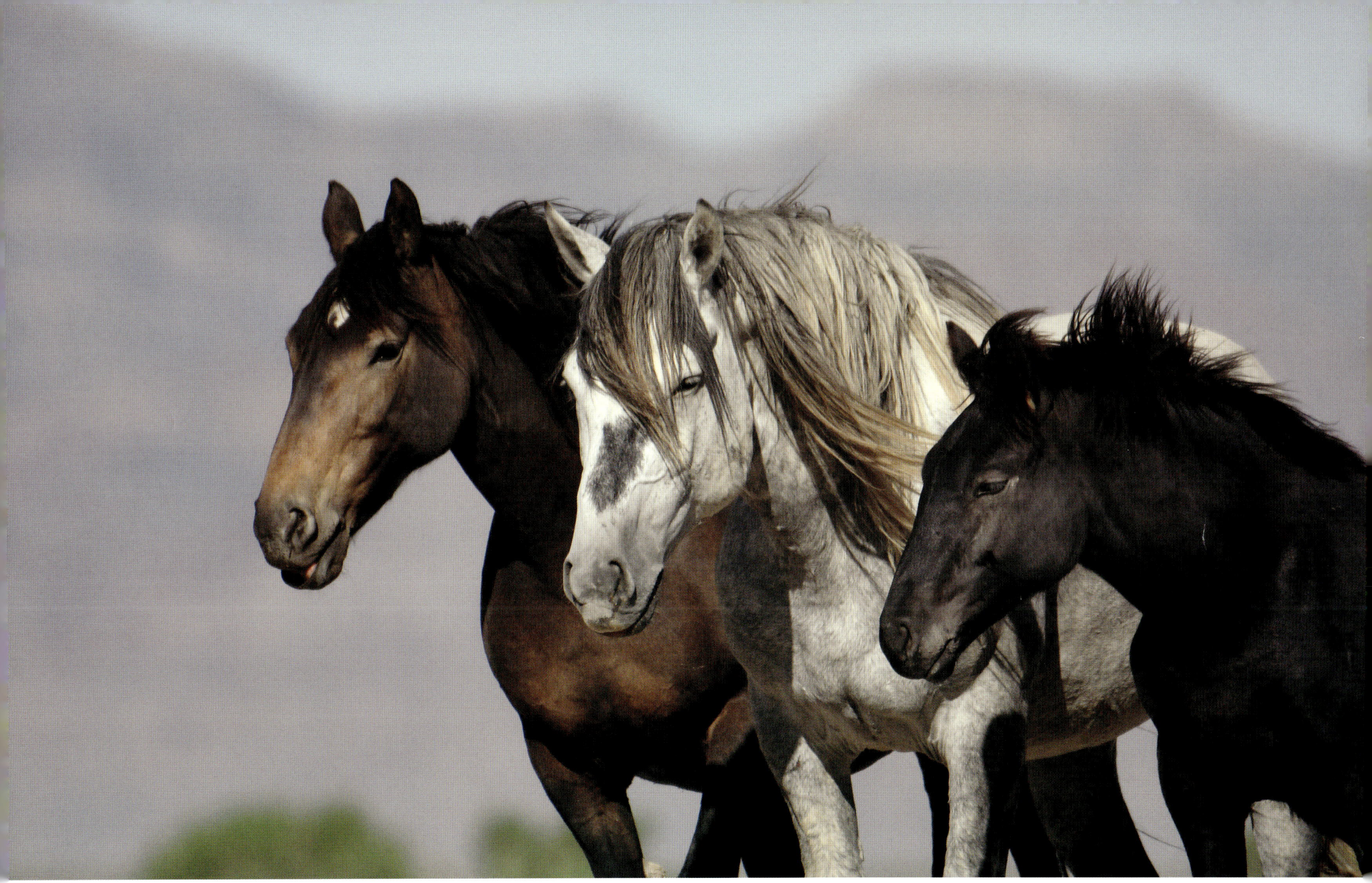

Opposite: A band stallion takes the opportunity for a quick splash in the muddy water before he returns to protect his band.

Above: A band stallion, "Goliath," with one of his mares and a young colt.

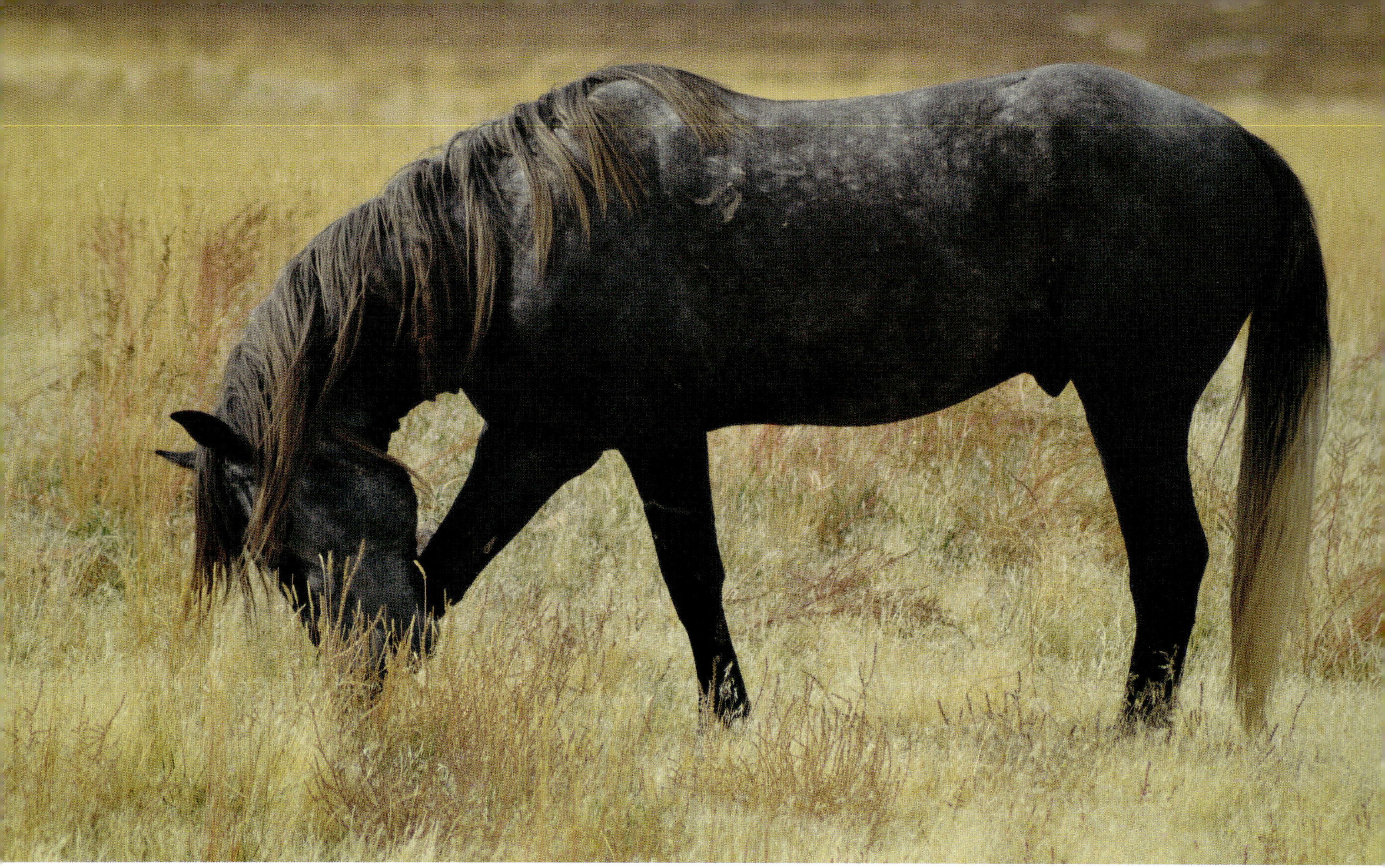

ABOVE: The band stallion, Goliath, in the fall of 2012 before his coat began silvering to the gray color it is today.

OPPOSITE: A band stallion rushes off to protect his band.

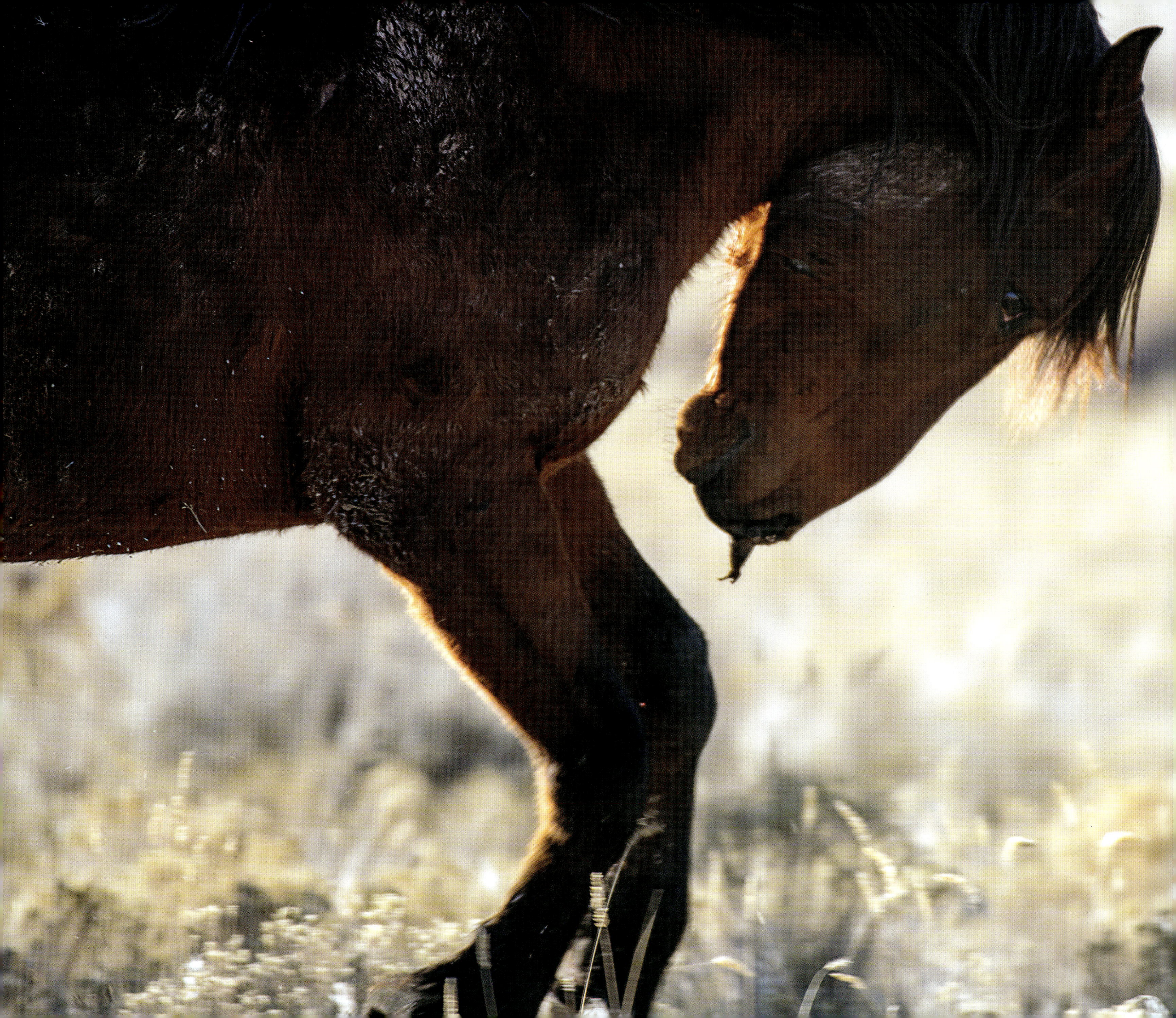

OLD MAN

Old Man is the most iconic stallion of the Onaqui herd and one of the most photographed horses on the range. Long in years, he has a fighting spirit that embodies the wild horses of these plains.

Nowadays, Old Man is contentedly living a solitary existence or traveling with another older stallion, usually close to the main herd. I have seen him with a couple of younger stallions, perhaps showing them the ways of the Great Basin Desert's strongest mustang. The winters are getting harder on him, but he seems to weather them well enough. When spring rolls around, his weight and coat bounce back as fast as the rest. He still sometimes takes on a challenge from a younger stallion, but those are few—the younger ones seem to know that he is not to be challenged.

Over years of photographing him, I have wondered about the many things he has witnessed—especially the changing herd dynamics, since the family bands have become a large, deeply intertwined herd. But I would most love to know what he thinks of all the visitors to the range these days. He seems to love the camera; I'd like to think that when he sees a camera, he poses just for you.

It will be a bittersweet day when I no longer see him on the range. The legacy he leaves will be rich a one, as he has enchanted many people over the years. It has been a pleasure and a privilege to photograph such a majestic creature.

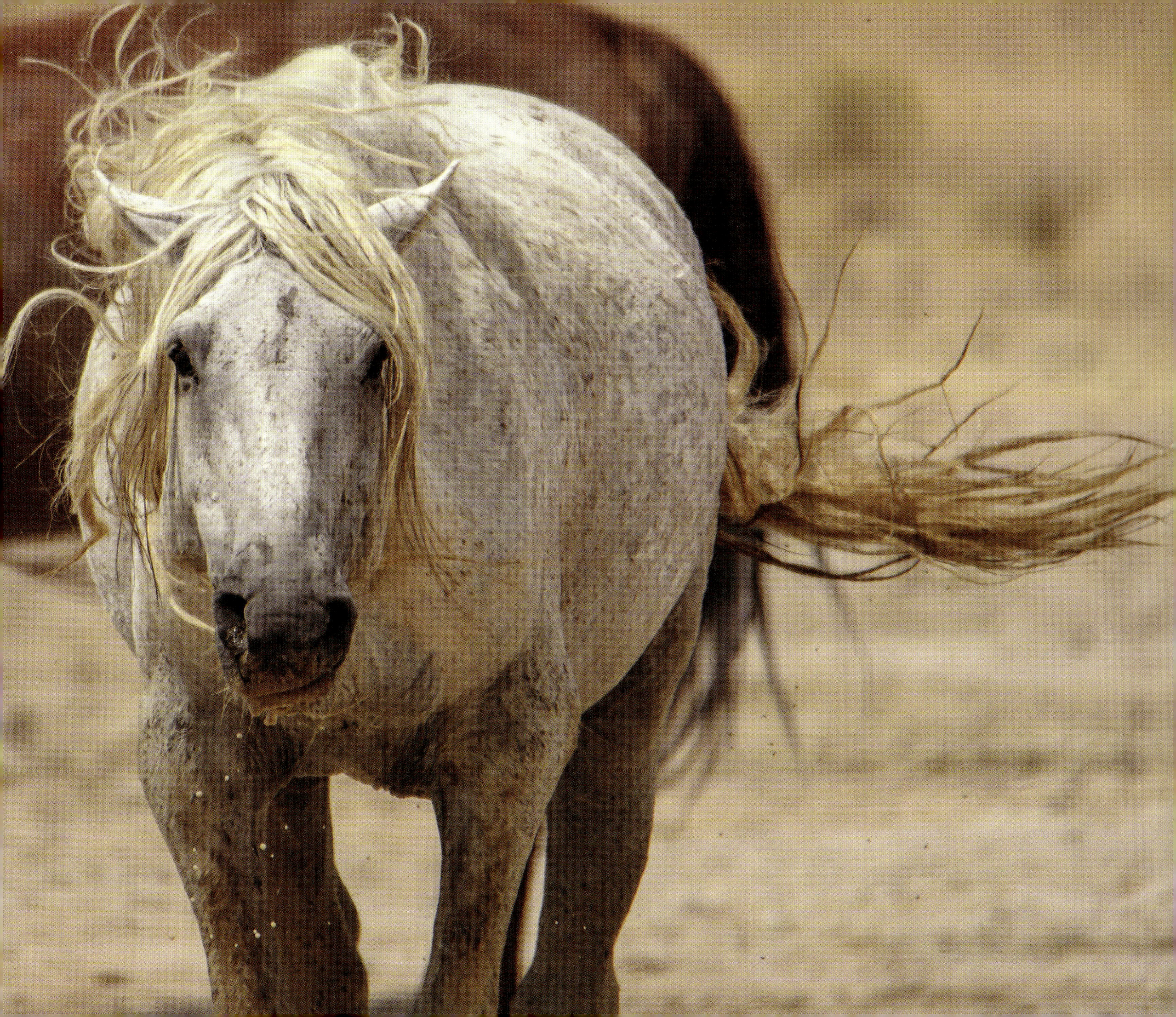

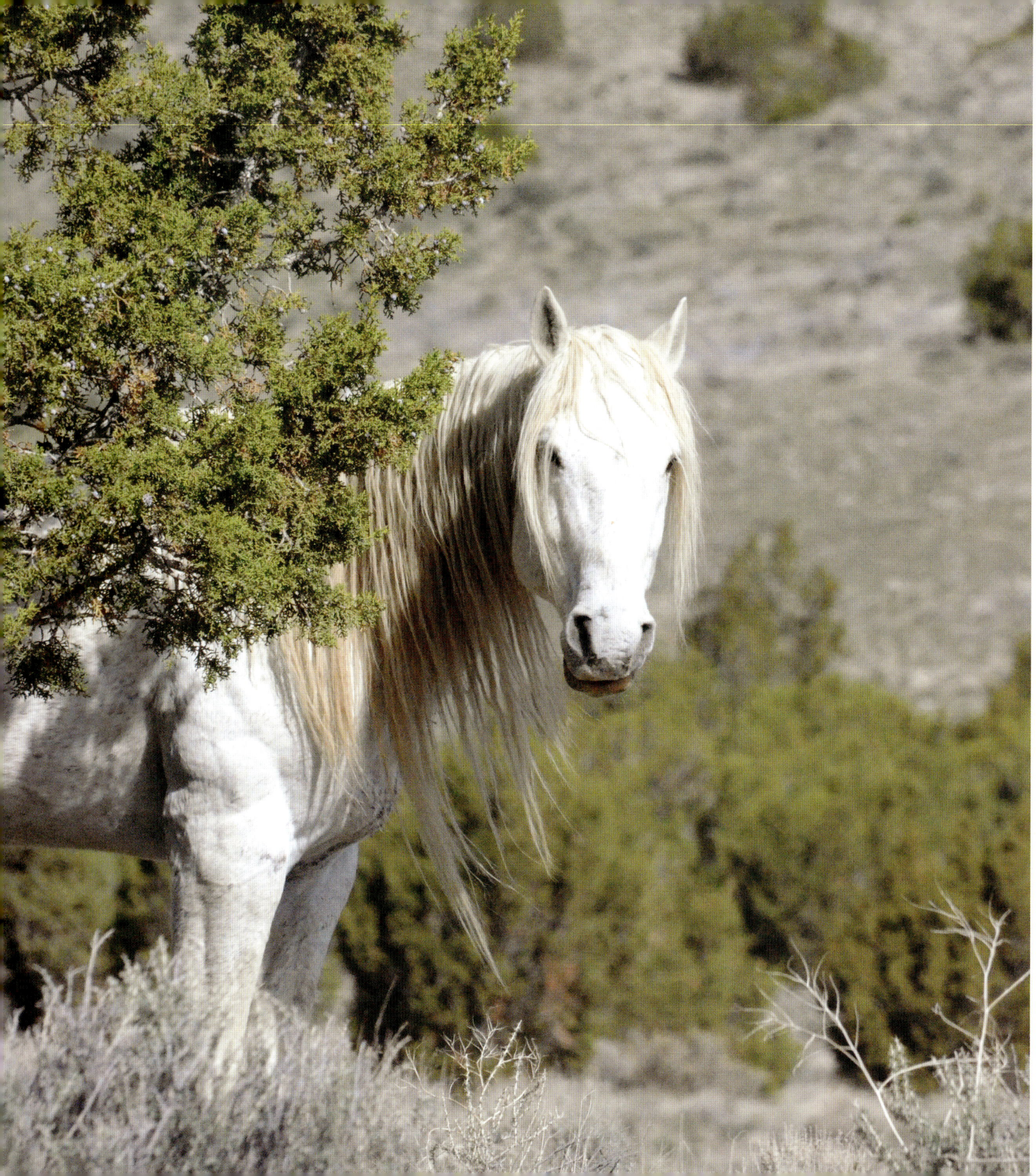

Left: Old Man hides in the juniper trees high up on Davis Mountain in Utah.

Opposite: Old Man during a hard winter.

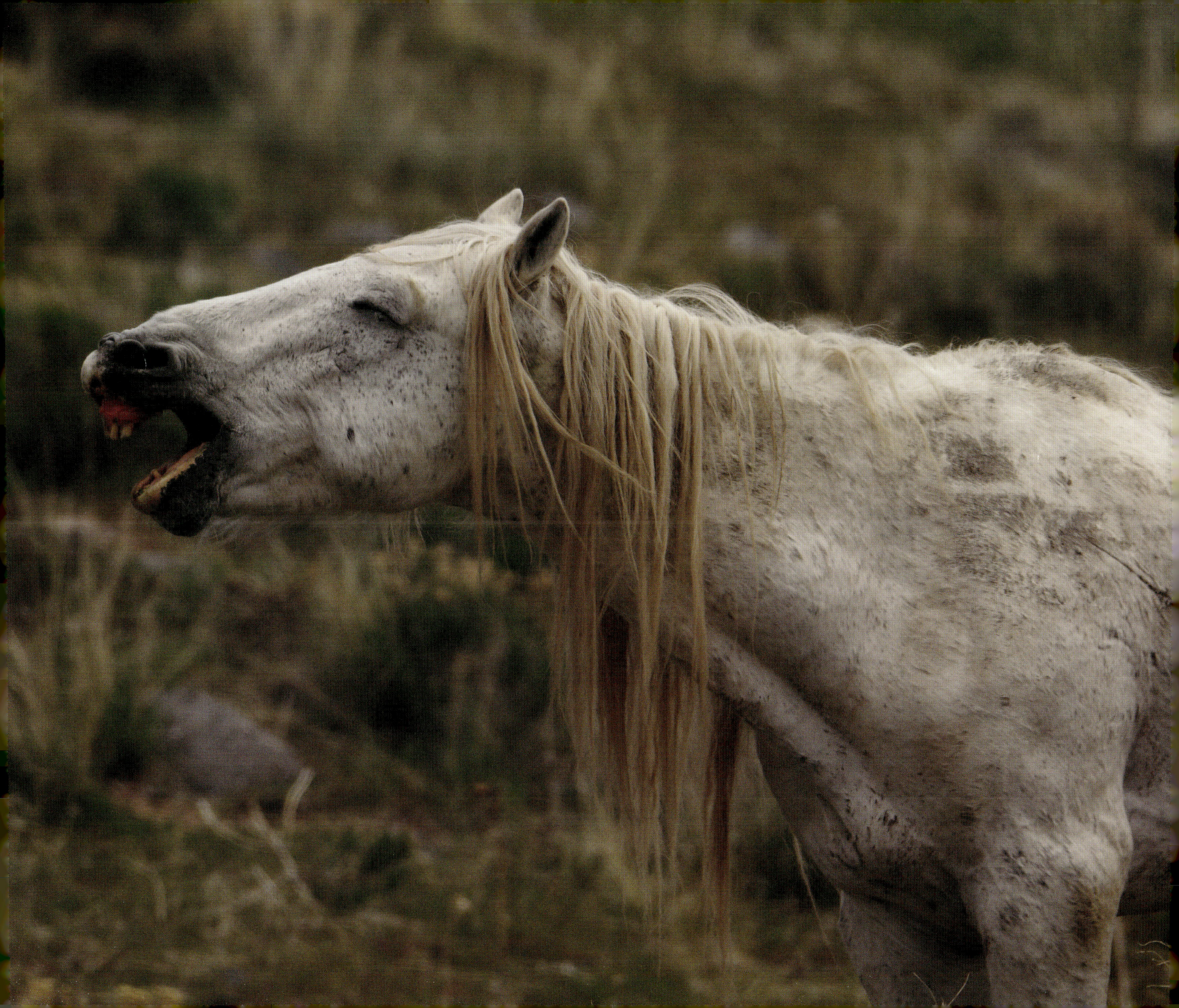

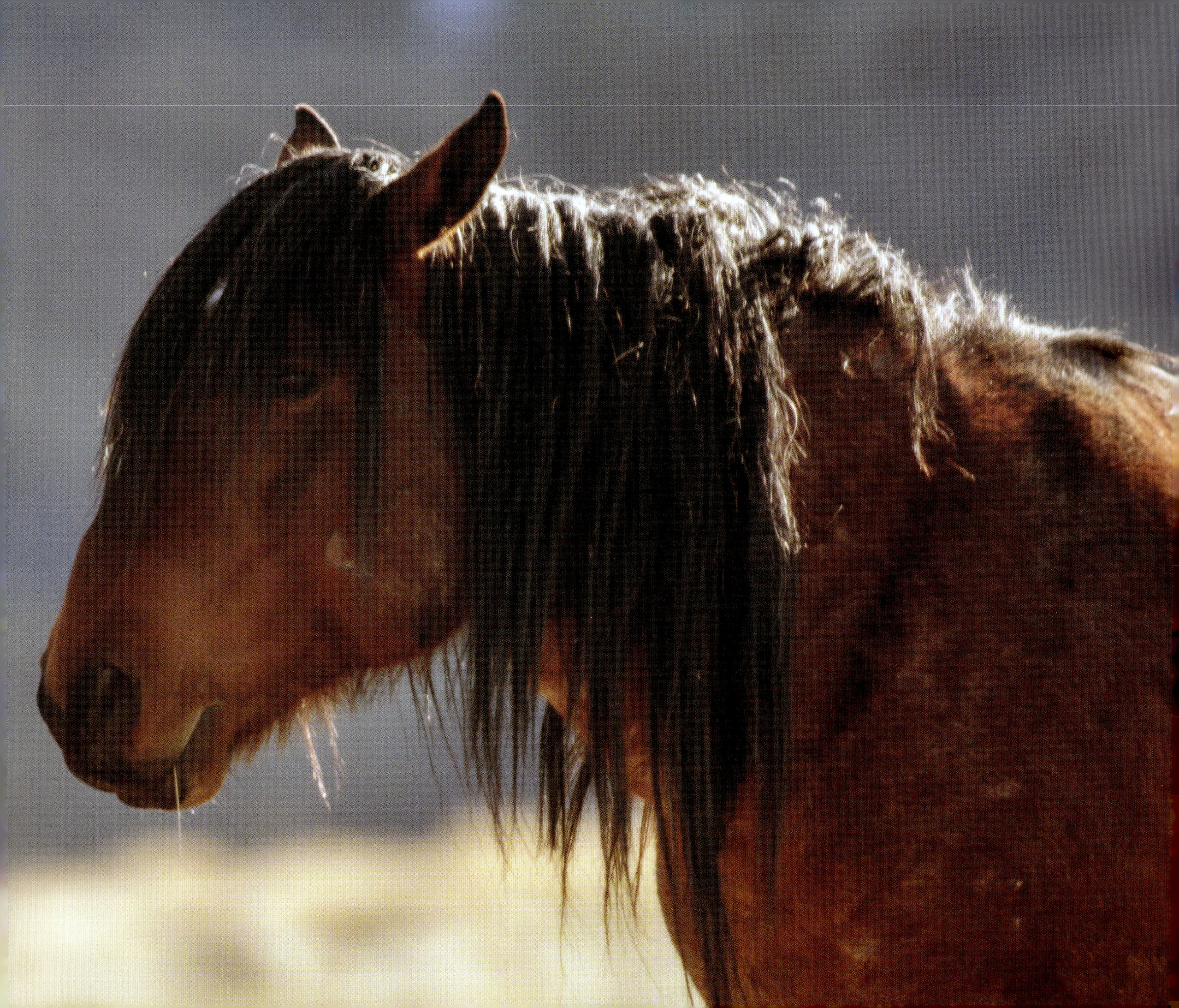

Opposite: A band stallion quietly keeps an eye on his band.

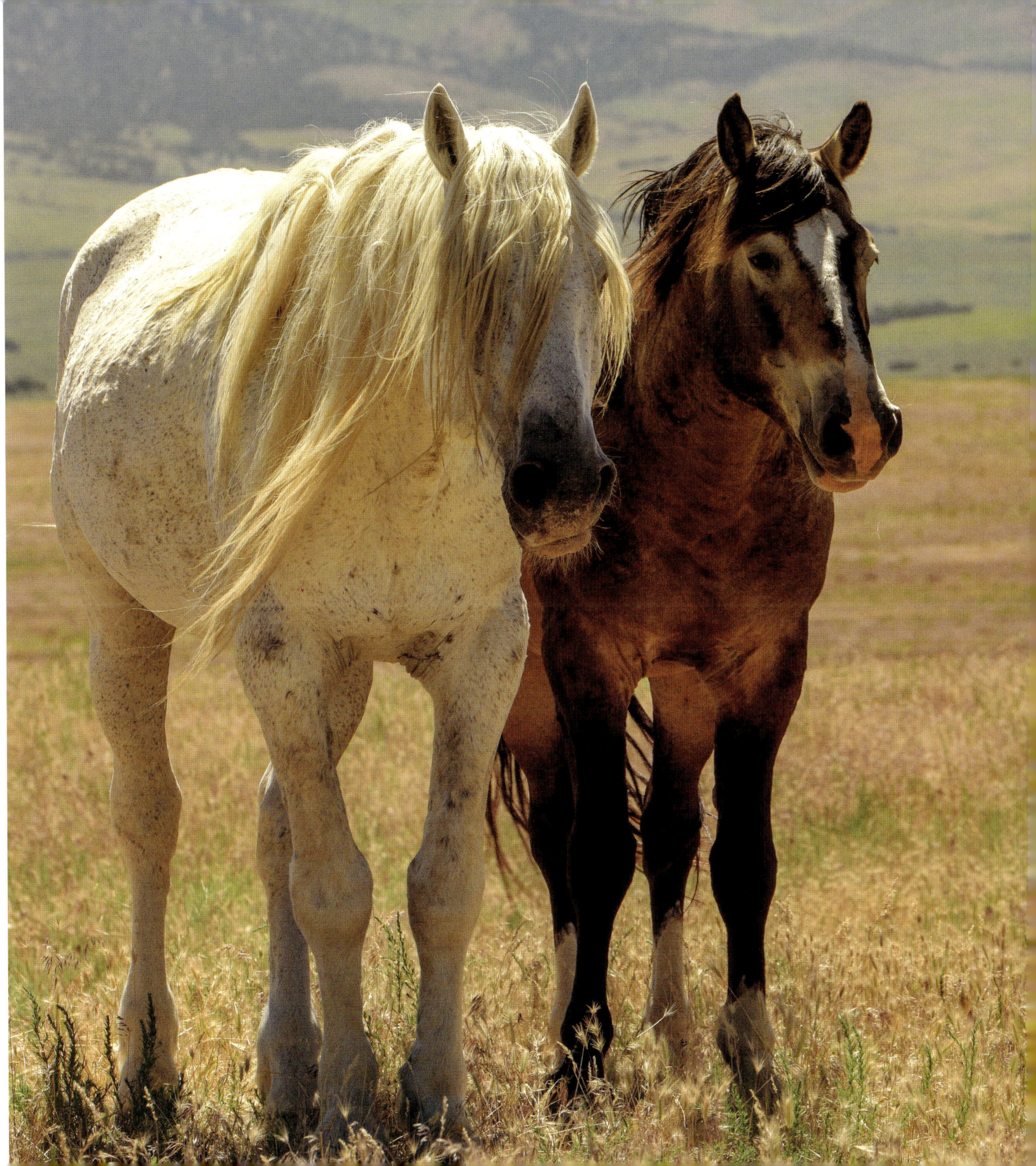

Right: Legends of the Onaqui range: Old Man and Buck.

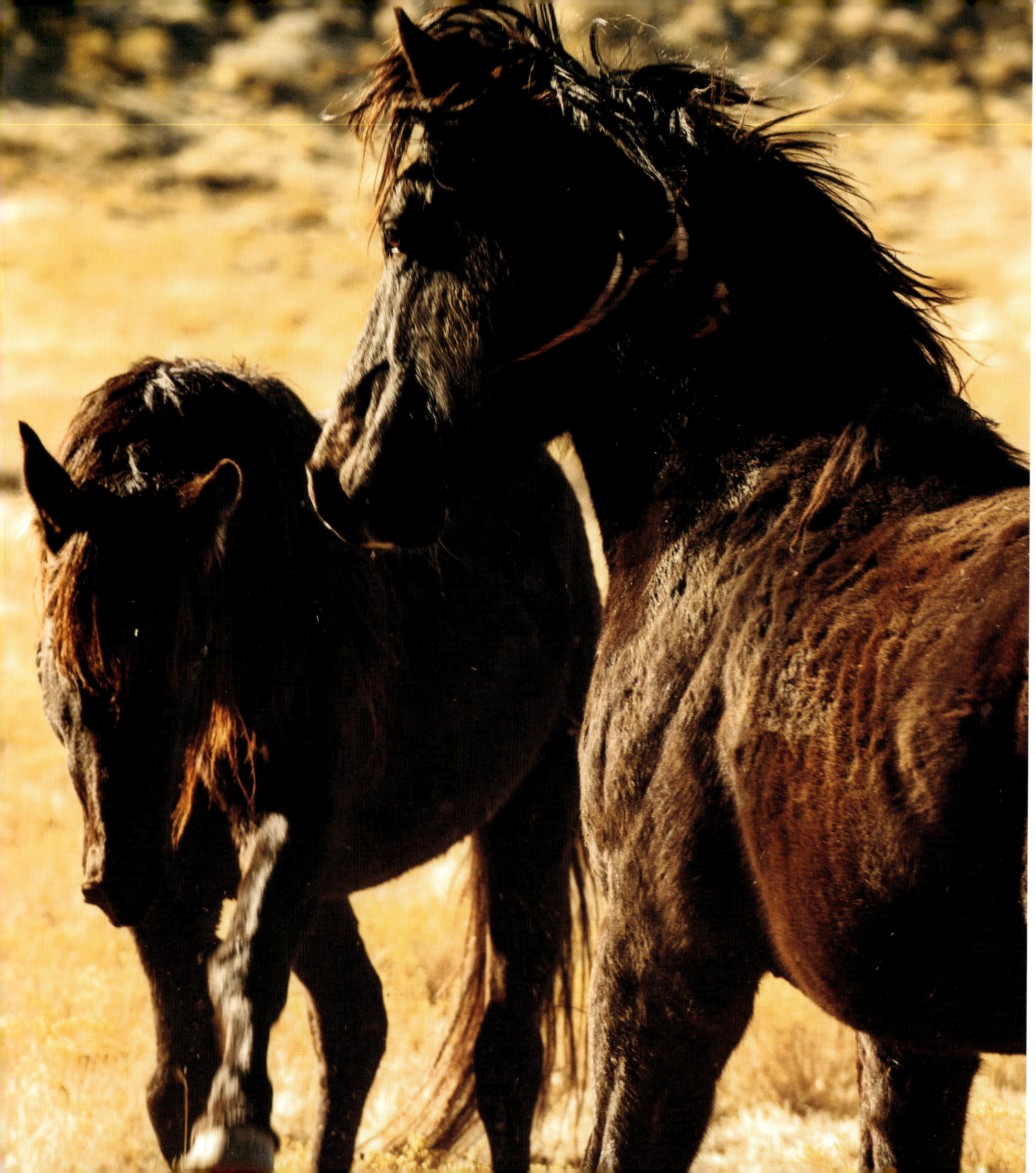

Left: Pawing and striking the ground with the front leg can be a form of dominance.

Opposite: Two old warriors still fight it out. Their scars and wounds will heal over time, but the rivalry between the two might not.

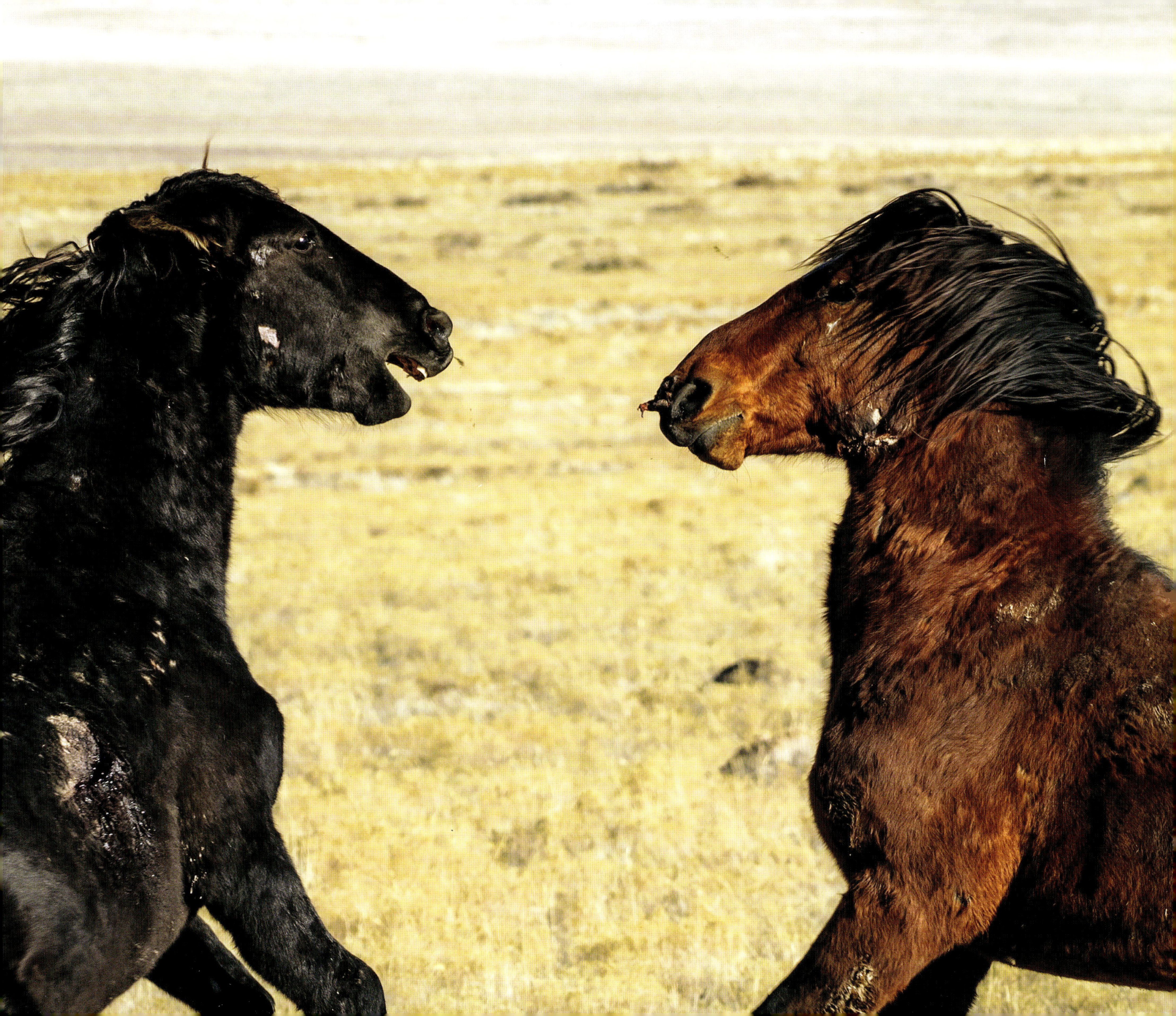

BLACK-AND-WHITE PINTO

This black-and-white pinto had a small harem band of about twelve to fifteen mares and foals. He protected them fiercely over the years, often clashing with the small bachelor bands, none of which were successful until the spring of 2009. He lost his band that spring, and I didn't see him again until the fall of 2010. He trailed across the flats with a red roan mare and a bay foal.

The black-and-white pinto was mysterious. I would see him for a few months, close to the band, and then he would disappear for some time again. I believe he was roaming the mountains—he seemed to like those quiet places.

As he got older, like the Old Man, I wondered if he would survive the winters on the range. When I last saw him in the late summer of 2017, his age was definitely showing, but he continued to take any challenges from the younger studs. He was solitary but enduring. I haven't seen him since—I like to think he found one of his favorite quiet places and passed peacefully there.

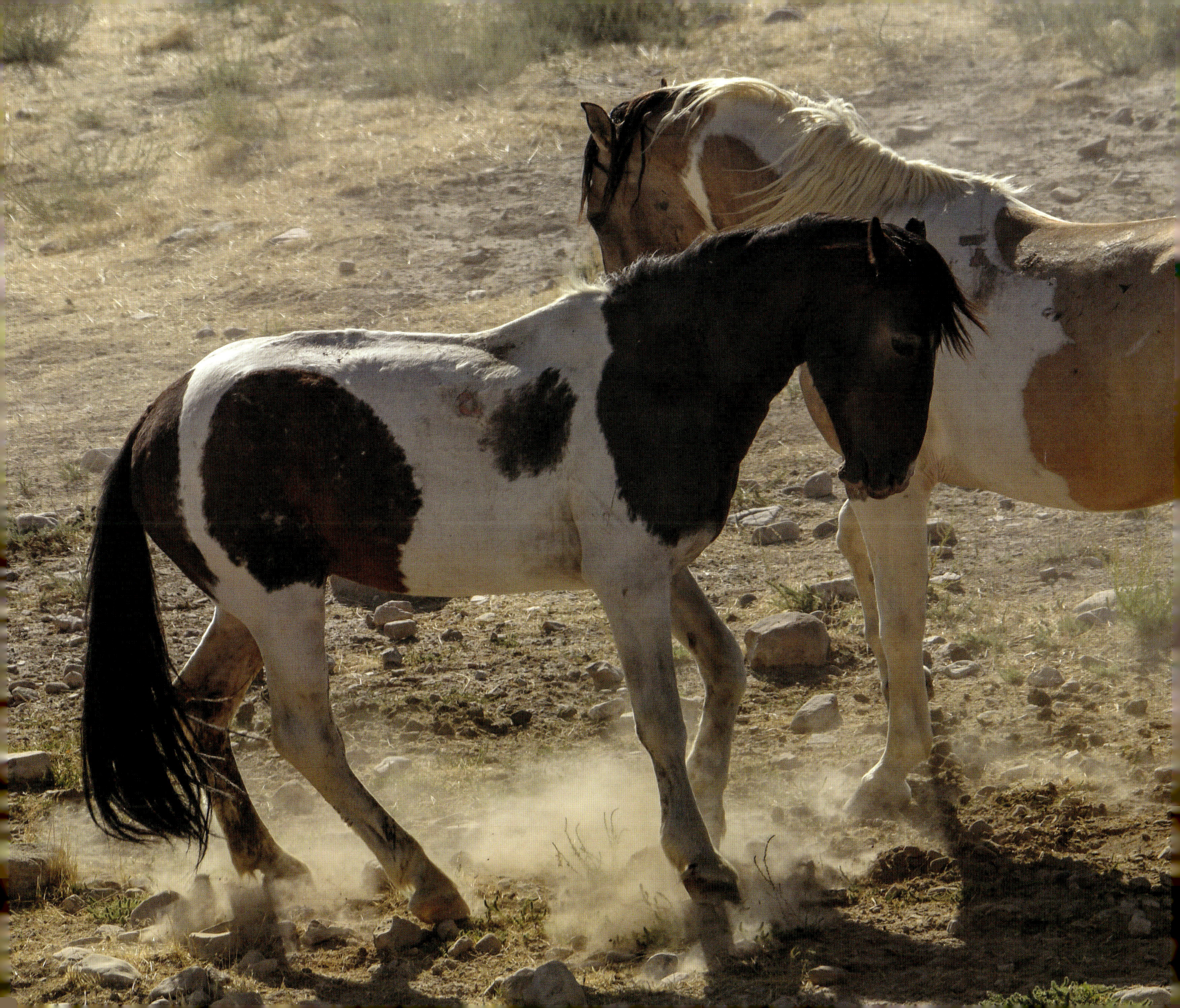

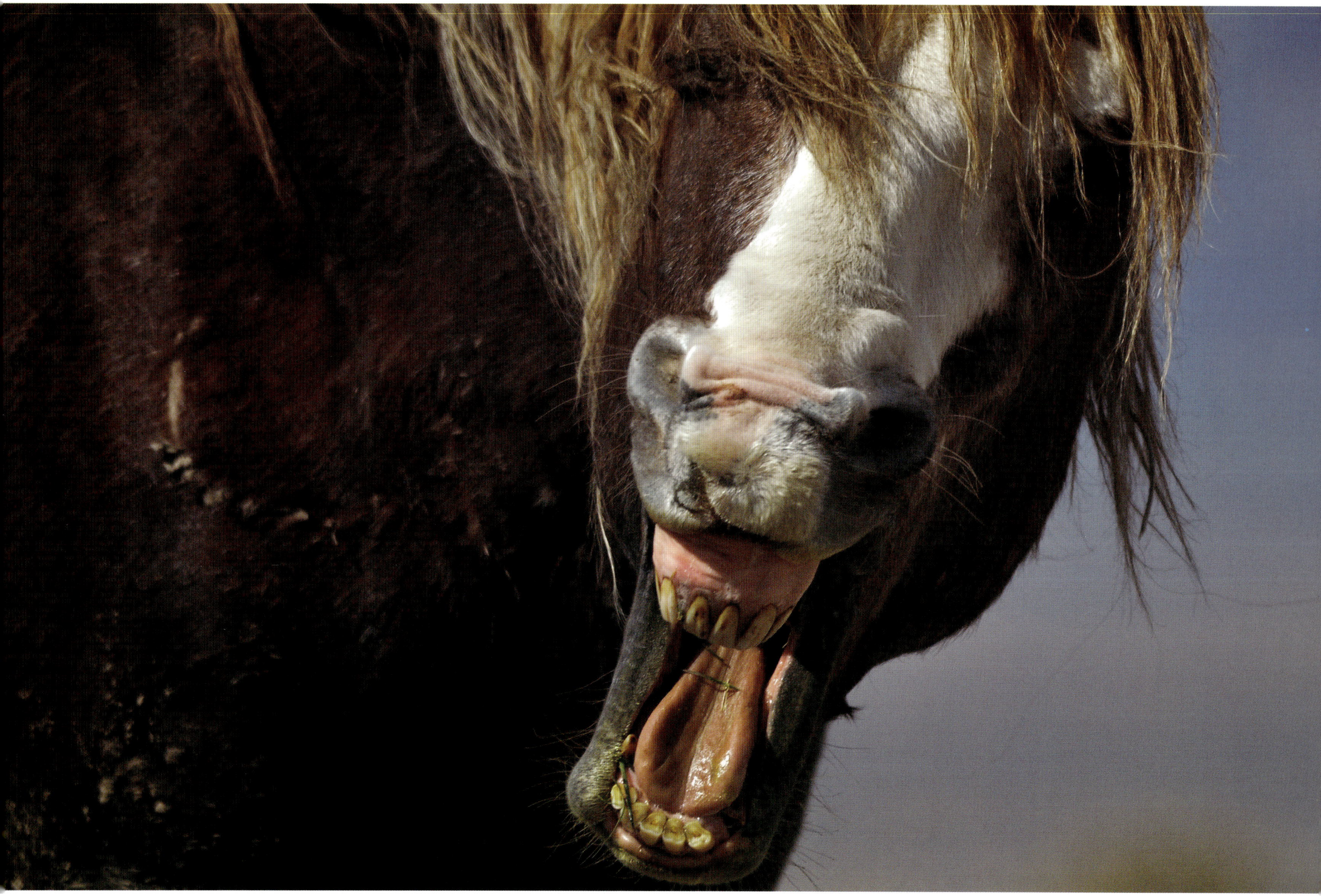

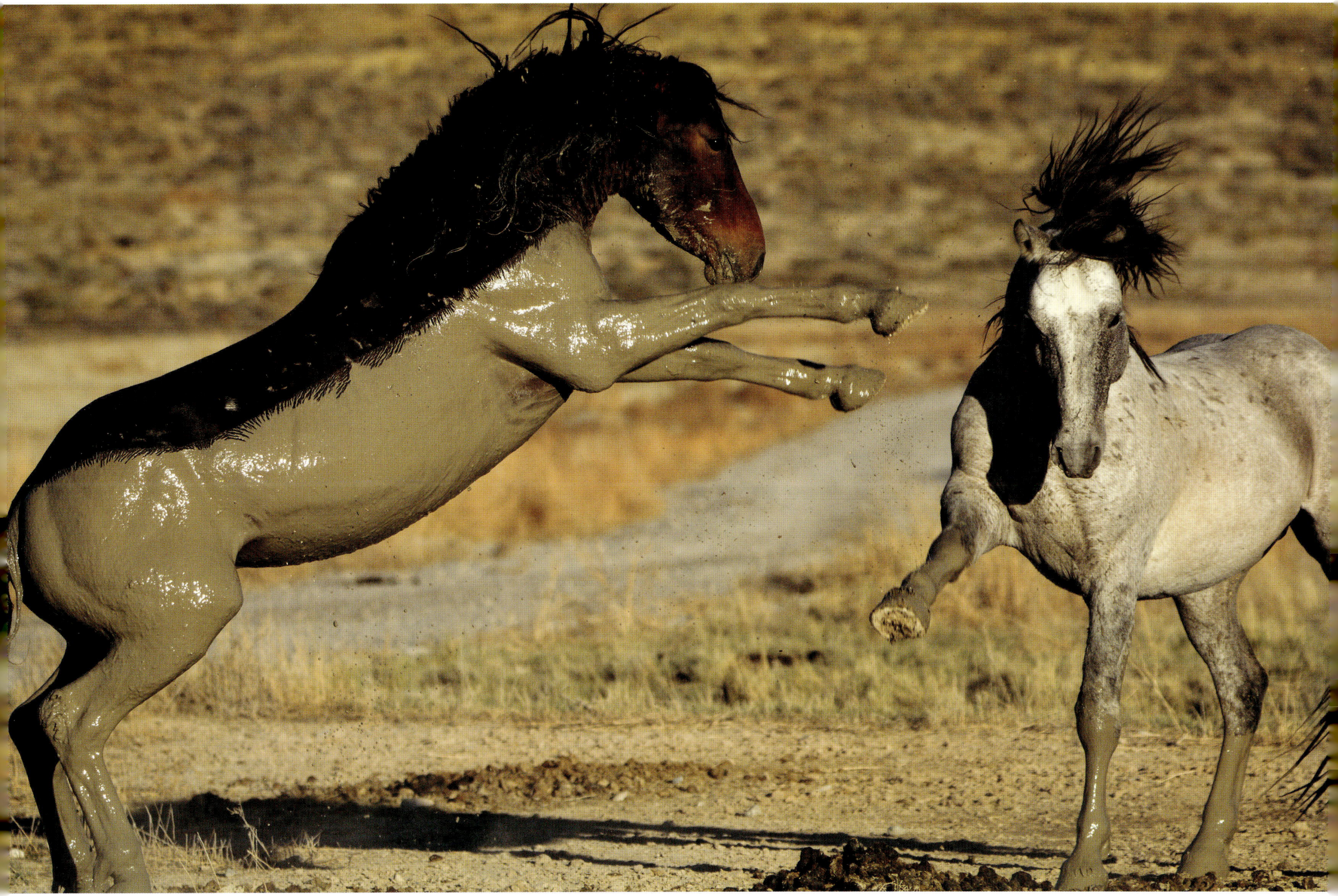

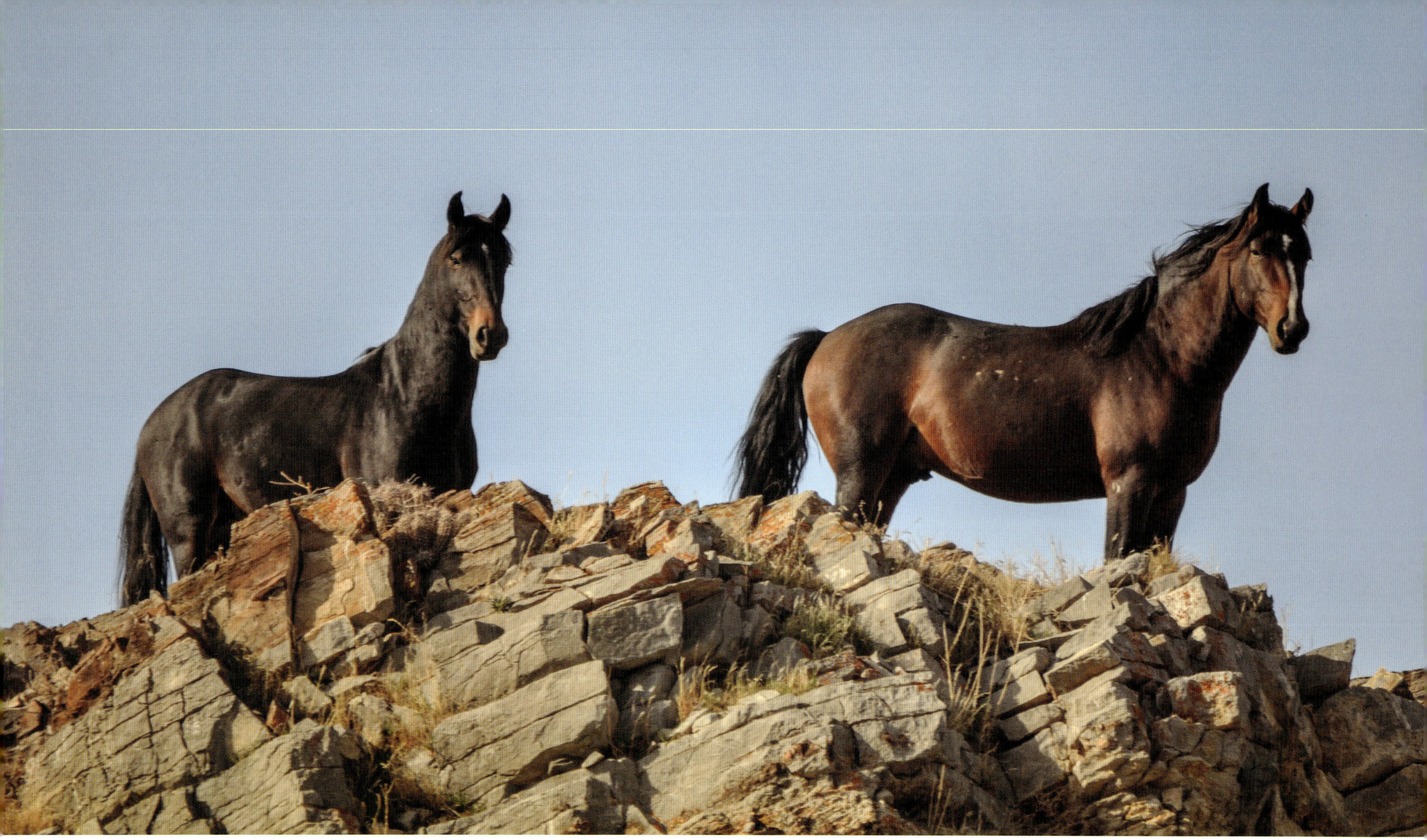

Previous page left: This big brown stallion seems to have something to say.

Previous page right: Sometimes a stallion doesn't even get a chance to roll in the dirt before someone challenges him.

Above: Two bachelor stallions watch the range from the rocks high above.

Opposite: A bachelor stallion makes a quick move to avoid a fight.

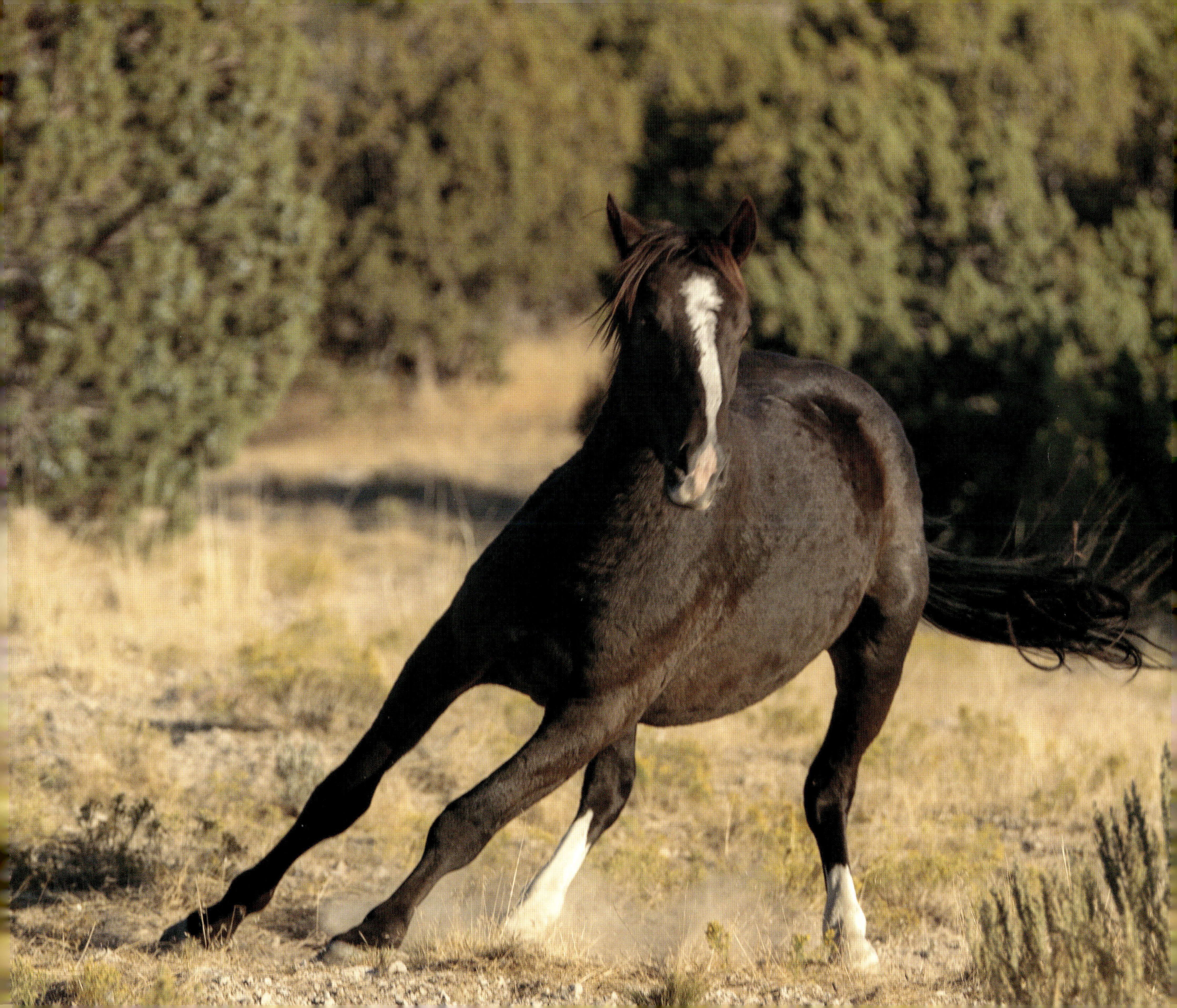

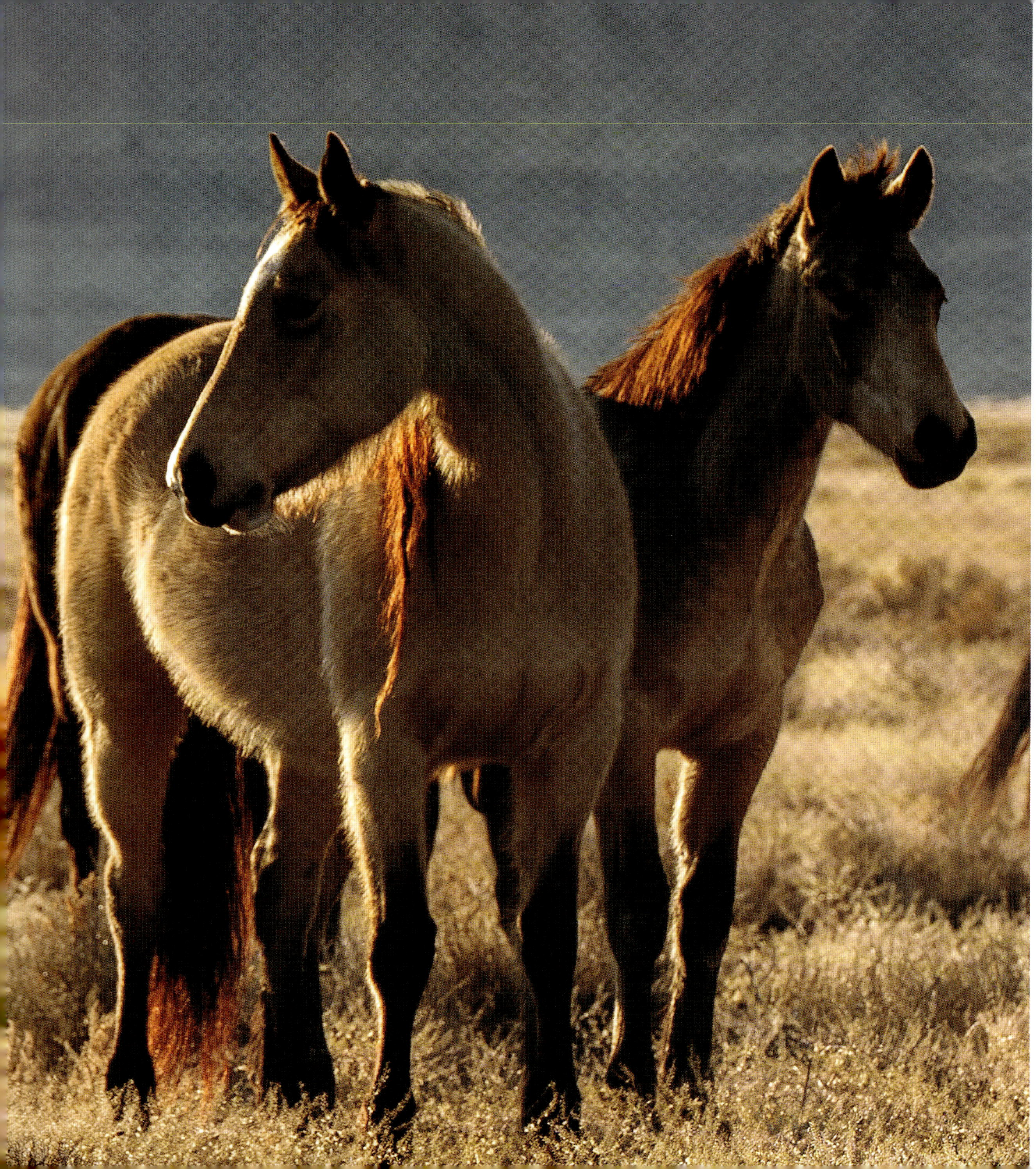

Left: The early spring evening sunlight reflects off the young colts.

Opposite left: This pinto mustang watches and waits for the rest of his band to make it to the waterhole.

Opposite right: The perfect reflection of this buckskin stallion at a pond.

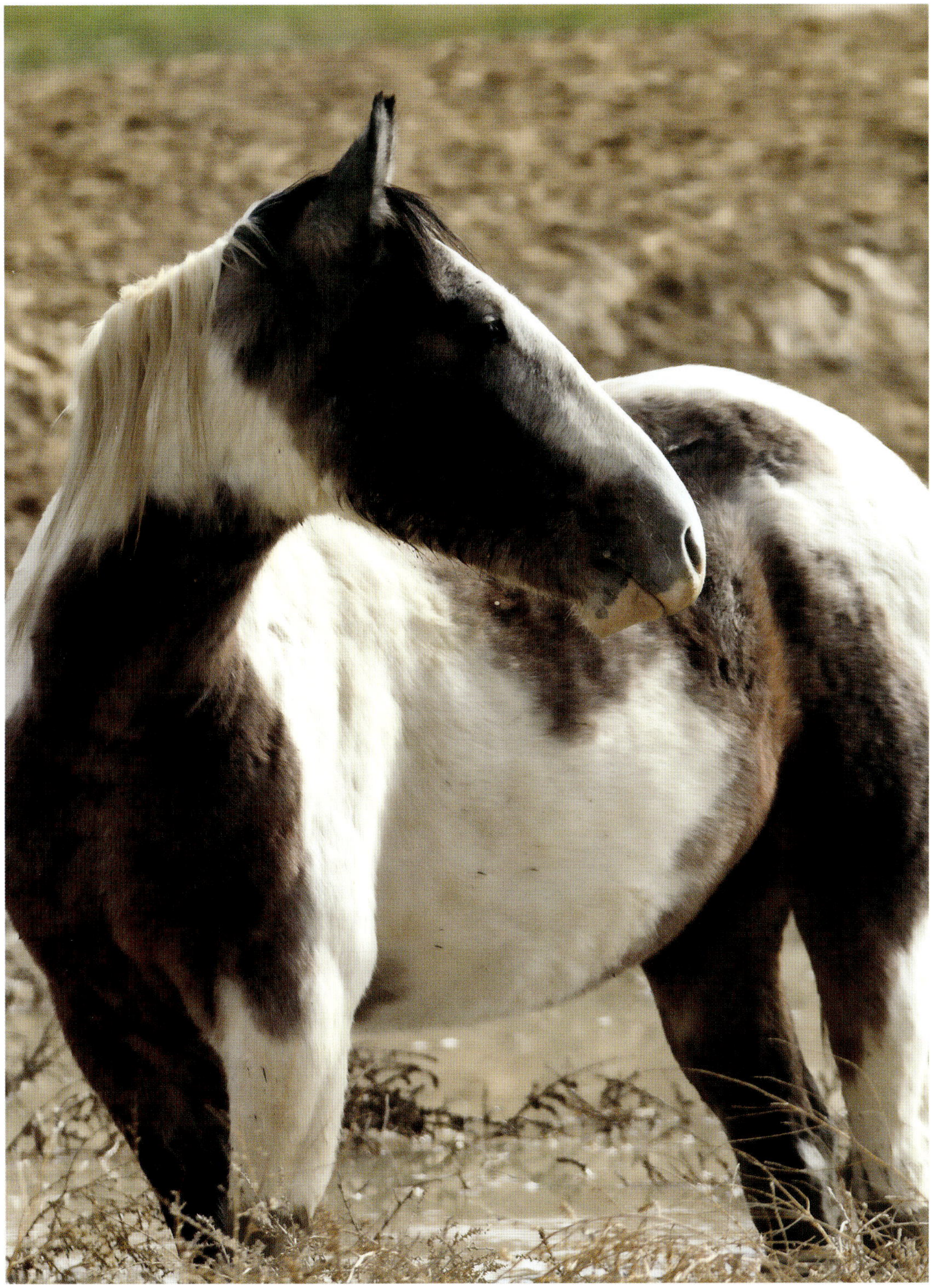

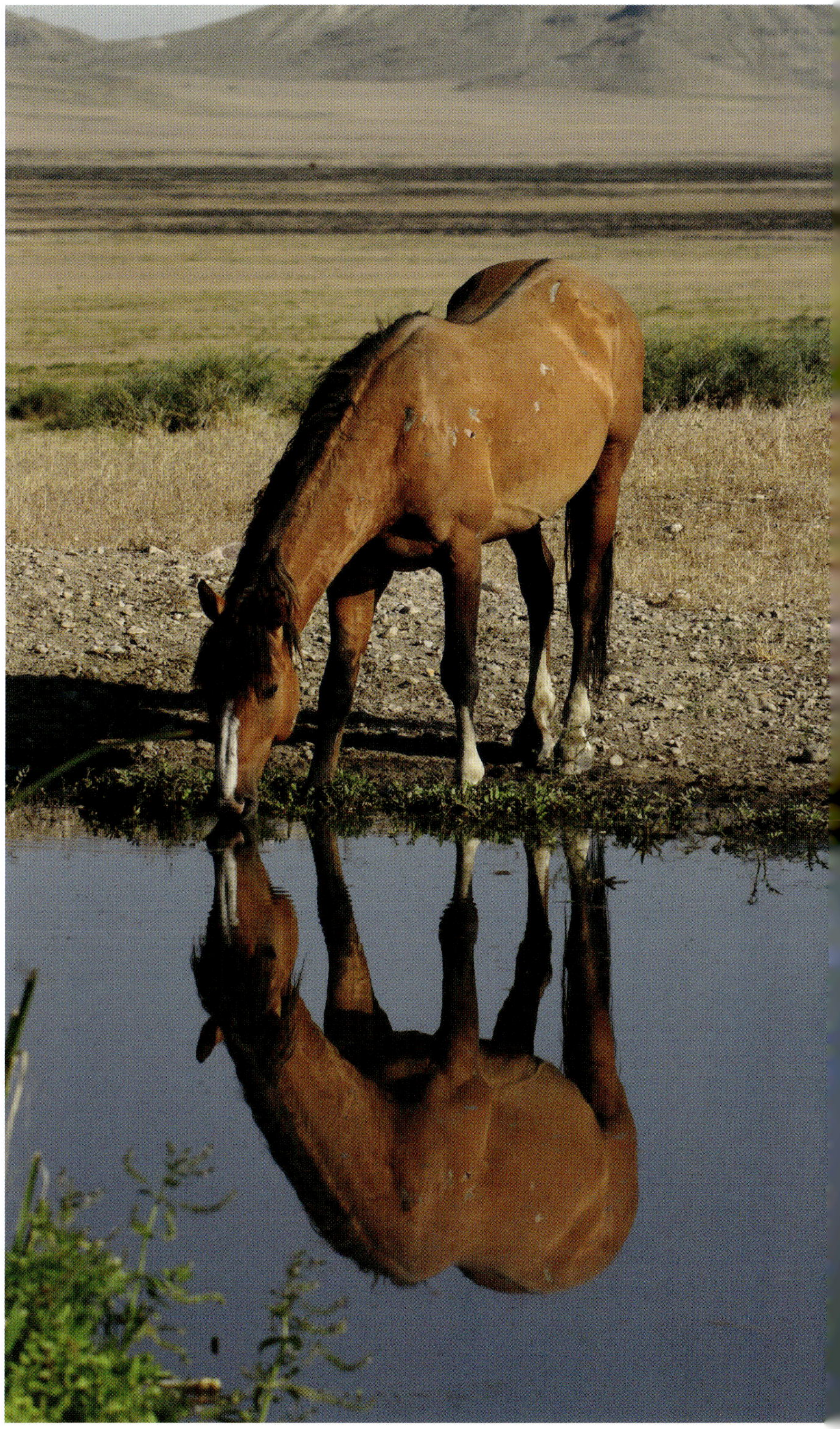

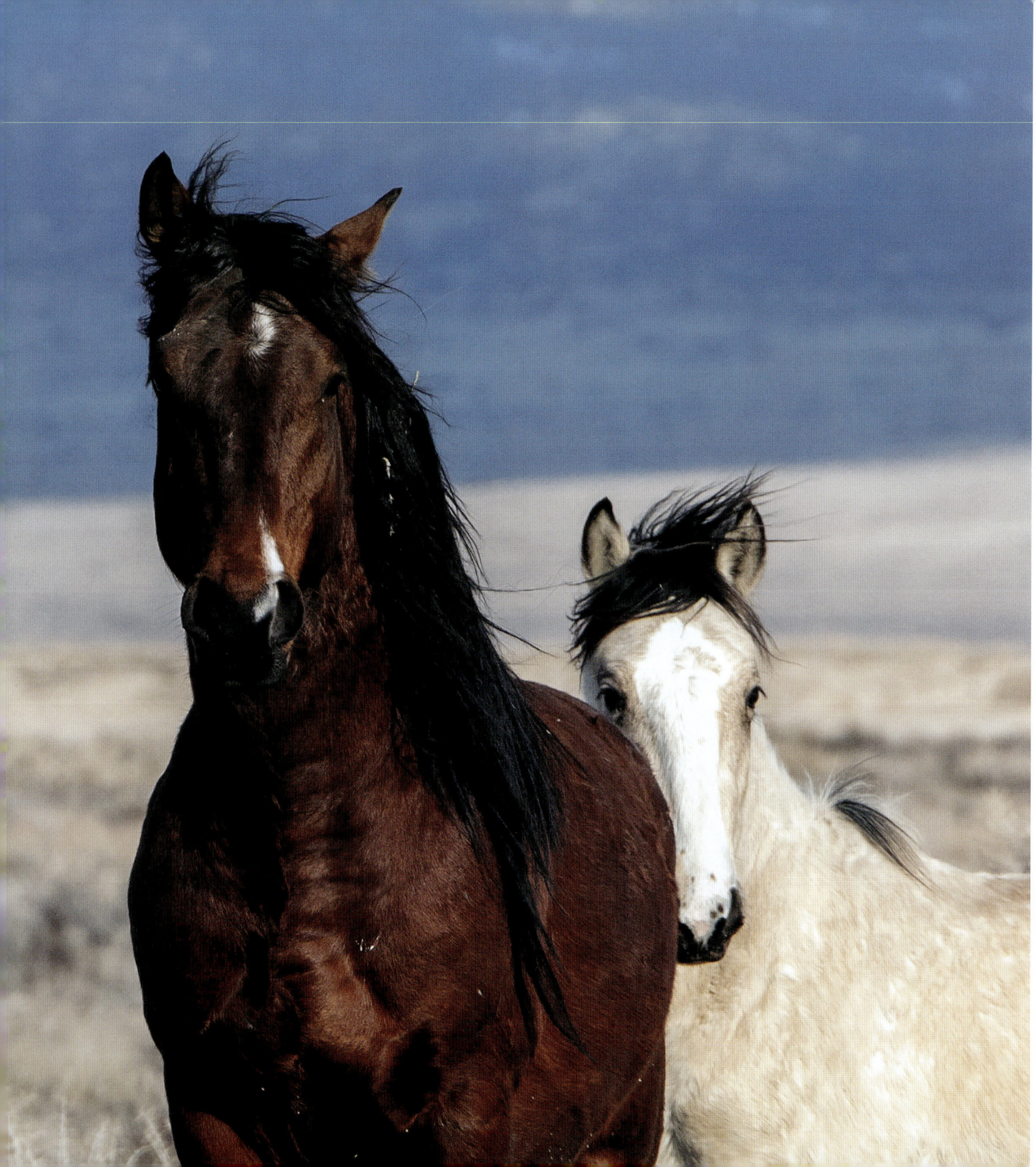

Left: A young buckskin colt hides behind an older bachelor stallion.

Opposite: A rarity for photographers: mule deer arrive over the ridgeline just above the wild horses.

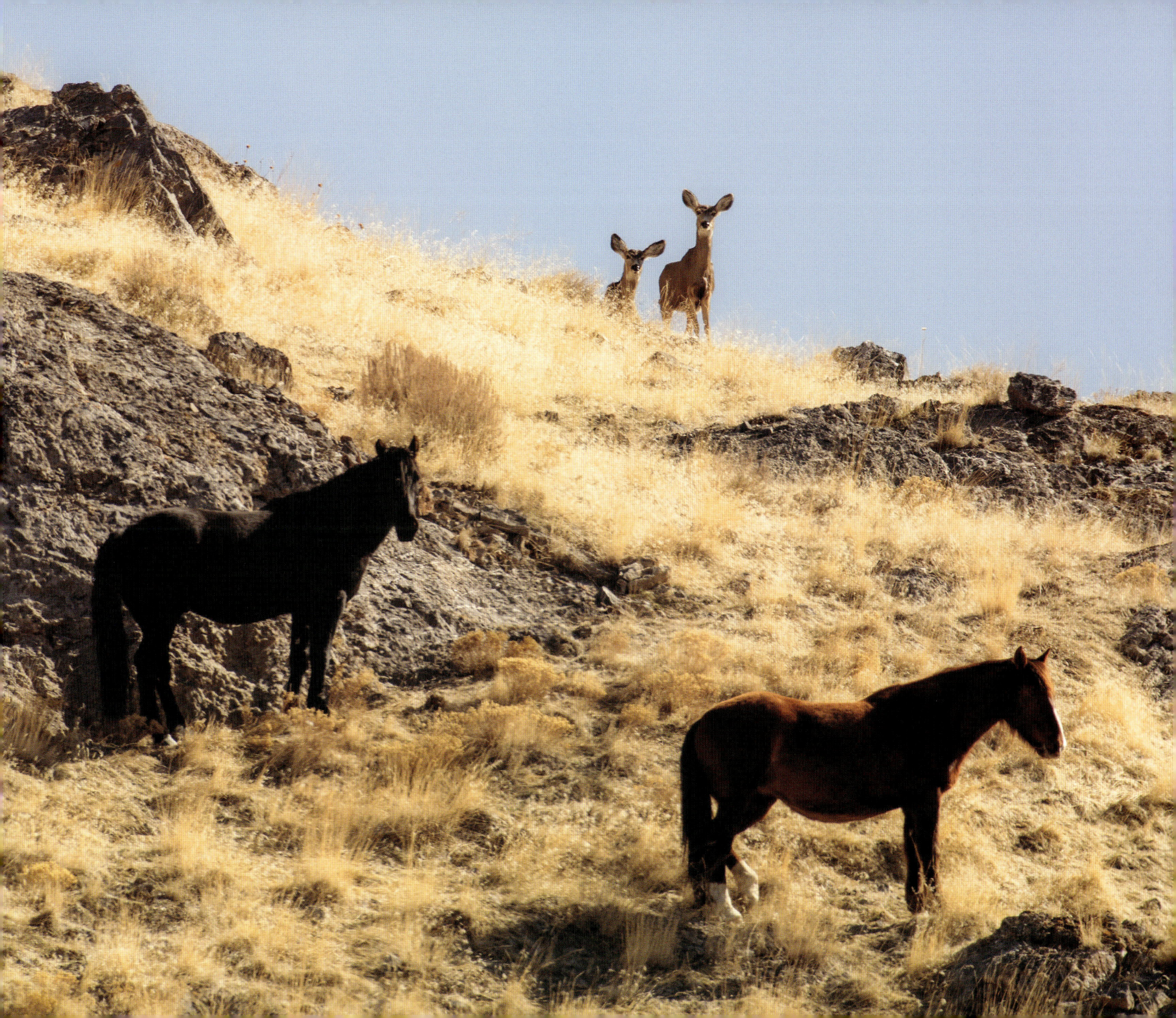

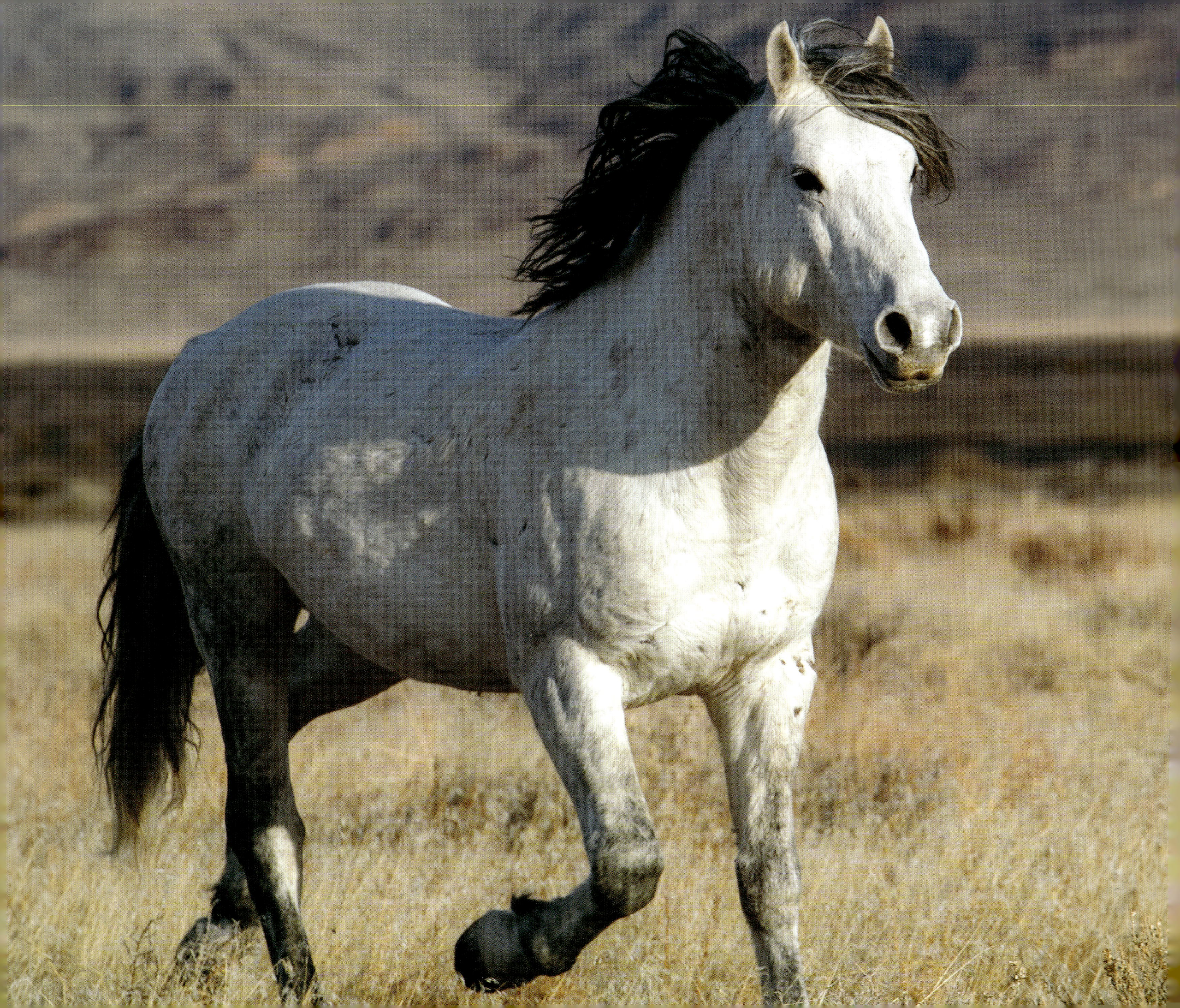

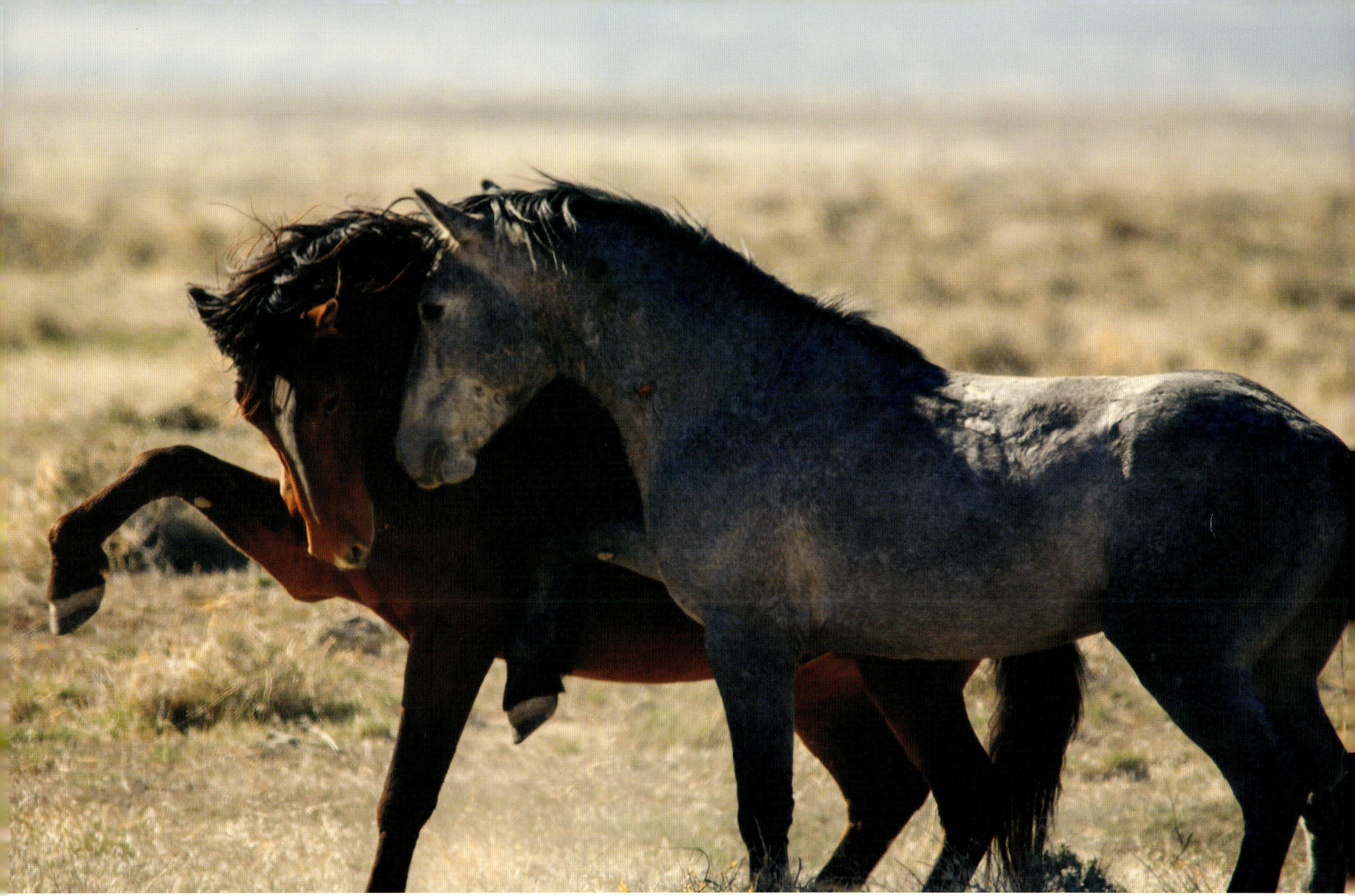

Opposite: A gray stallion runs toward a challenge to protect his band.

Above: Another form of posturing by the stallions—this one makes it look like a well-planned dance.

CHASING SNOW

Finding a water source is a challenge during the winter months when the water holes are frozen and dried up. But with the frigid winter comes snow—a challenge and a blessing for the herds. With no exposed food, the horses must either paw and dig up the ground to forage or move to the ridgeline where the wind carries the snow off of the forage. Despite these setbacks, the wild horses will eat the snow for hydration—thus, "chasing snow."

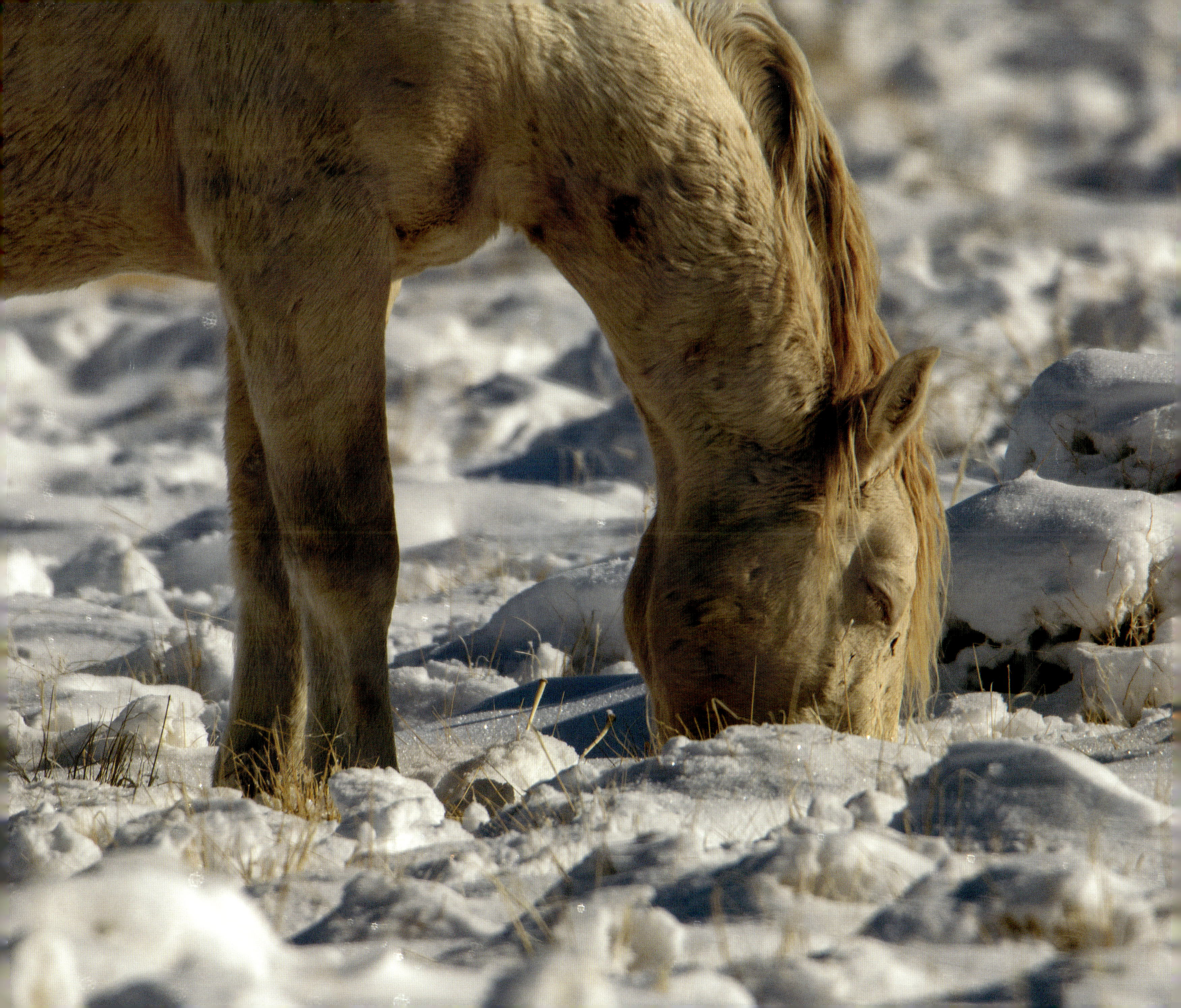

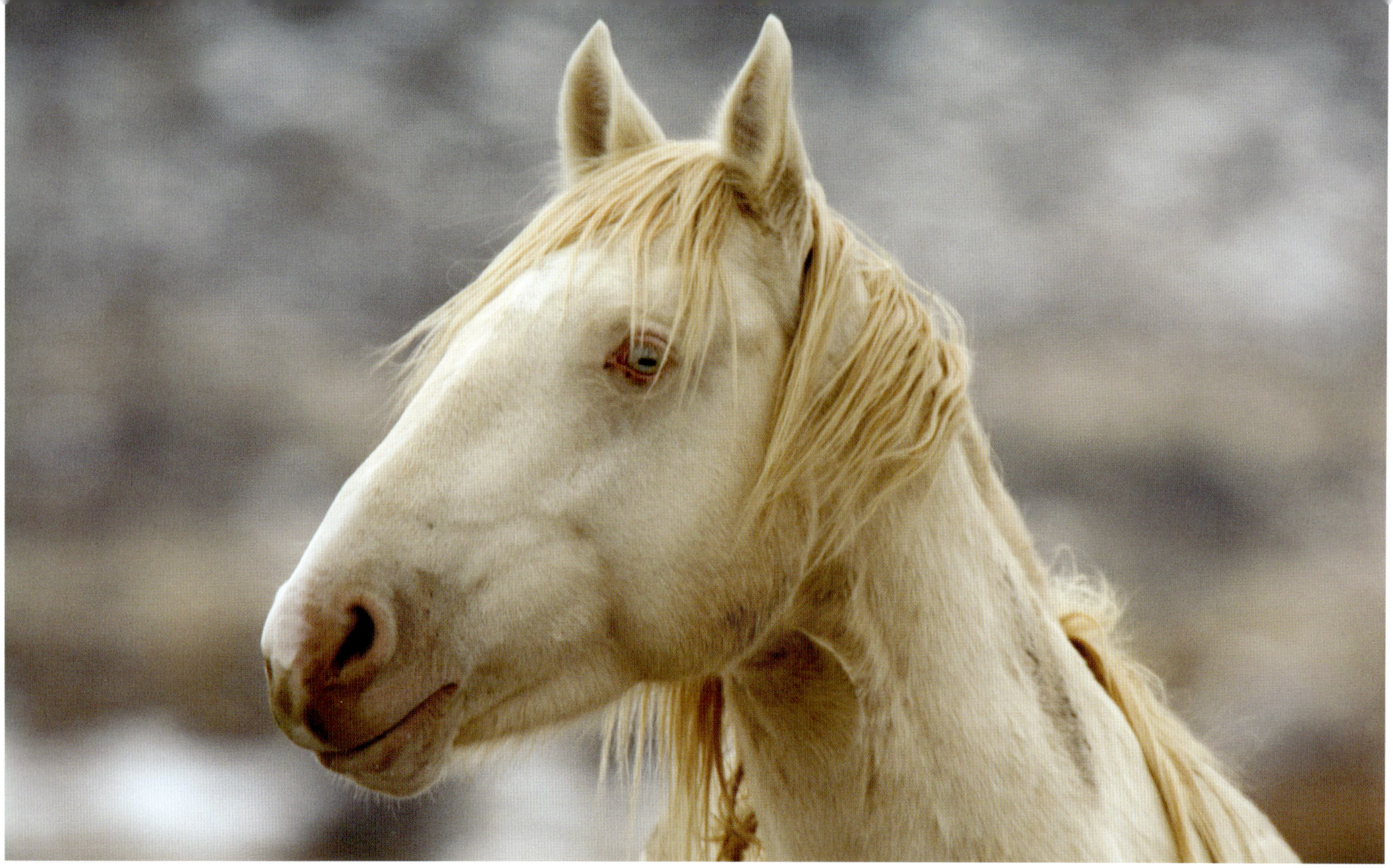

Clockwise, from top left: The cremello bachelor stallion on high alert. An interesting thing about stallions fighting is that you can always plan on a good photograph of their manes going wild. Birds provide a little grooming on this wild horse—or perhaps seek a free ride.

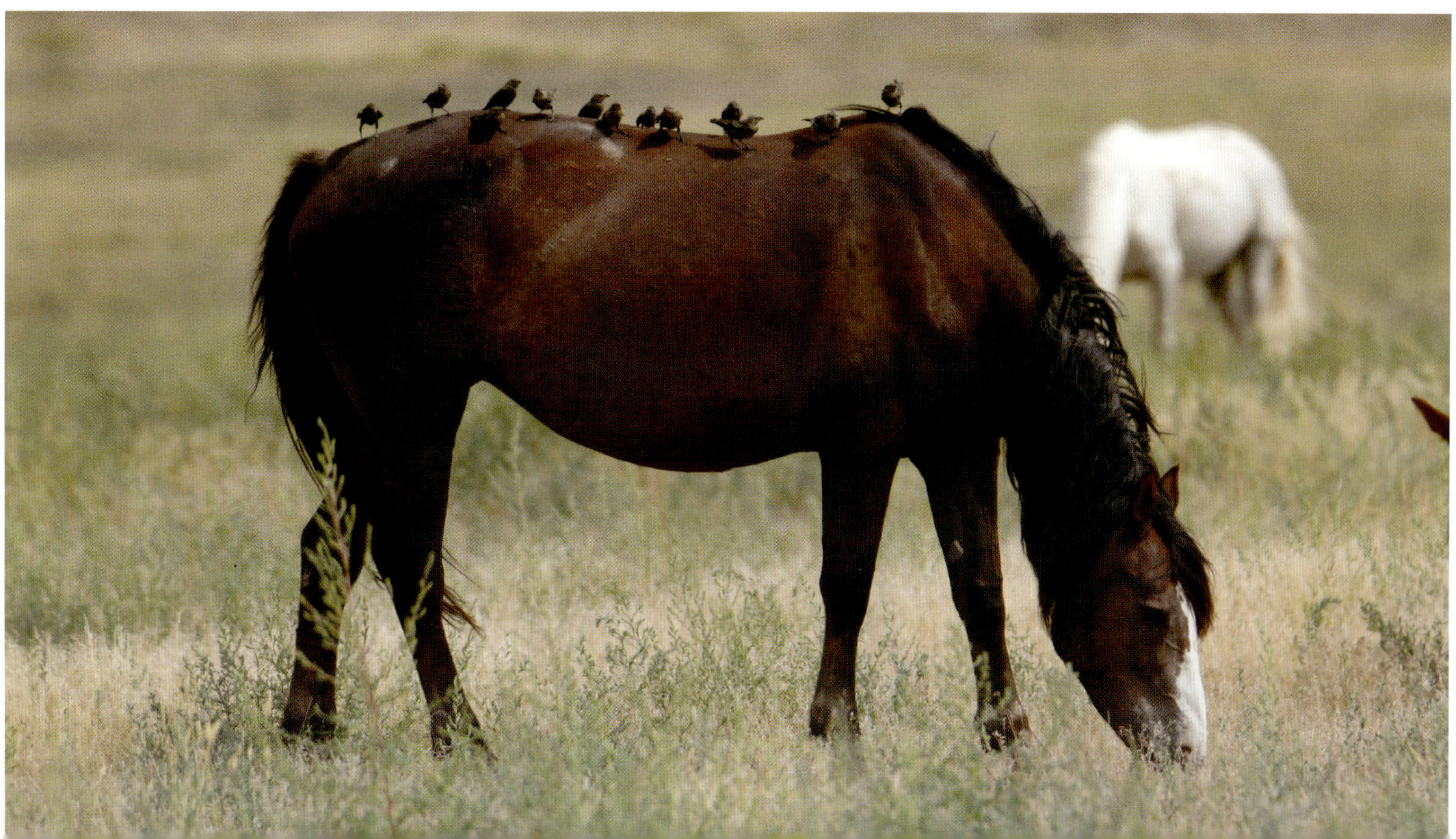

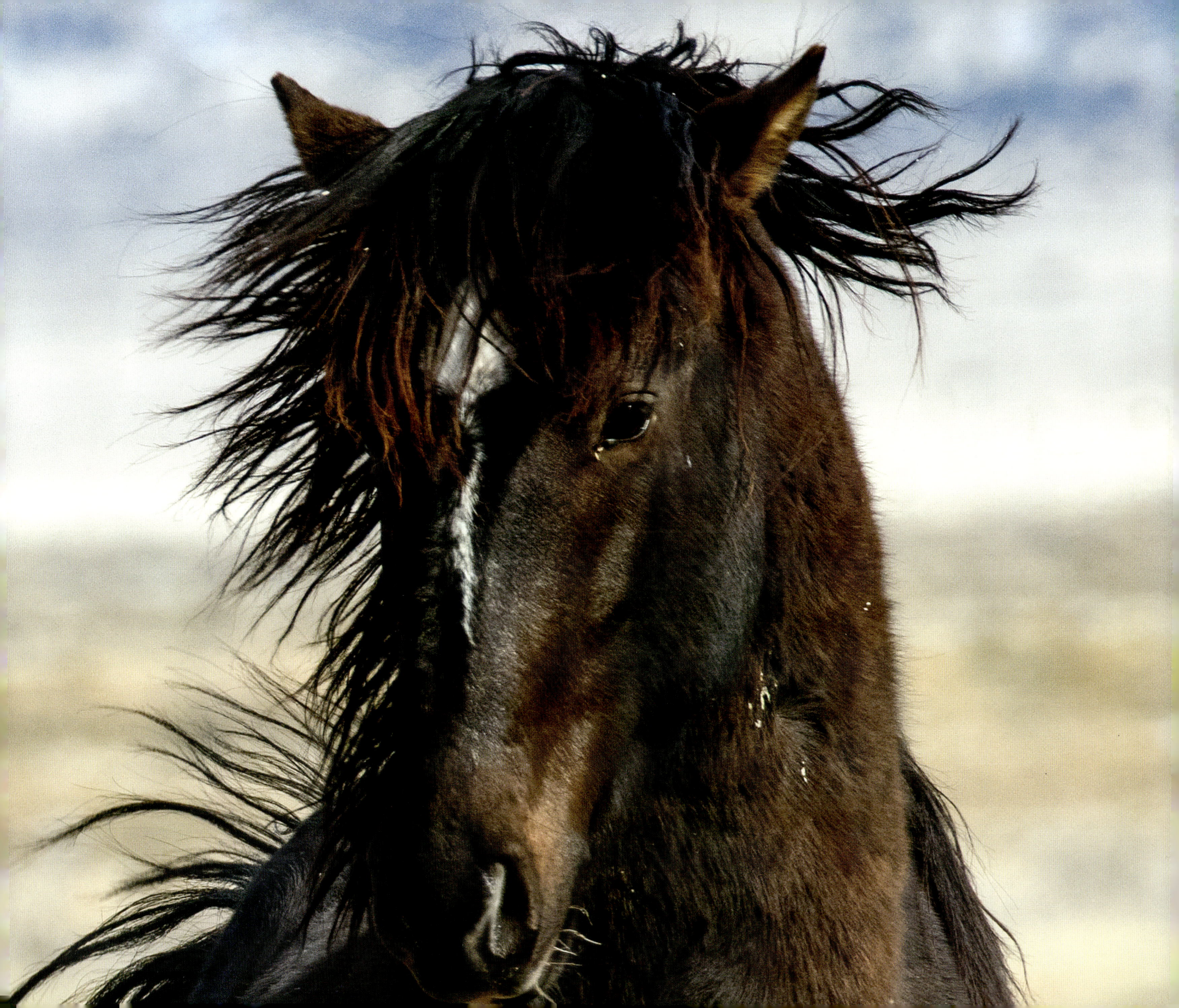

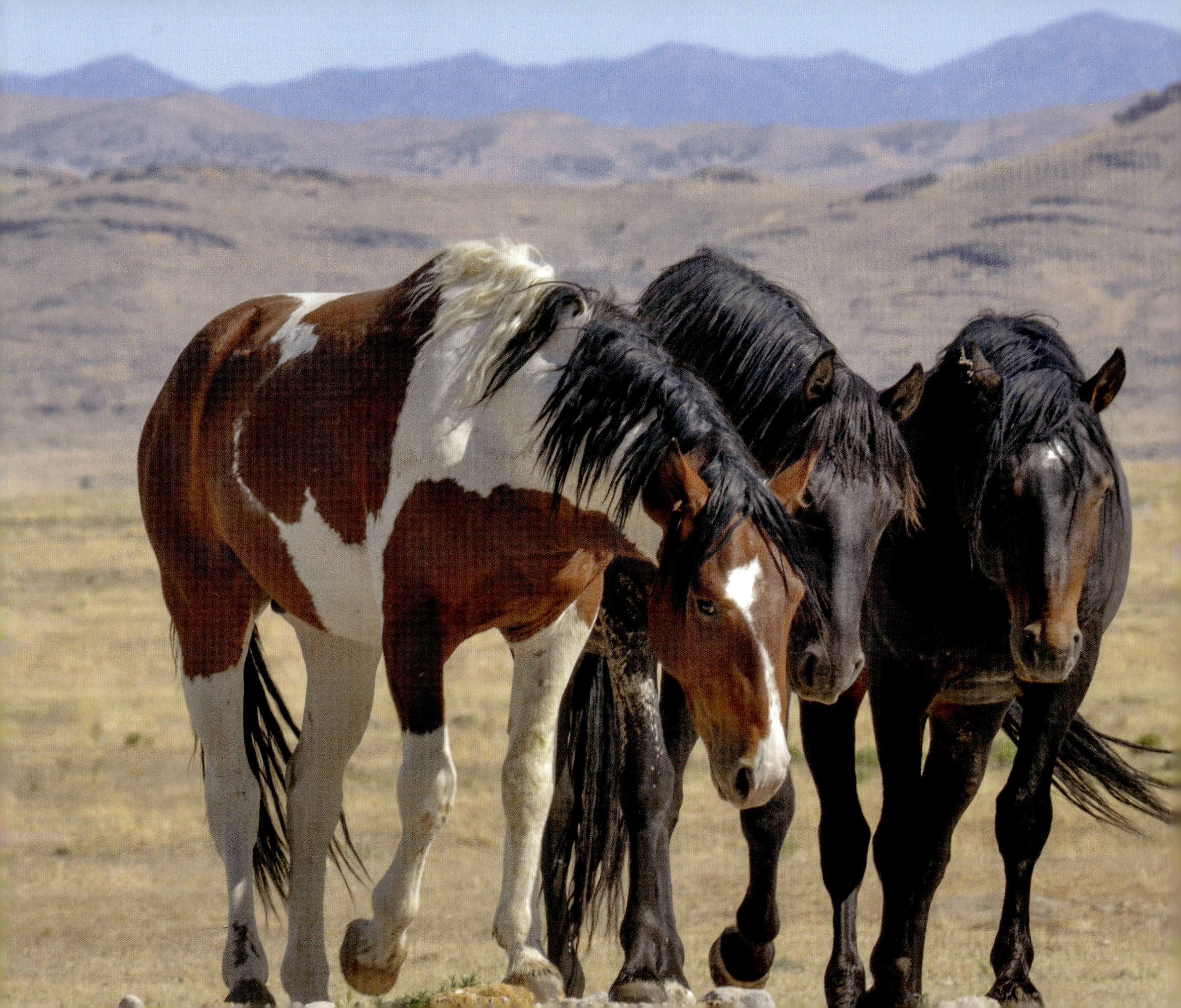

Left: A young group of bachelor stallions look mischievous as they approach a watering hole.

Right: The softness of a young bachelor stallion's eye.

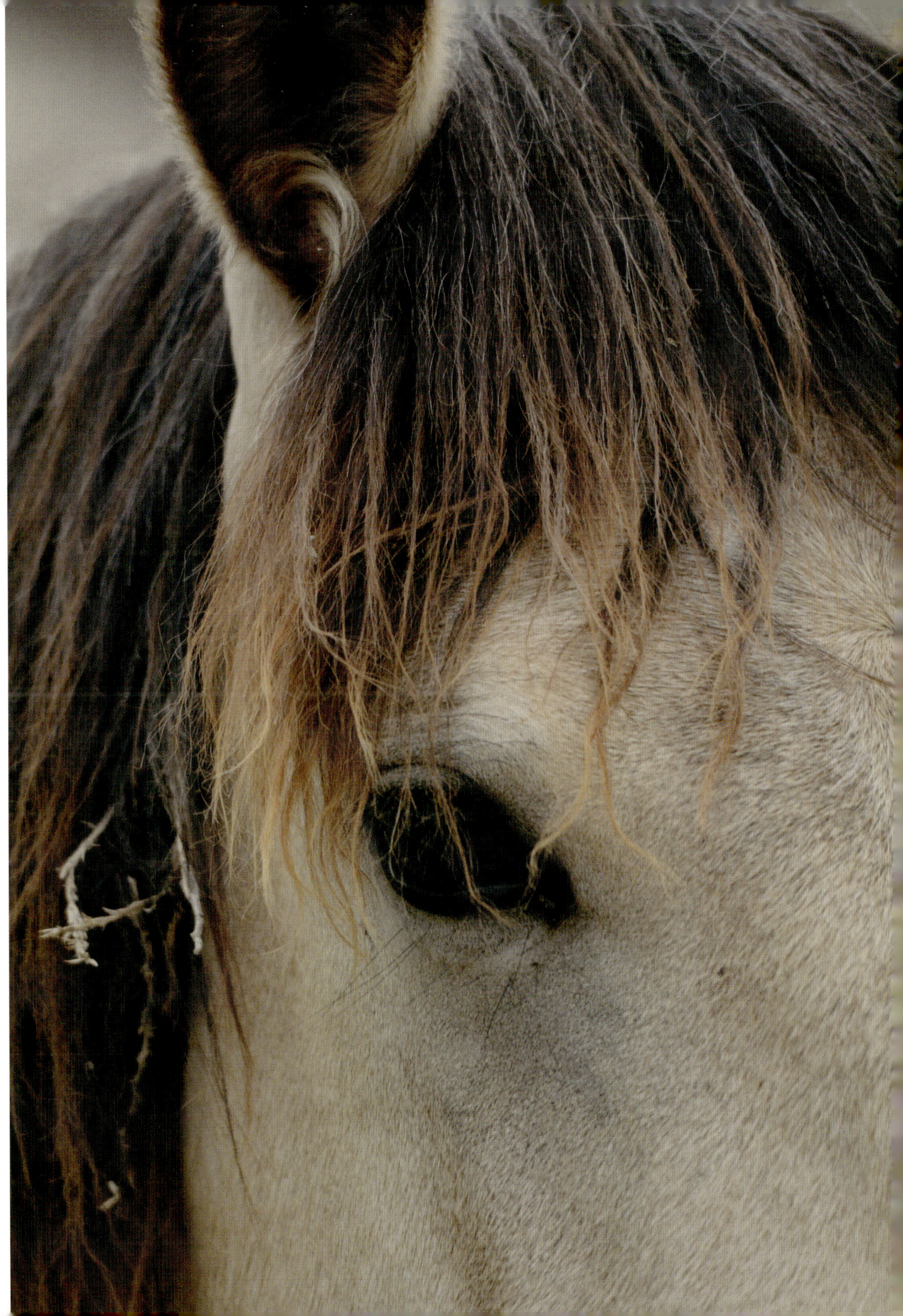

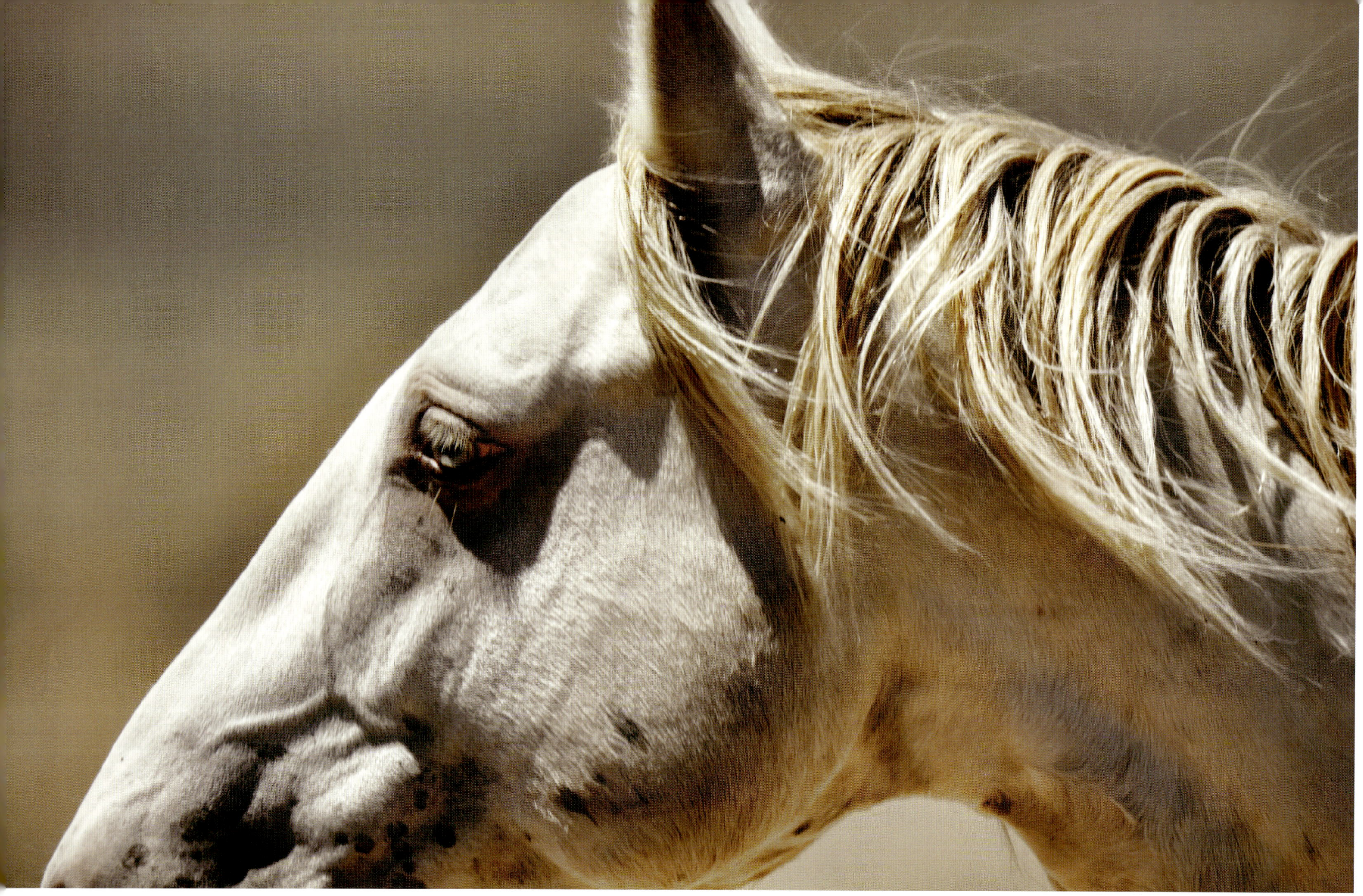

ABOVE: A cremello bachelor stallion.

OPPOSITE: It may appear as if these two stallions are on good terms, but they are smelling each other prior to a fight.

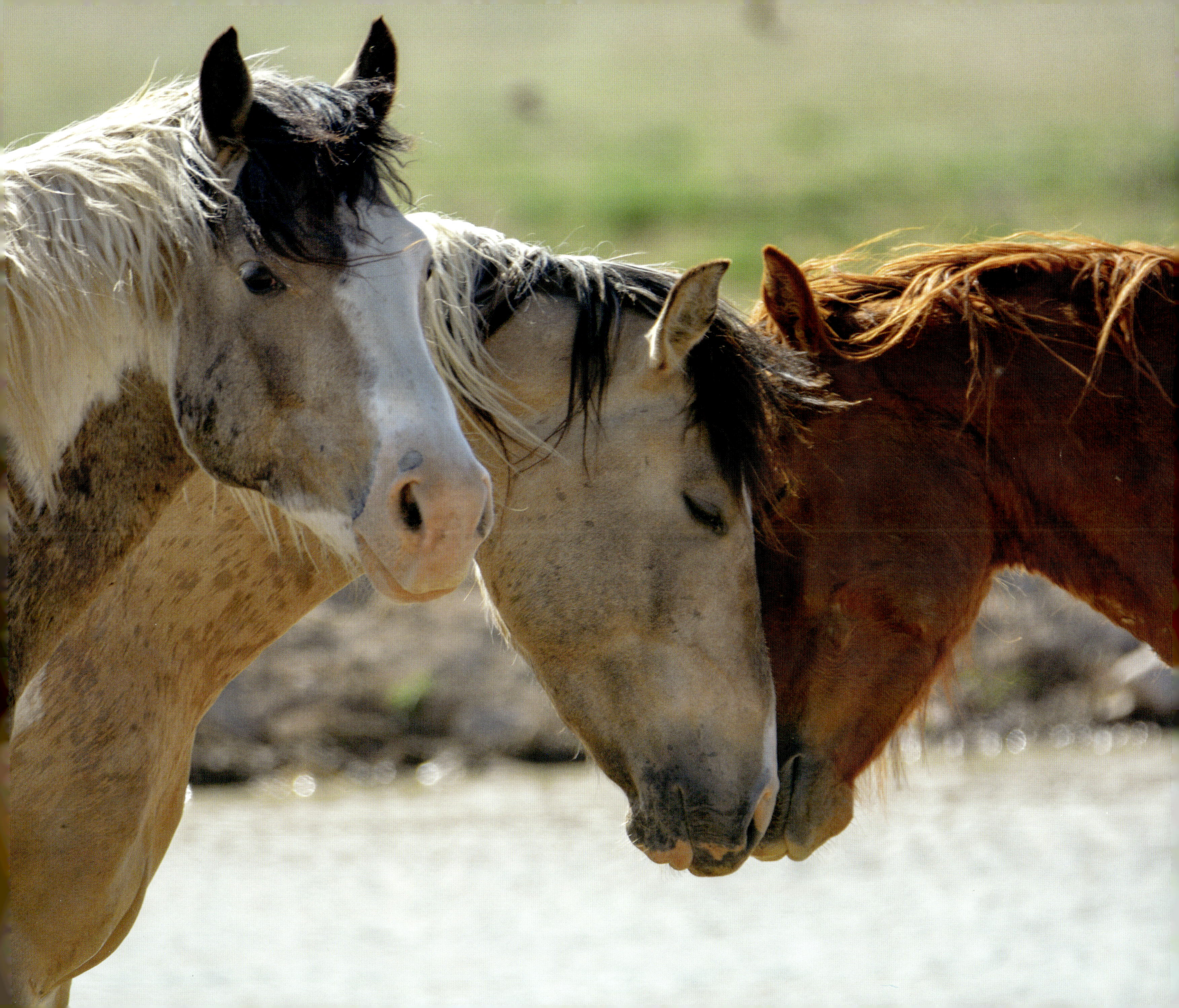

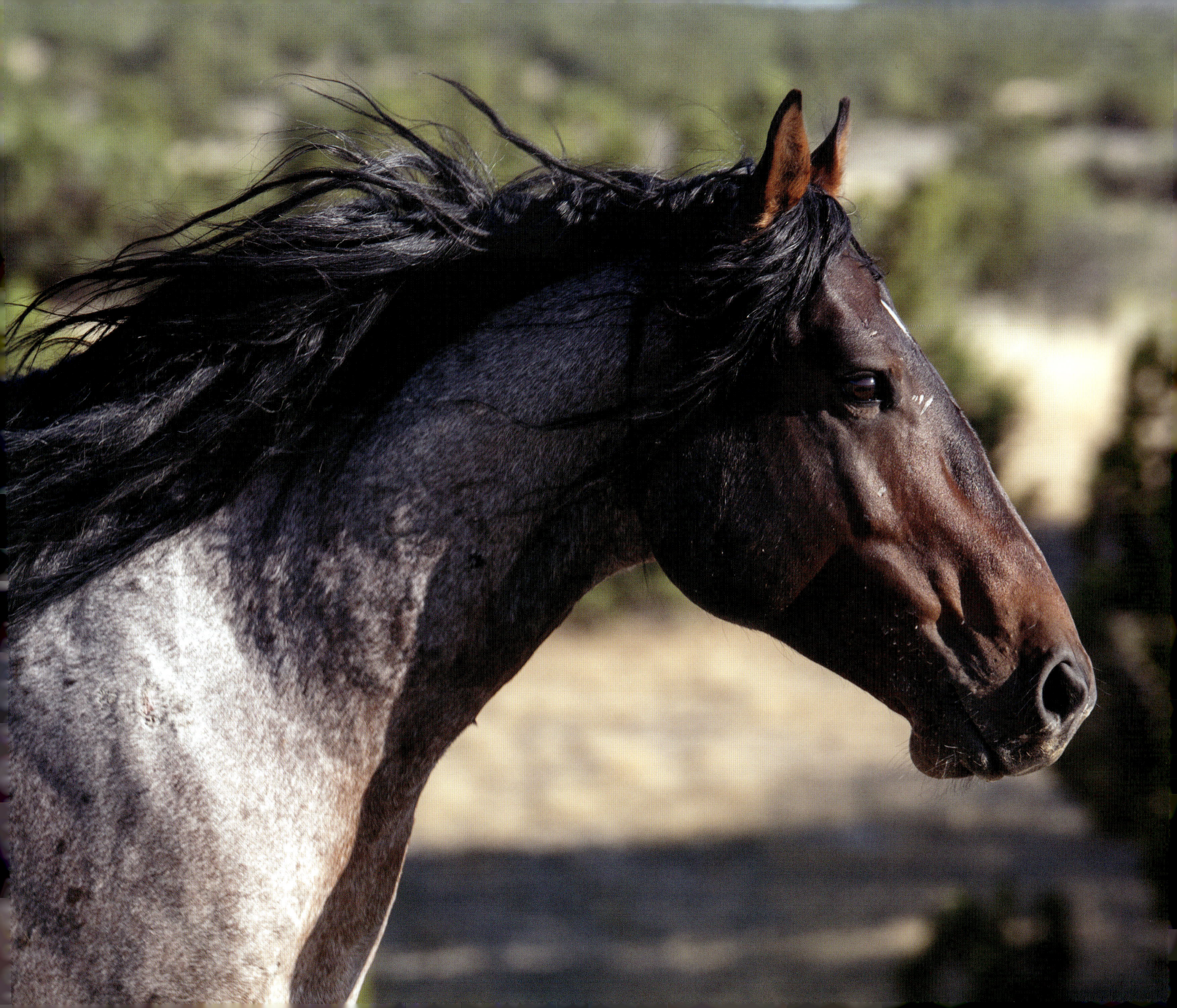

Opposite: A red roan bachelor stallion departs from the waterhole.

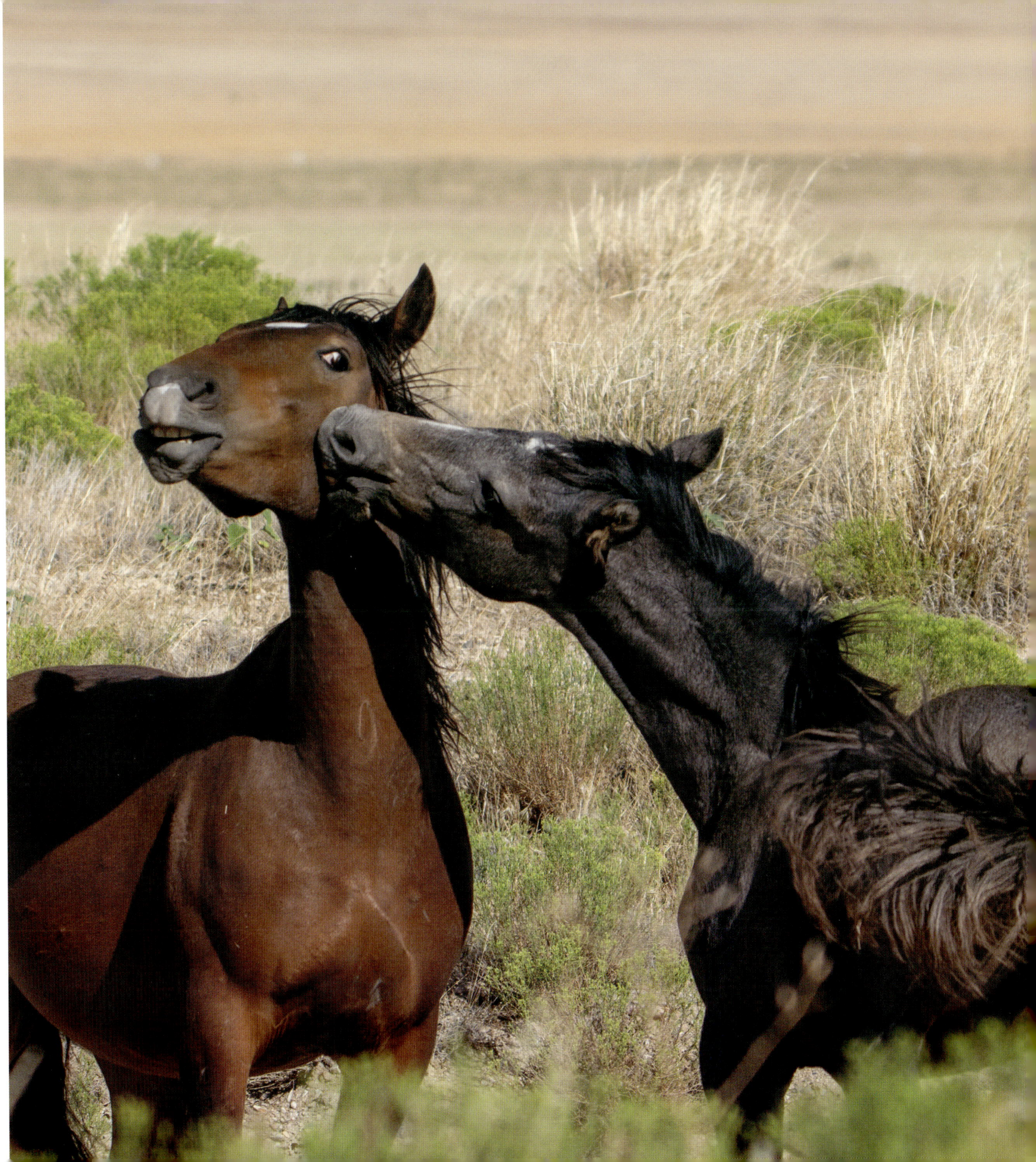

Right: Two young colts play fight.

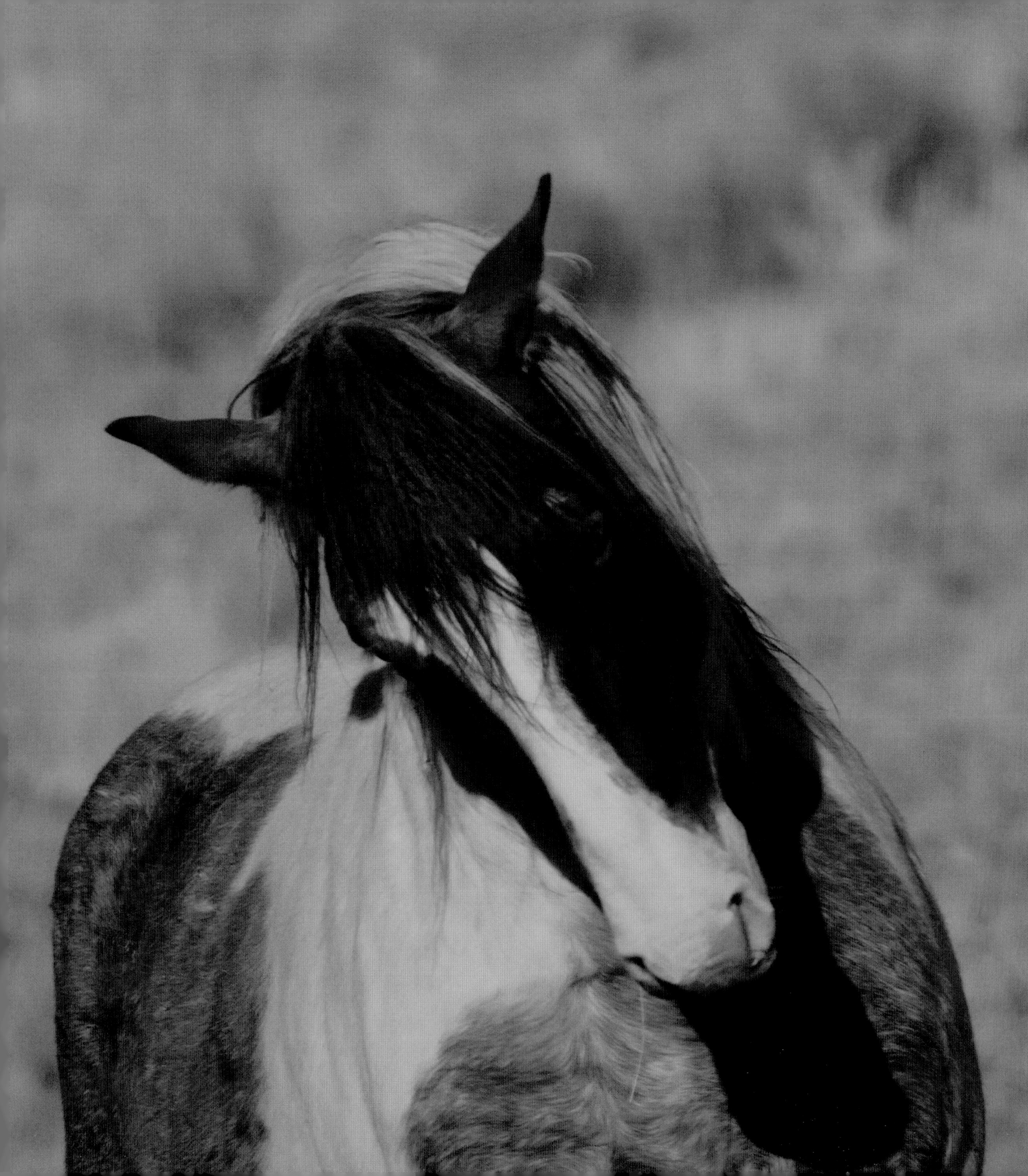

LEFT: Stallions will often swing their heads back and forth as they're posturing to fight.

OPPOSITE: A colt hurries back across the range to catch up to his band.

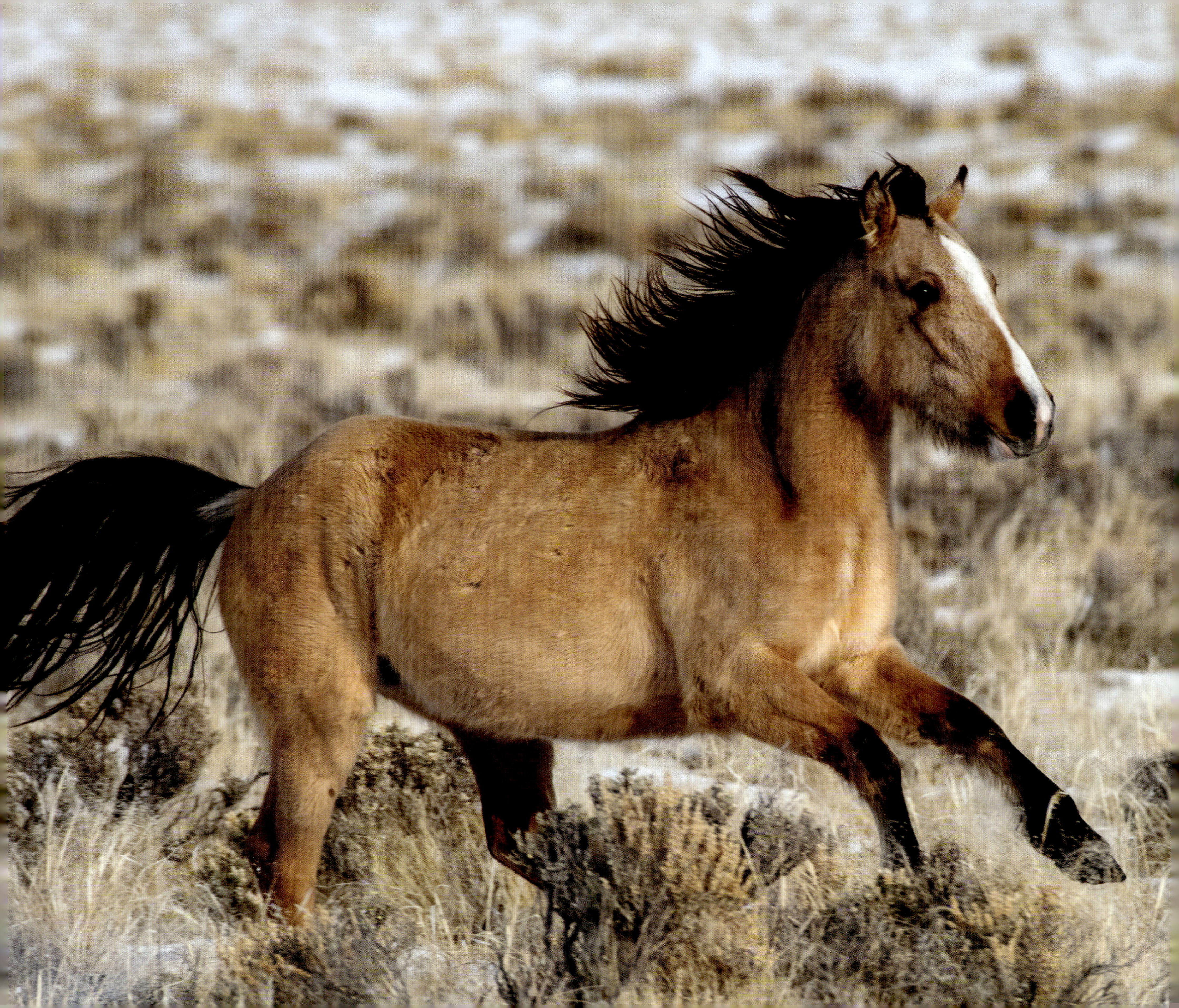

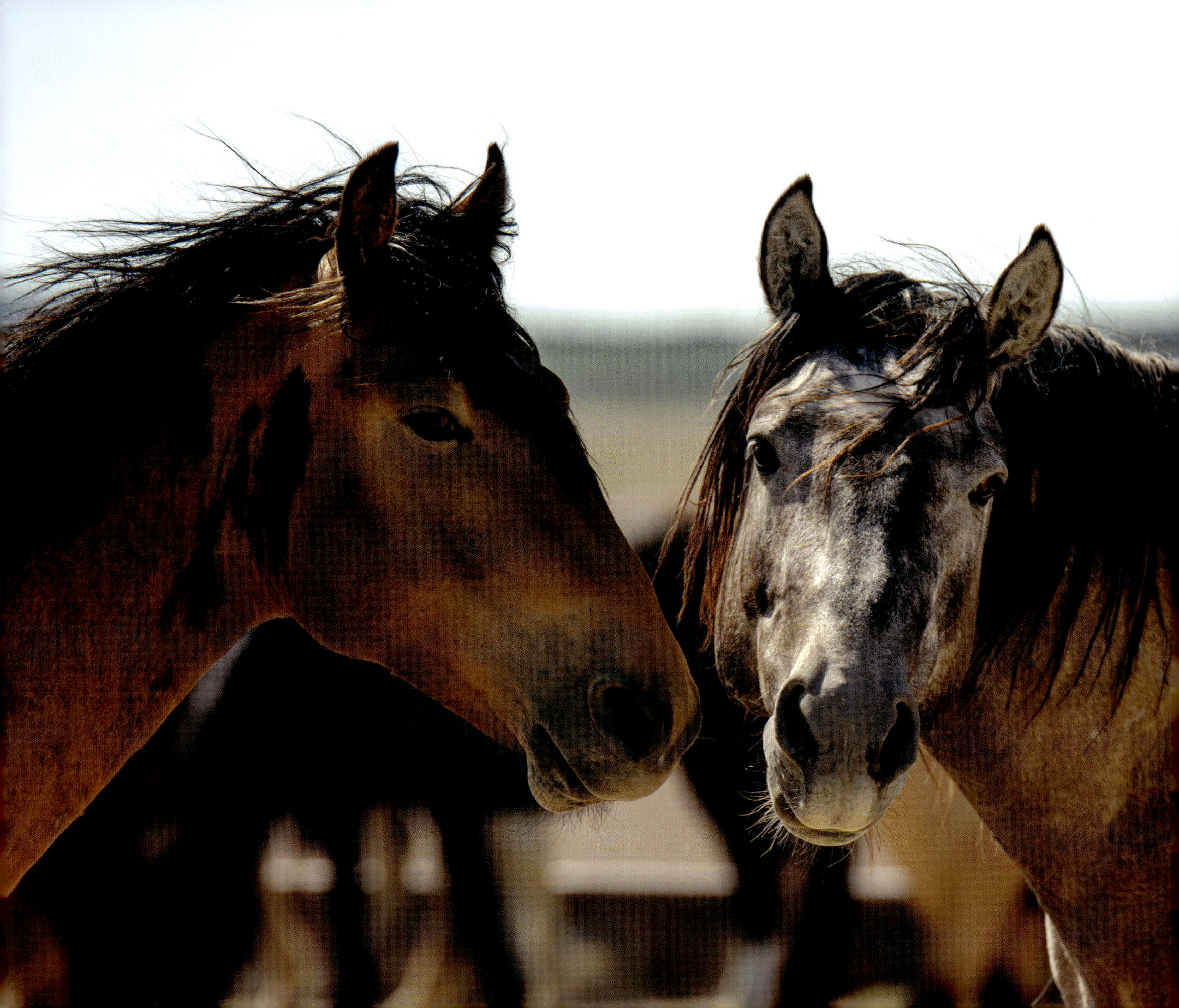

Clockwise from opposite: A pair of bachelors pose for the camera at the Winter Springs water trough in Utah. One Ear exhibiting the flehmen response. A stallion will use this courtship behavior of rolling back his upper lip to smell if a mare is in the estrus state (in heat). The flehmen response is also used by mares to explore their surroundings. This black bachelor stallion seems to have something to say to the gray.

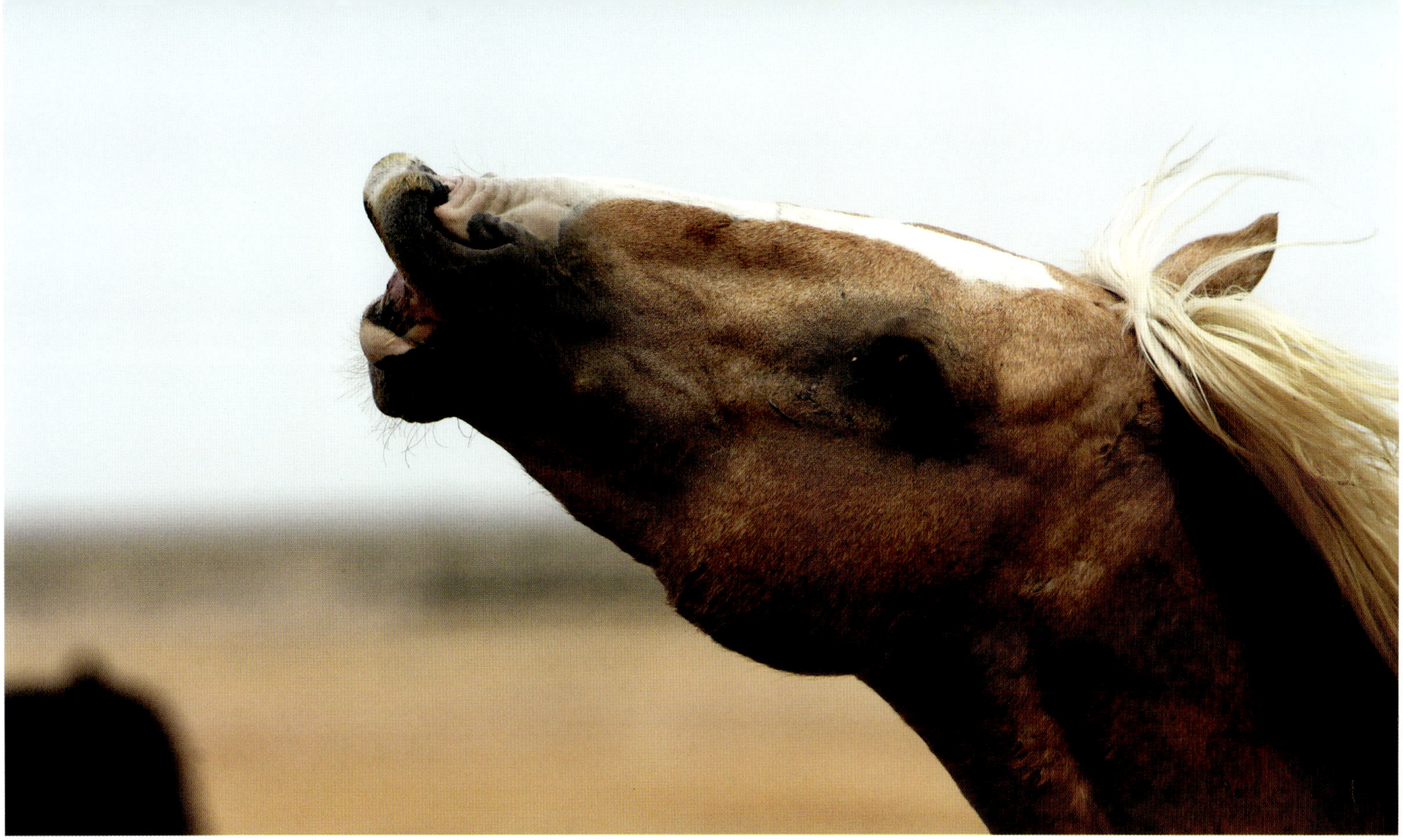

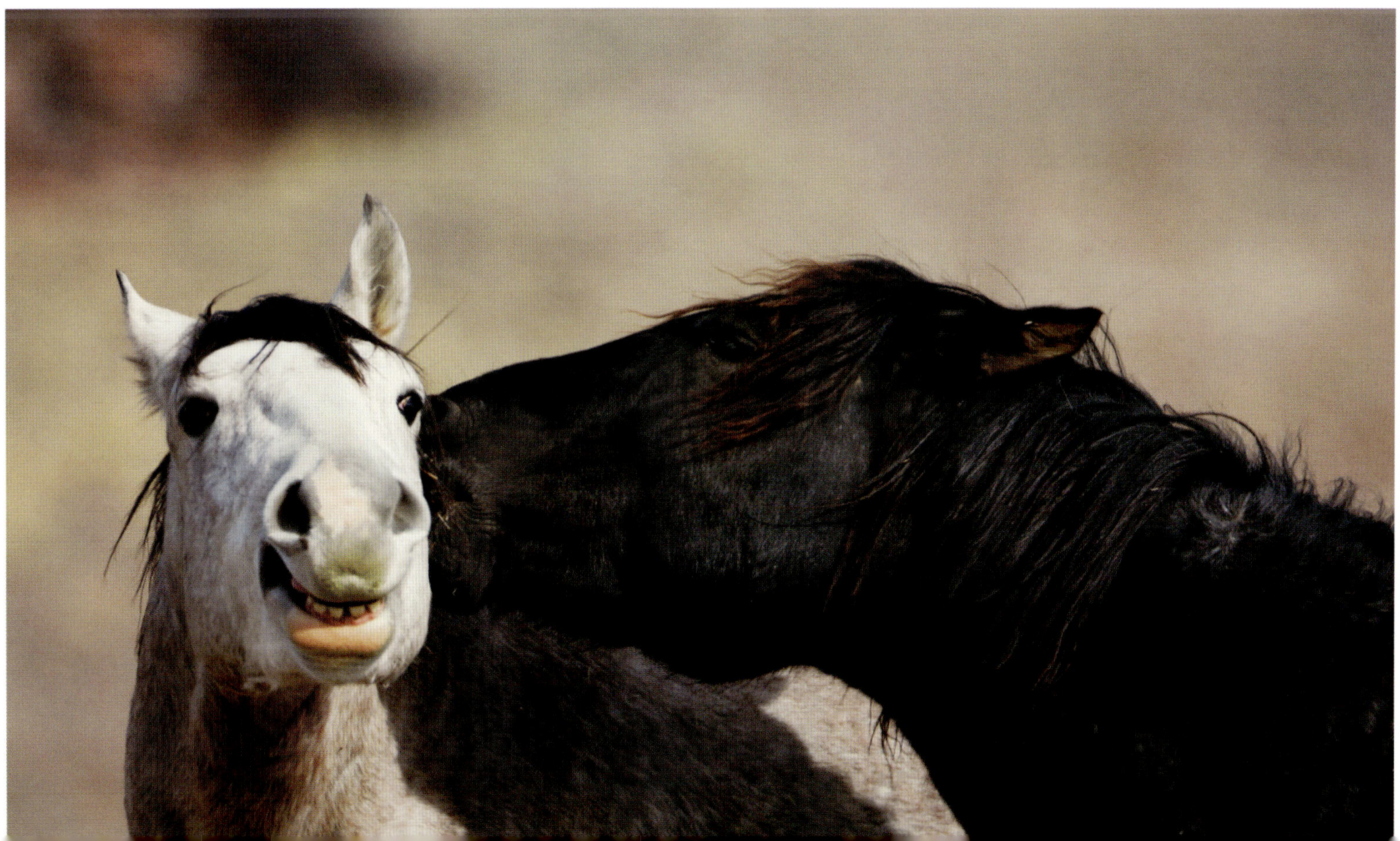

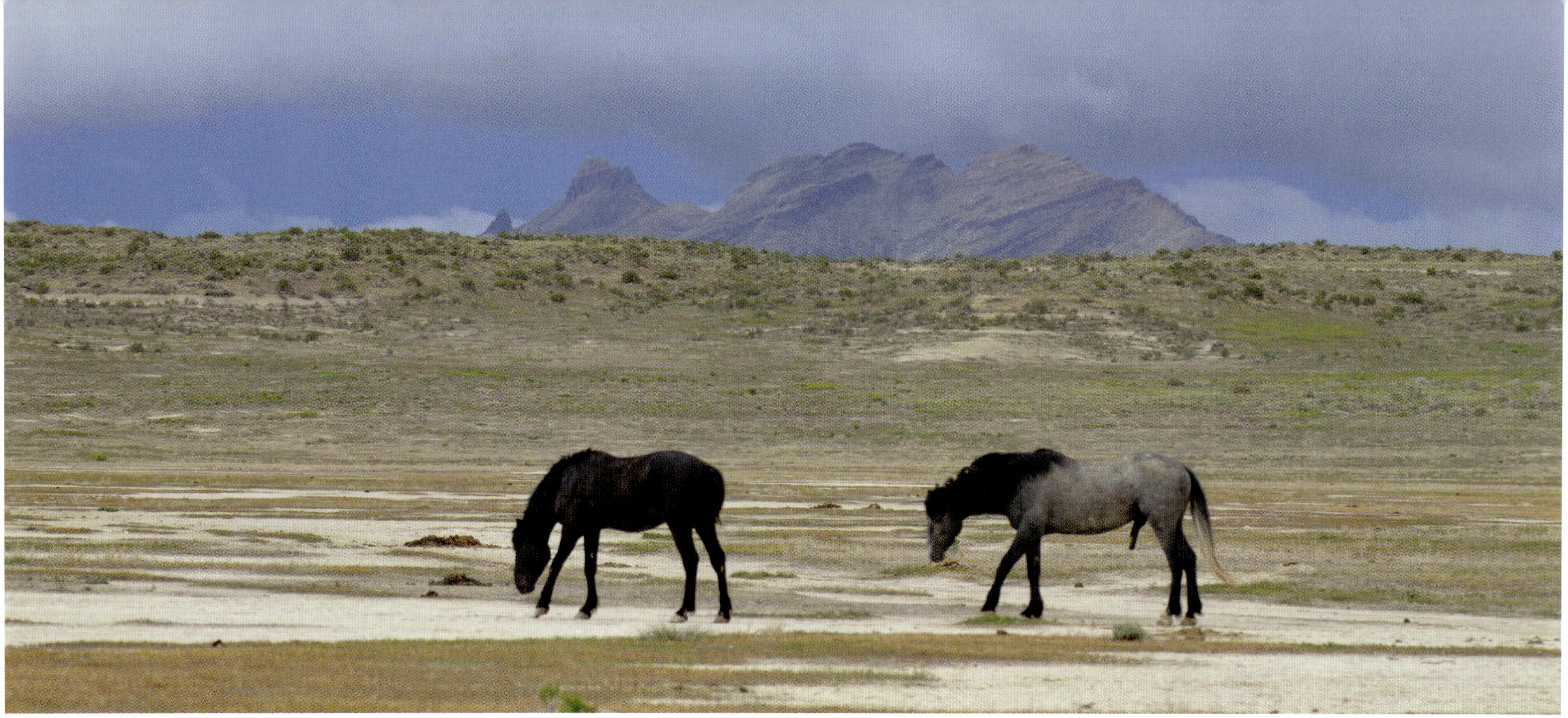

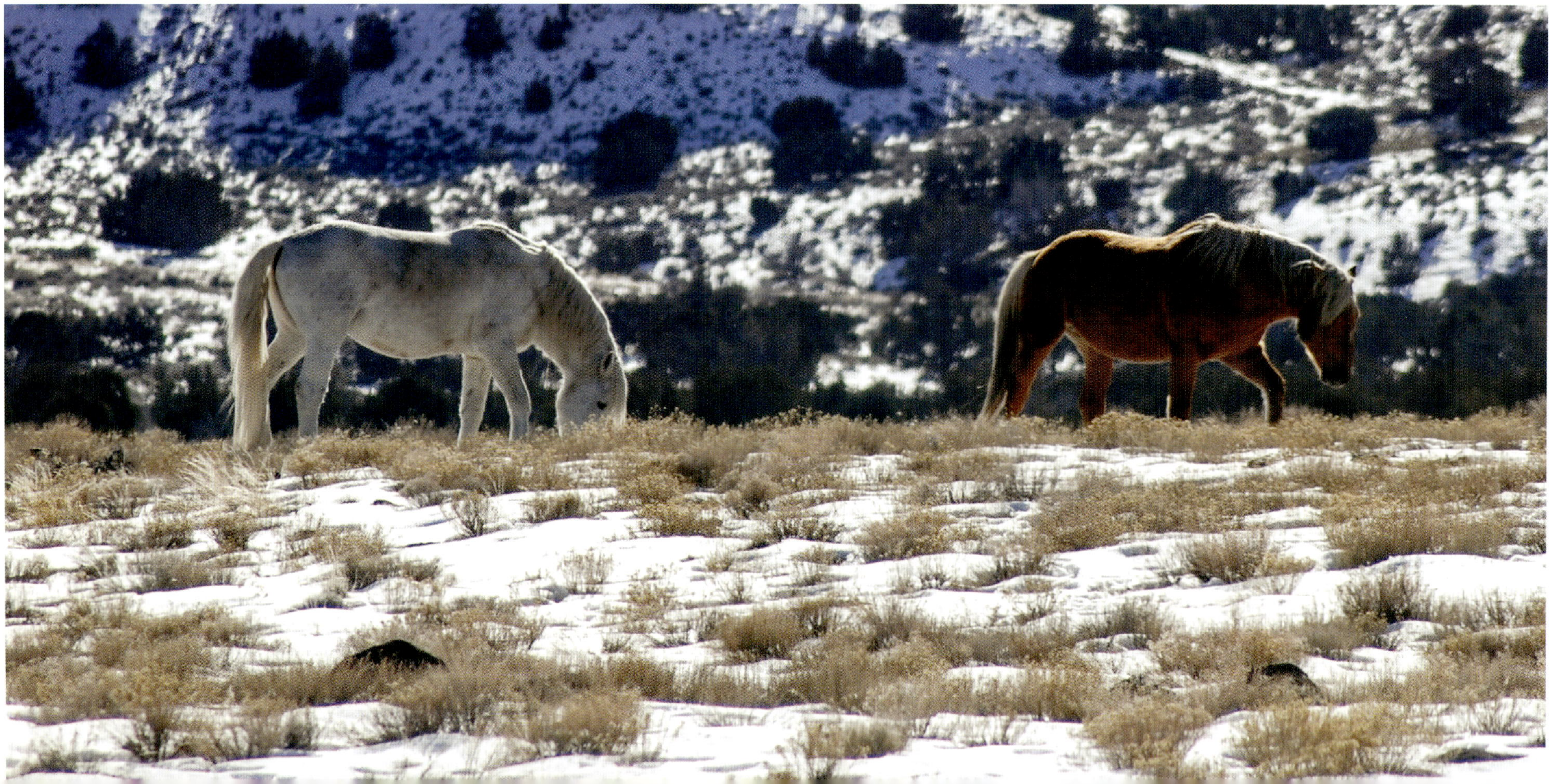

Opposite above: Bachelor stallions head across the range before a storm rolls in.

Opposite below: Two bachelor stallions forage through the snow.

Right: A band stallion charges toward a challenge.

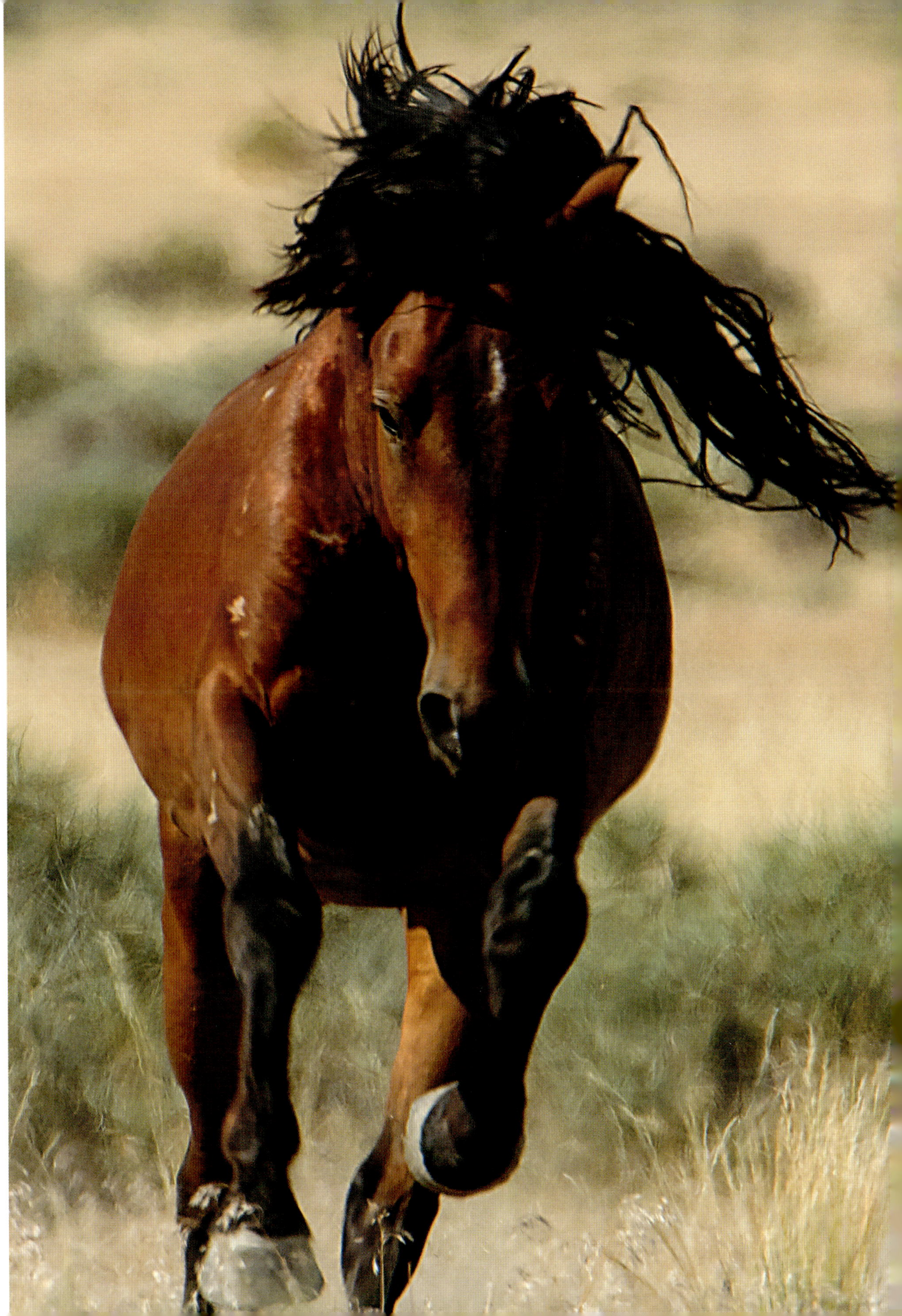

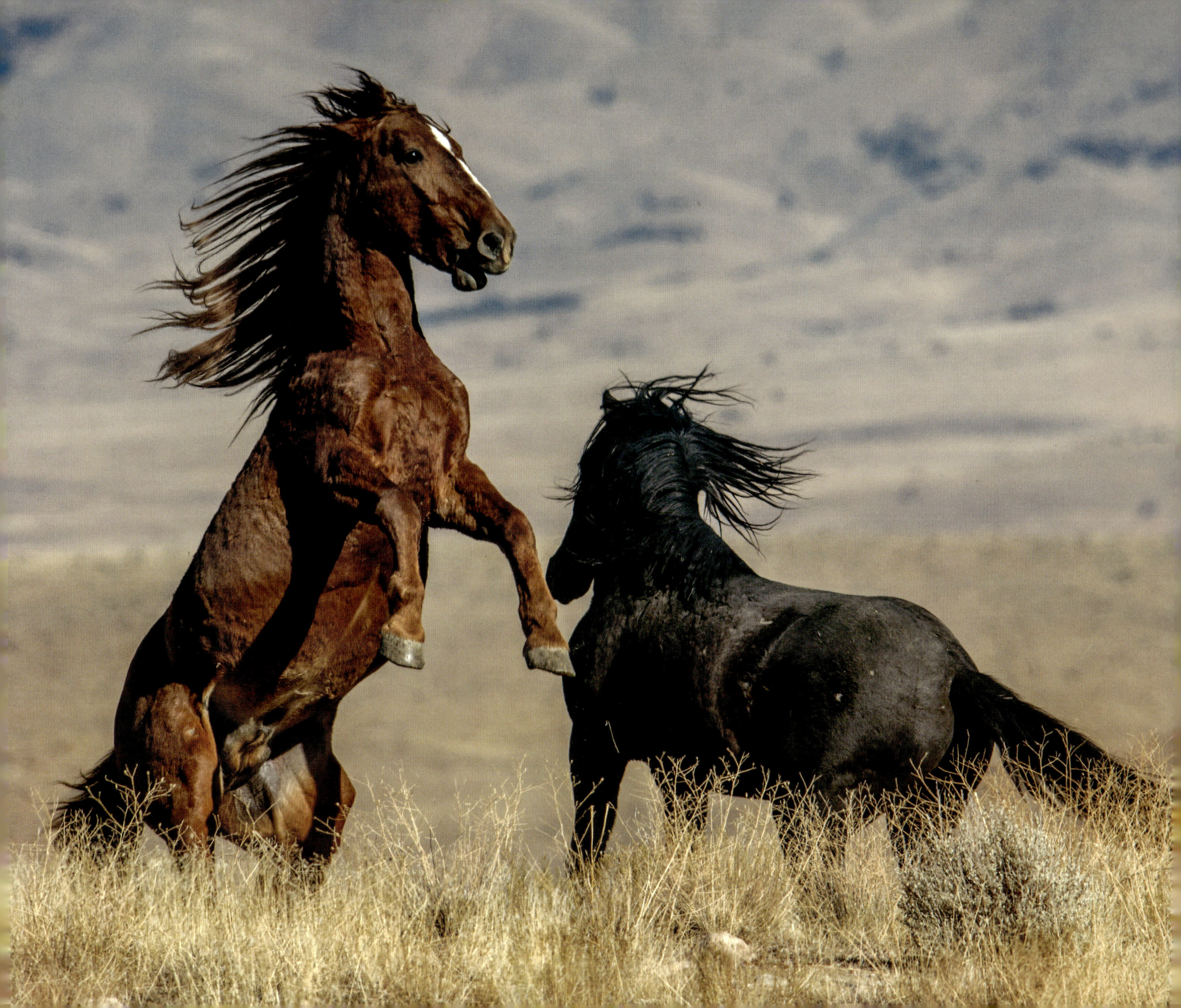

MUSTANG CHALLENGES

♦ ♦ ♦

Bachelor stallions straying too close to a band may spur a brief, uneventful clash. Stallions are most severe when an opposing stallion tries to steal their mare; these longer, aggressive fights usually end in blood. Fights between mustangs can be brief or span several minutes. No matter how long they take, they are always vicious. The horses bite and strike at each other with powerful teeth and hooves, emerging with deep wounds in their hides—and, in at least one case, an ear bitten off.

The onset of a fight is the most interesting part to watch. The stallions snort, posture, and kick up dust with stomping and pawing. It is a threatening display of power and sets a stunning stage for photographers to catch these stallions at their most wild.

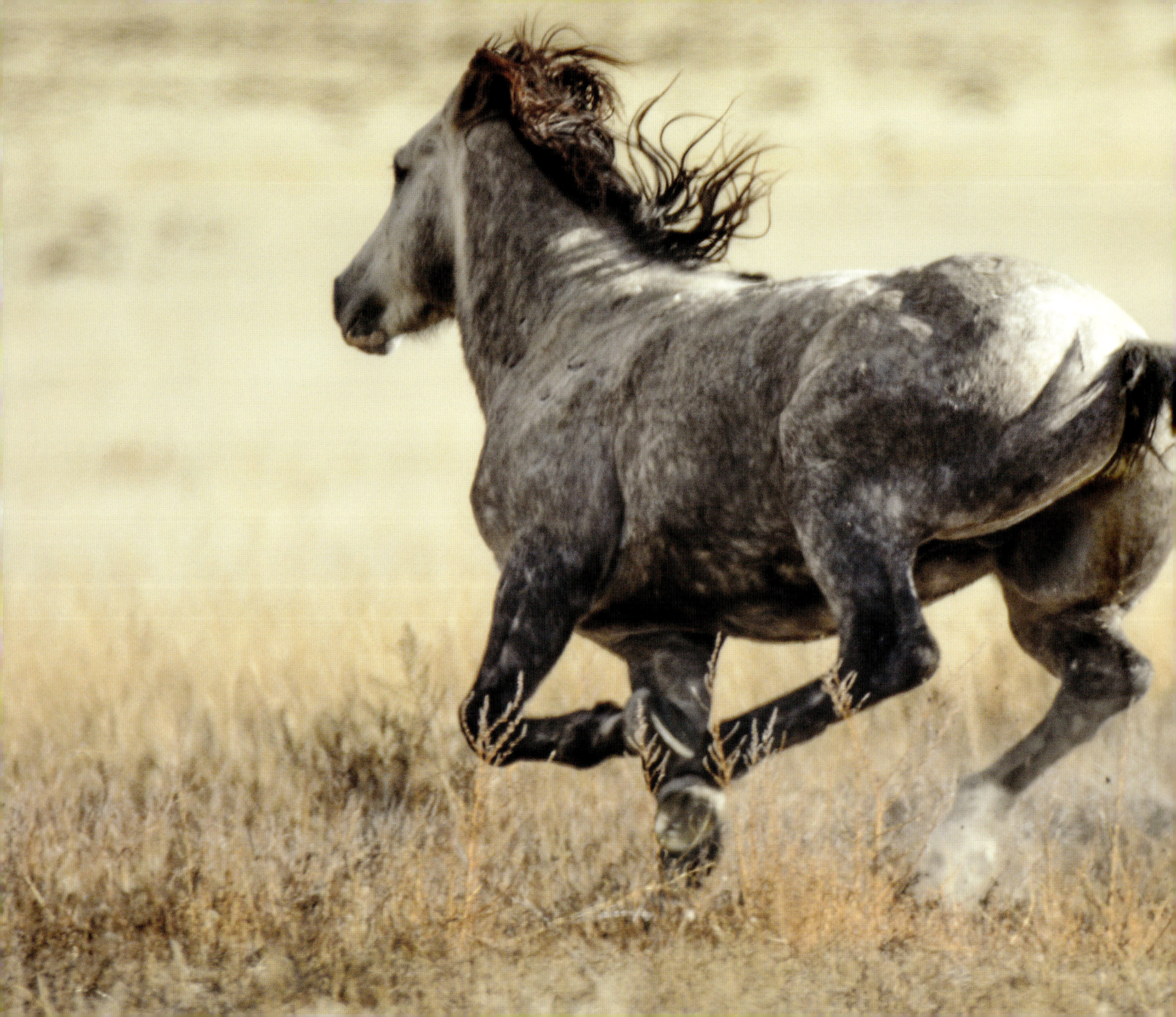

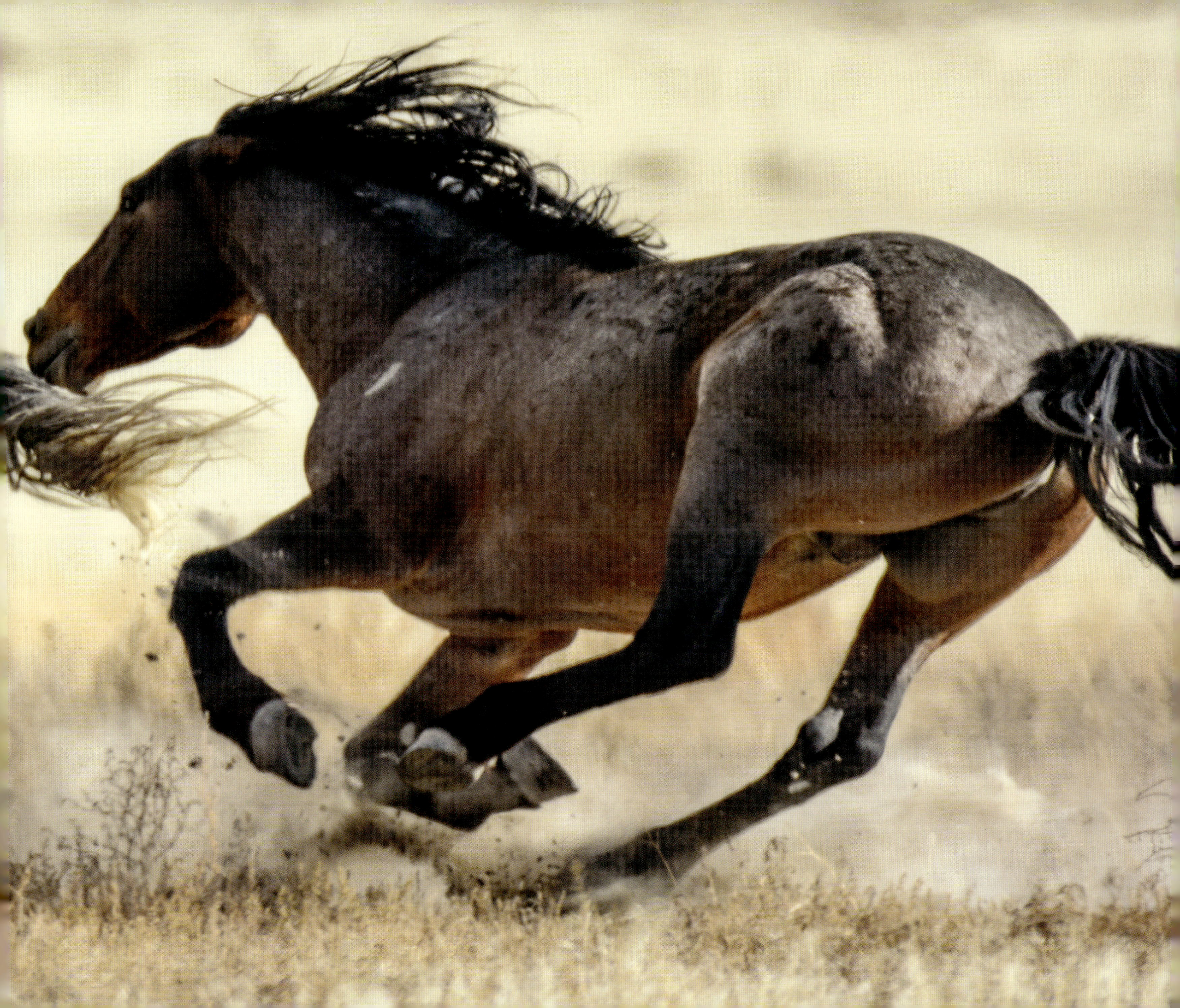

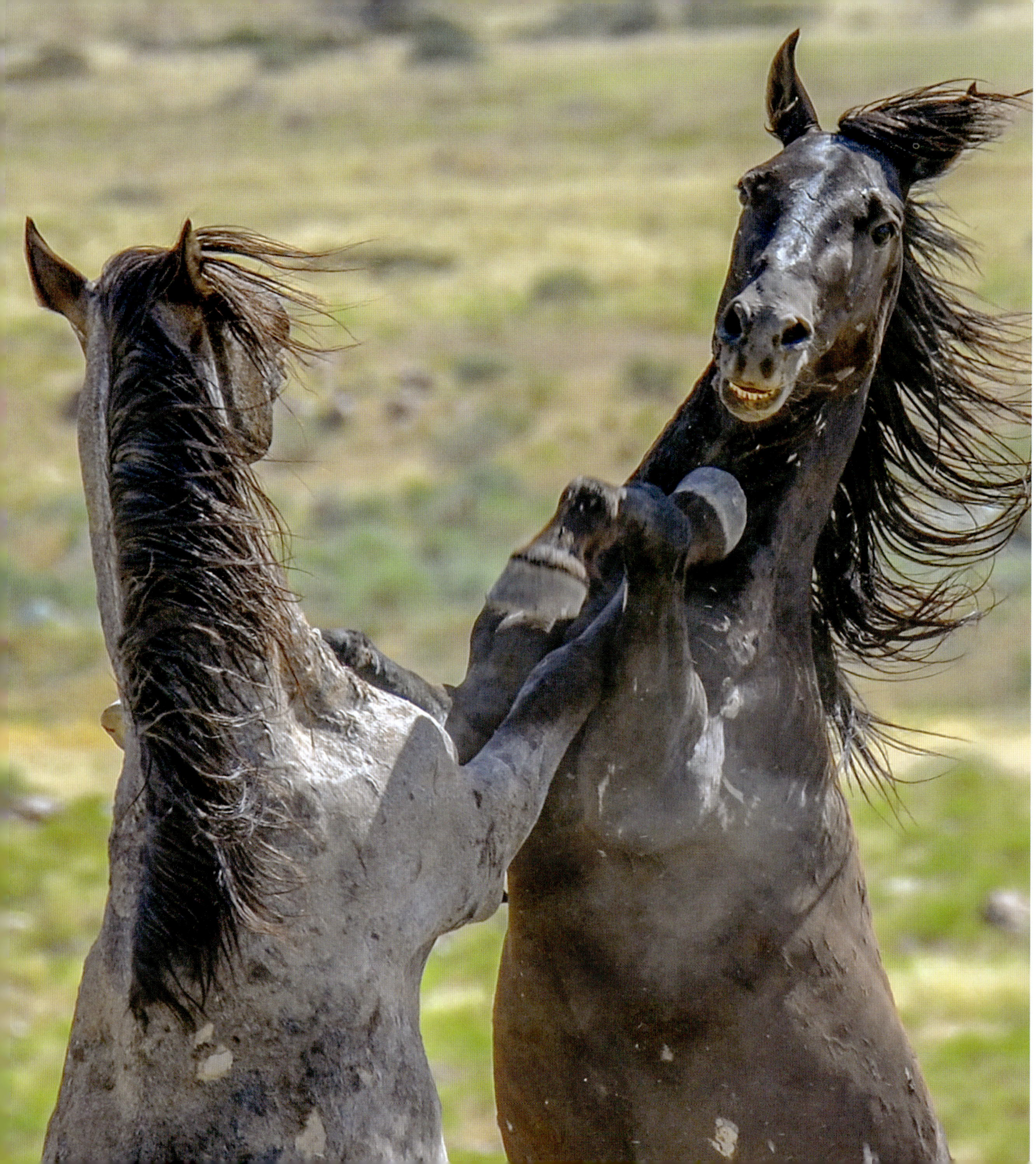

Previous page: A band stallion chases off a challenger.

Left: Fights among bachelor and band stallions involve standing up on their hind legs with their front hooves pounding on the chest and head of their challenger.

Opposite: One of many fights the gray and cremello bachelor stallions have had over the years. Neither had a band to fight for; this was just a territorial battle.

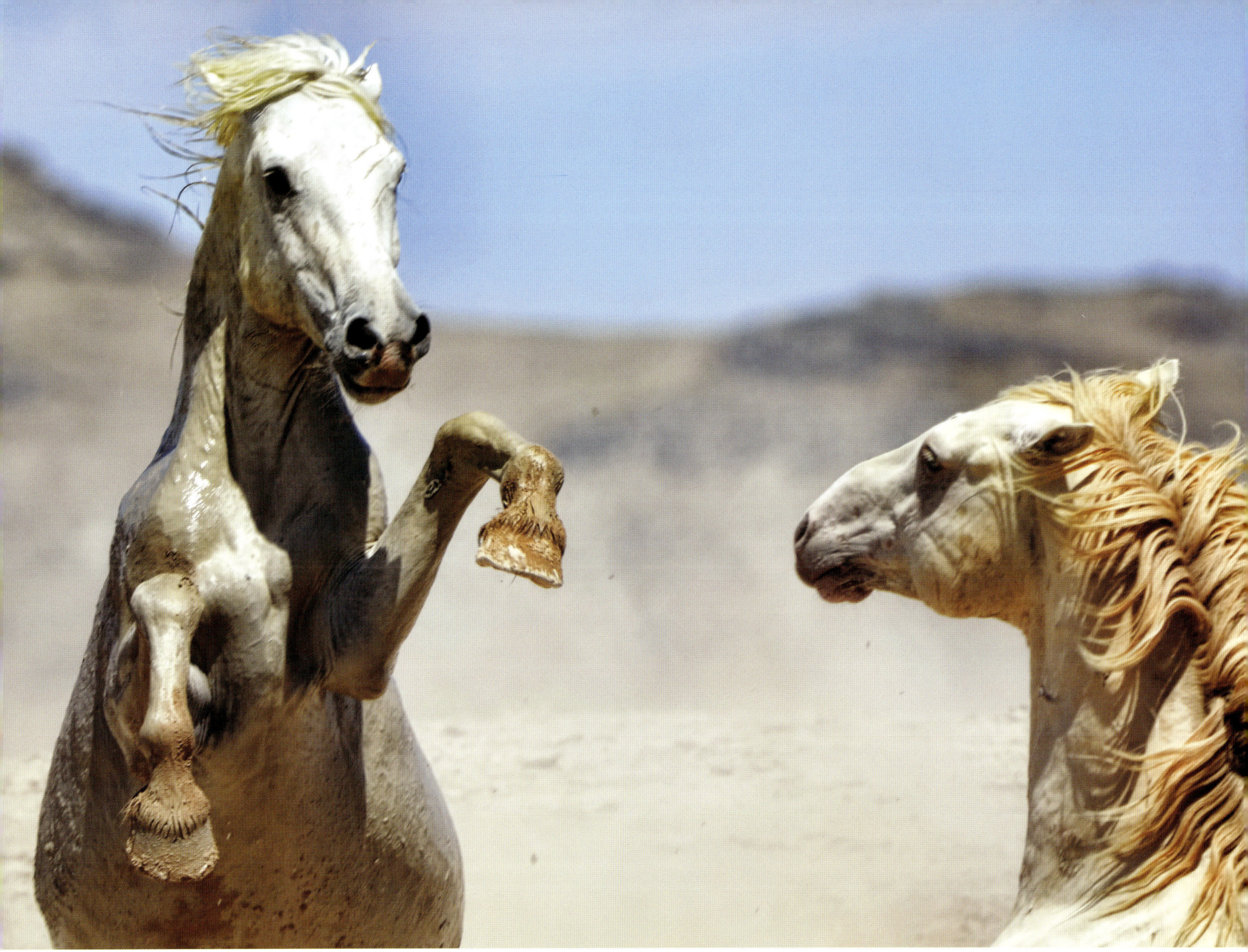

ONE EAR

I first saw One Ear in 2007. Back then, this stunning palomino was probably four or five years old; he was a bachelor stallion traveling alone. He had both his ears and an unconquerable spirit. He followed one band for the next year, eventually overpowering the band stallion and taking over. His new band continued to grow, and he sired many foals in the following years.

The story of his name comes from that determination. It's said that his large band of mares drew challenges from many other bachelor stallions. The palomino emerged the victor again and again, until a fateful challenge with a large, aggressive stallion.

The fight was violent. It cost the palomino his band of mares and his left ear.

He disappeared for some time, returning with a single goal: to regain his band. It took time, grit, and many clashes, but One Ear eventually drove off the gray stallion and reclaimed his band.

The past couple of years have been challenging. Many younger, stronger stallions have challenged him, and he has lost his band once again. He now travels with another older stallion or alone. Because he usually travels close to other bands, ol' One Ear can go weeks without being seen.

Still, his heritage is felt throughout the range. The foals that he sired today have produced their own foals and run other bands. When you do catch sight of him, it's humbling to be reminded of a stallion with so much history of courage and strength.

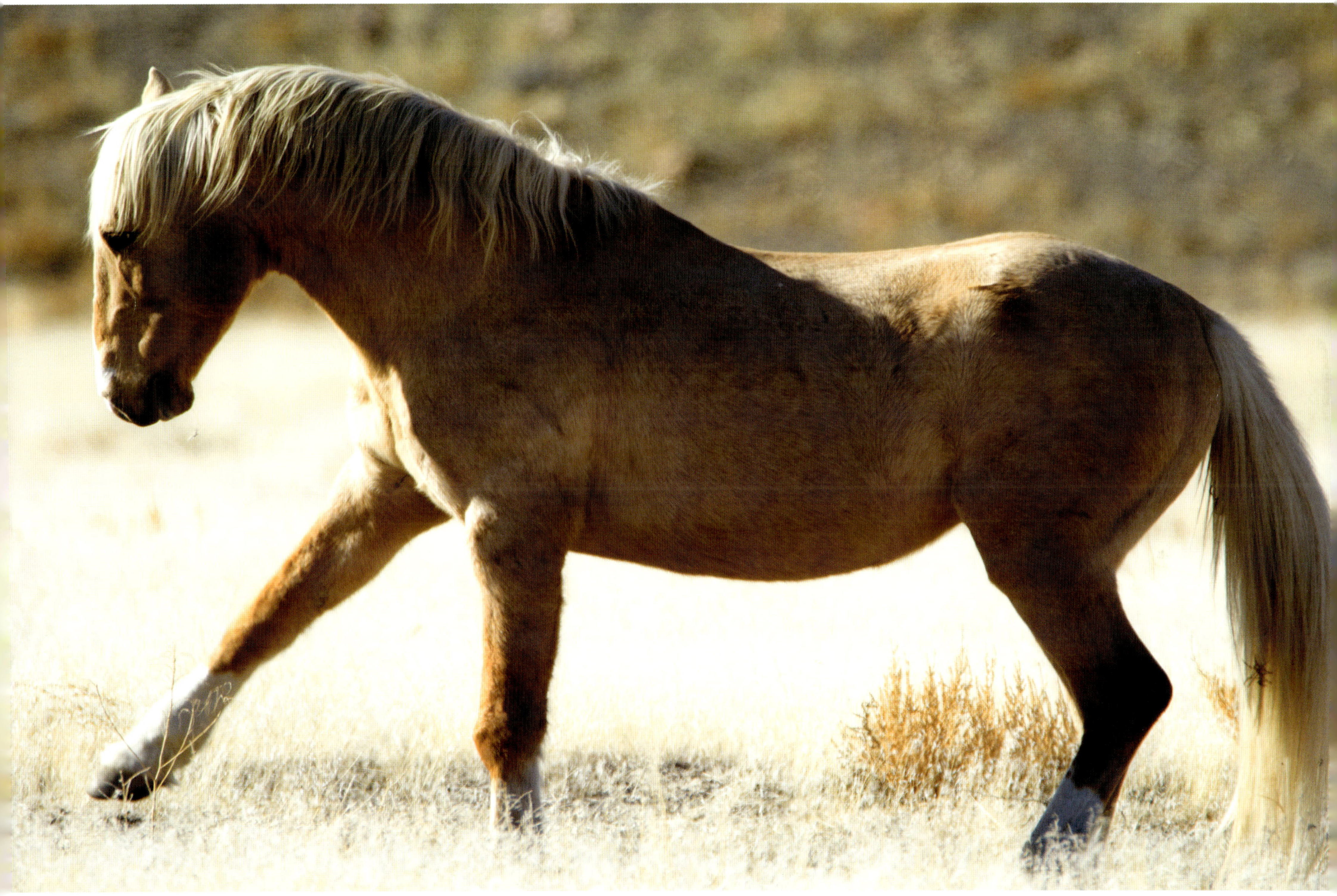

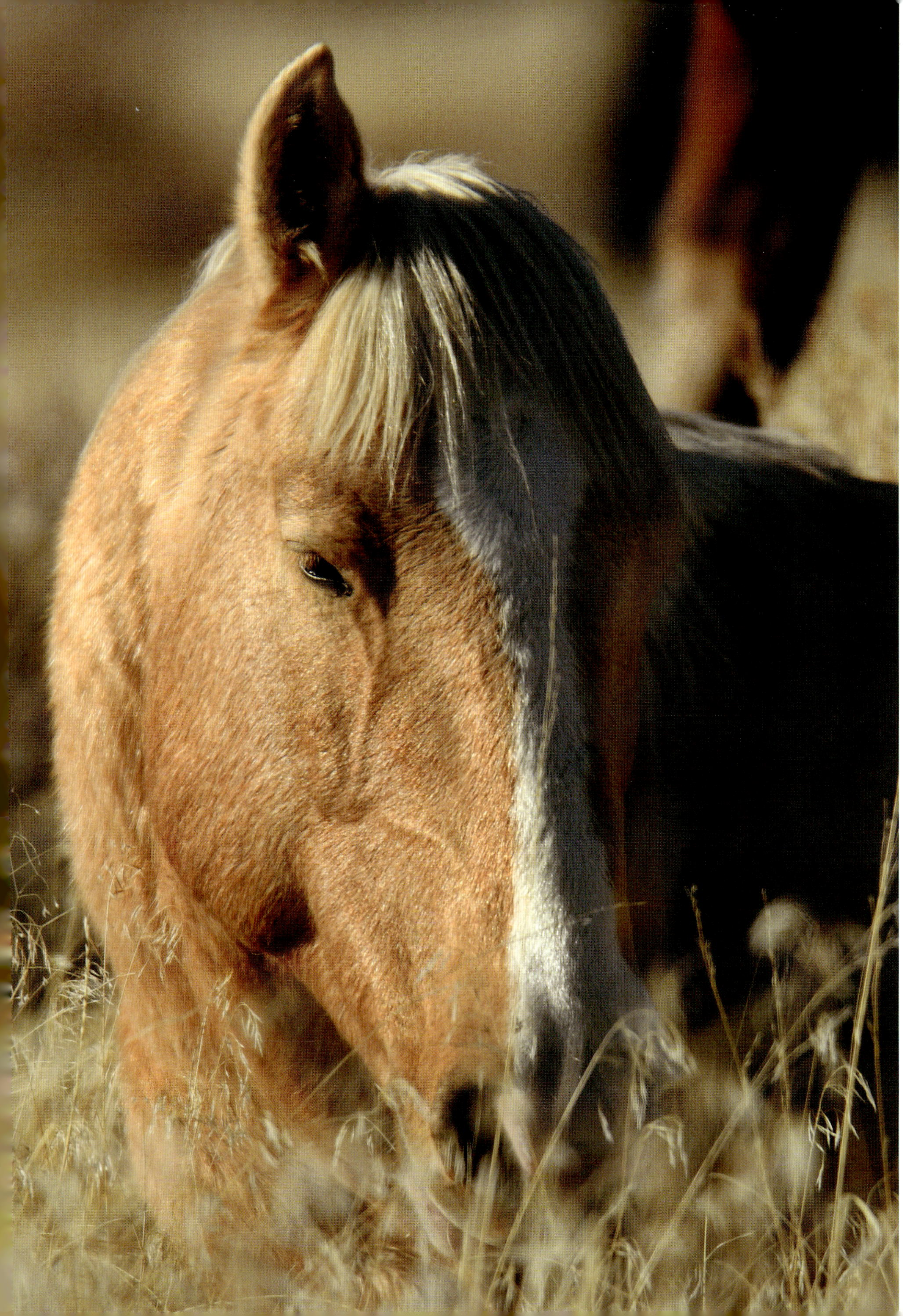

Left: Even band stallions need to enjoy a warm winter's afternoon nap.

Opposite: One Ear runs to chase off a threat to his band.

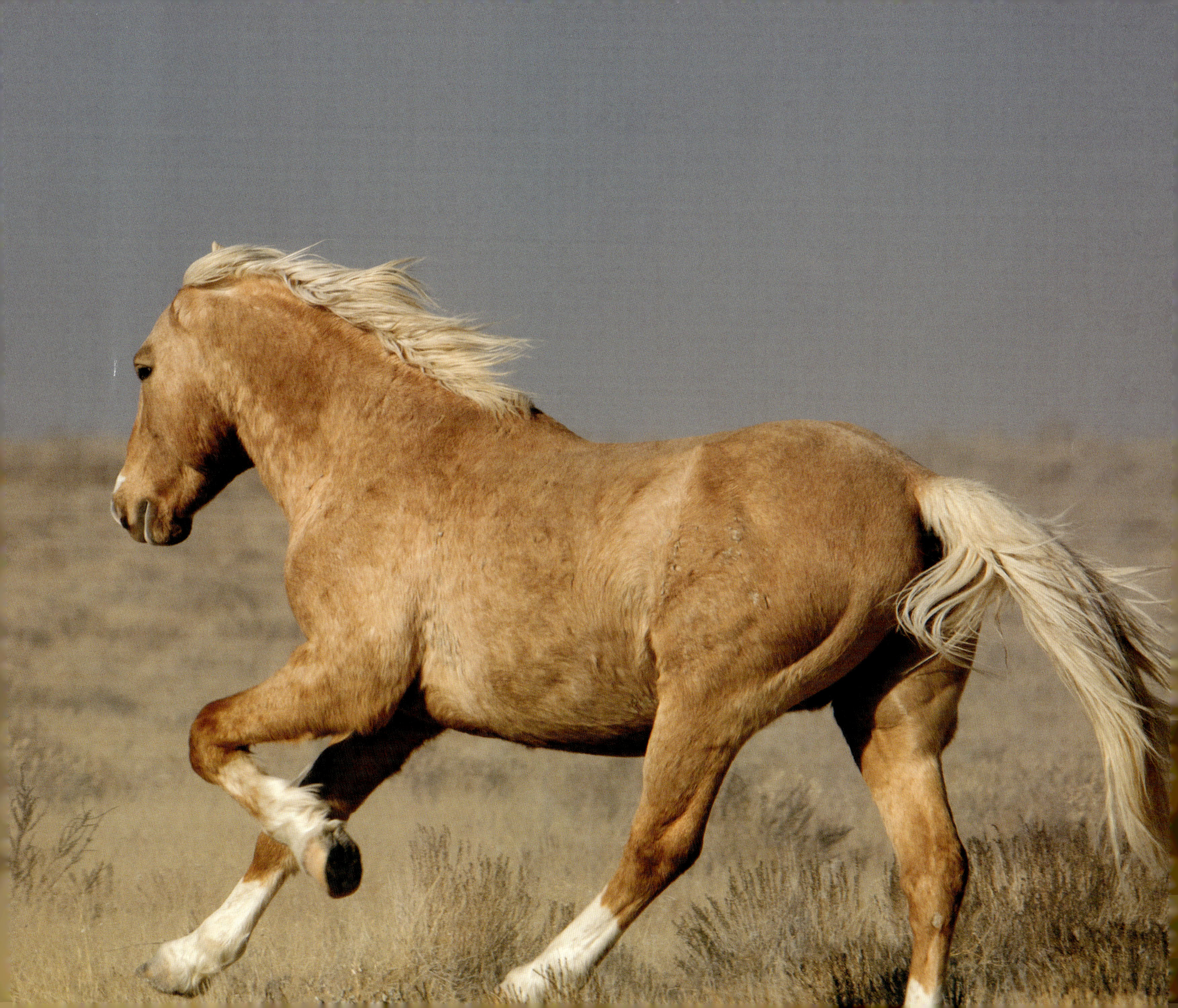

A GOOD ROLL IN THE MUD

Rolling in the mud is part of a wild horse's natural grooming for many reasons. A good roll in the mud will cool off the horse, provide protection from the sun and various insects, and relieve an itch when the horse can't find another horse to scratch it. And maybe they think it's fun—it certainly provides some great photos.

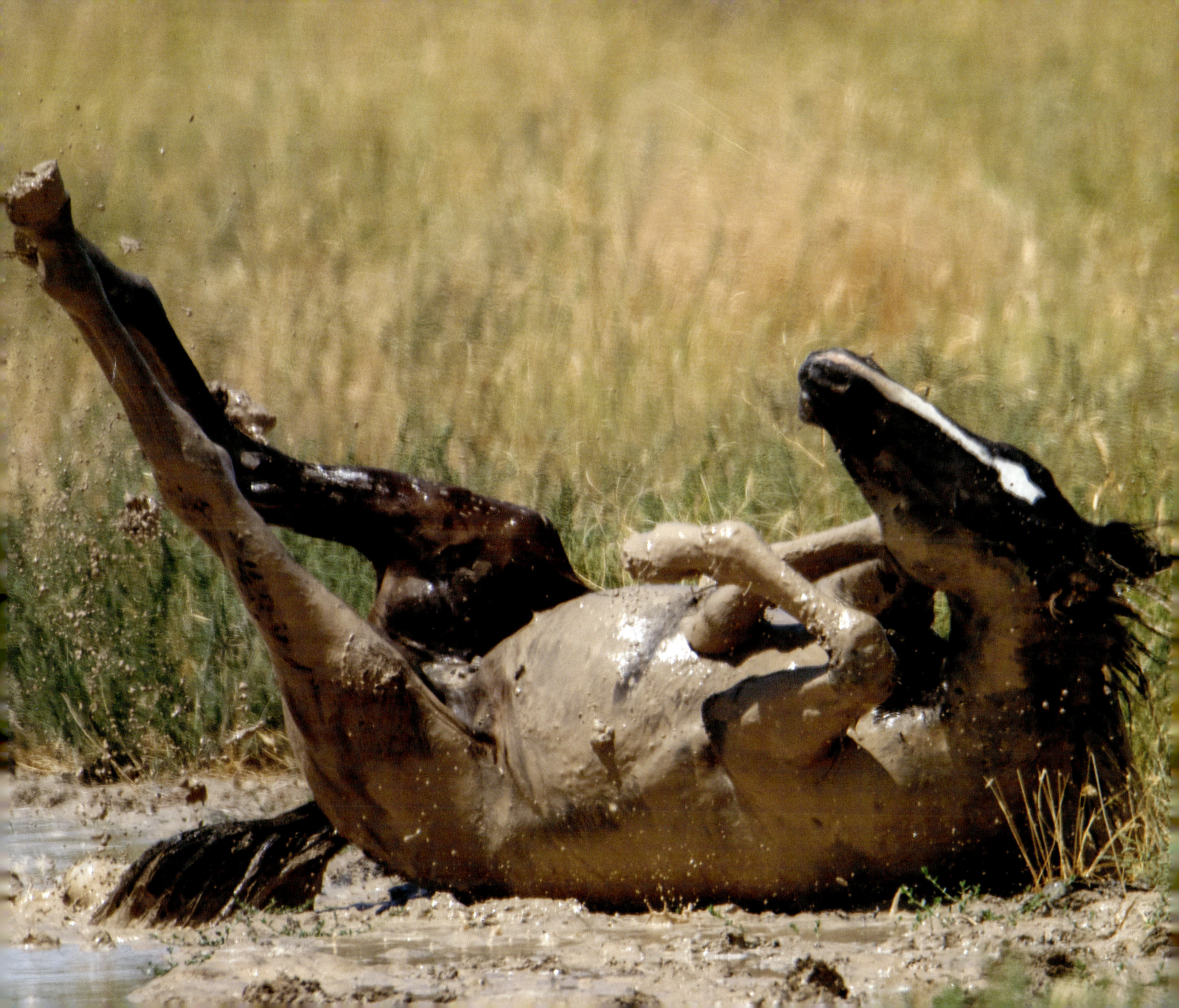

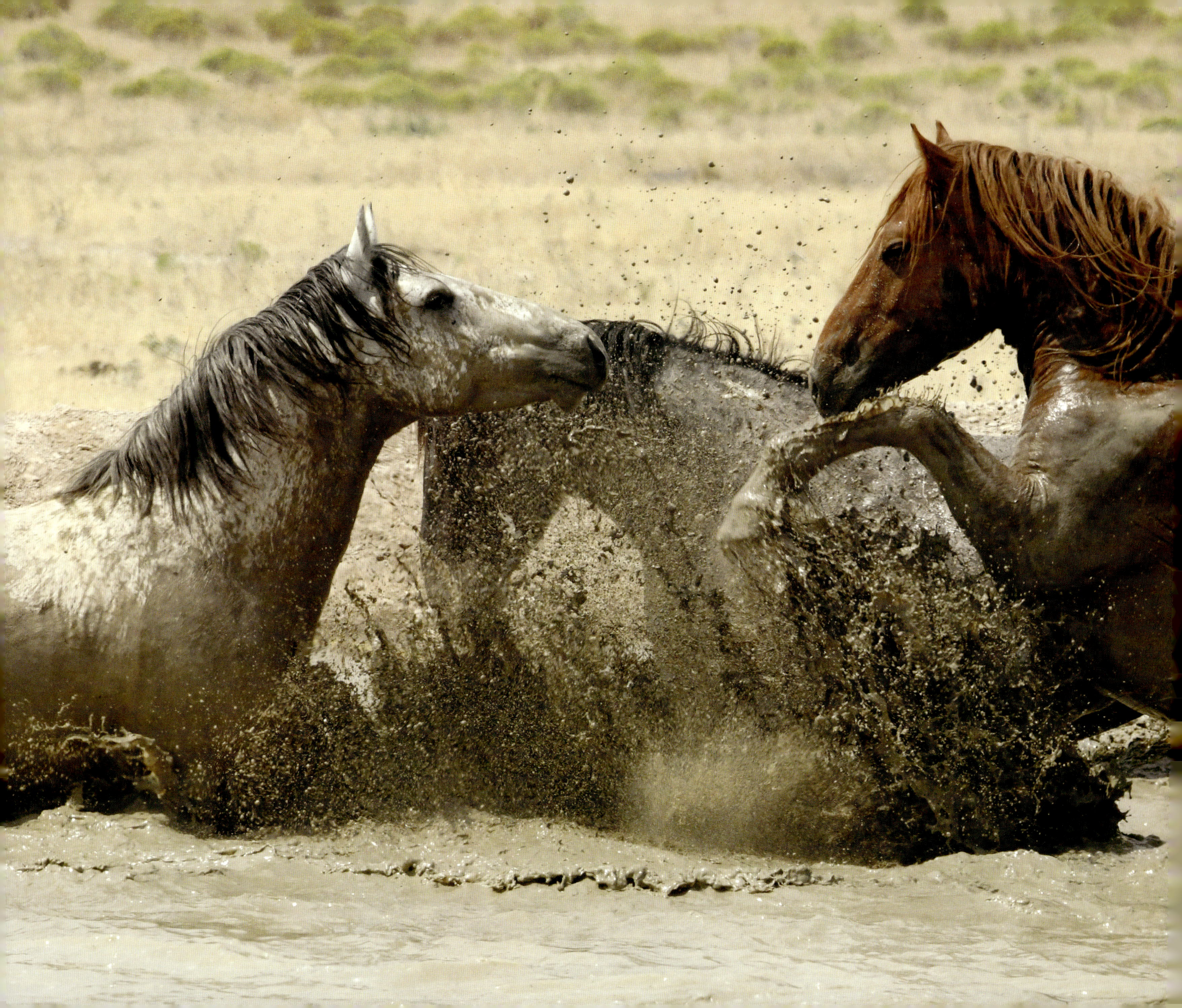

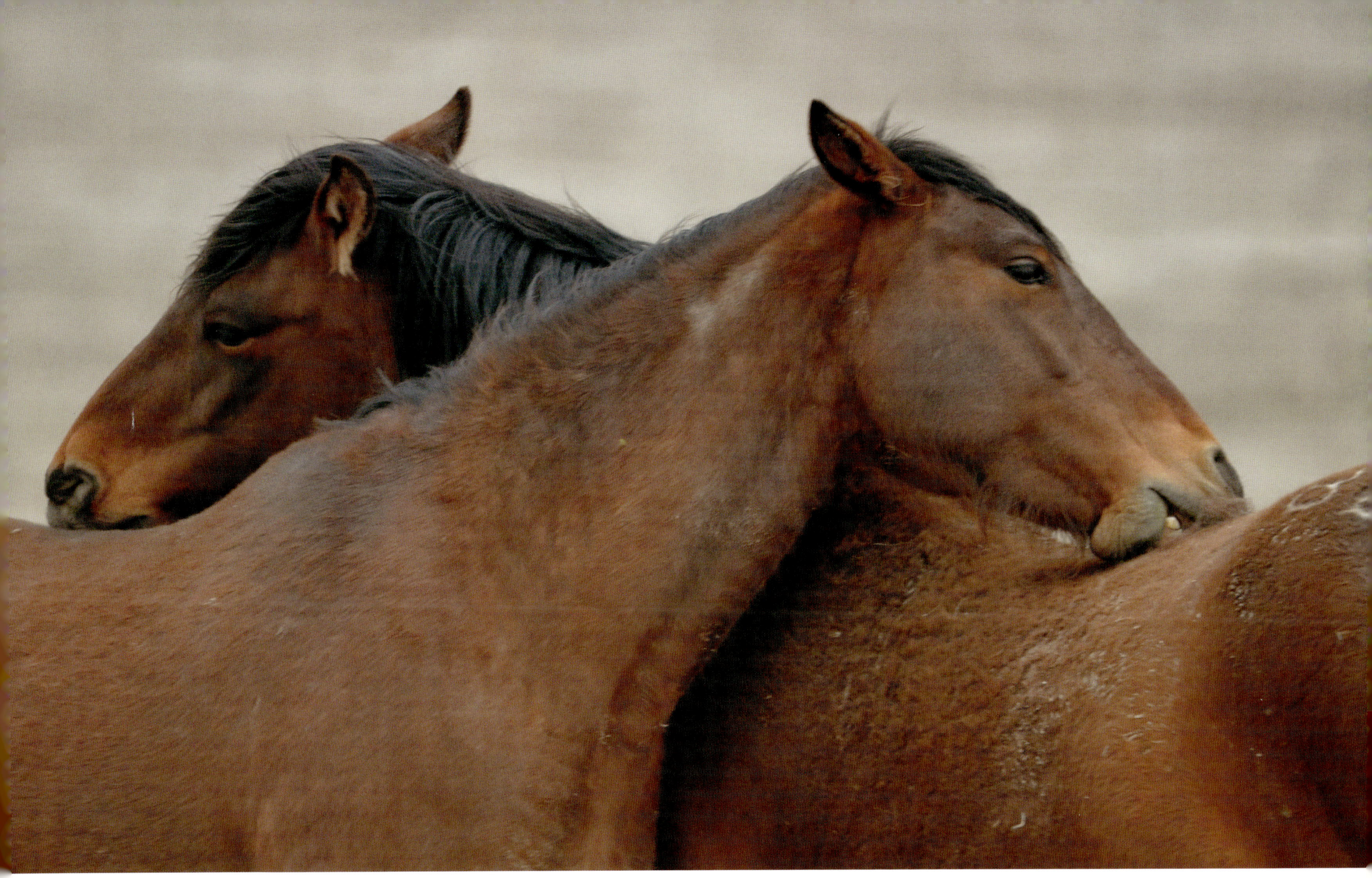

Opposite: Challenges will sometimes take place in the waterhole as the other horses stand by calmly, as if nothing were happening.

Above: Harem band mares give one another some grooming.

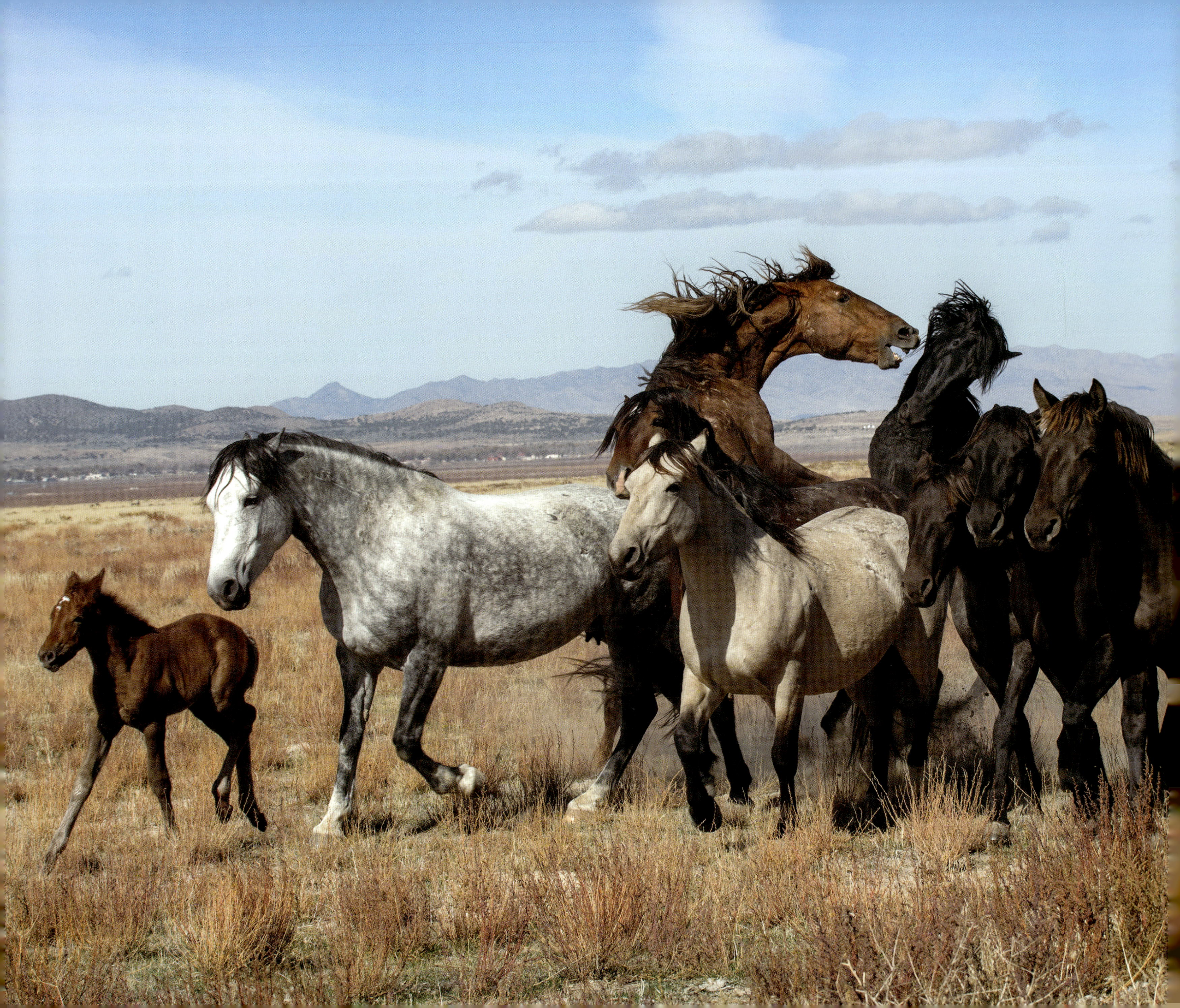

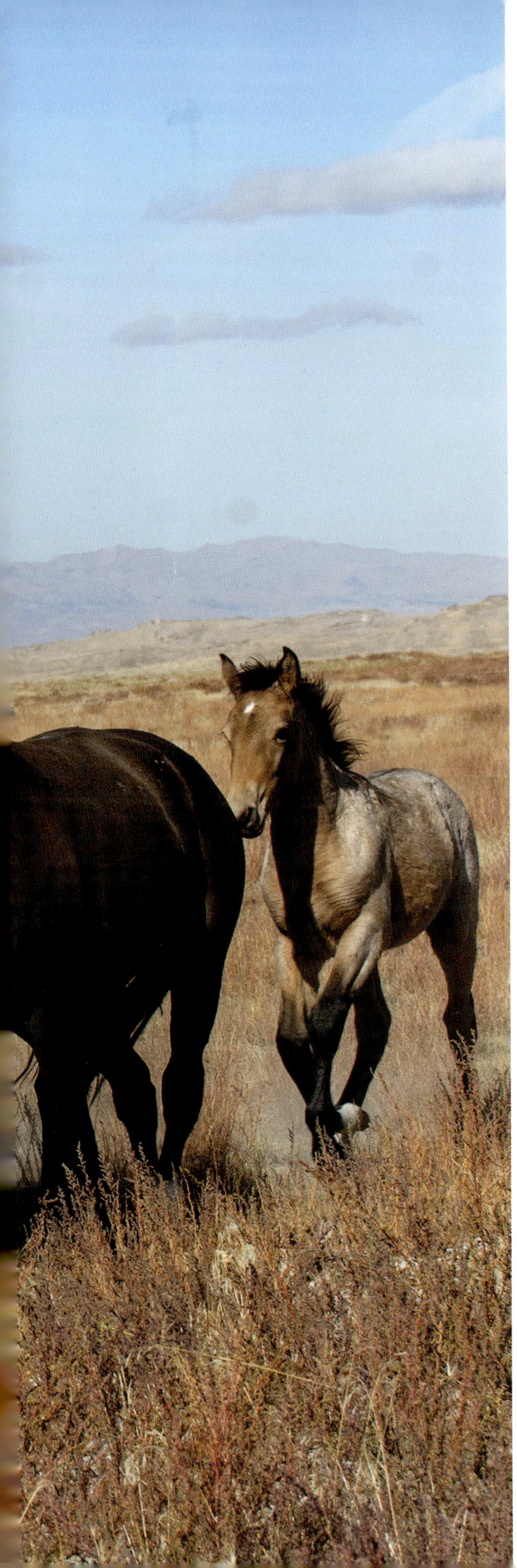

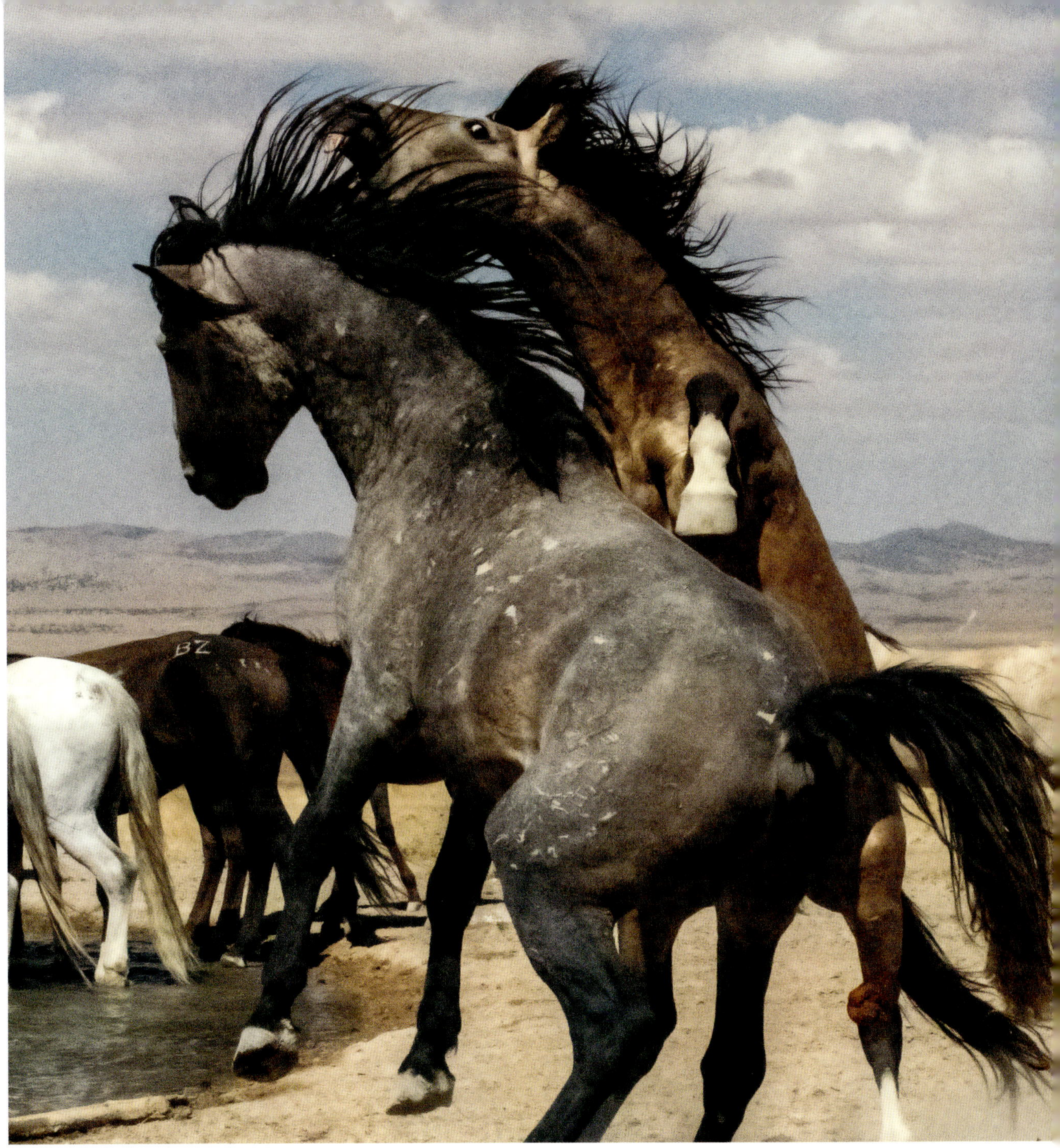

LEFT AND ABOVE: The waterholes are a frequent spot for bachelor stallion fights.

NEXT PAGE LEFT: Sometimes fighting will involve one horse kicking out with its hind legs. The hind legs inevitably provide a more powerful blow to the head of the other horse.

NEXT PAGE RIGHT: Fighting stallions always provide great shots of their manes flying in all directions.

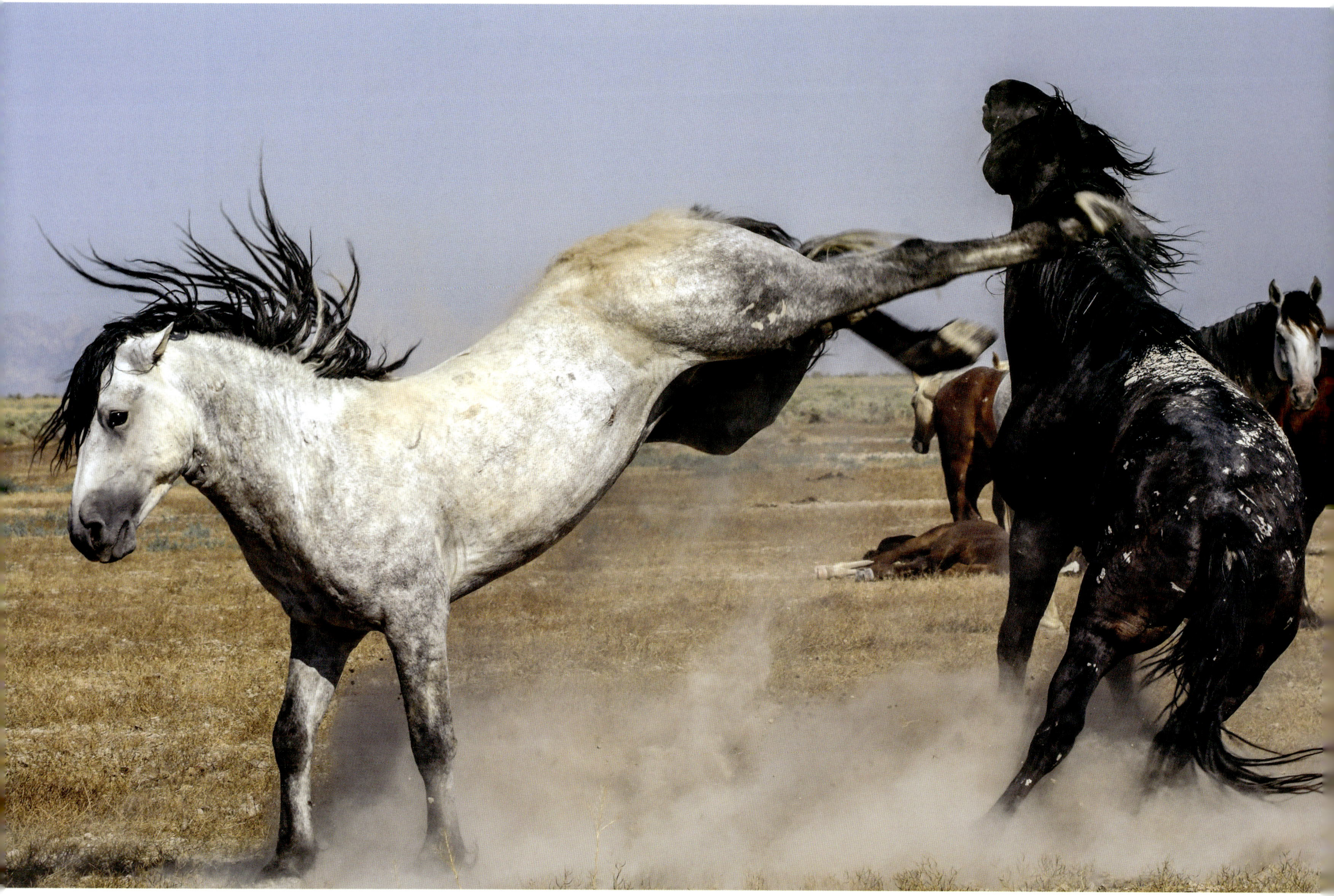

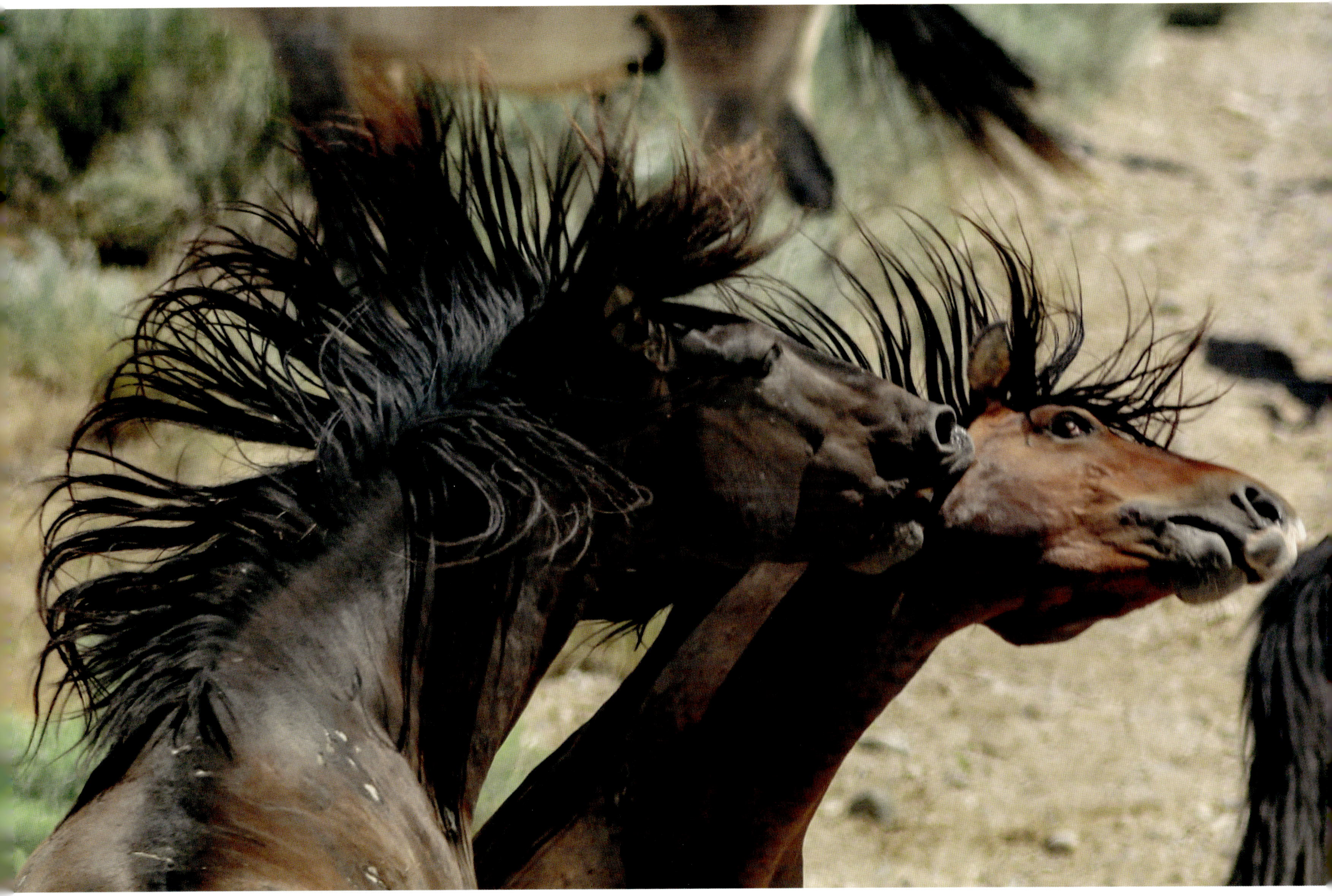

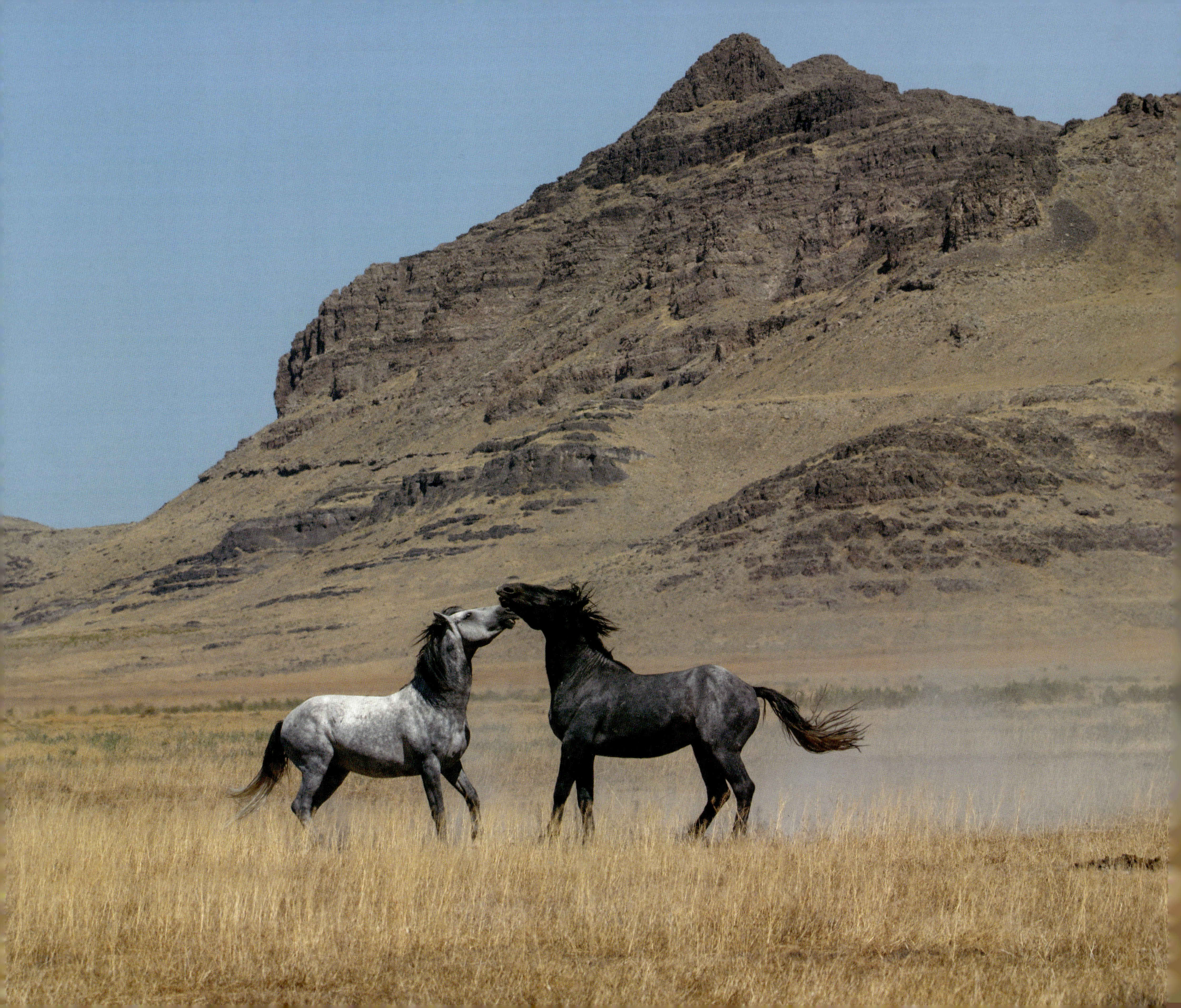

Opposite: Two shades of gray bachelor stallions posture before a fight, with one of the many unique rock formations of the Great Basin Desert in the background.

Right: This stallion seems to have an advantage over the other, smaller stallion.

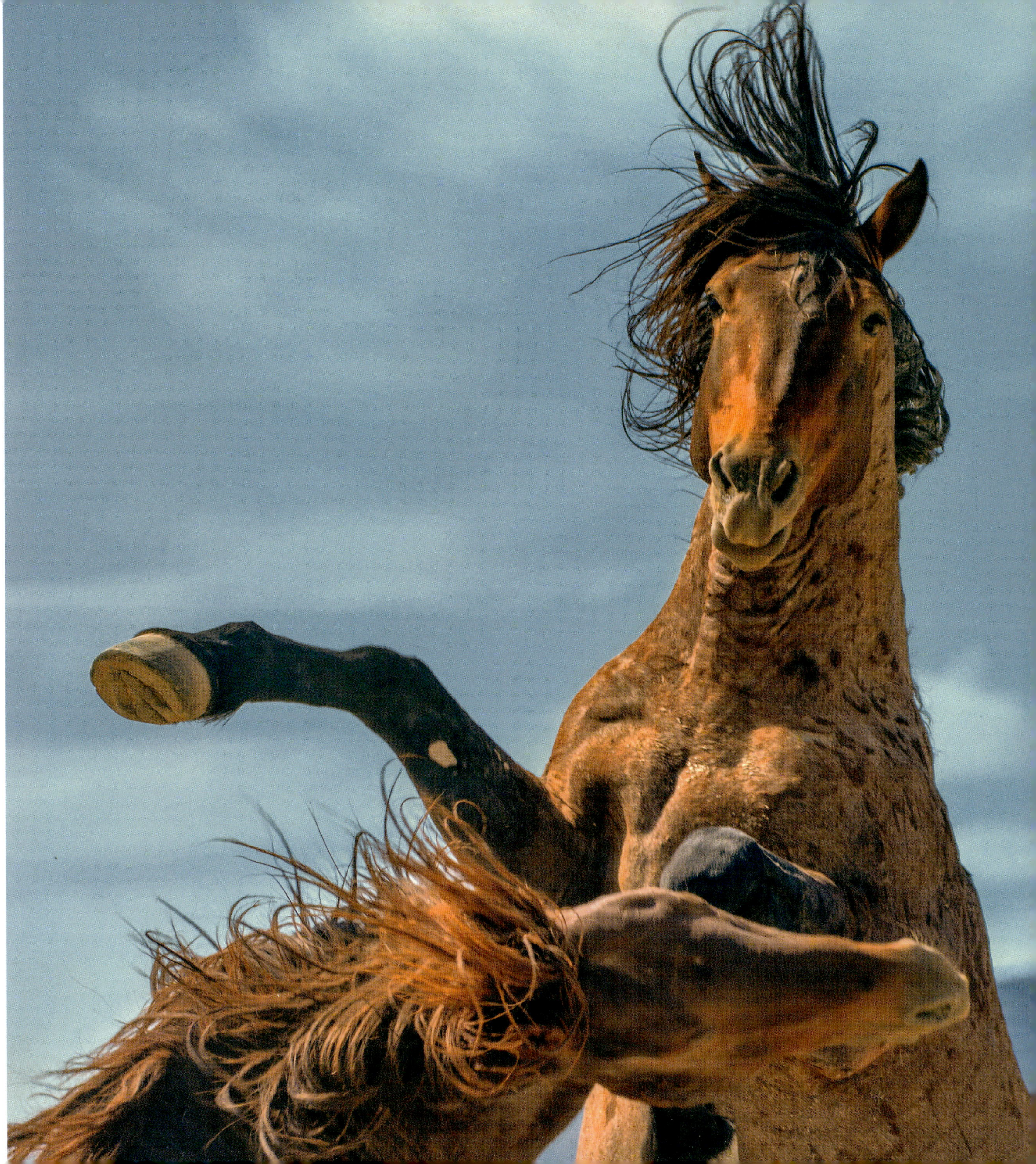

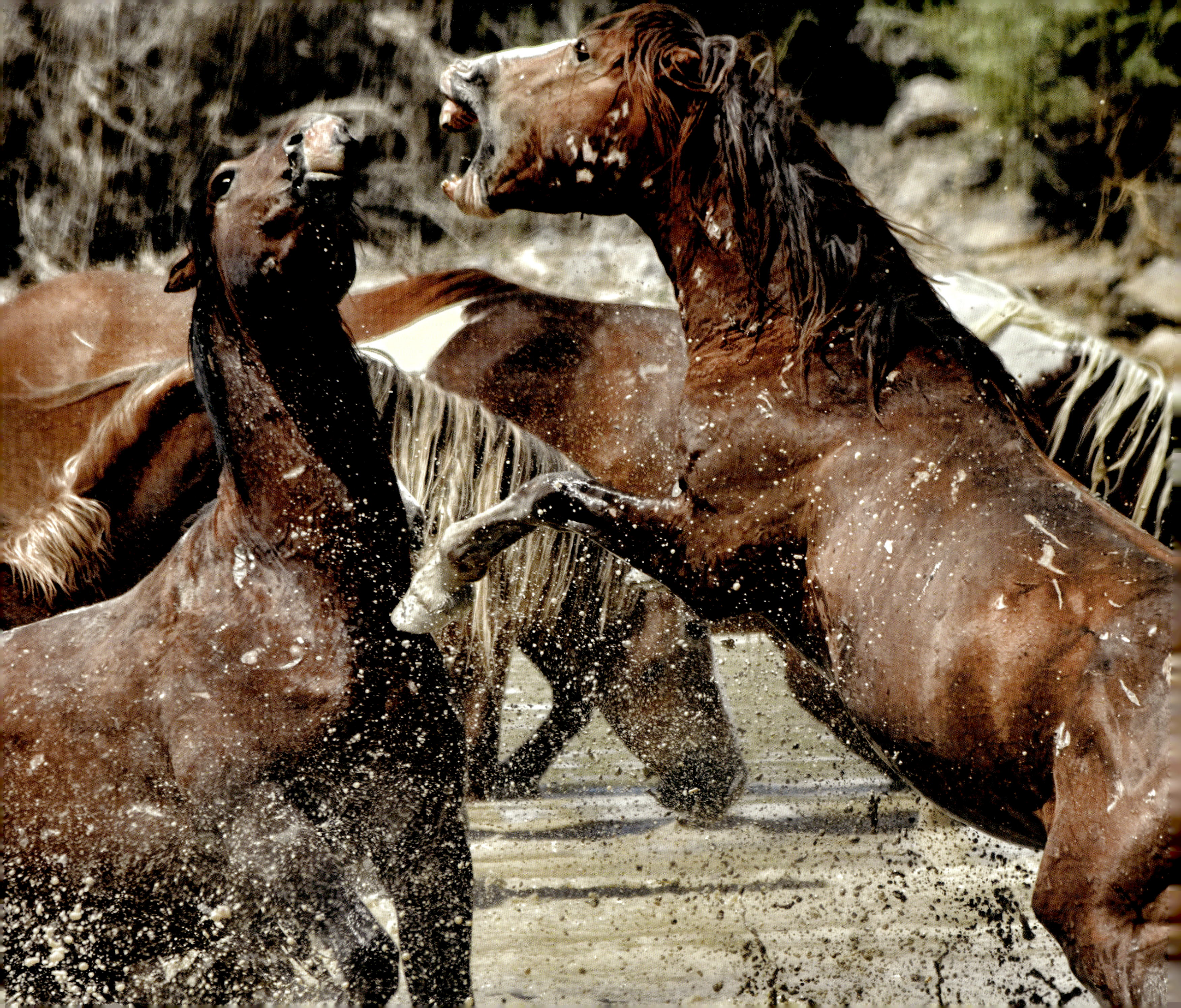

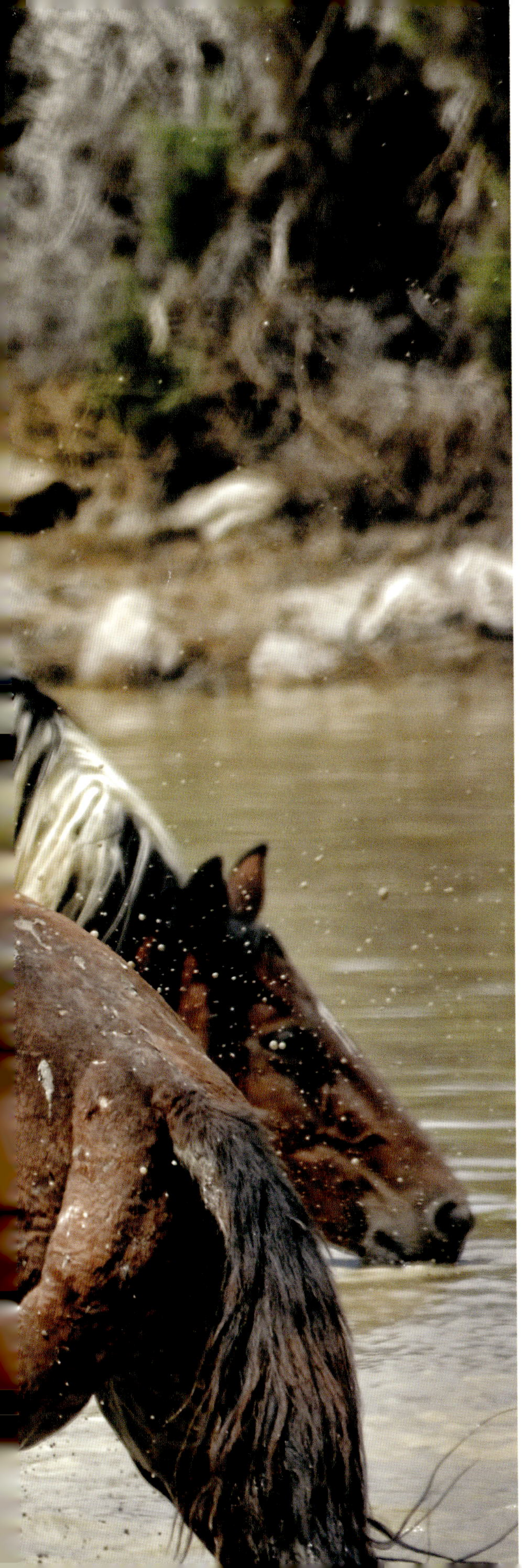

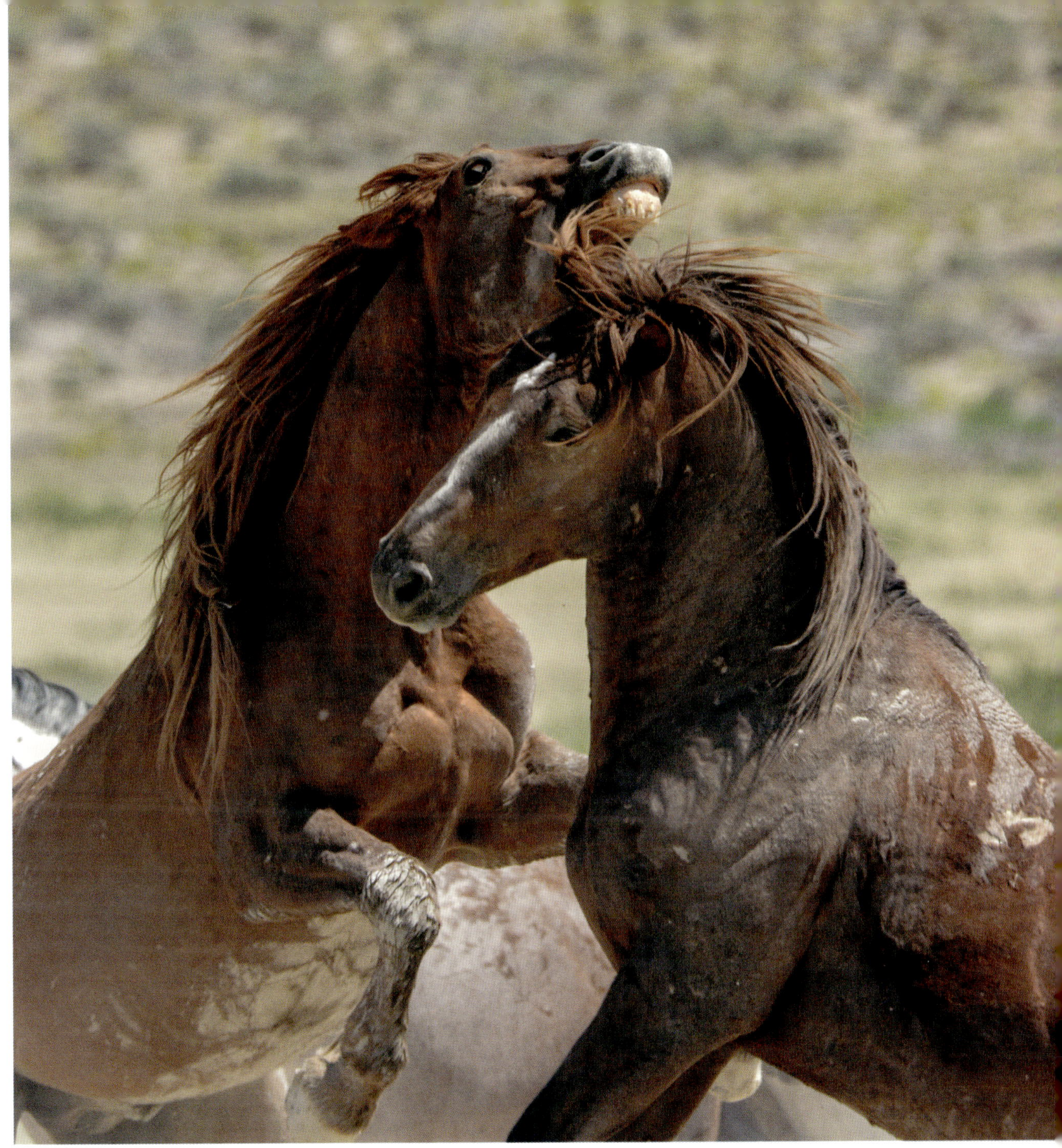

LEFT AND ABOVE: Fights often involve ferocious bites to the ears and face, which tend to leave serious battle scars.

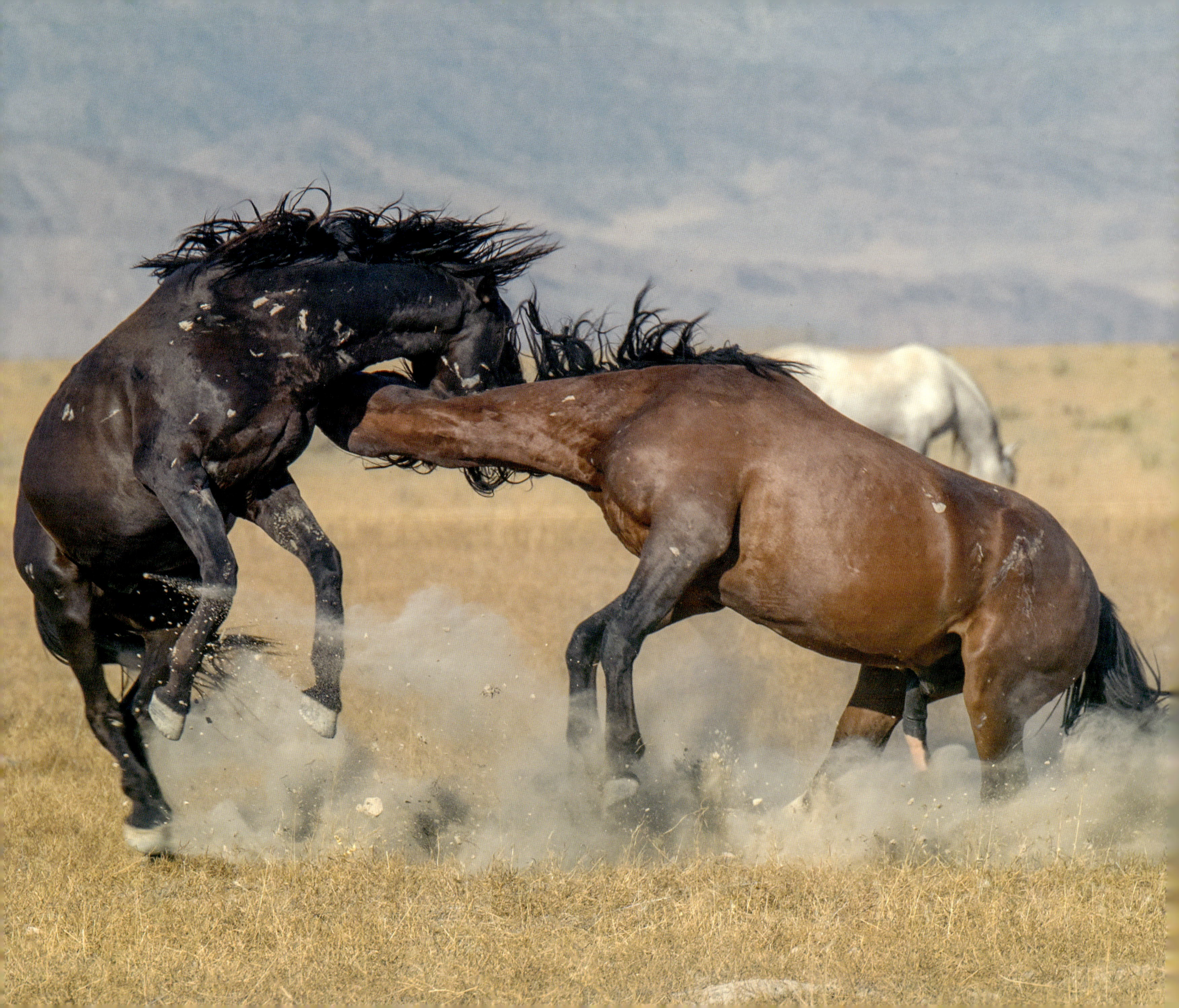

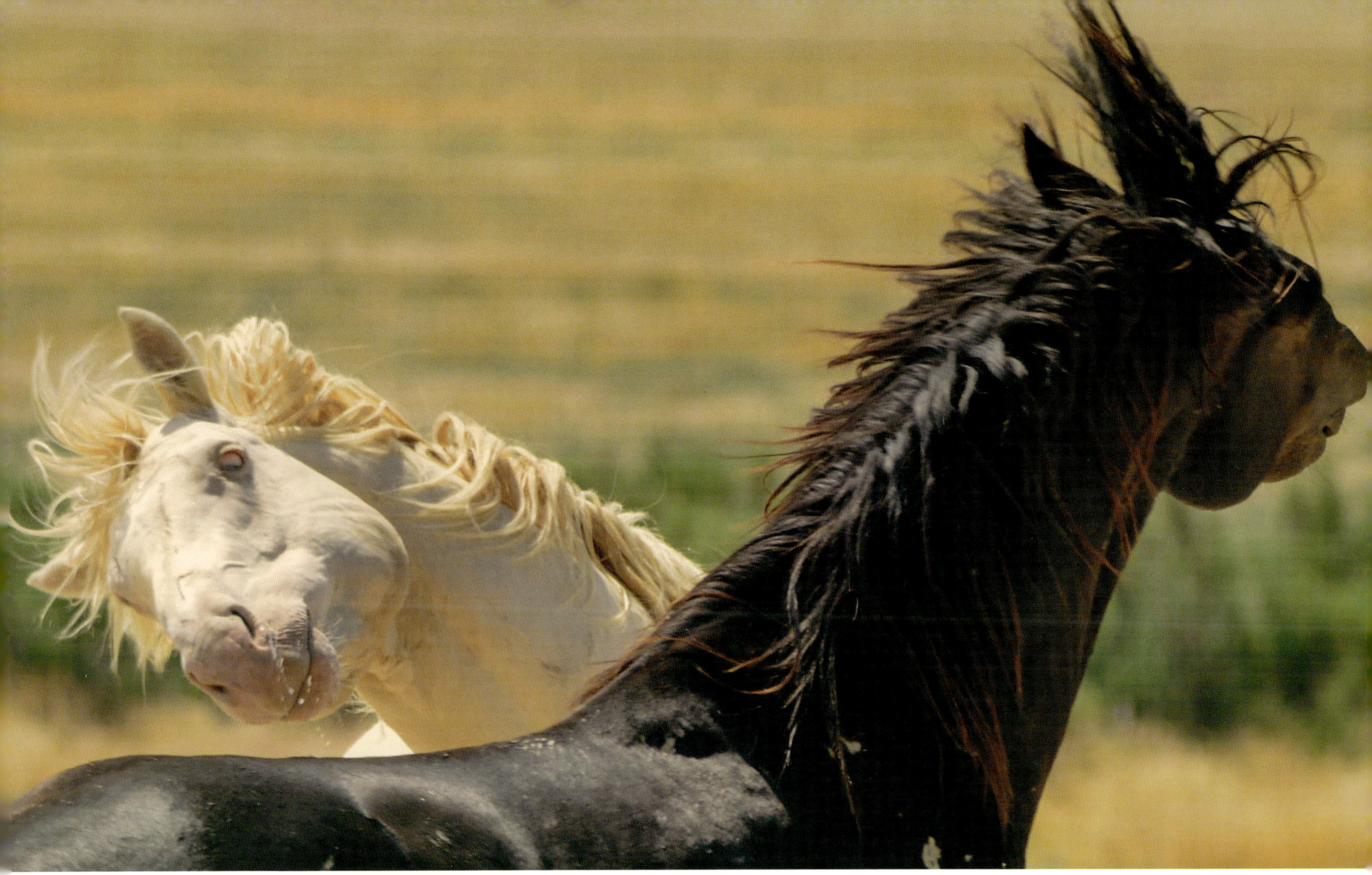

OPPOSITE AND ABOVE: Bachelor stallions seem almost as if they are performing a dance as they fight.

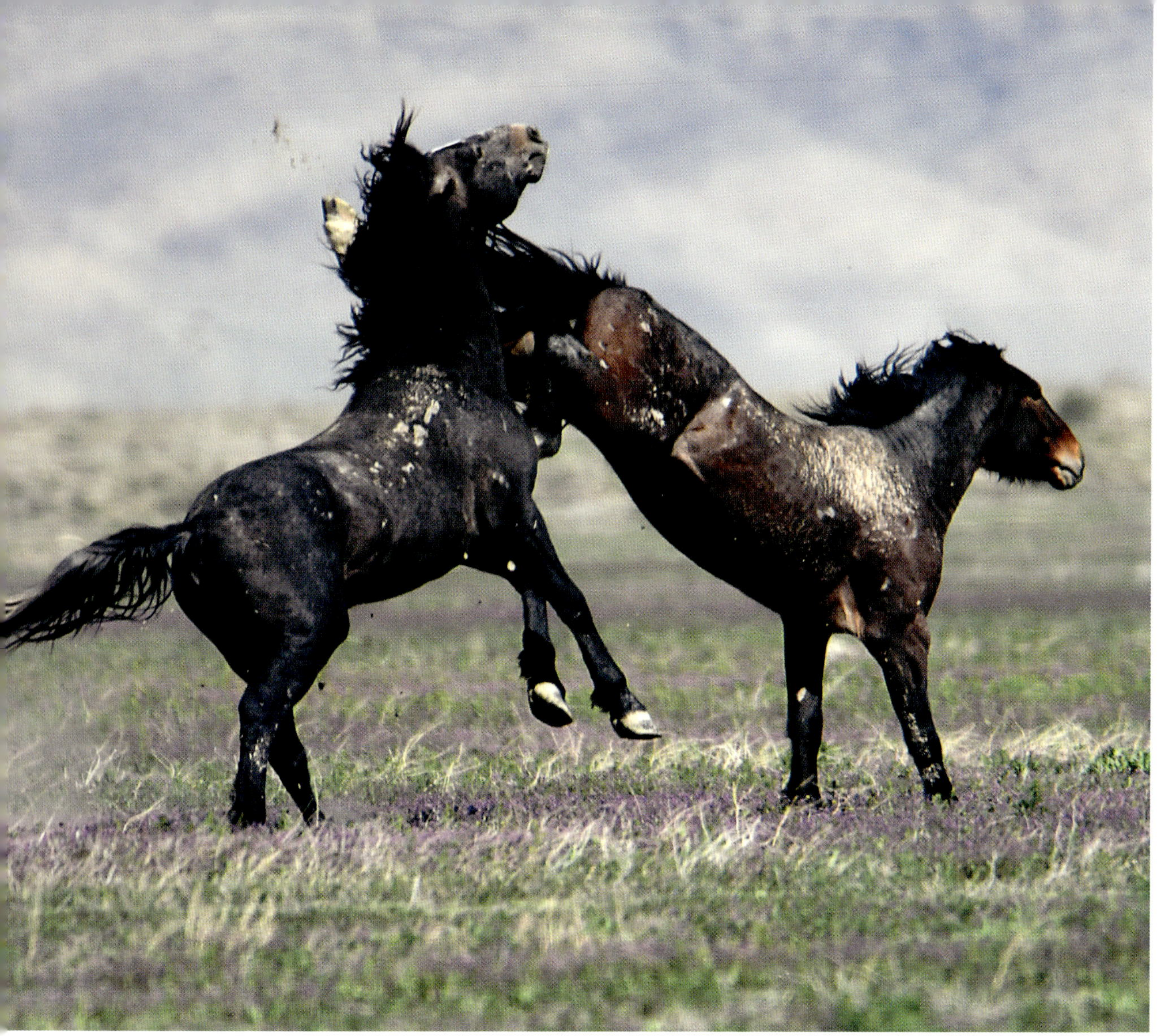

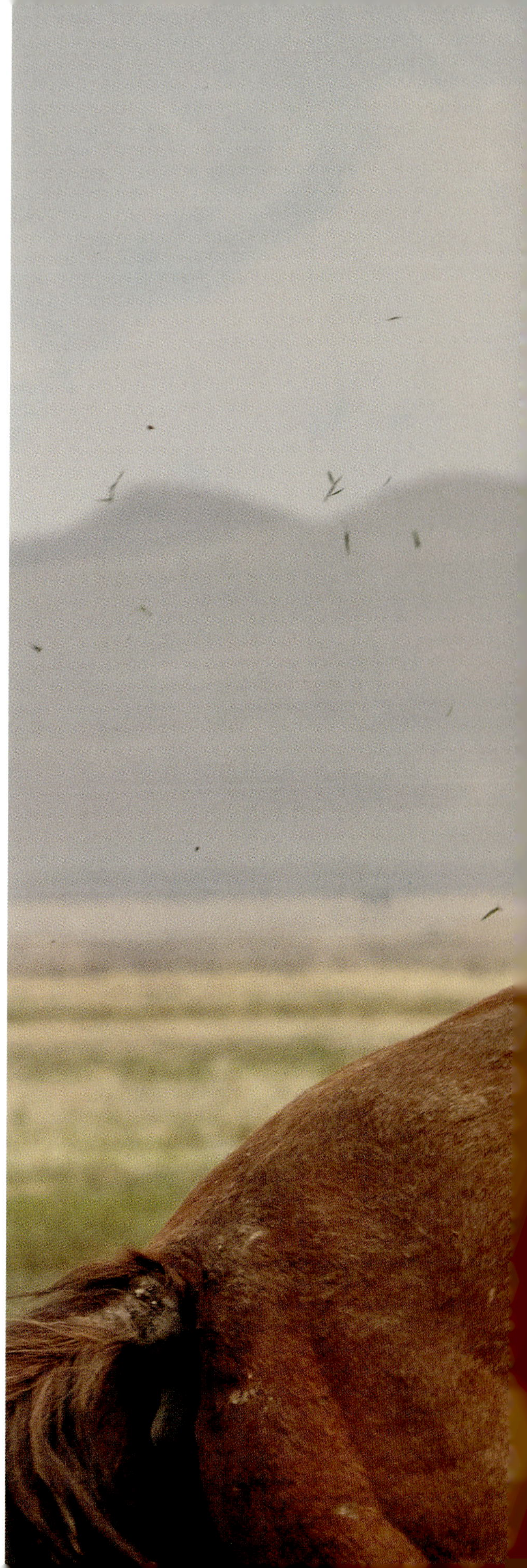

ABOVE: Fights sometimes involve one stallion chasing another when, suddenly, the one being pursued will double barrel the pursuer with his hind legs.

RIGHT: The dominance of a band stallion over his challenger.

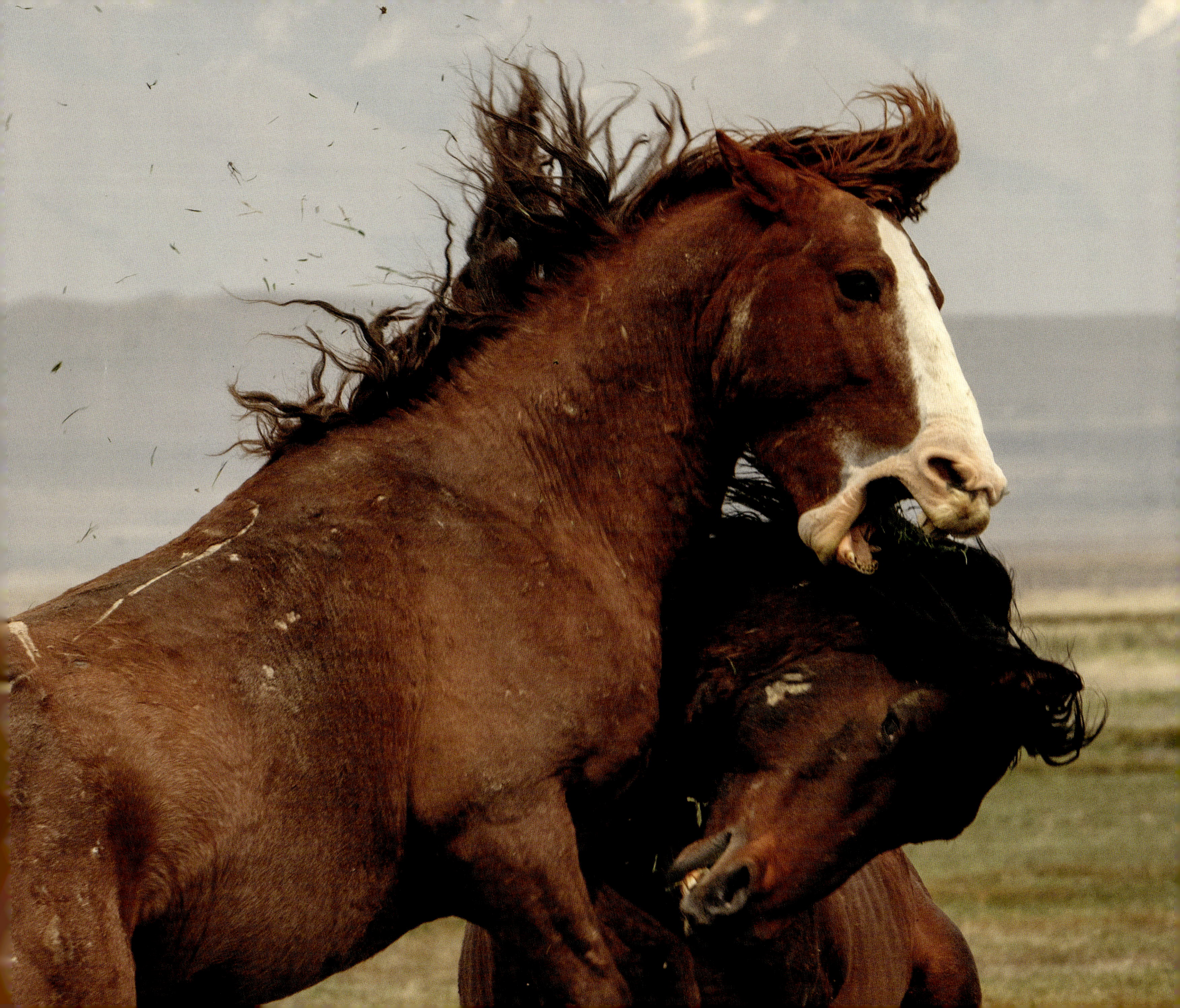

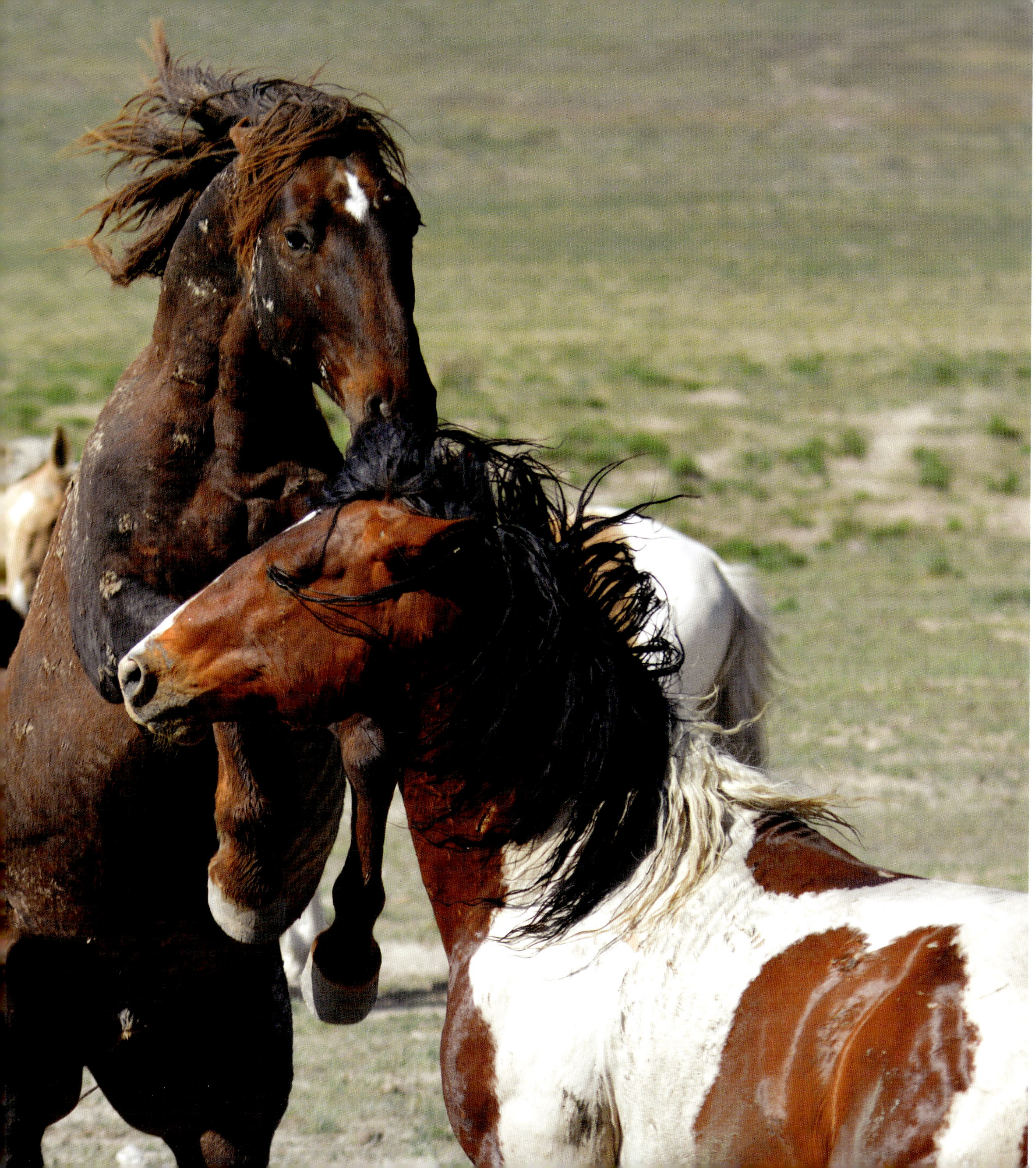

Left: The liver chestnut (brown) stallion appears to have the upper hand on this pinto stallion.

opposite: Two young bachelor stallions fight, but not too seriously.

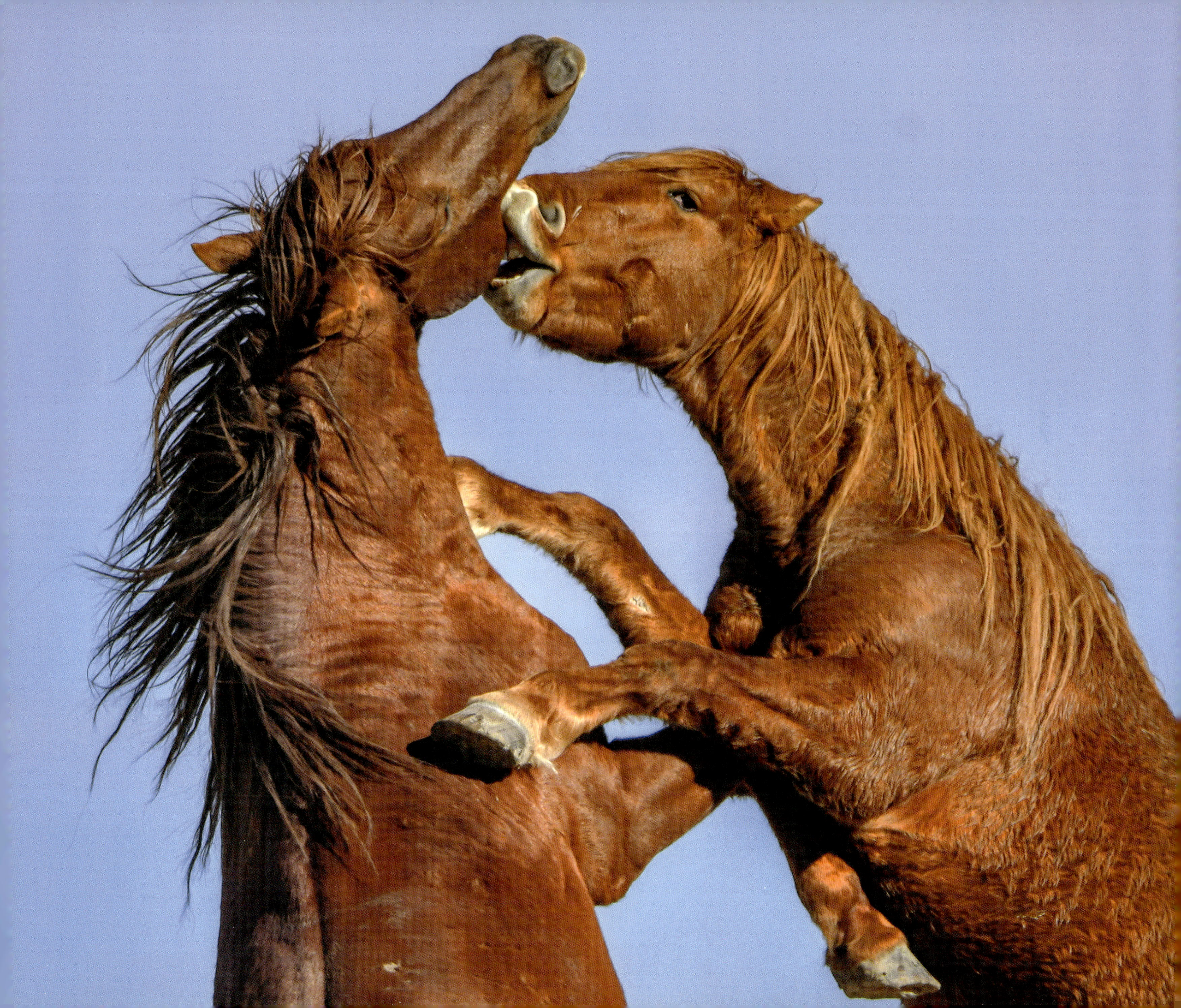

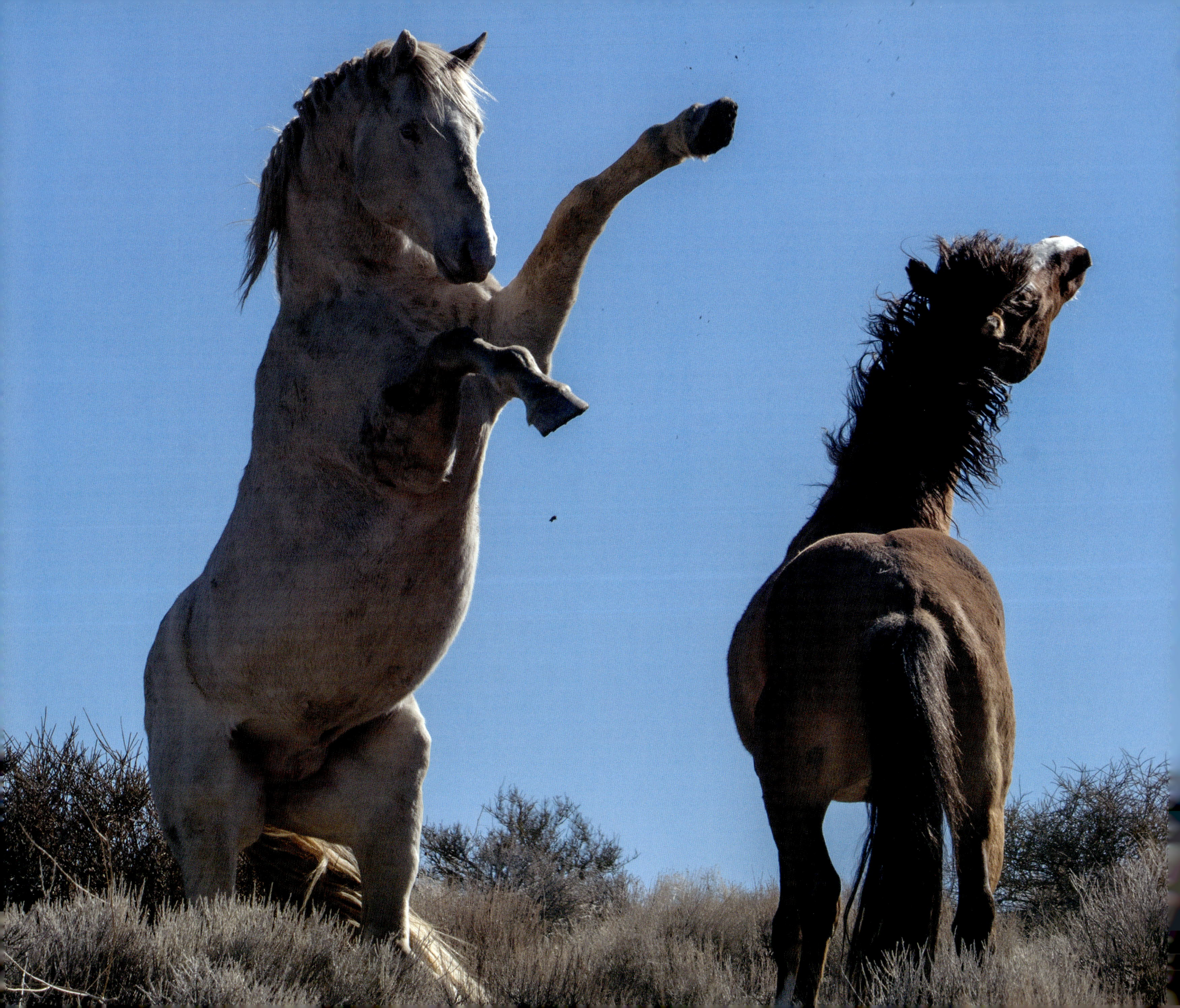

Opposite: A cremello stallion shows his dominance over another bachelor stallion.

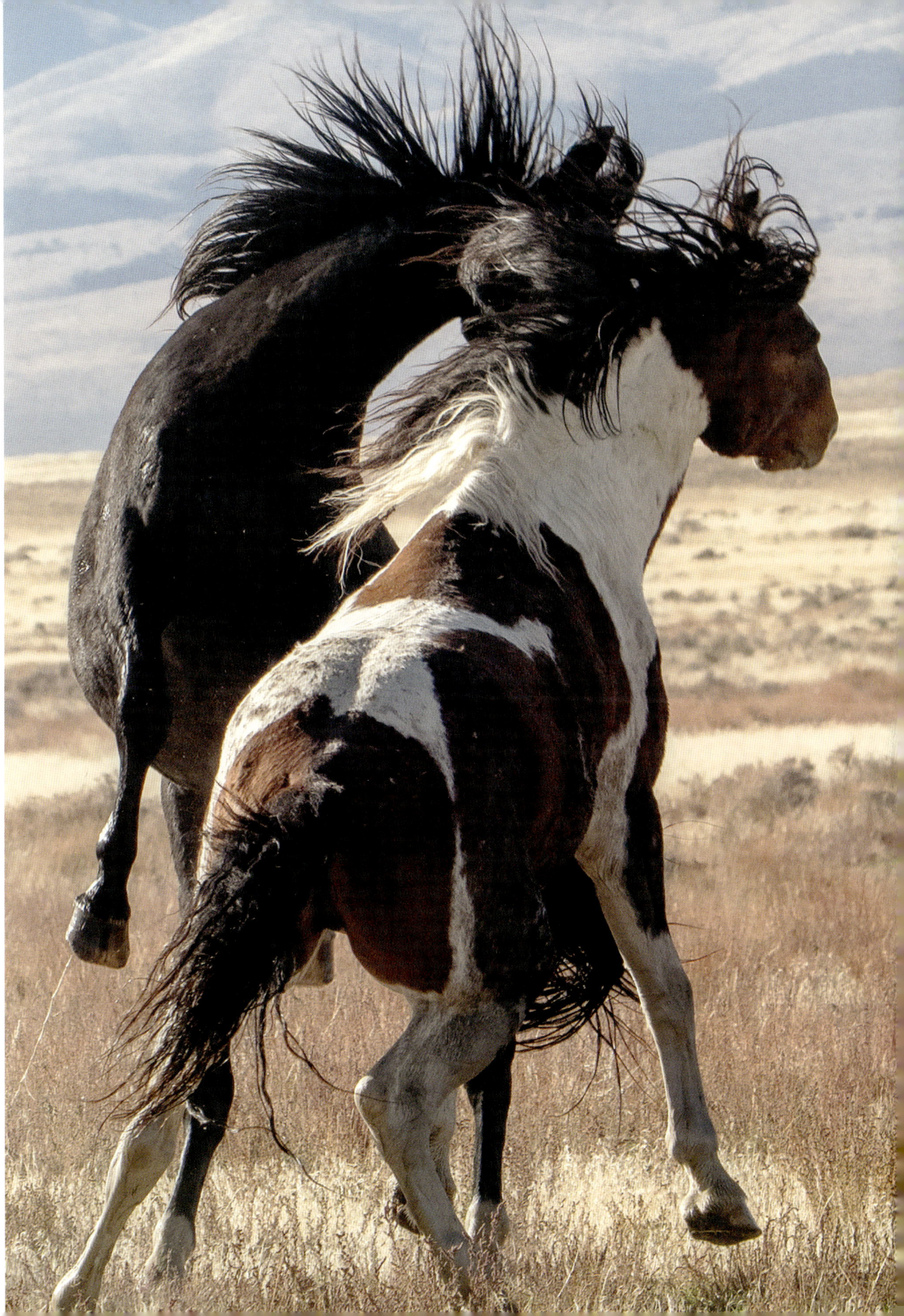

Right: Often during a stallion fight, the stallion rearing up will throw his front legs and whole body at the opposing stallion with a powerful force.

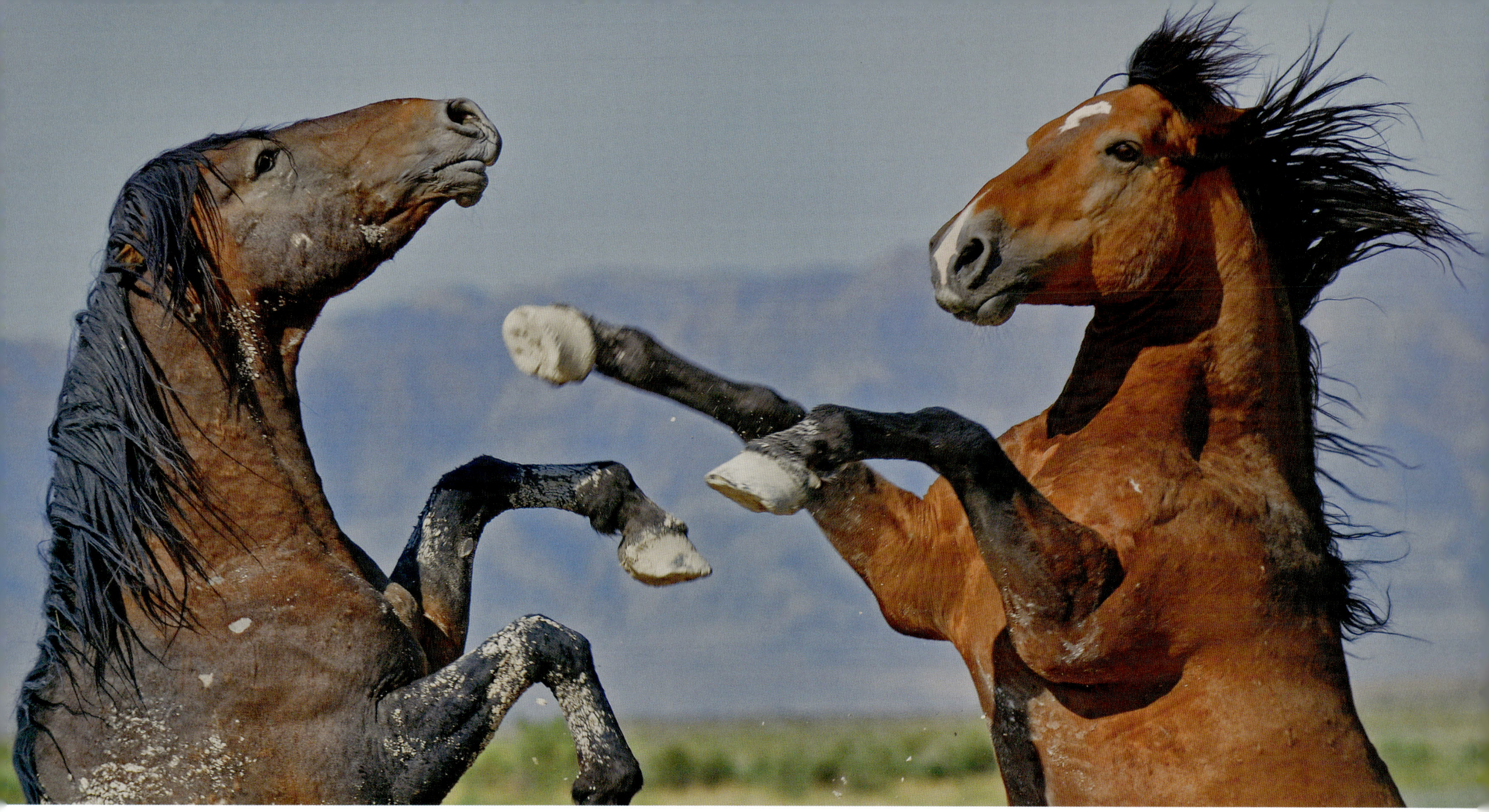

Above: The stallion with the longer legs clearly has an advantage when the fights are done on their hind legs.

Opposite: After having just rolled in the mud, the marks on this buckskin's face and chest make him look almost like an Indian war pony prepared for battle.

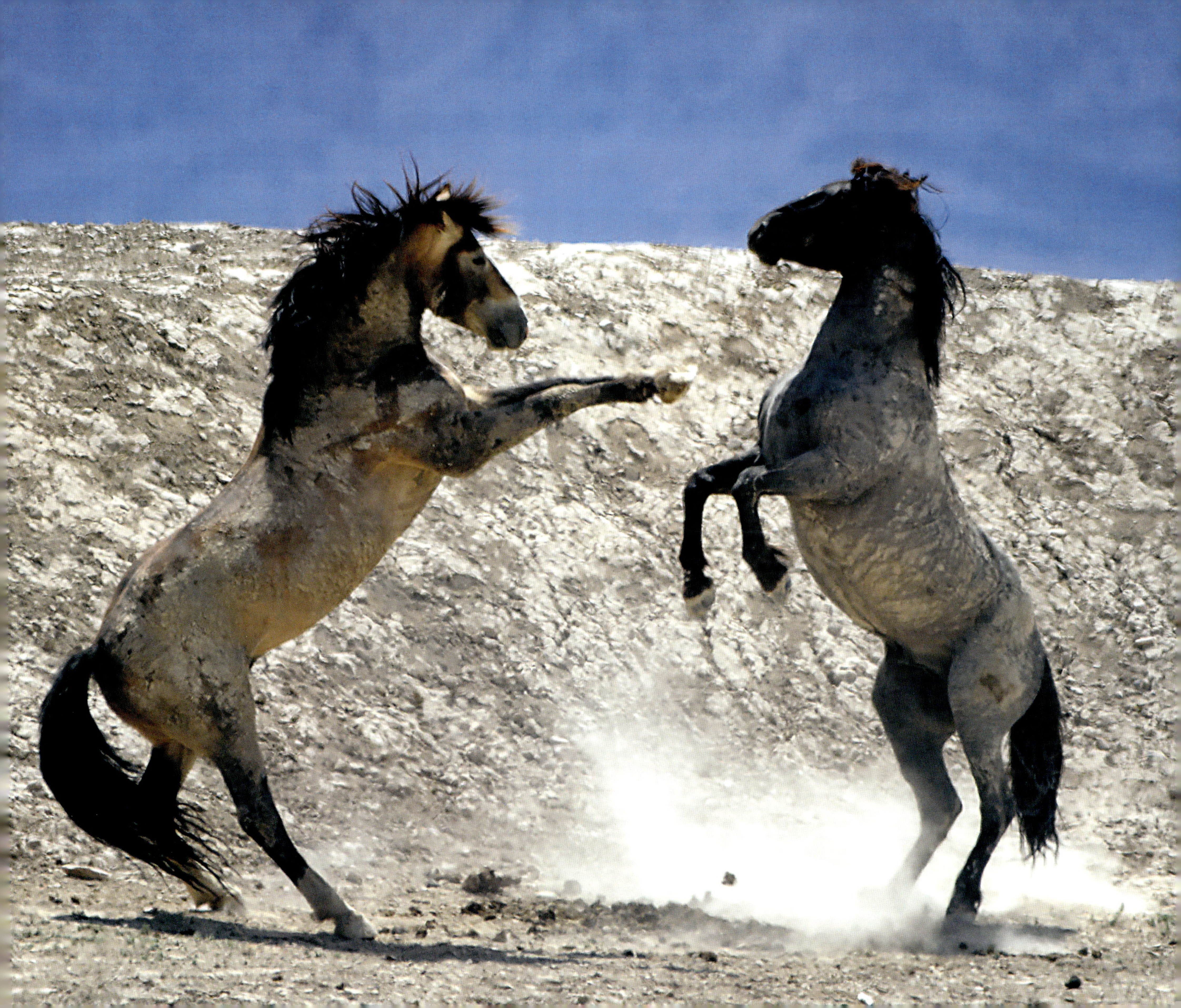

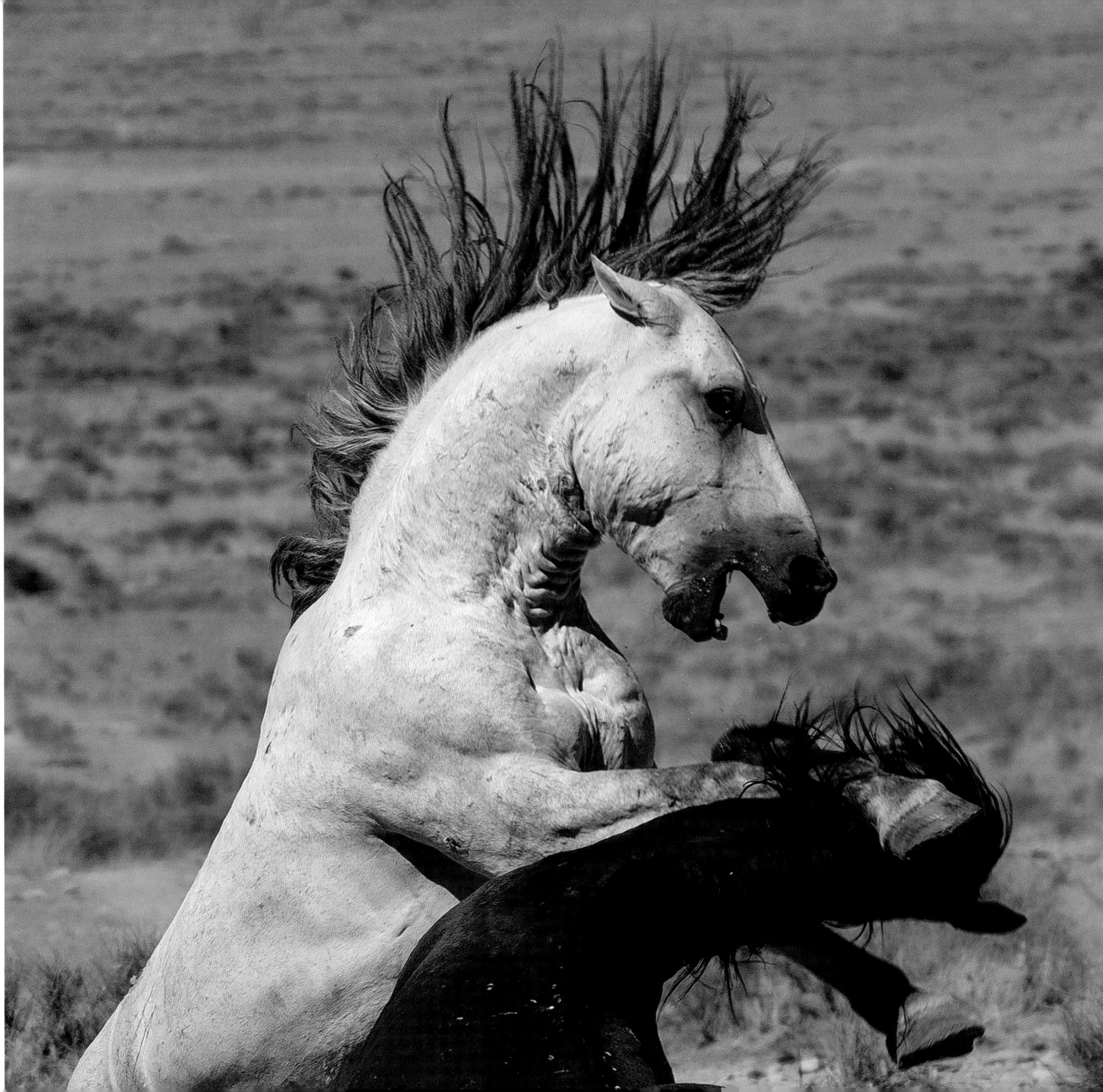

Clockwise, from left: A gray stallion puts his challenger into a headlock. Fights generally always involve one of the stallions getting punched in the head with the other's front hooves. The band stallion Buck defends his mares against the blue roan bachelor stallion.

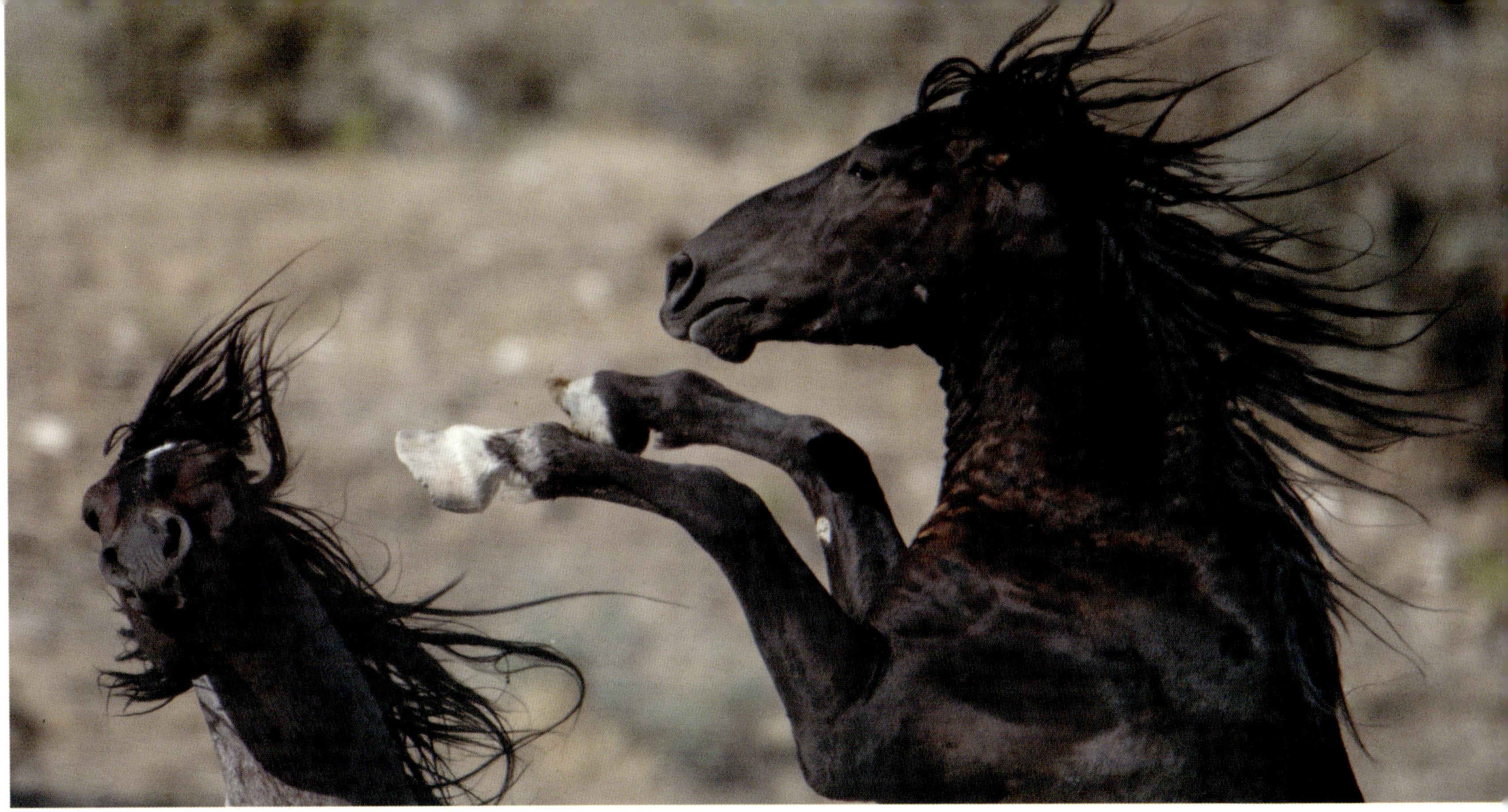

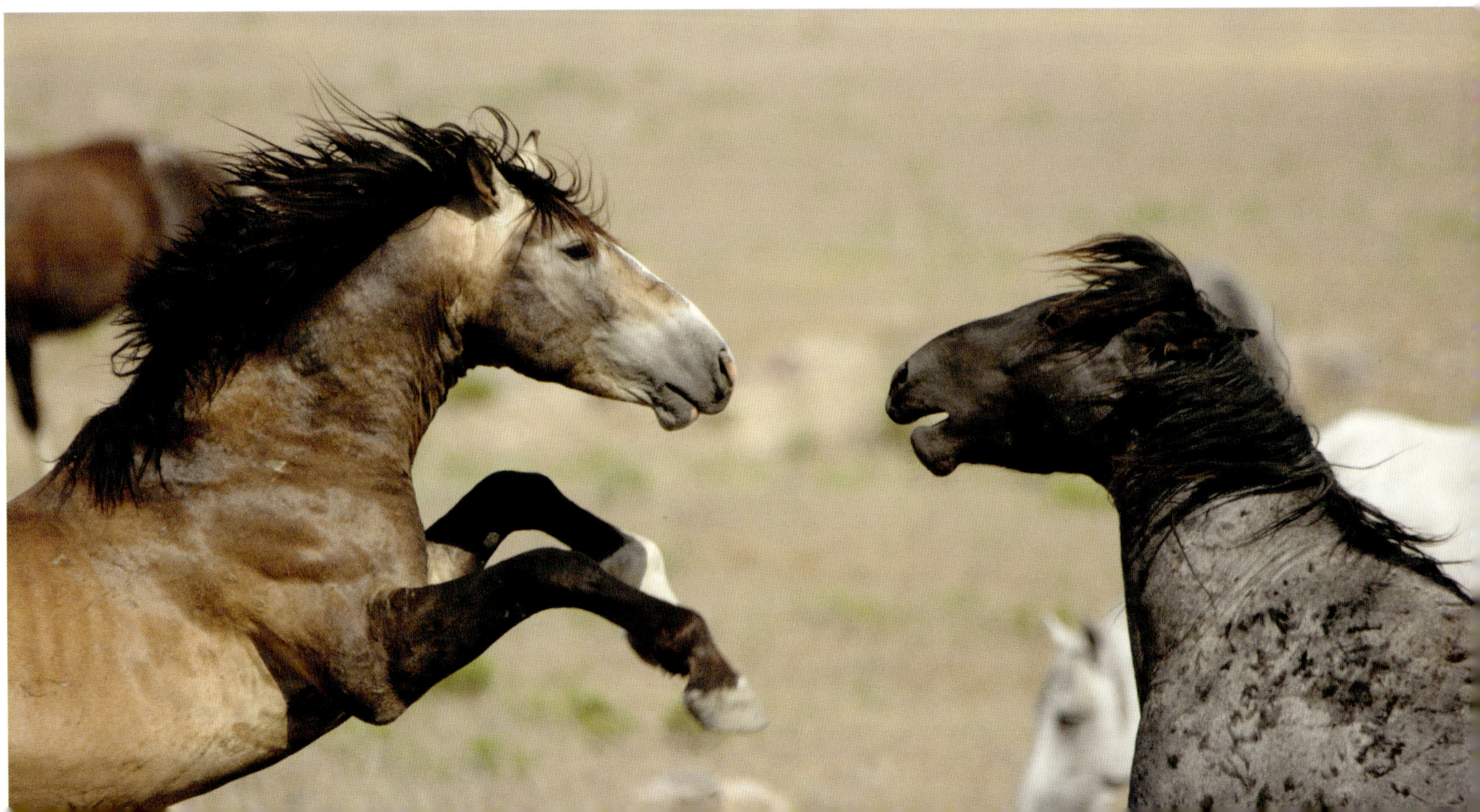

Next page left: Typical fights involve the horses rearing on their hind legs, allowing for a more forceful blow to the other horse.

Next page right: This black bachelor stallion's face and neck show the results of many battles.

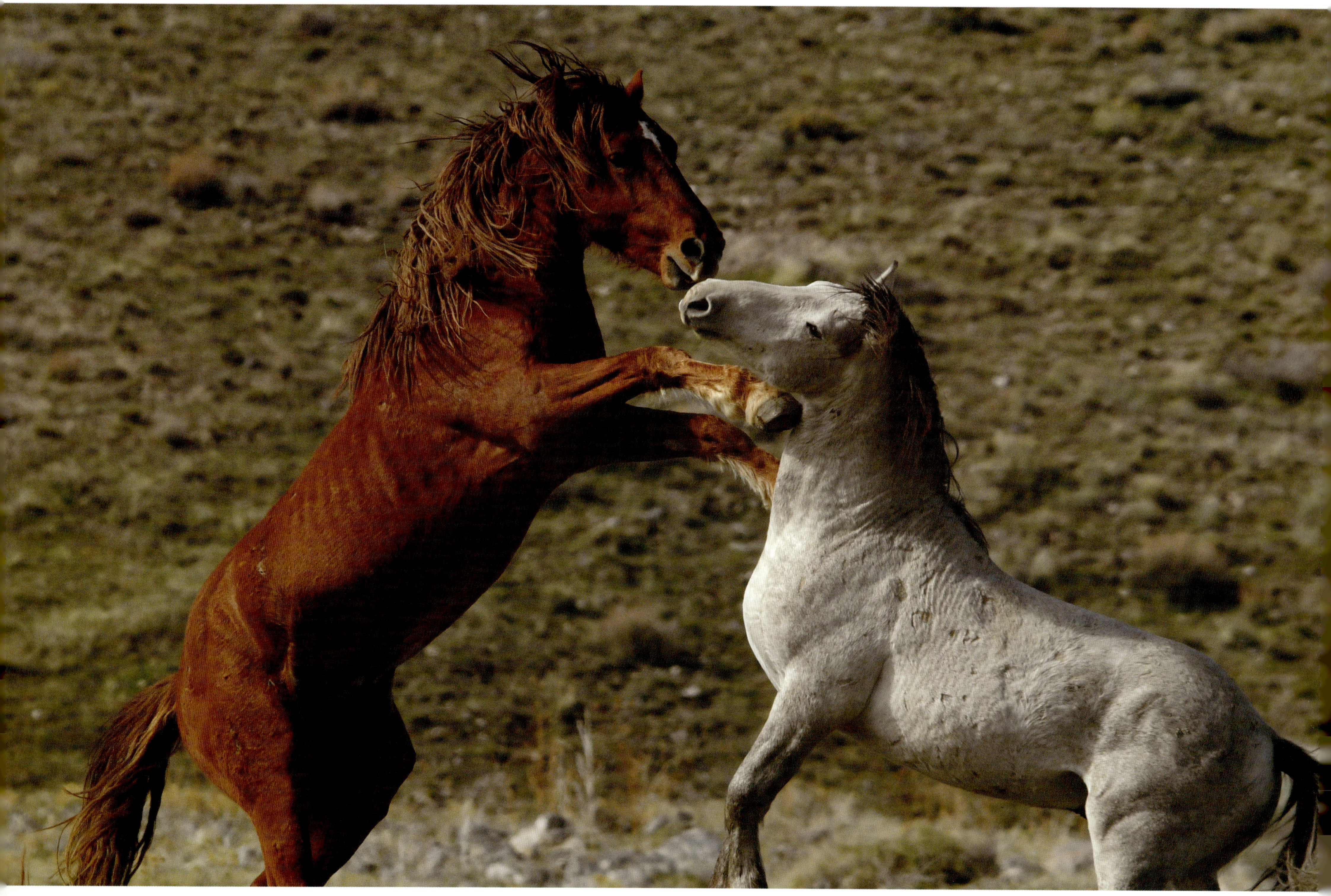

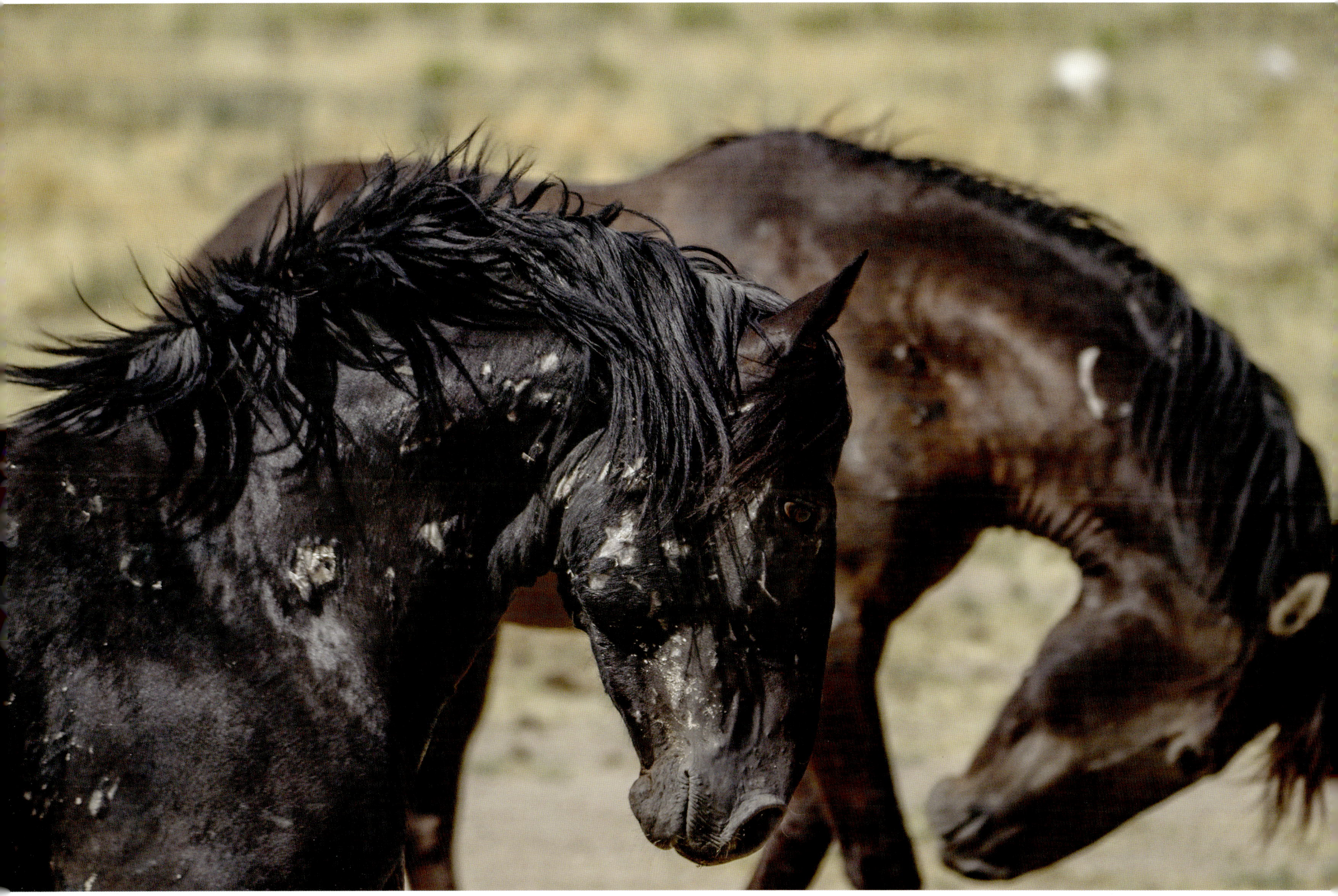

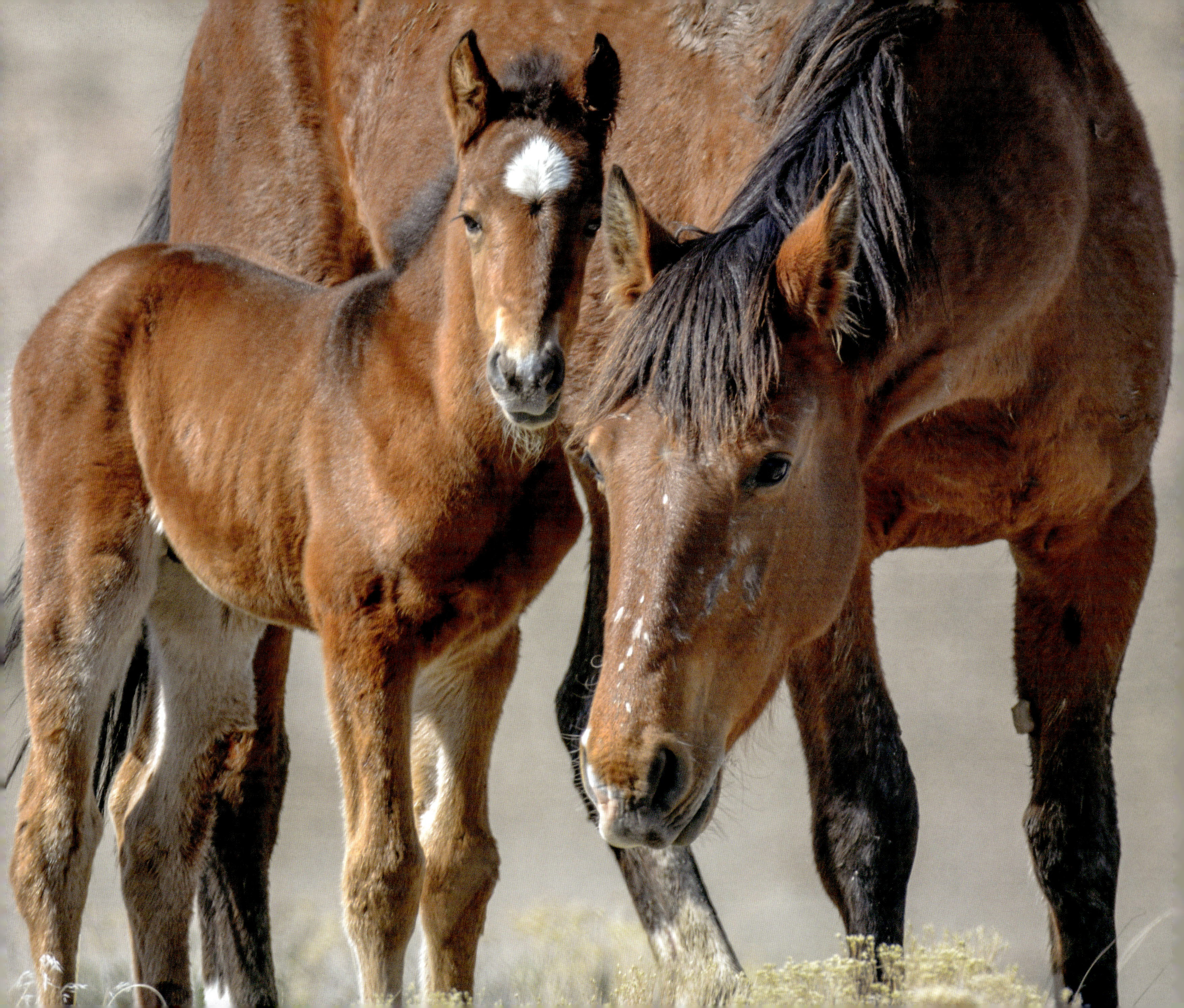

MARES & FOALS

Mares and foals are among my favorite group of horses to photograph—they're not only adorable, but they have so much spirit and personality.

The mare usually leaves to deliver the baby by herself, but the protective band stays near while she gives birth. It only takes three to four hours for the newborn foal to walk—their ability to move with the herd immediately is necessary for survival. While wild horses give birth at any time, new foals are usually born in the early to late spring; foals born in the winter months have a lower chance of survival.

The foals form bonds with other foals in the band as they age. The young colts play together, learning to fight in preparation for their departure from the herd. The fillies stay close to their mothers until they are old enough to be sought after by bachelor stallions hoping to form their own band.

Foals tend to be more curious than older horses—a boon for photographers, who find that adventurous foals are a delight to capture.

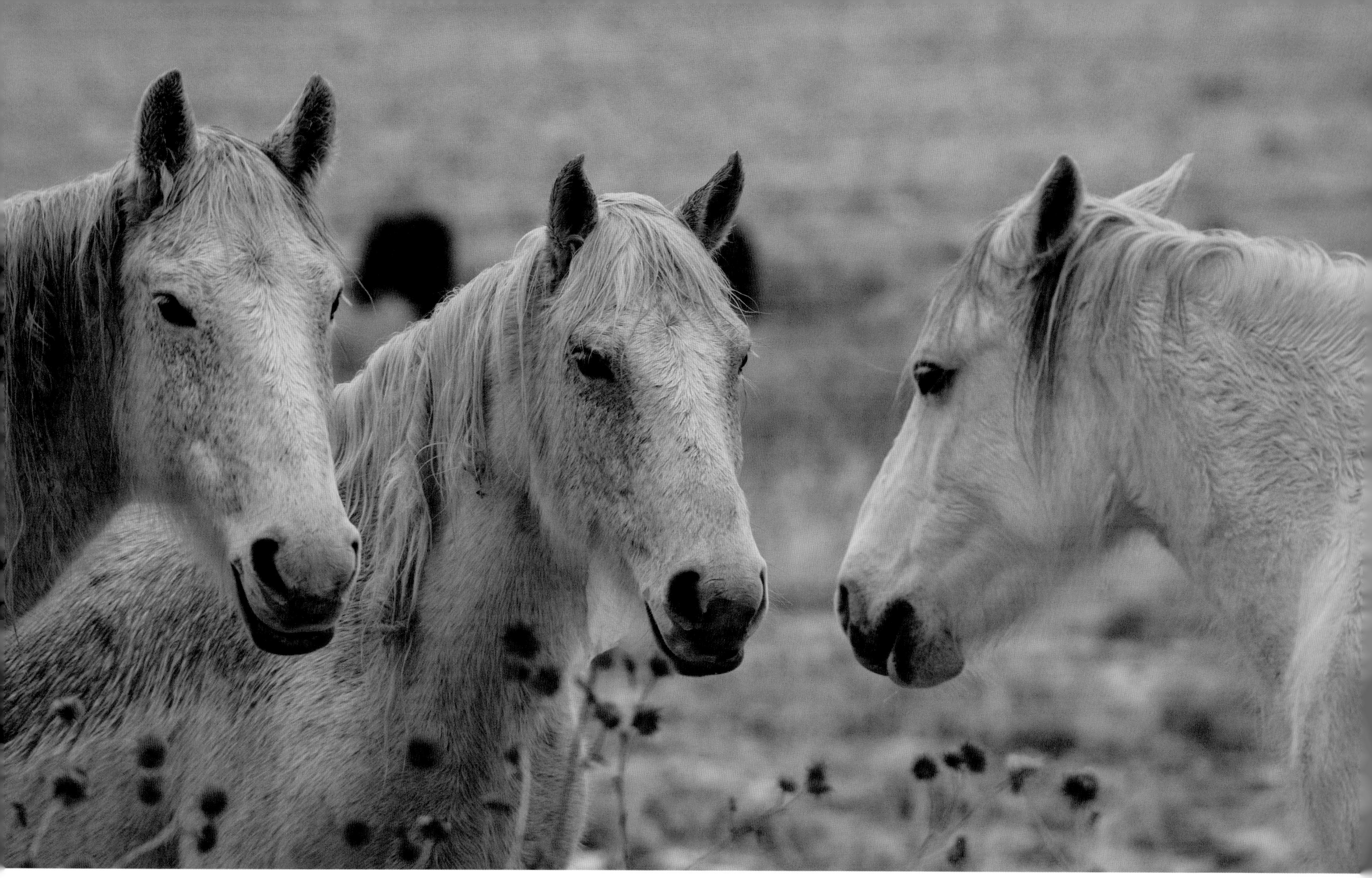

Above: Older mares within a harem form strong bonds with each other over the years.

Opposite: The pinto foal stretches his legs while his mother watches.

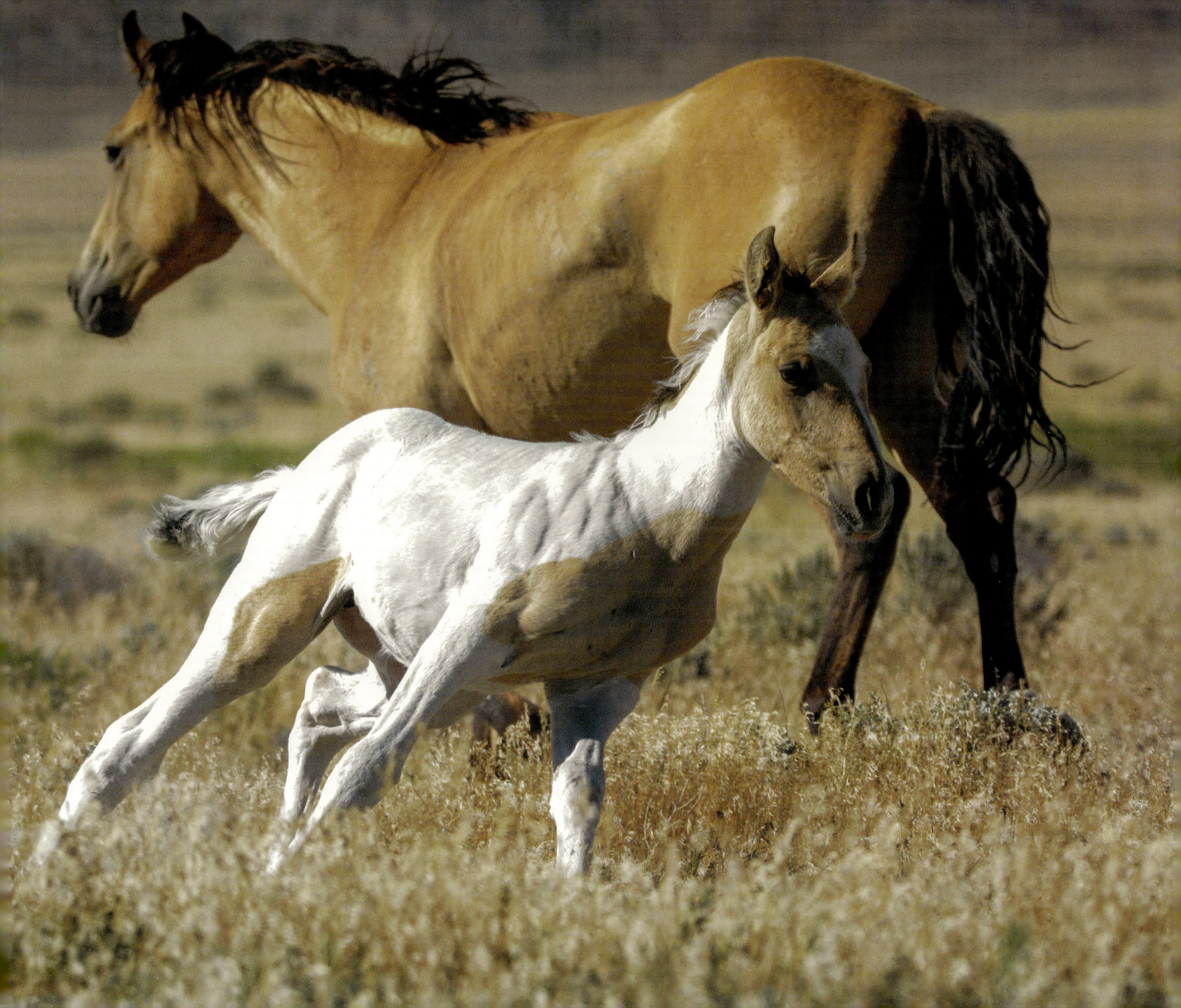

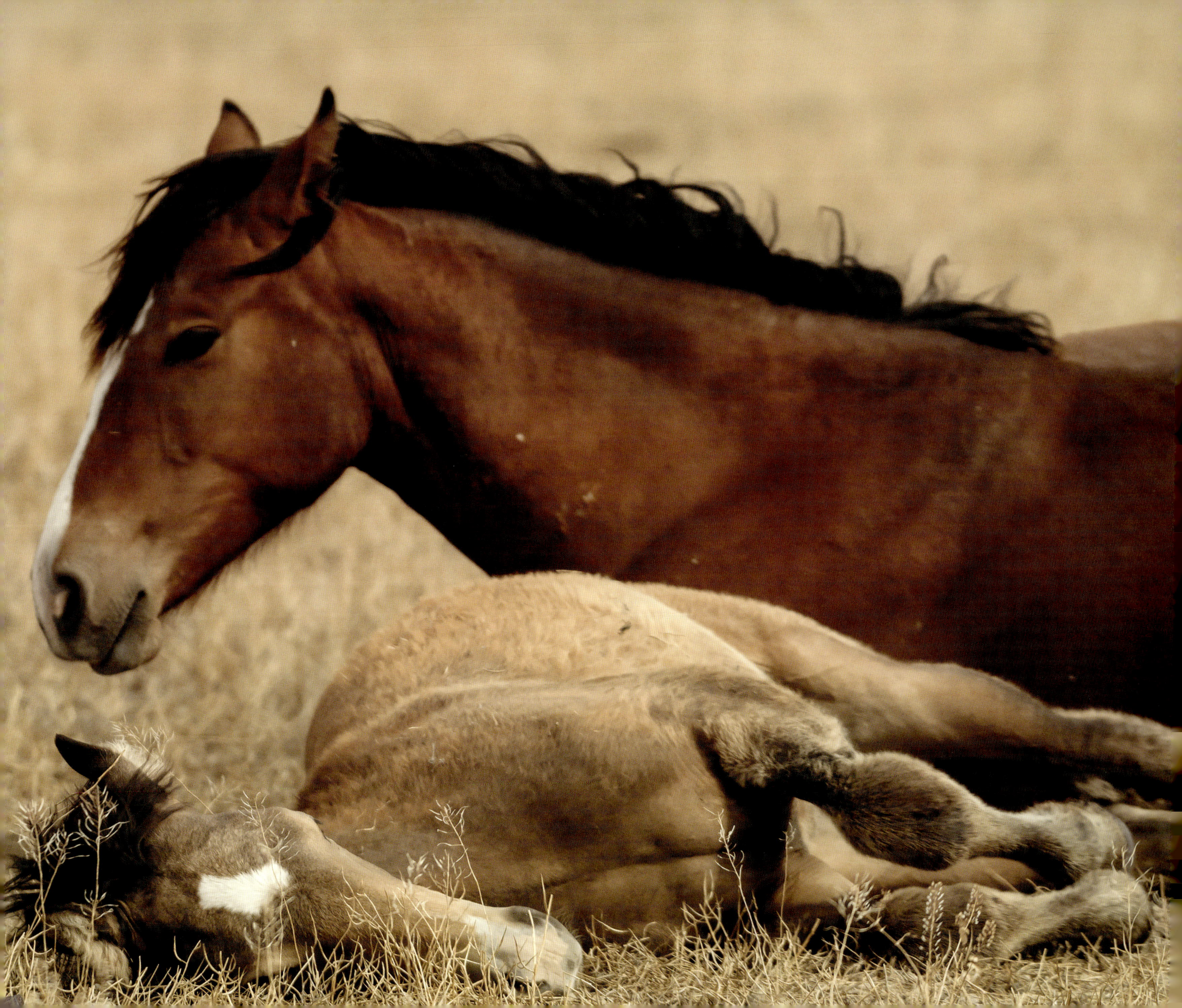

Clockwise, from left: The peacefulness of a young colt napping while being watched over by an older mare. A grulla filly naps; the word *grulla* comes from the Spanish word for gray horse. This gray colt would be called a *grullo* (word for the male). The coat of a grullo (or grulla) horse is a mousy gray color.

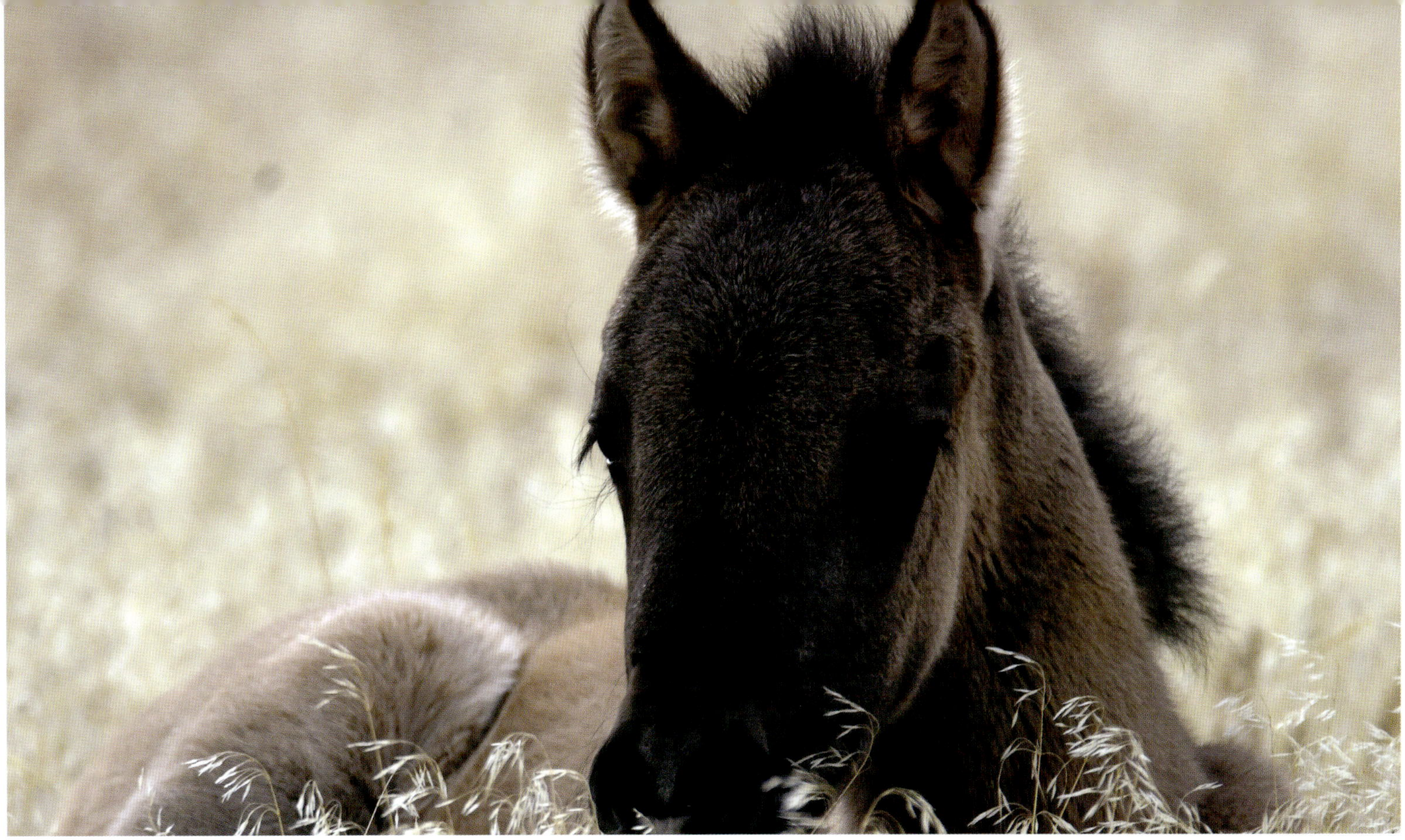

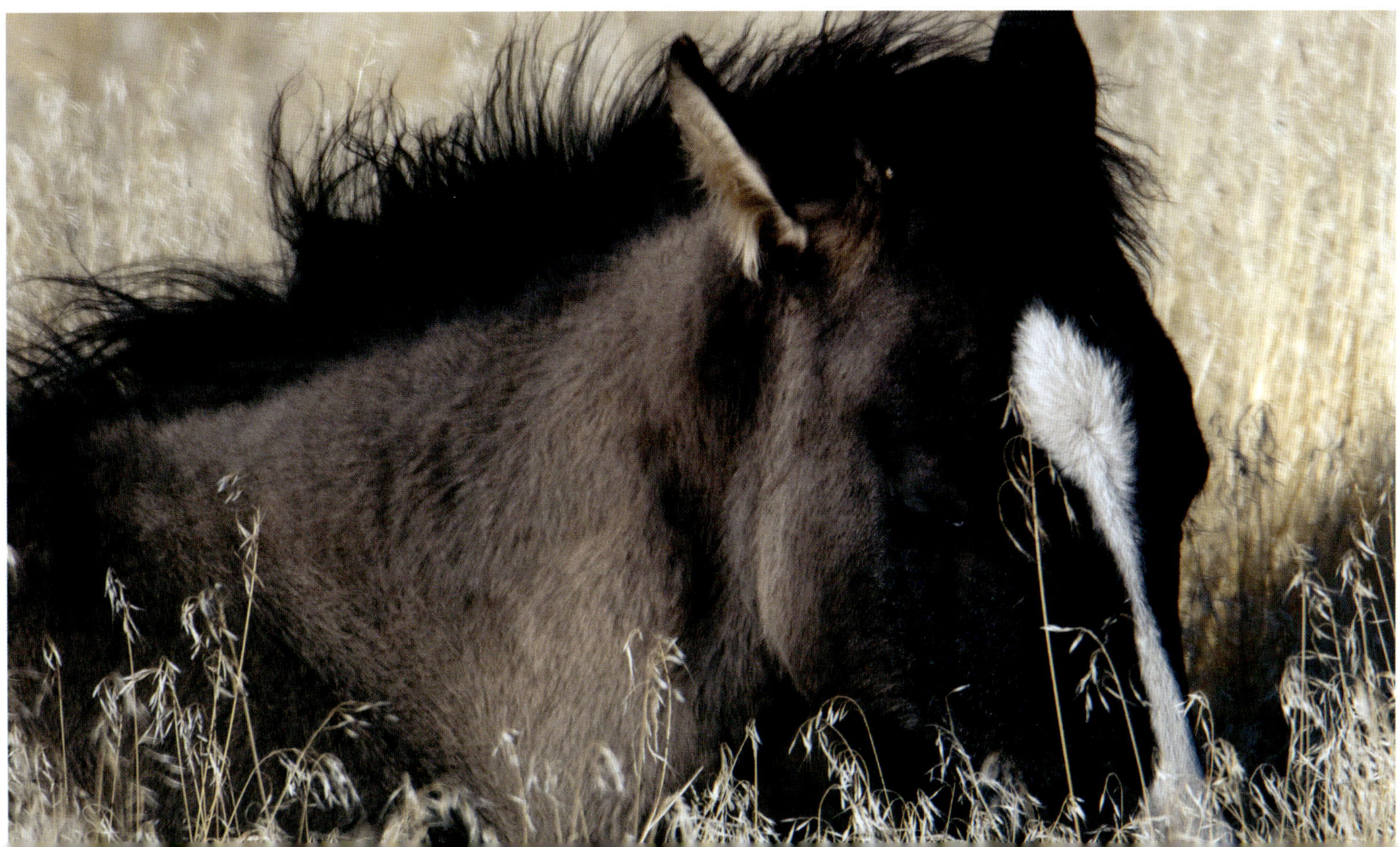

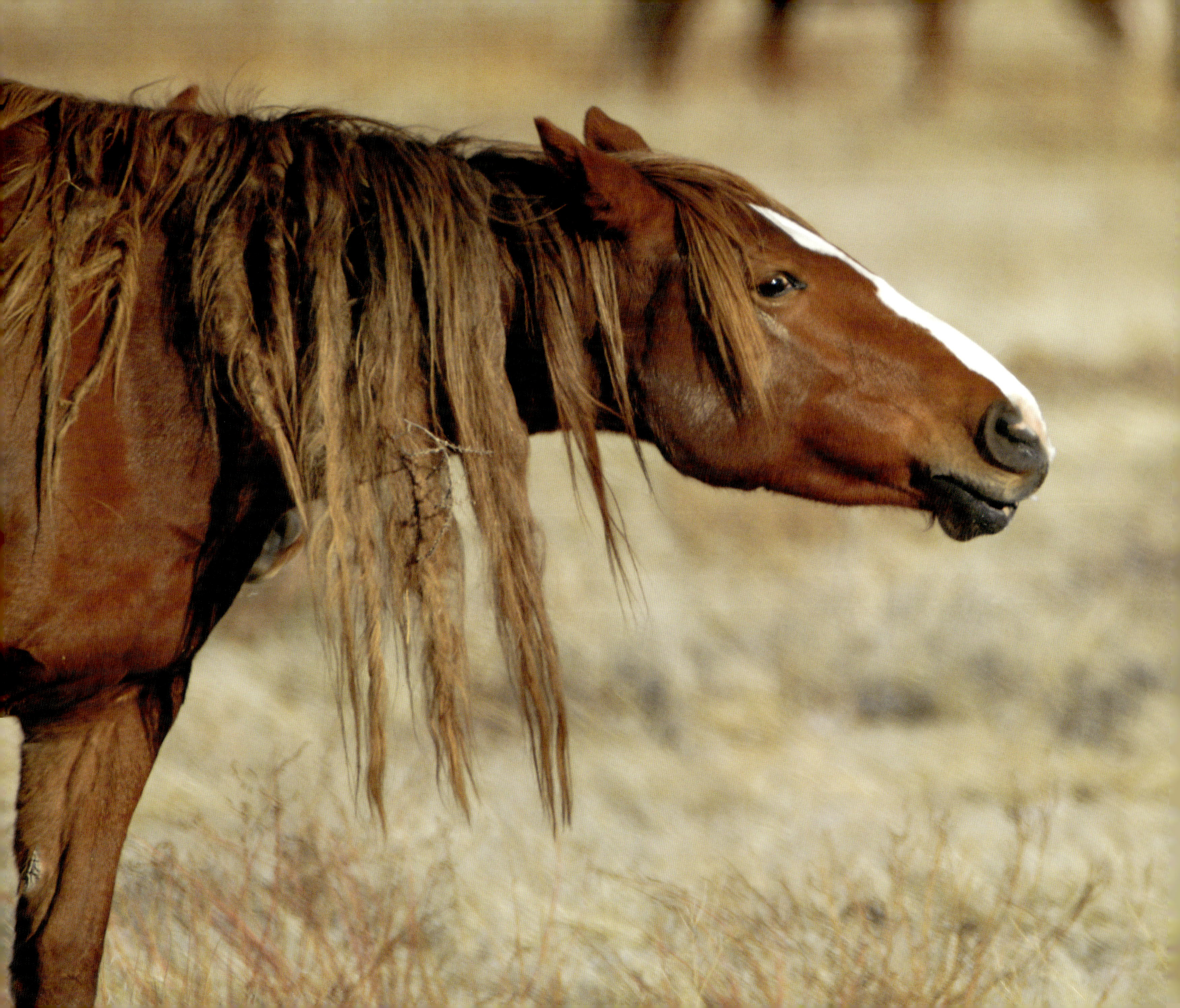

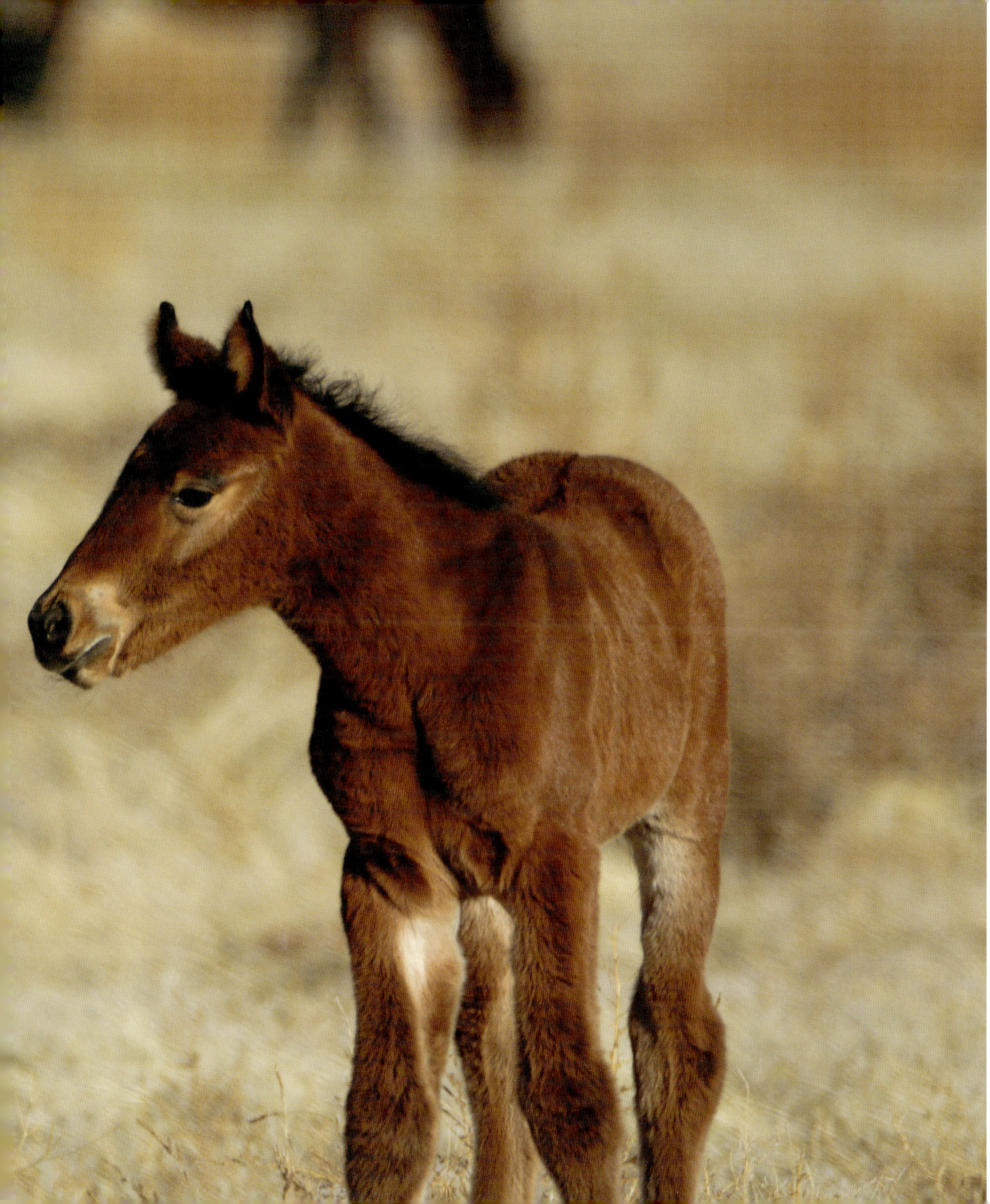

This young colt appears to be getting a scolding from his mother.

THE BIRTH

One of the most rare sights on the range is a mare giving birth. I have never witnessed a birth, but I was lucky enough on one early morning to witness a foal's first steps as the mare and stallion welcomed him into the band.

We were out photographing at sunrise when a solitary pair caught my eye. A mare had left the band, and a stallion stood vigil close by. I was shocked to see a newborn foal lying at his mother's feet. He could not have been more than an hour old—he was cleaned up, but the mare had yet to pass the afterbirth.

I watched in awe as the colt stood on wobbly legs and, with a nudge from his mother, took his first tentative steps.

The first interaction with the stallion is tenser—stallions have been known to injure or kill a foal if they sense that something is not right or that another stallion has sired the foal. I waited apprehensively. After observing the mare and new colt for a while, the stallion finally wandered over to join the new family and accept the foal as his.

The colt moved with the band mere hours after birth. Foals are ever a testament to the tenacity of wild horses—how lucky I am to have seen one in his earliest hours, before he thundered across the range with the rest.

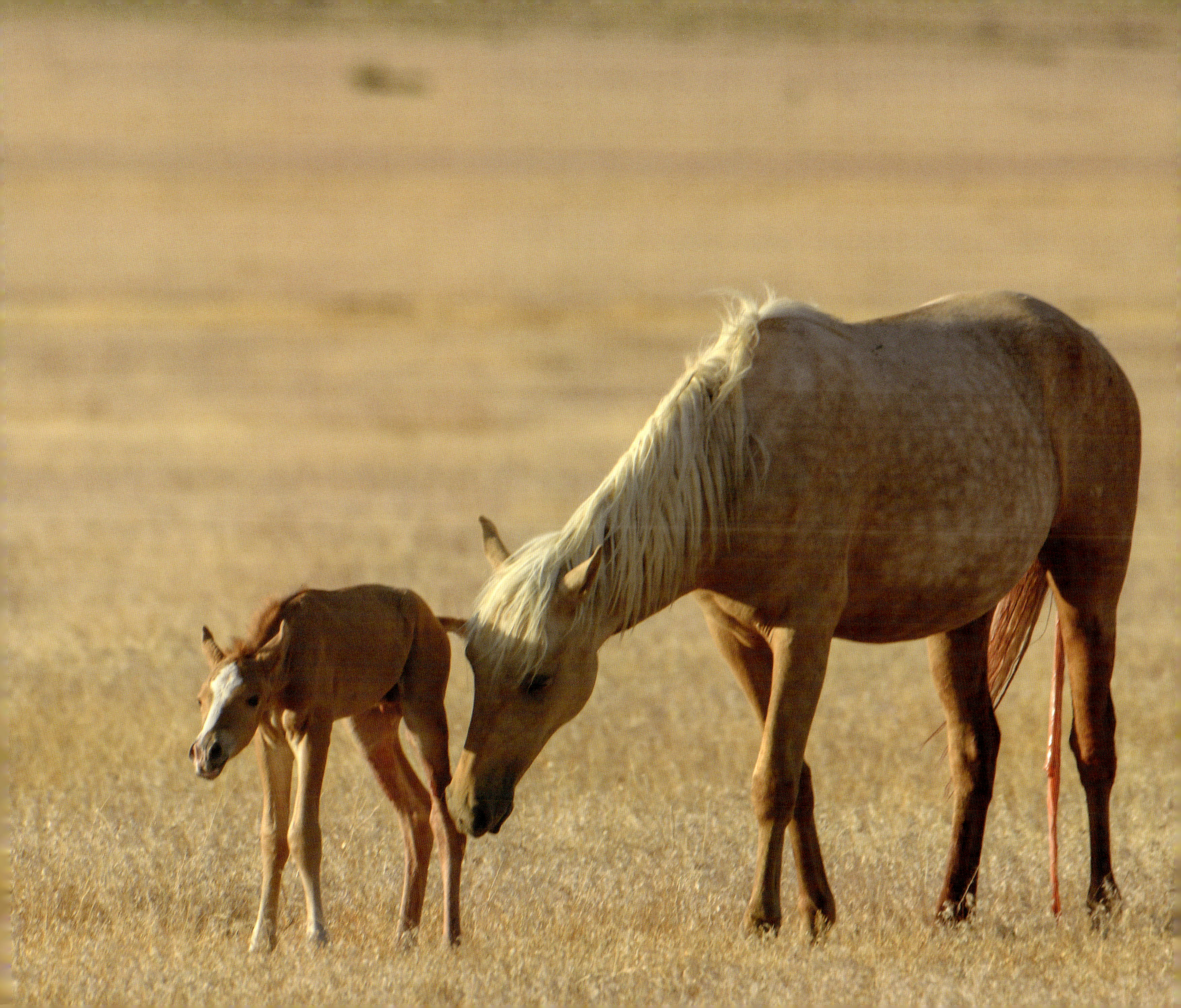

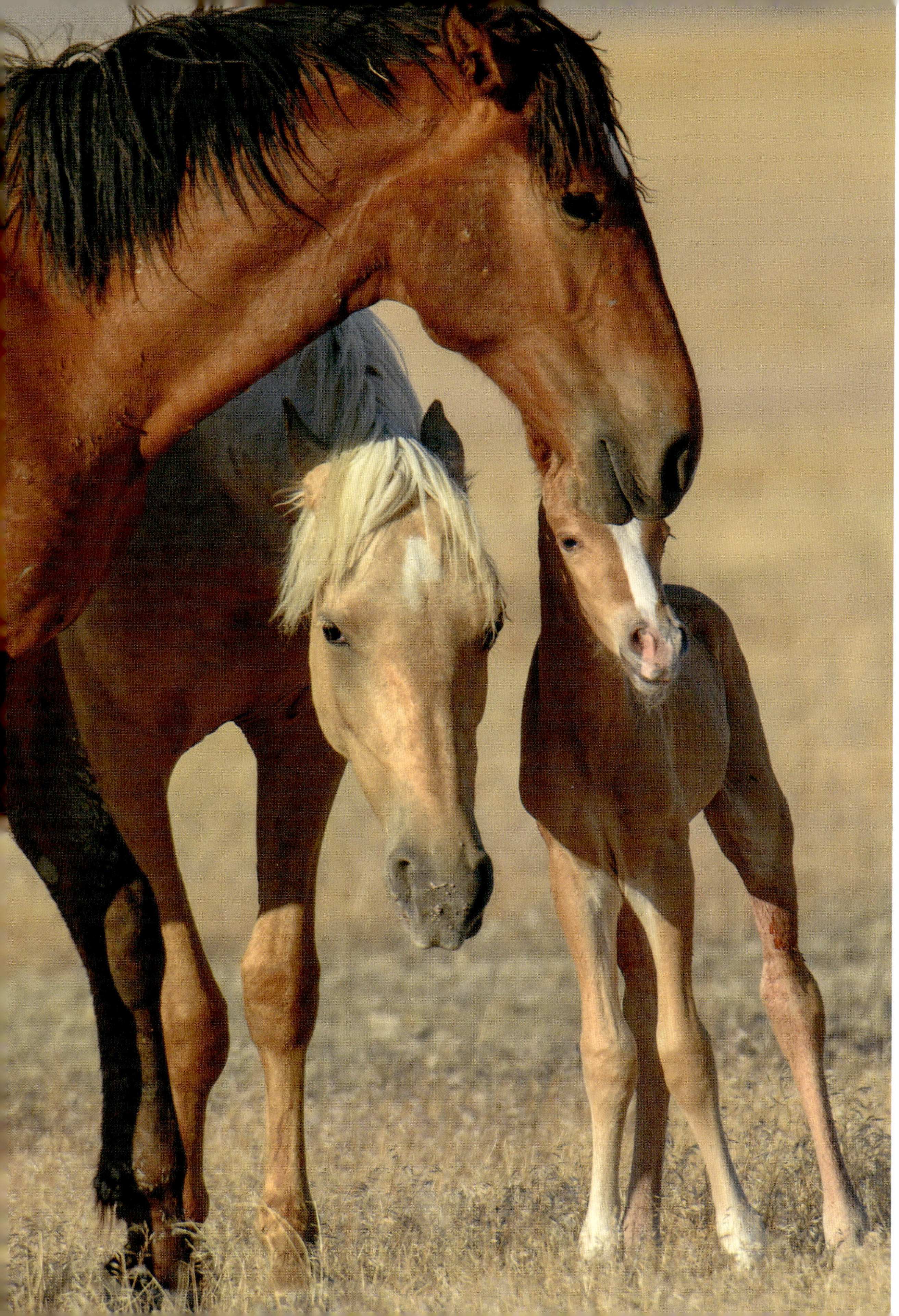

Left: The proud band stallion with his newborn colt and his mare.

Opposite: The palomino mare nuzzles her newborn colt.

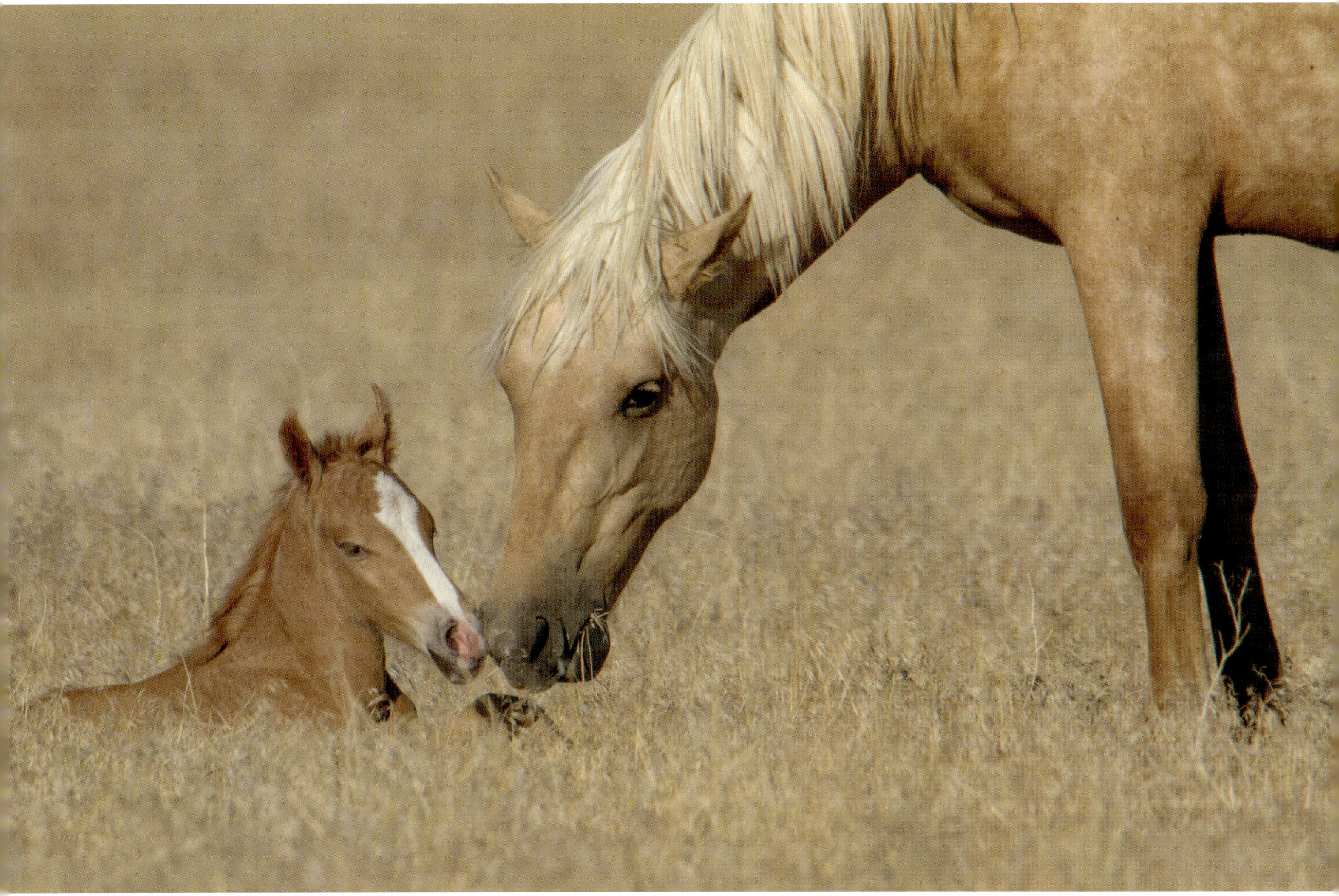

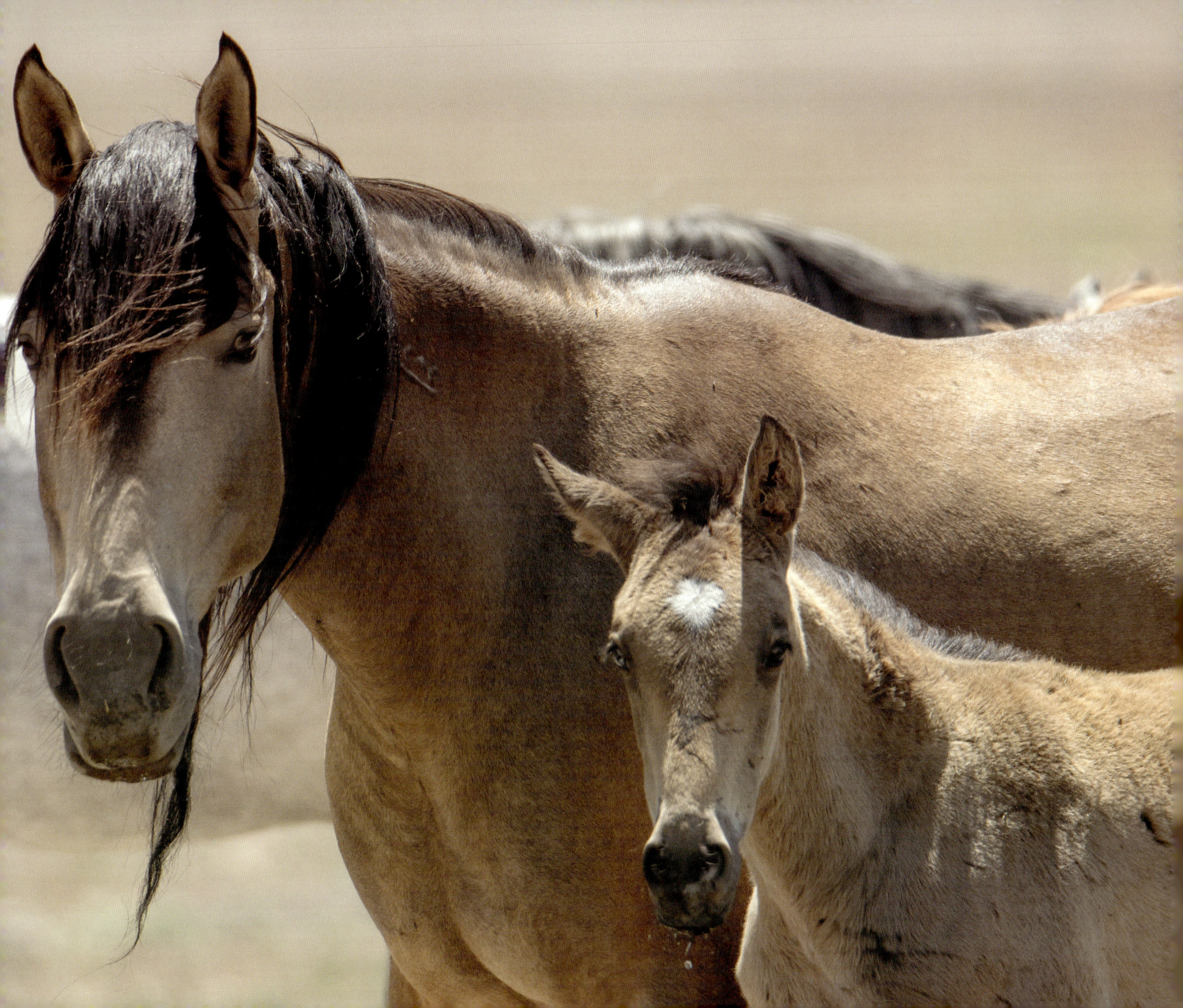

Opposite: Often a mare will have a foal with the same coat color and marking as her; this mare and foal are of the buckskin coat color.

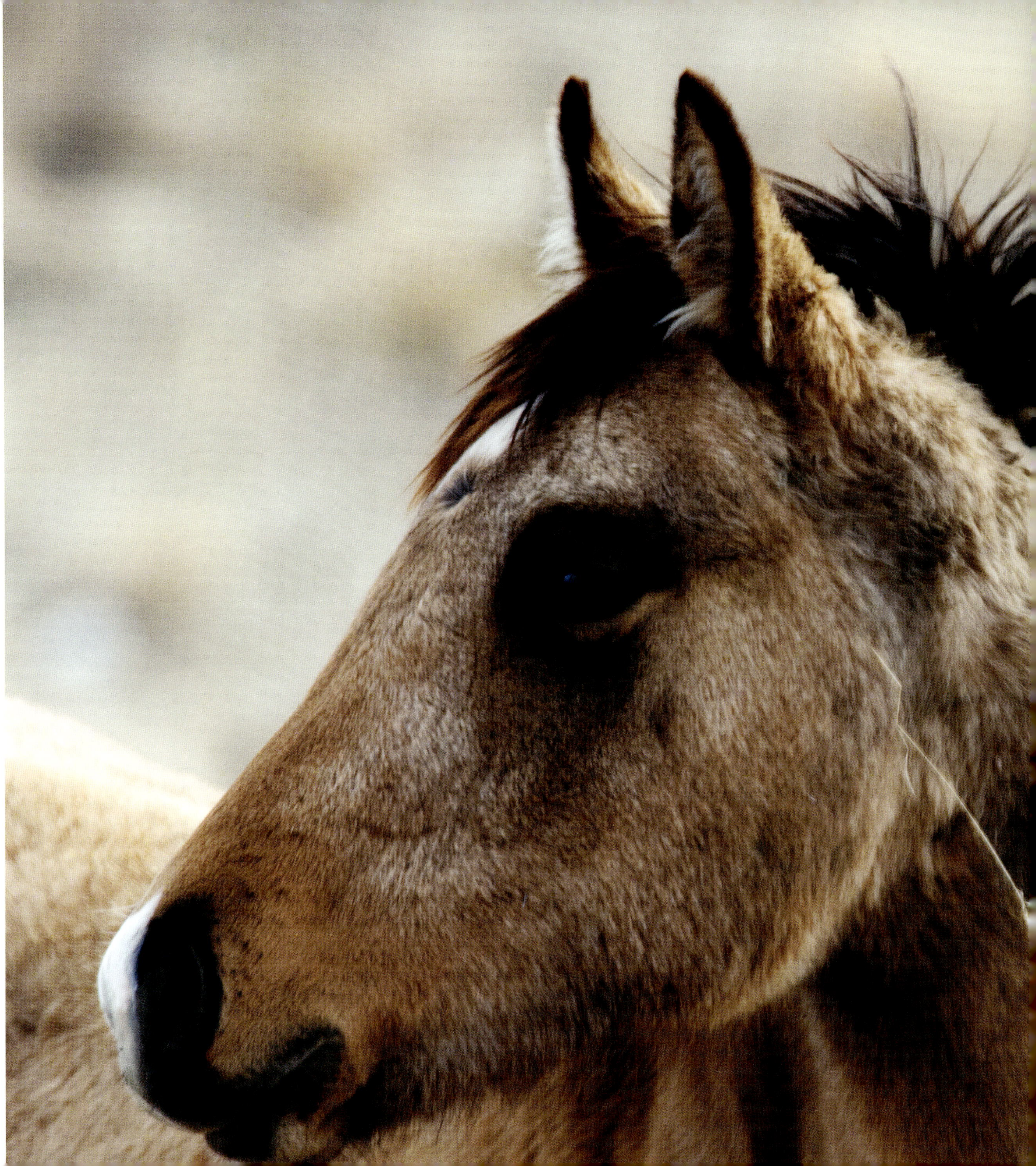

Right: This little filly's coat is buckskin, which resembles certain shades of tanned deerskin. Buckskin horses have a tan- or gold-colored coat with black points on their mane, tail, and lower legs.

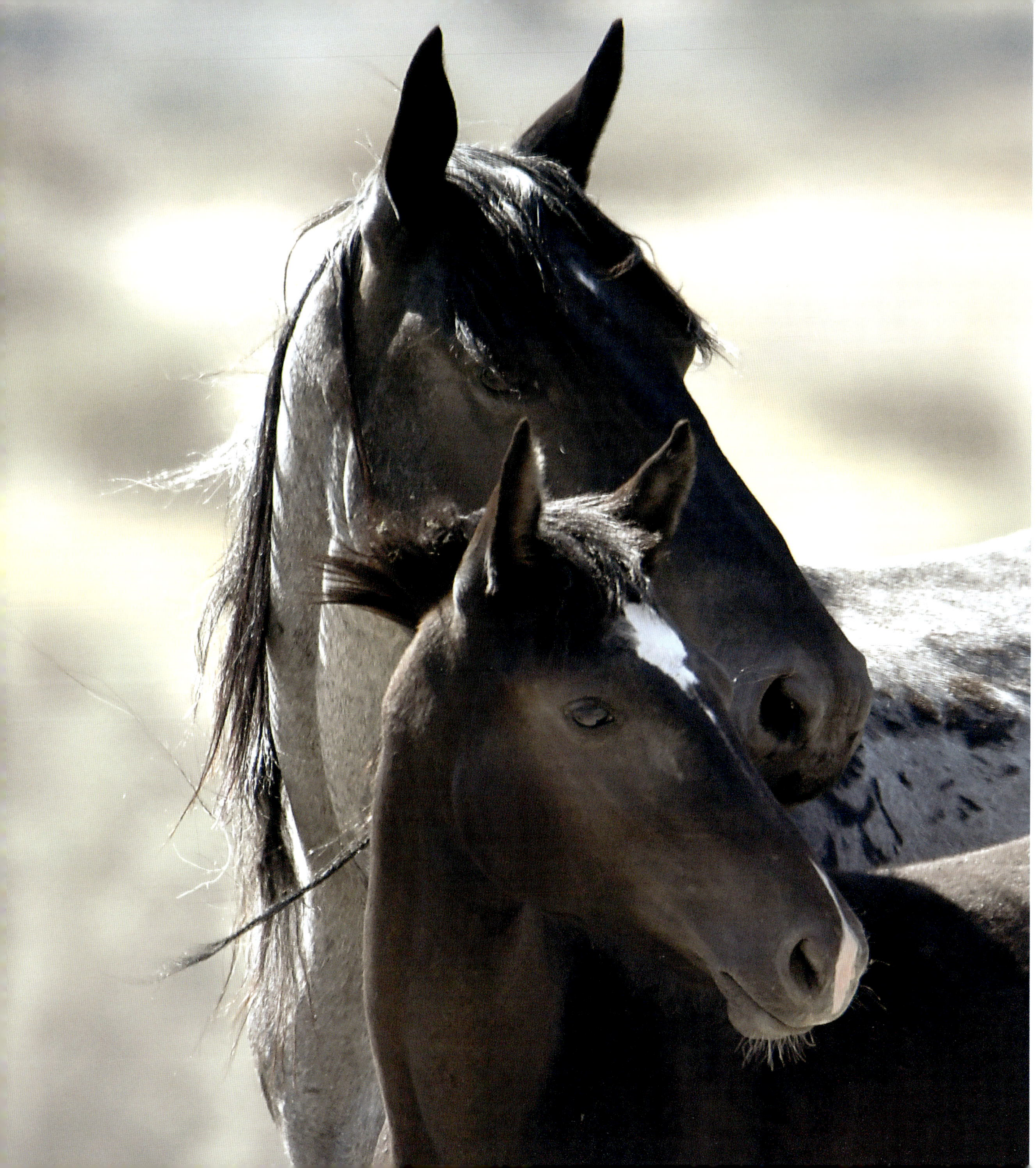

LEFT: A mare and foal watch the rest of band.

OPPOSITE: The red roan stud gives his foal some attention.

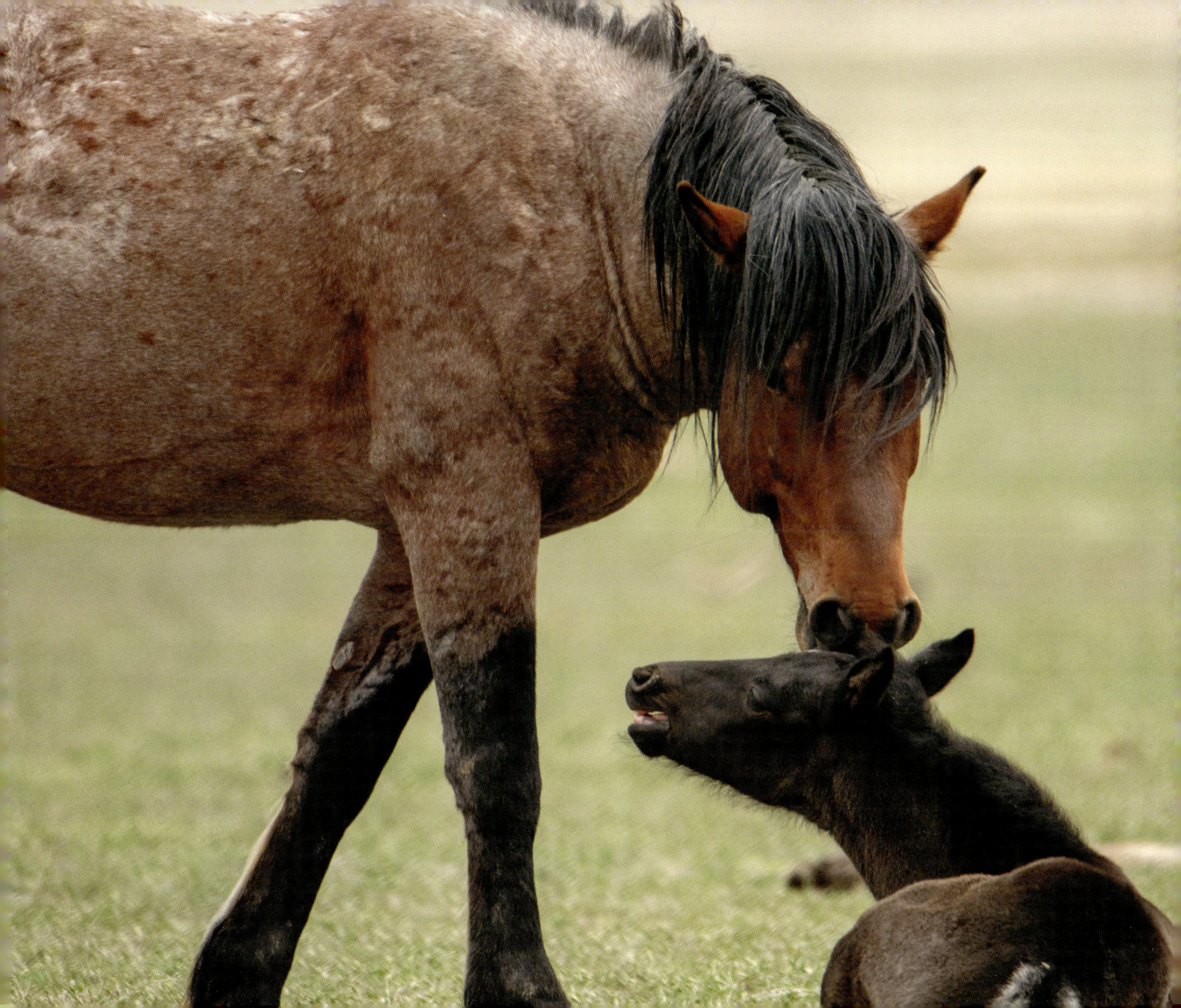

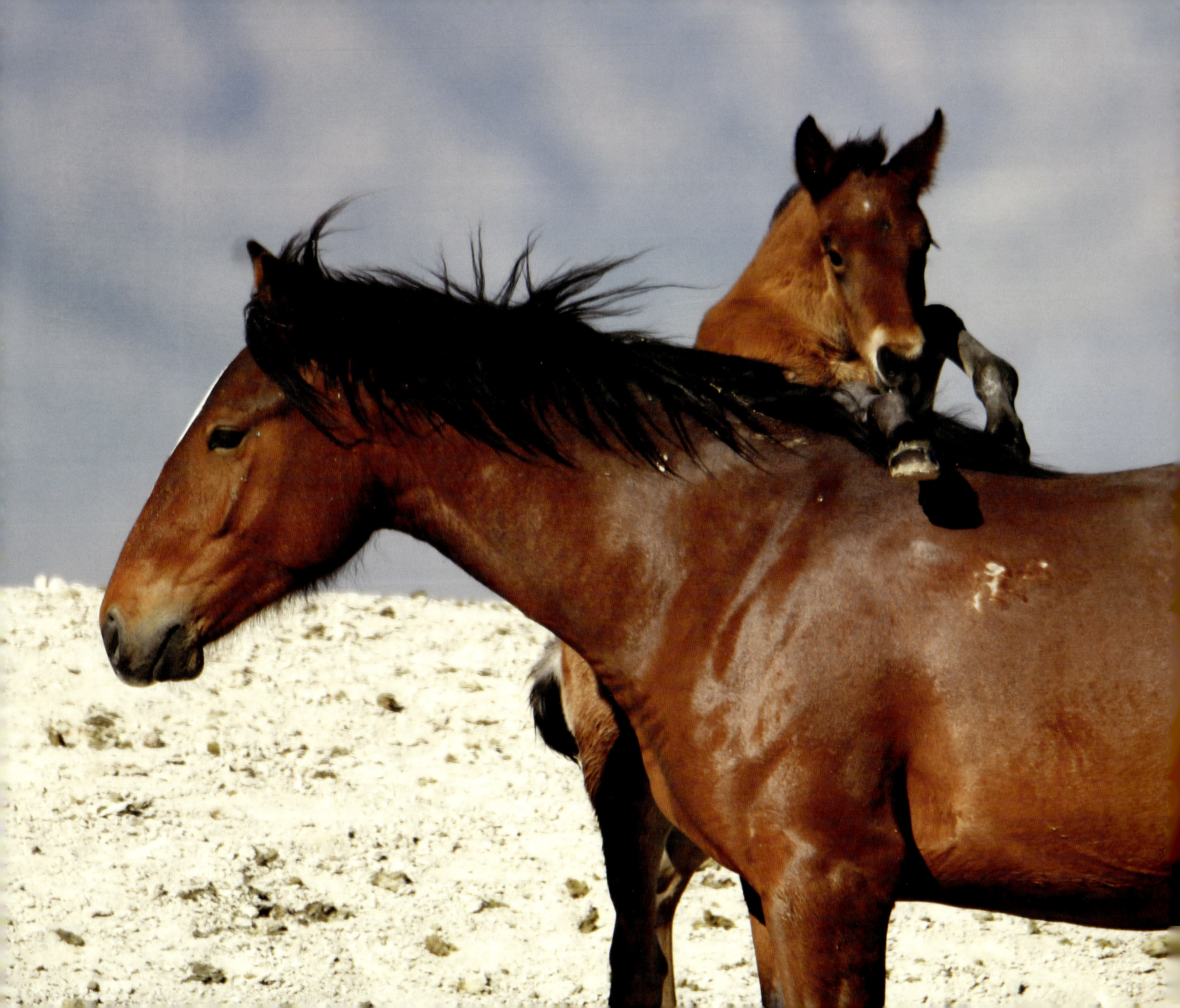

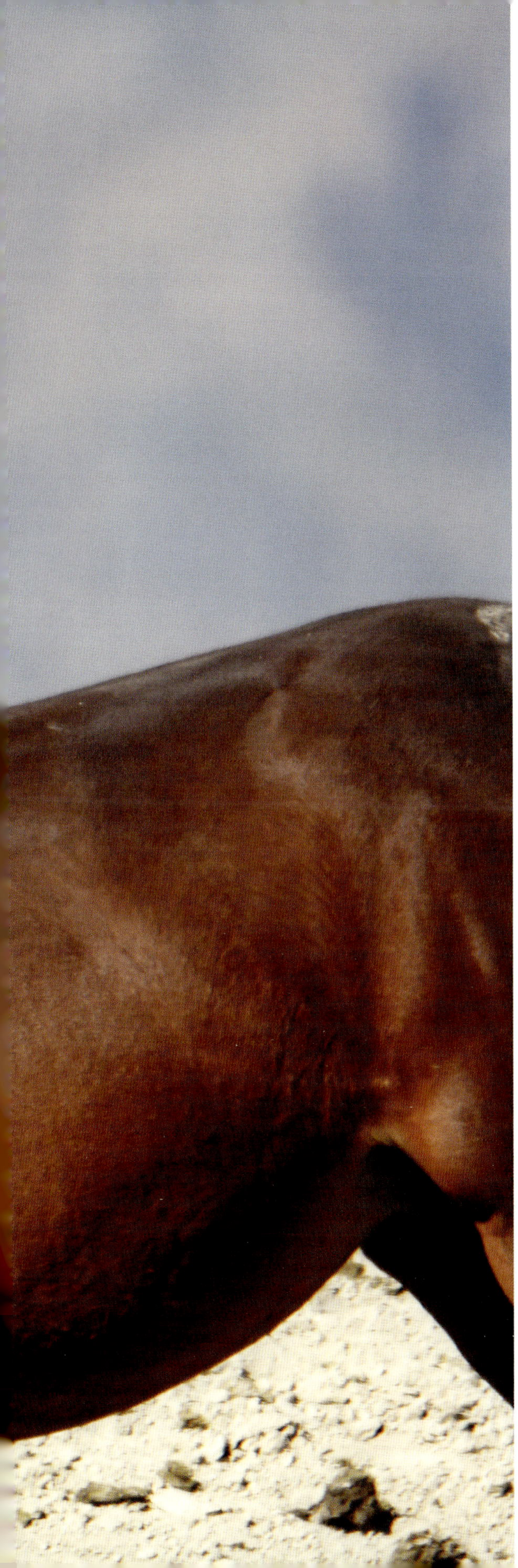

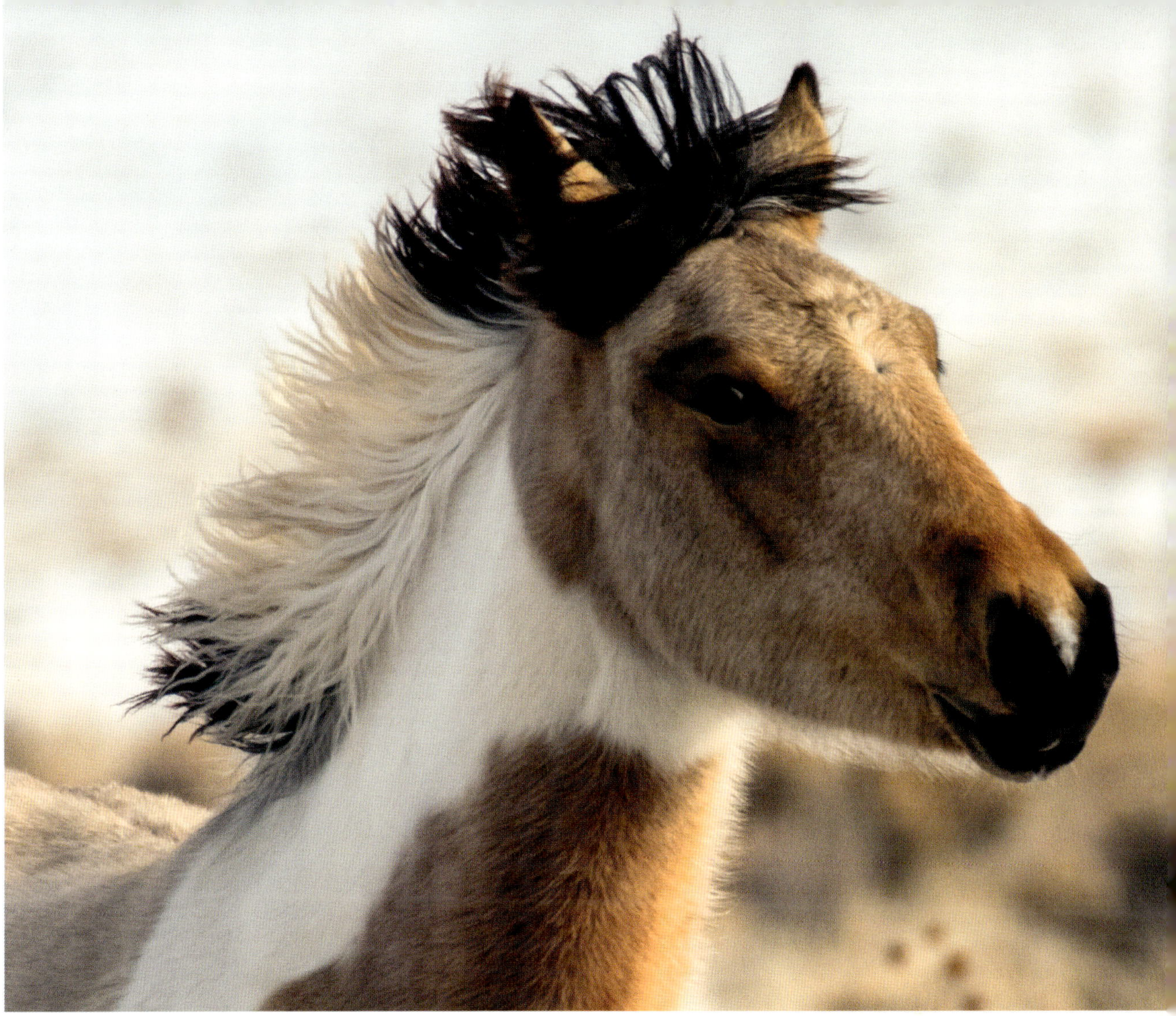

Left: The enduring patience of a mare is evident here as her young foal enjoys playing on his mom's back.

Above: This pinto foal runs wild and free.

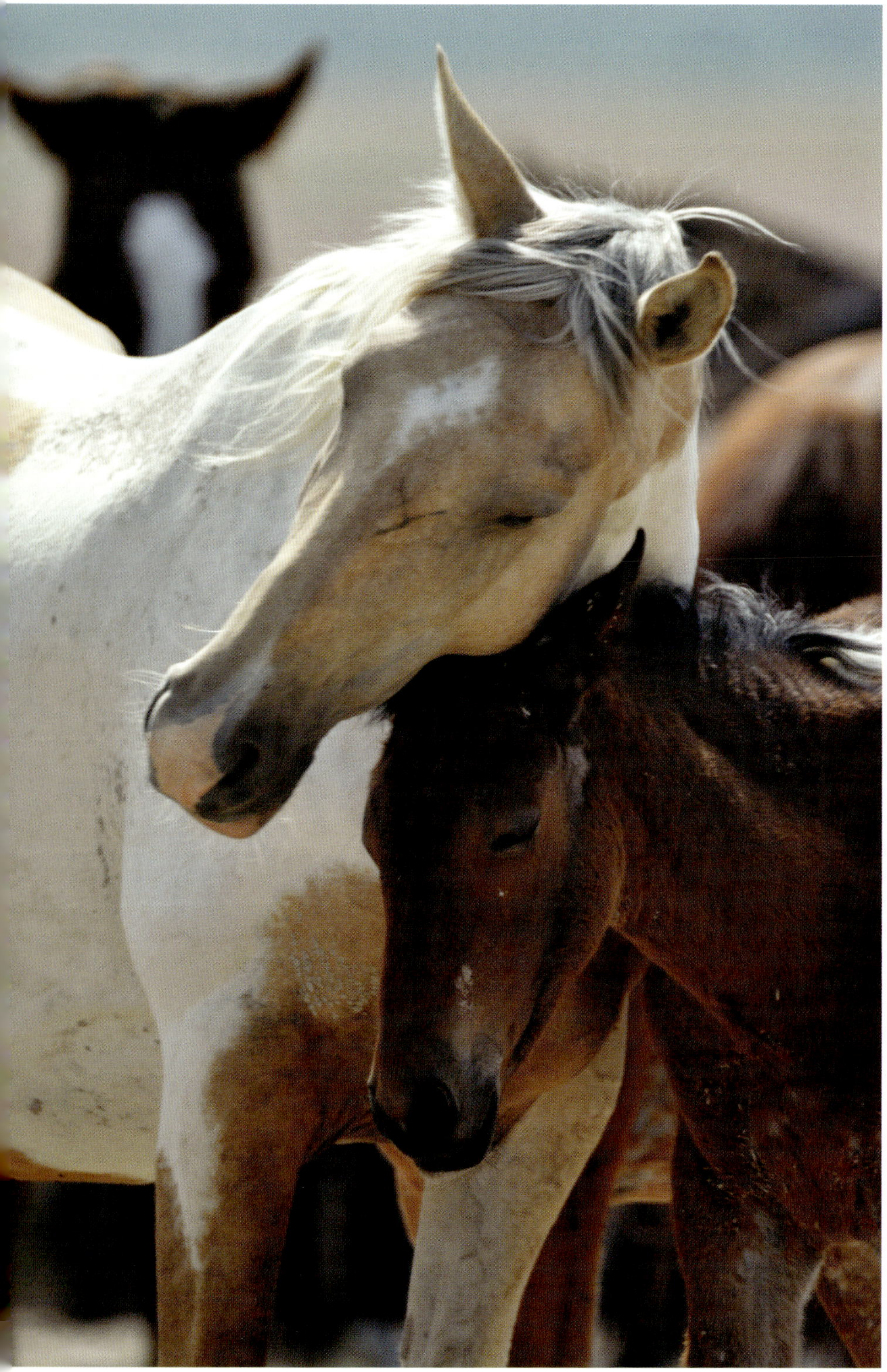

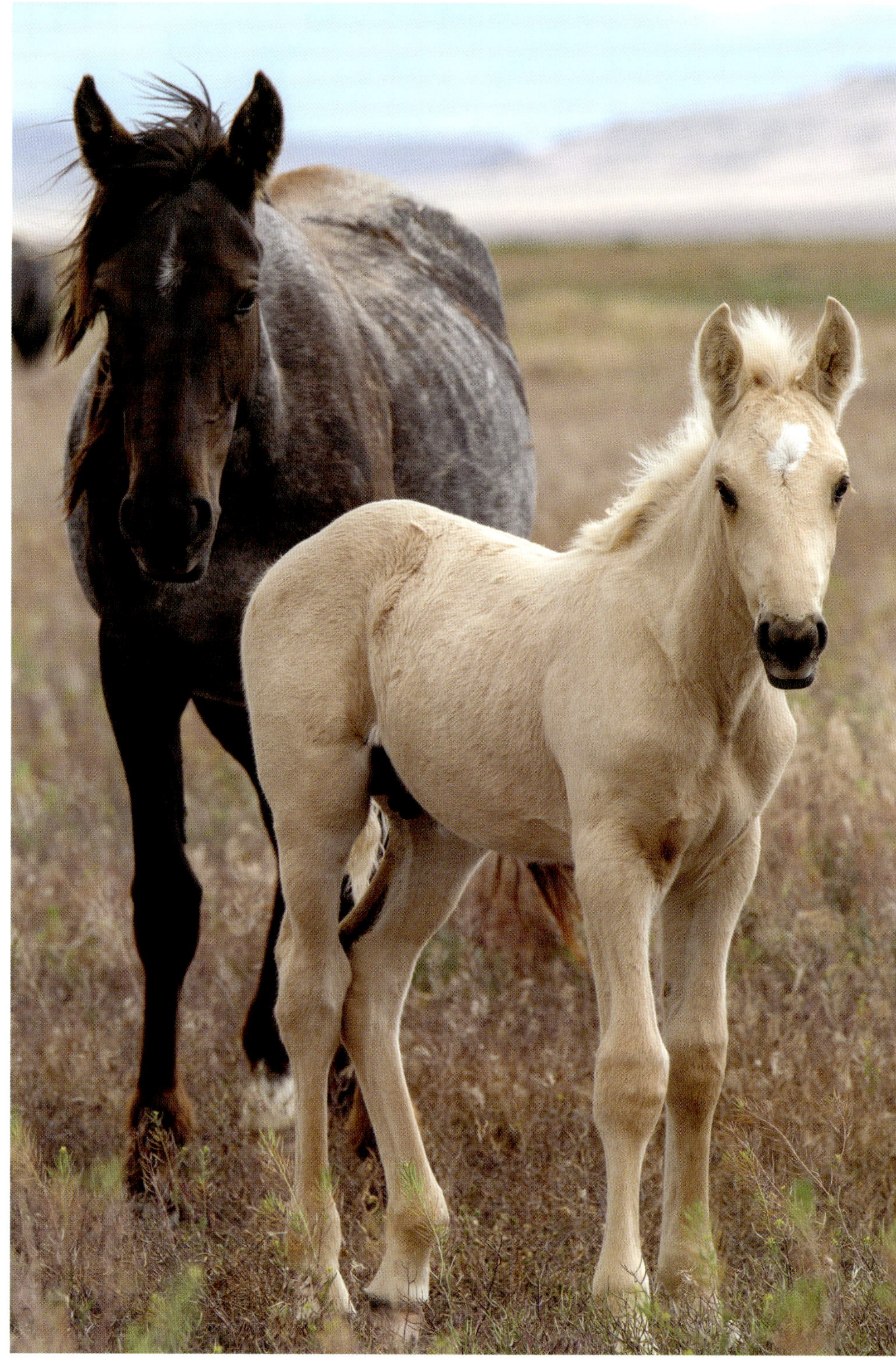

Opposite left: The affection between a mare and her foal is a special bond.

Opposite right: A palomino colt with his mom.

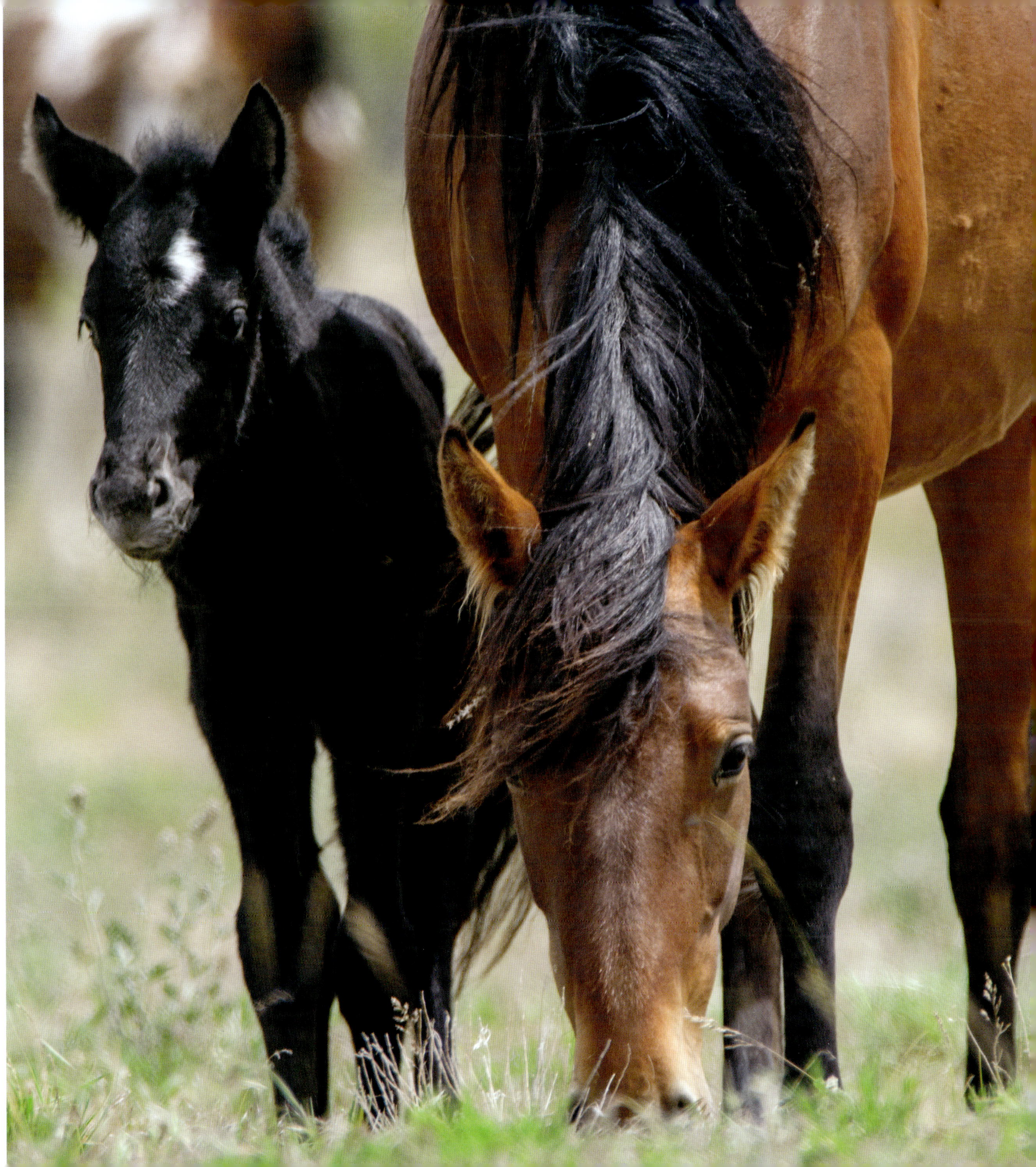

Right: There are many kinds of markings on a horse's face; this little black foal has what is called a star.

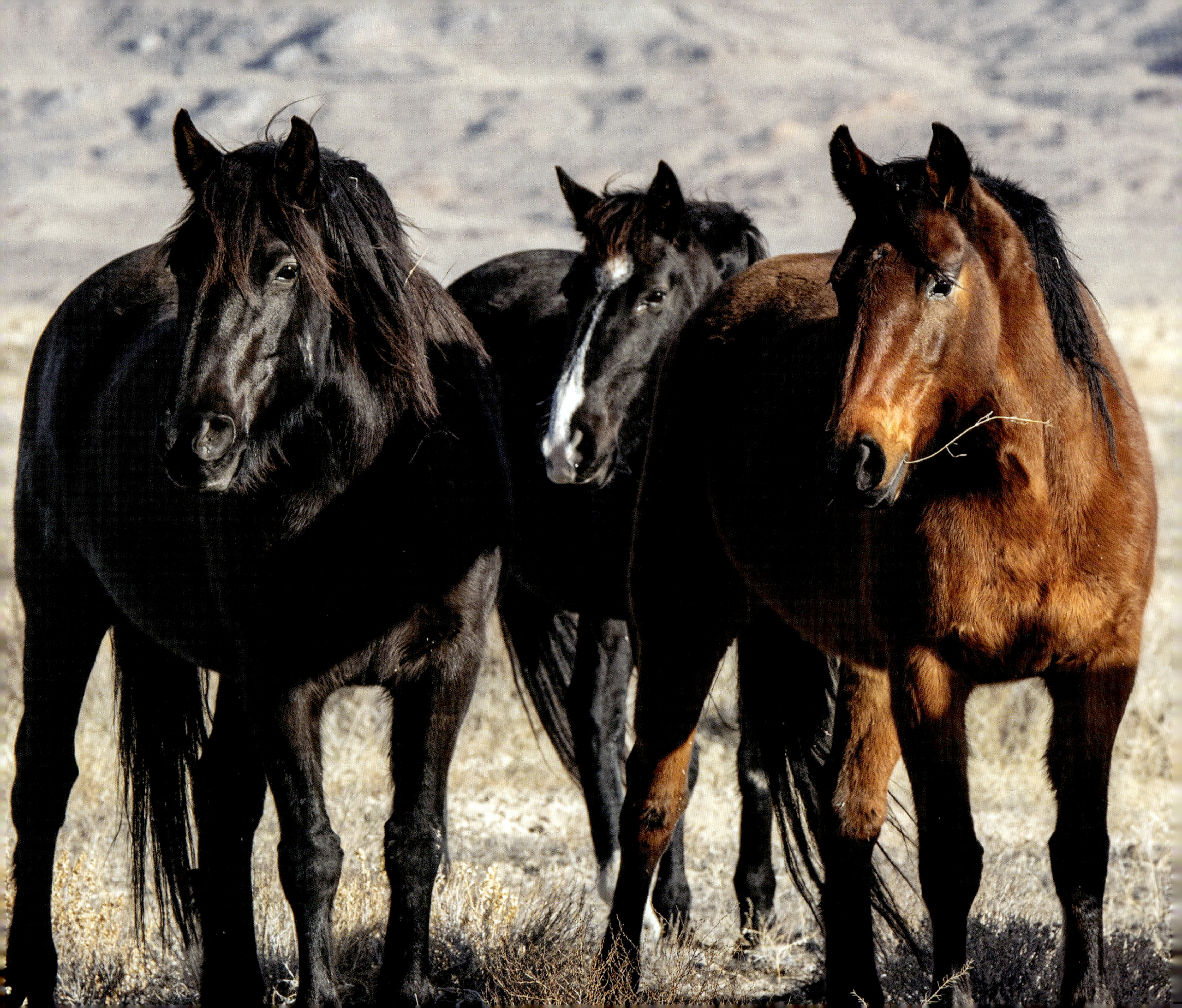

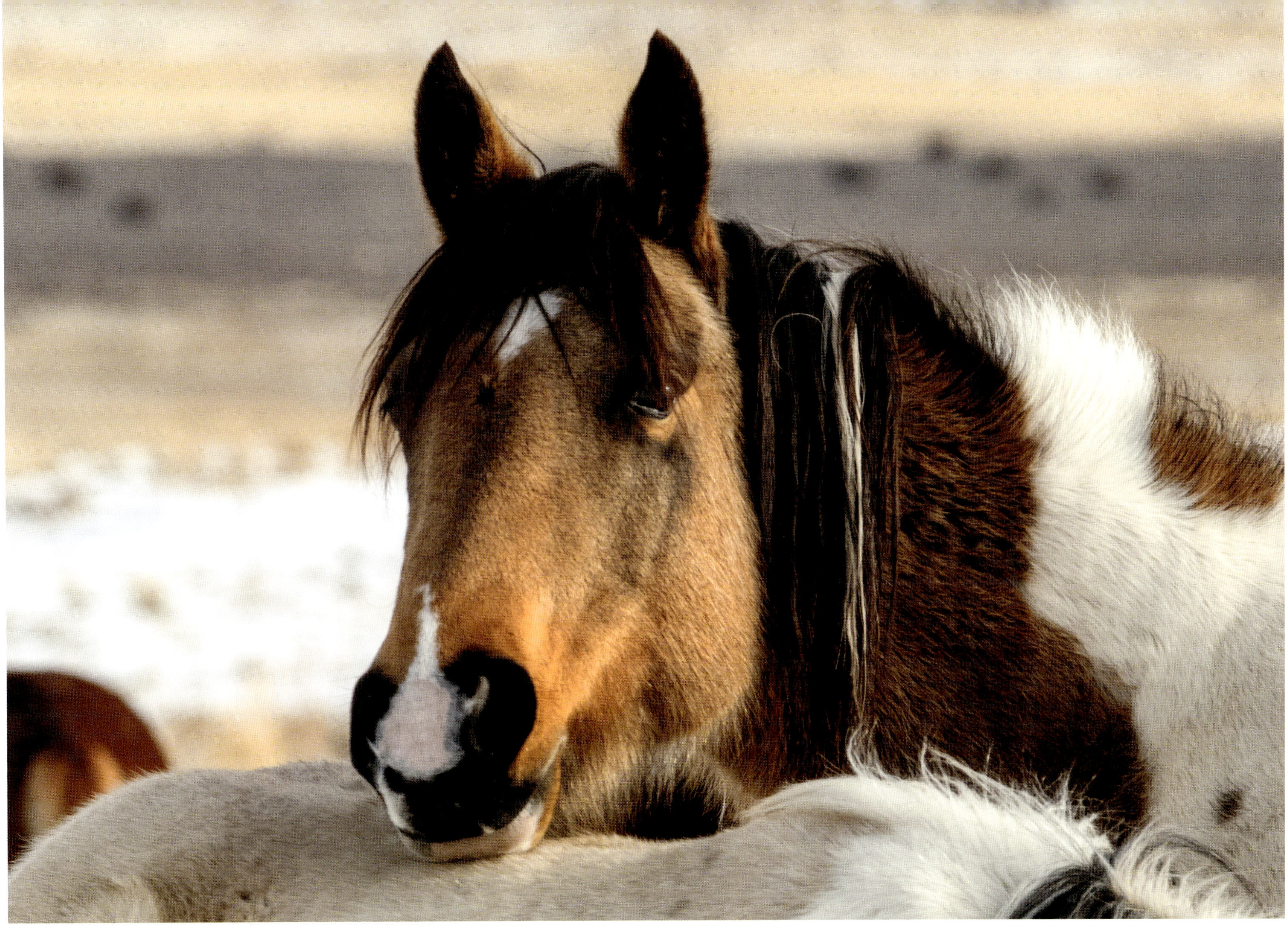

OPPOSITE: A group of young bachelor stallions observe the action on the range.

ABOVE: This tricolored pinto mare has found a convenient resting spot.

MOCK FIGHTING

Colts tend to strike bonds with other colts in the first two to three years of their lives before they are forced out of their family band. During this lively period, the colts are preparing themselves for life on their own. They run, play, and antagonize one another, and as they start to mature, this playful spirit becomes mock fighting, mimicking what they see from the band stallion. As the colts hone their fighting skills, they also show dominance amongst themselves—dominance that will prove beneficial when they leave the band to form new bachelor bands.

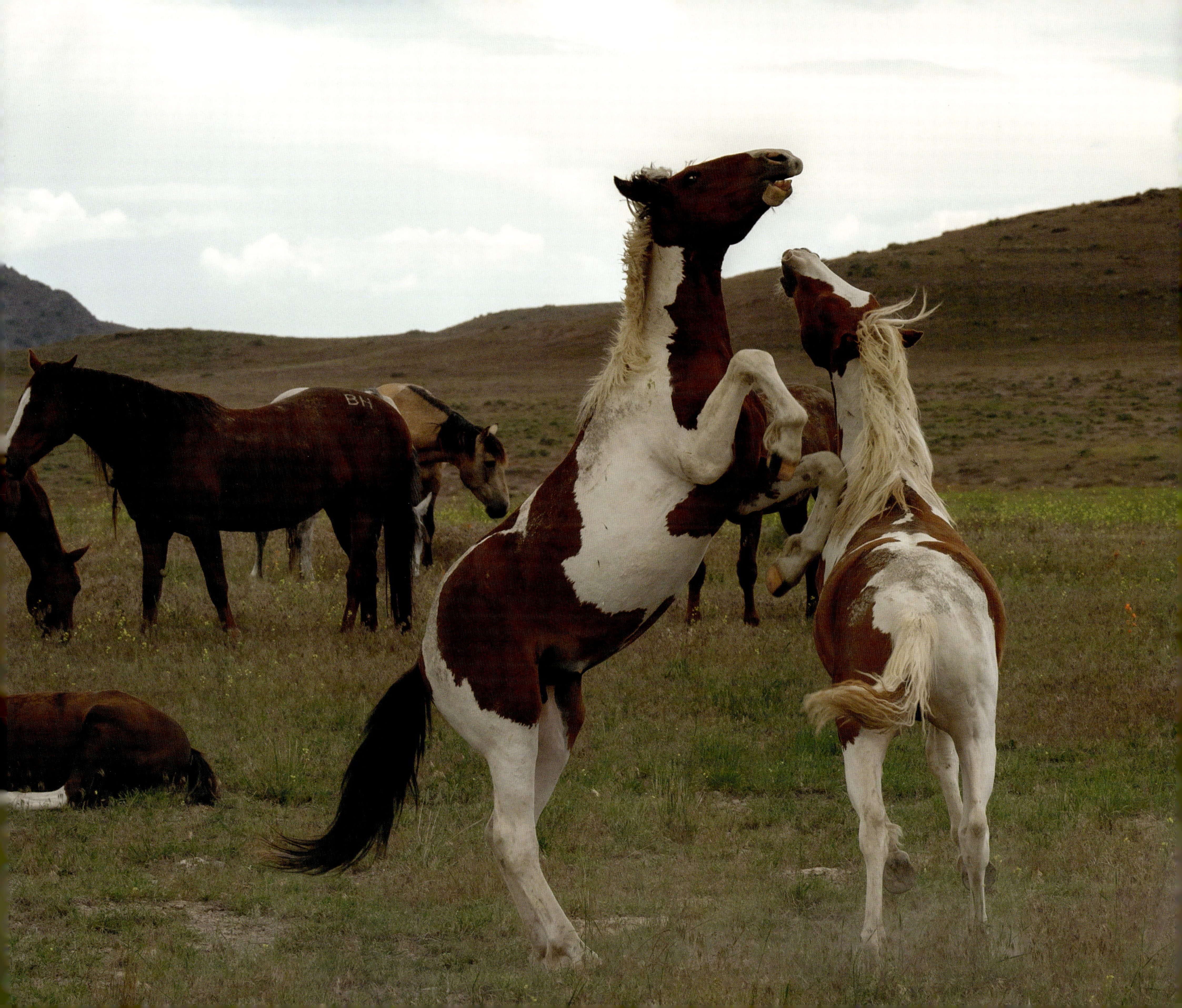
BH

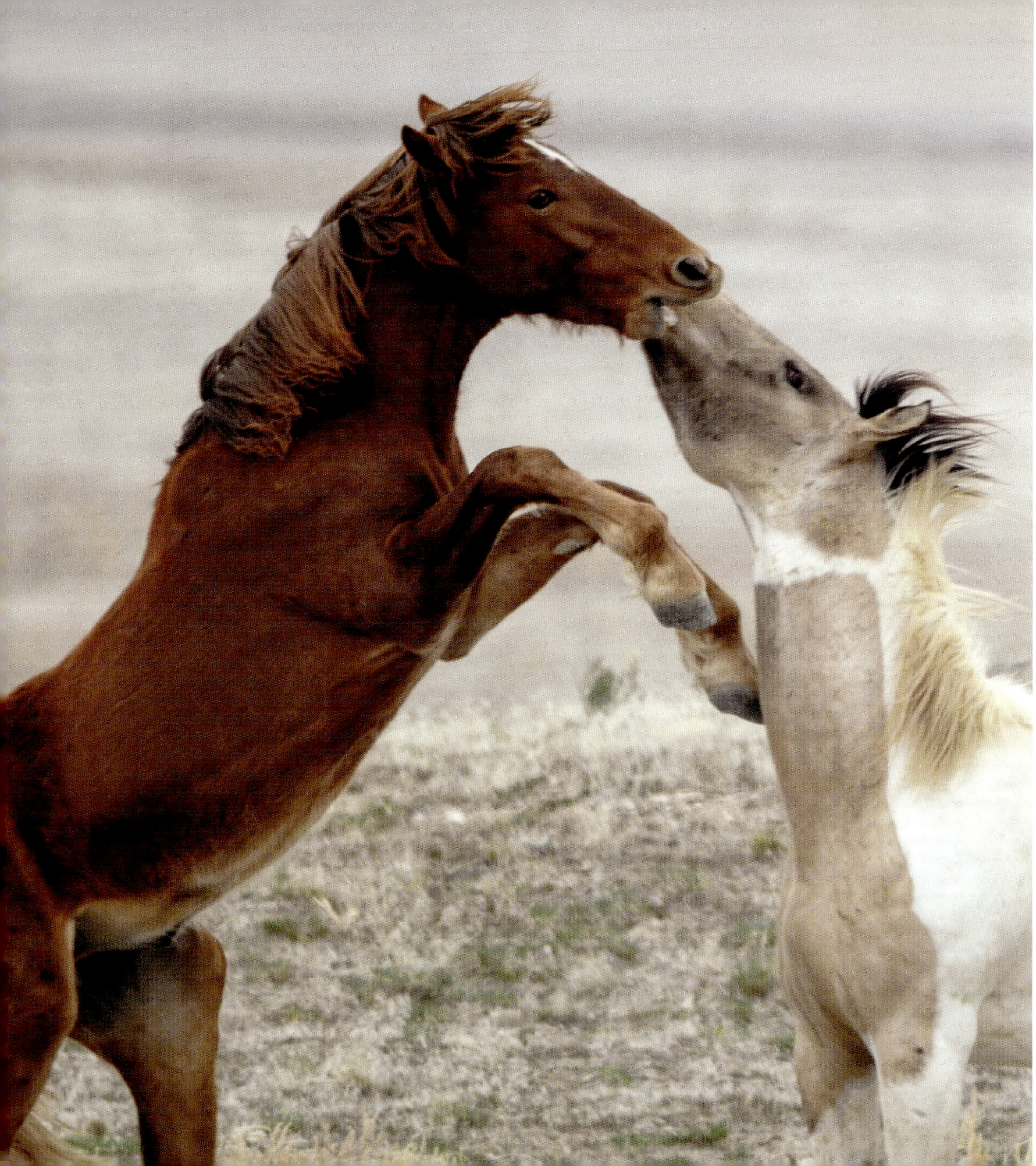

LEFT: The playfulness of young colts will eventually prepare them for life as a stallion.

OPPOSITE: This little foal will do just about anything to get the sleepy one up to play.

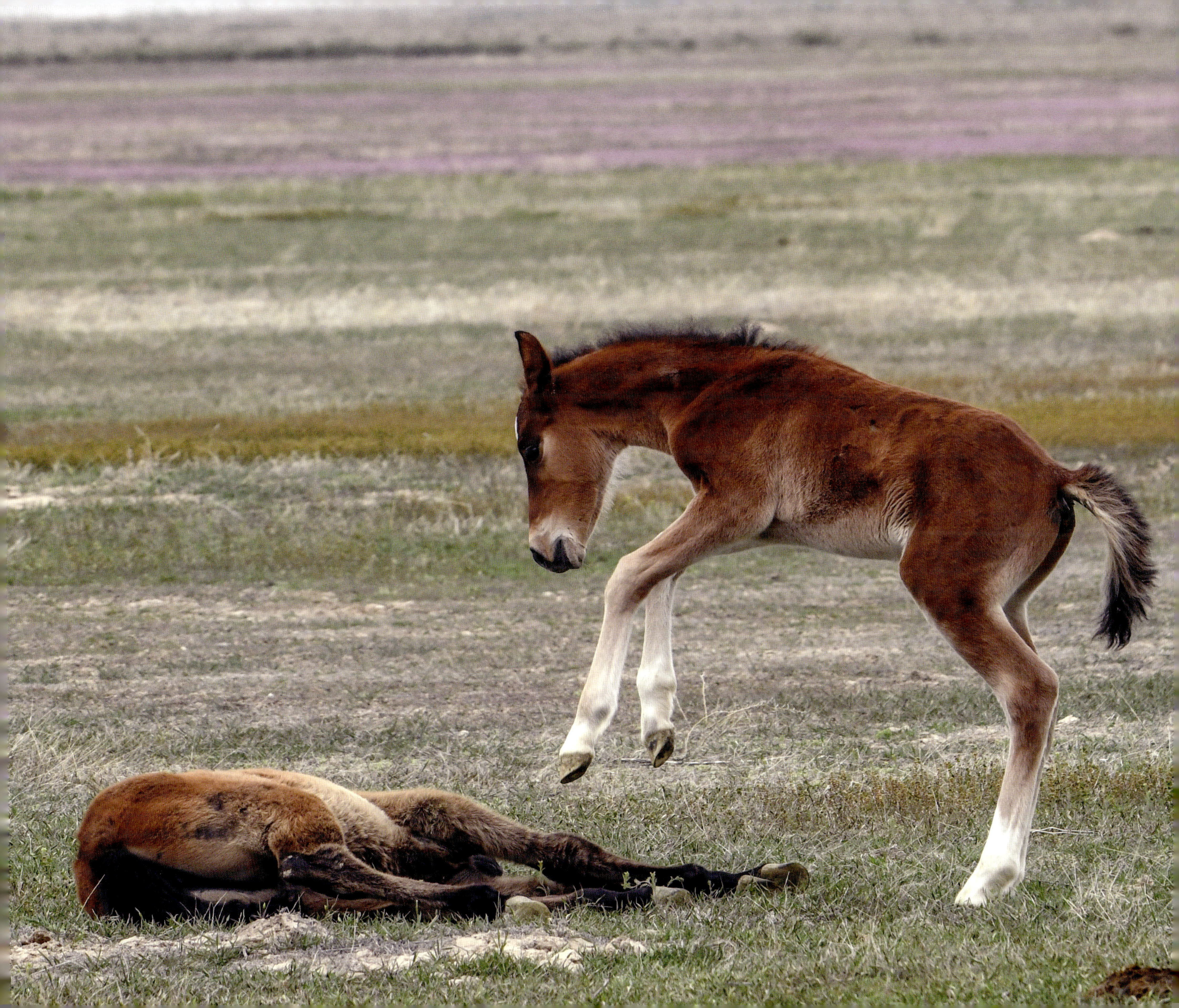

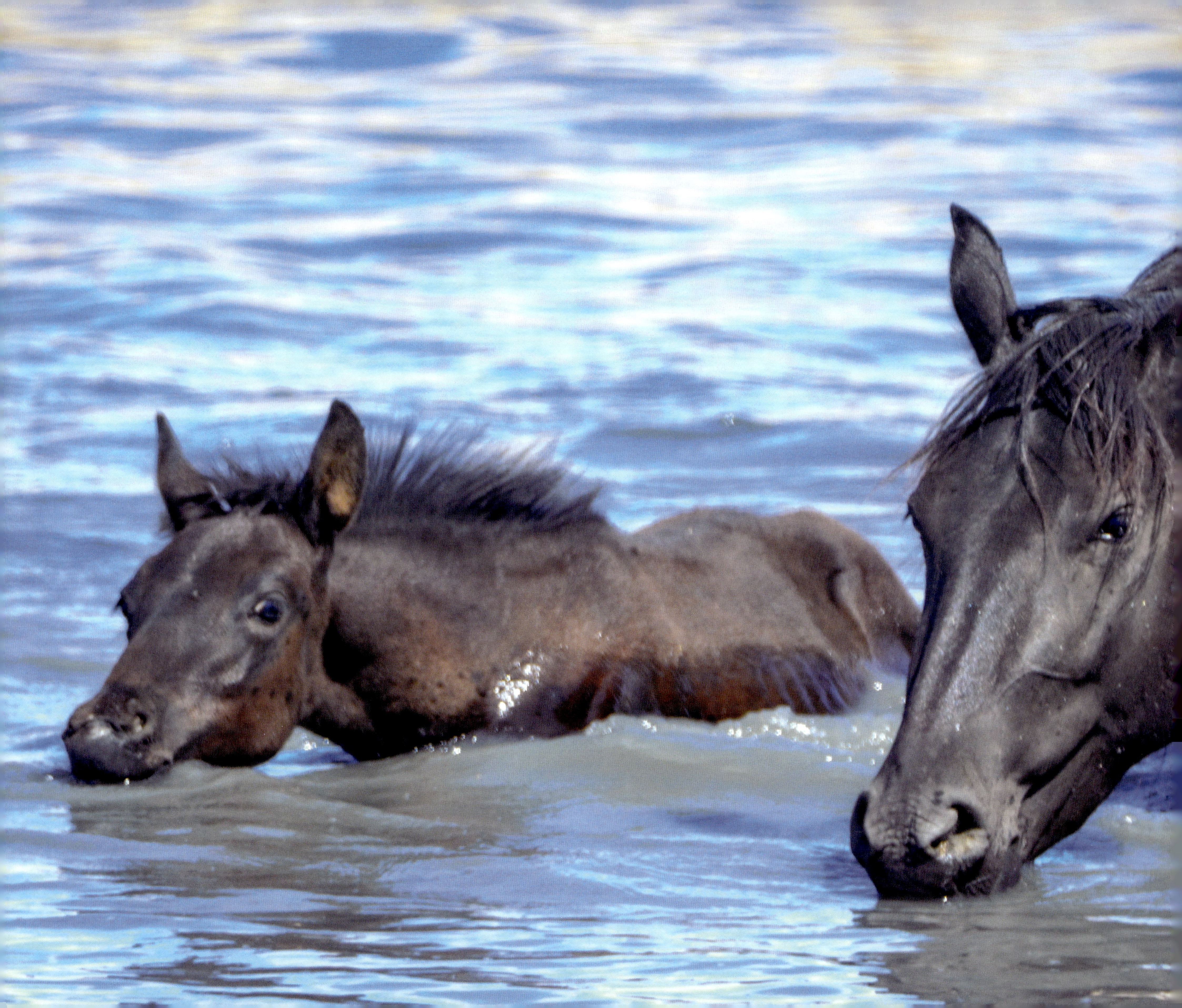

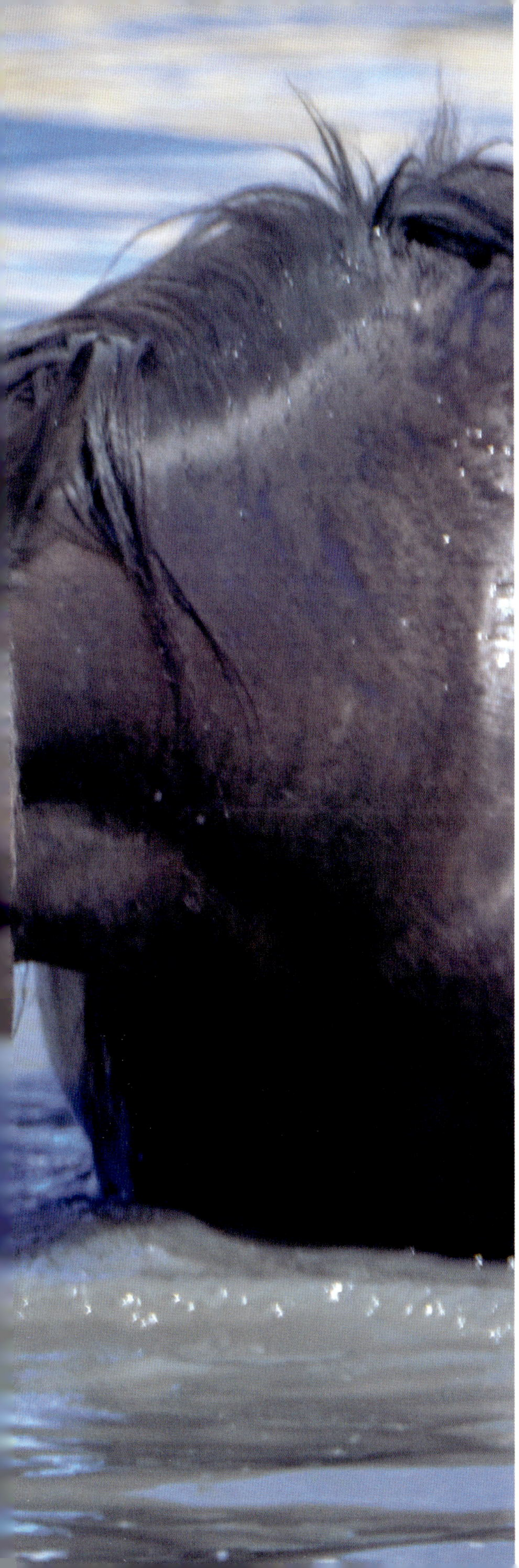

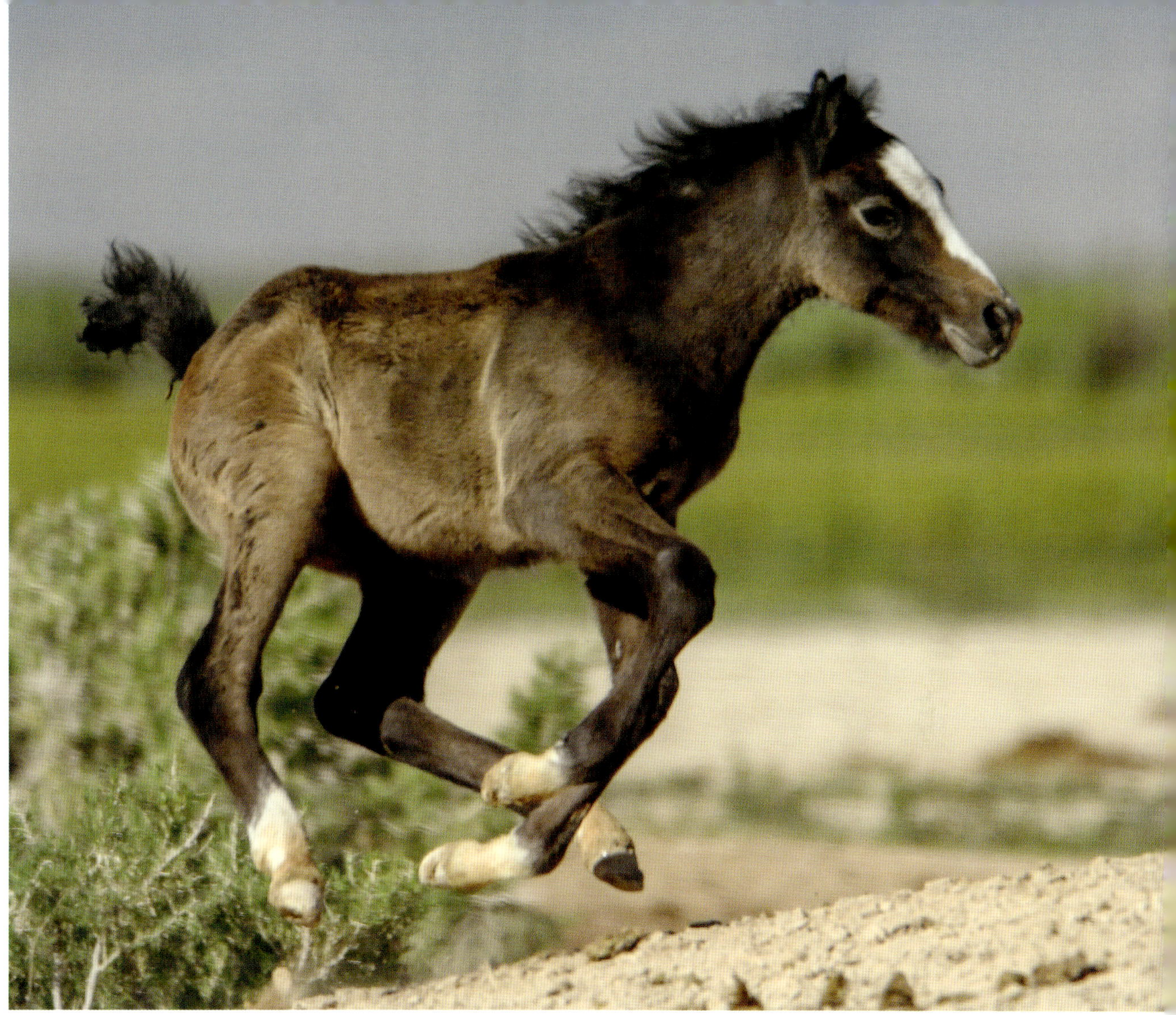

LEFT: A mare and her foal enjoy a cool drink and a refreshing dip in the waterhole.

ABOVE: All four legs off the ground and playing hard.

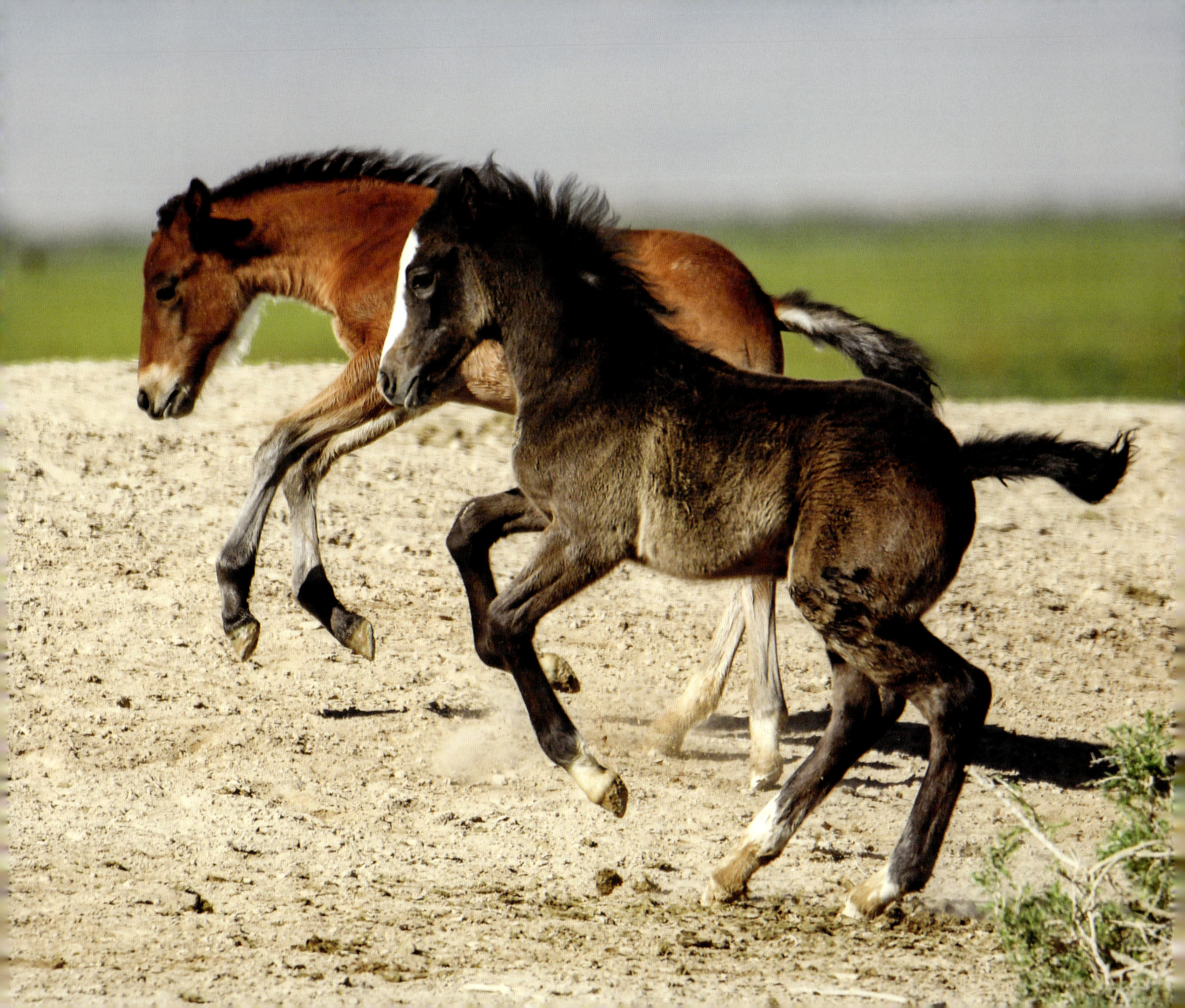

Clockwise, from opposite: A pair of young foals in the band enjoy their playtime. A cremello filly delights playing in the new snowfall. Often young foals will race around the waterhole, enjoying themselves.

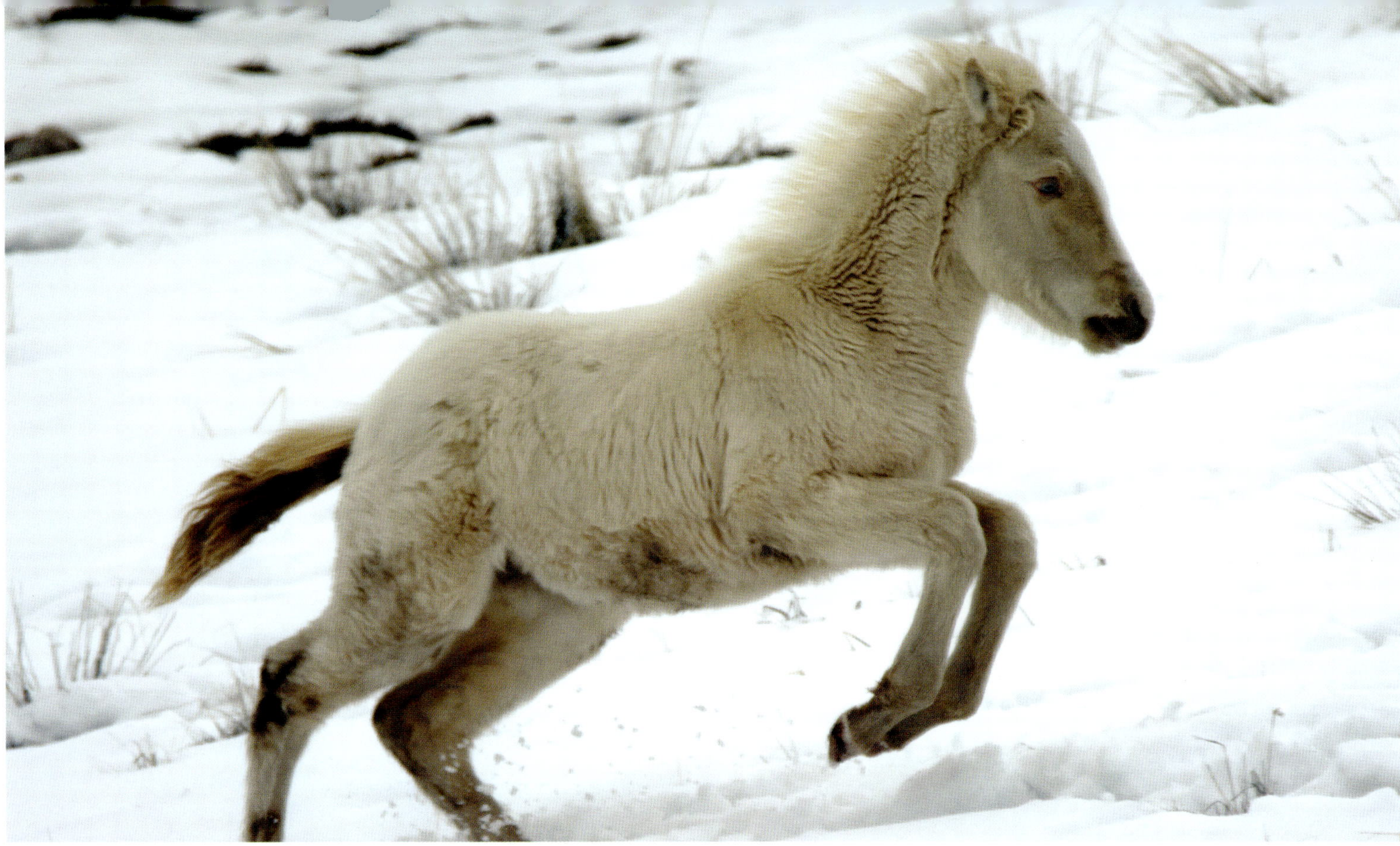

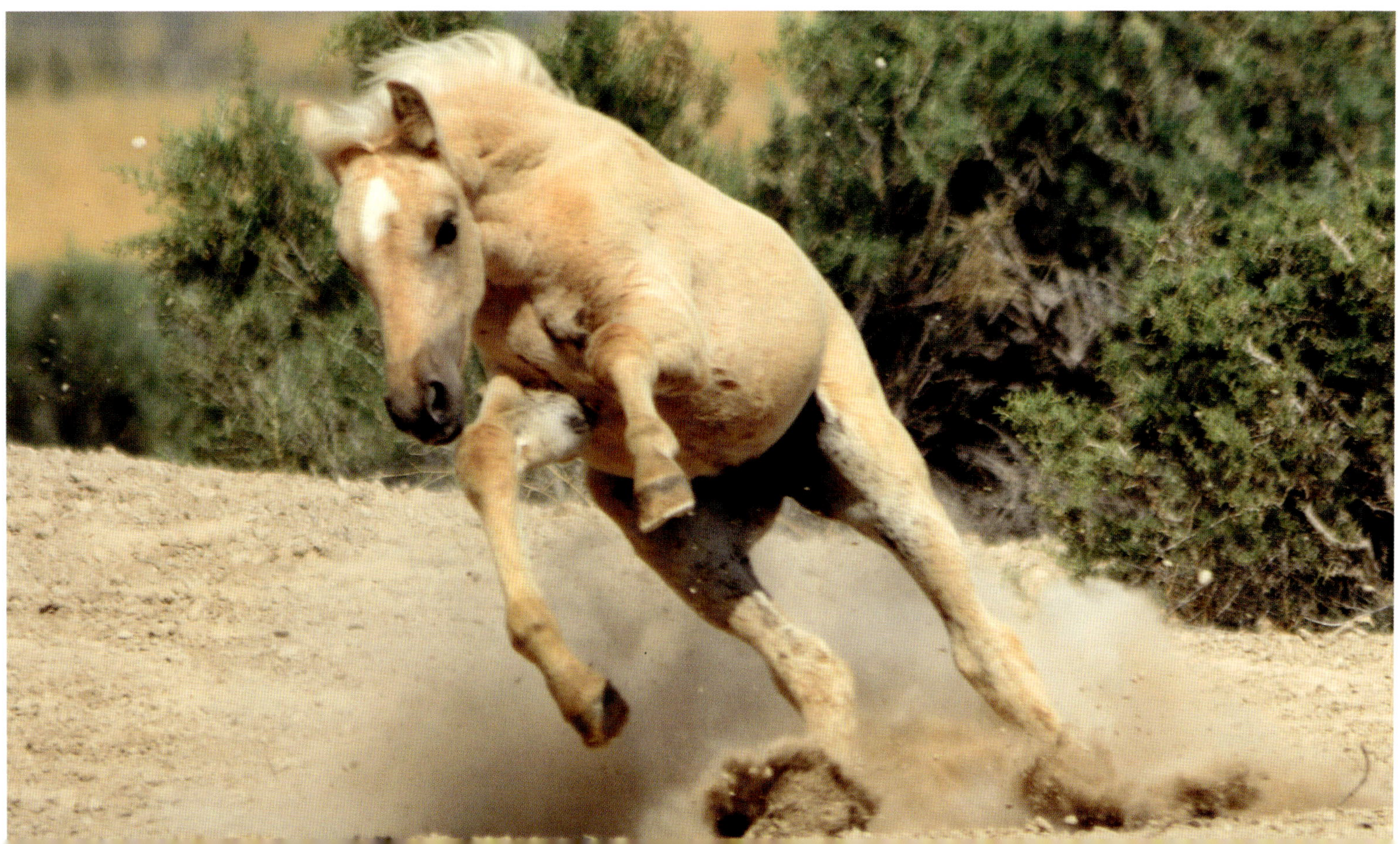

Next page left: A mare and her newborn foal travel together.

Next page right: Even at just a few days old, a wild mustang foal must be able to keep up with its mother and the rest of the band.

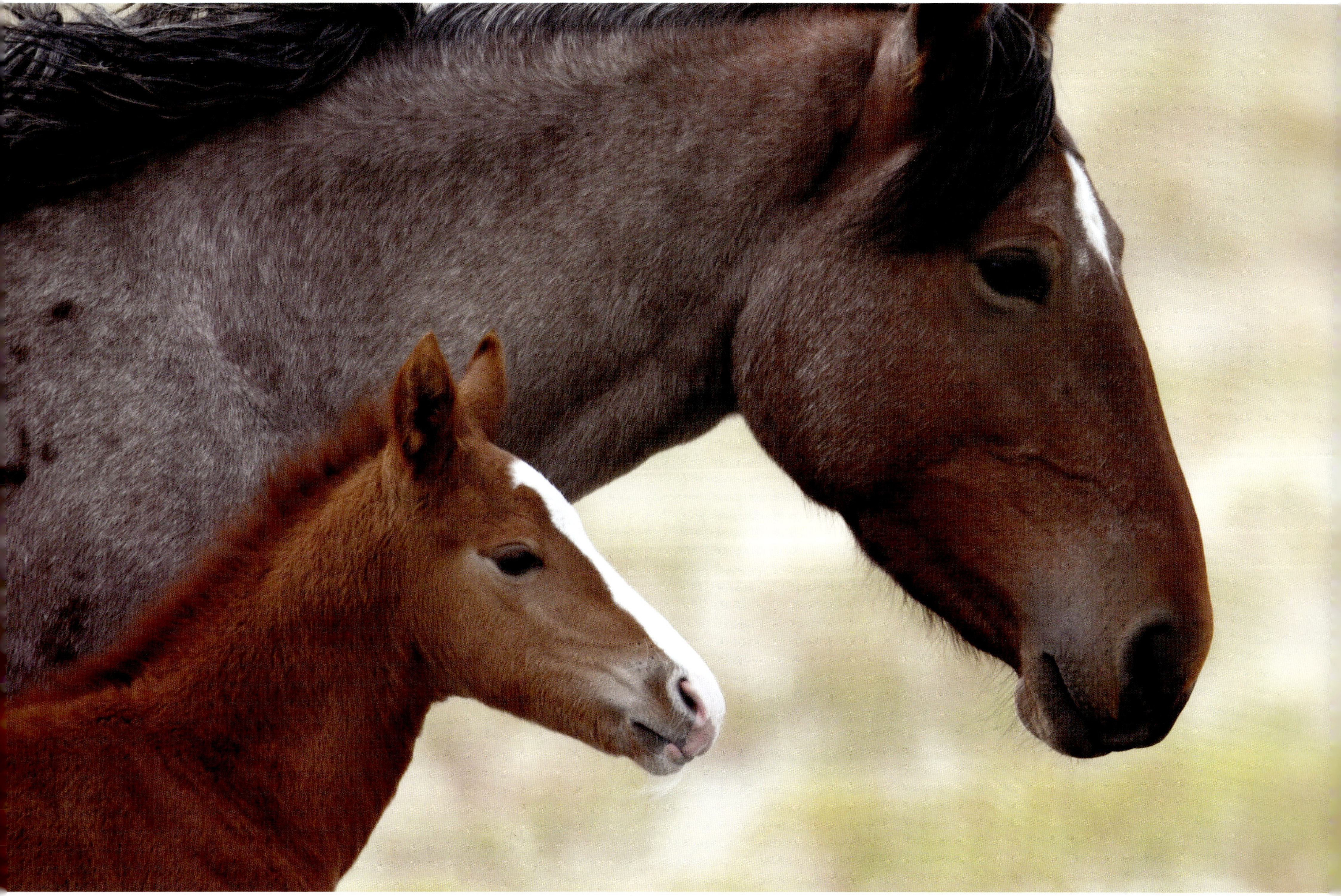

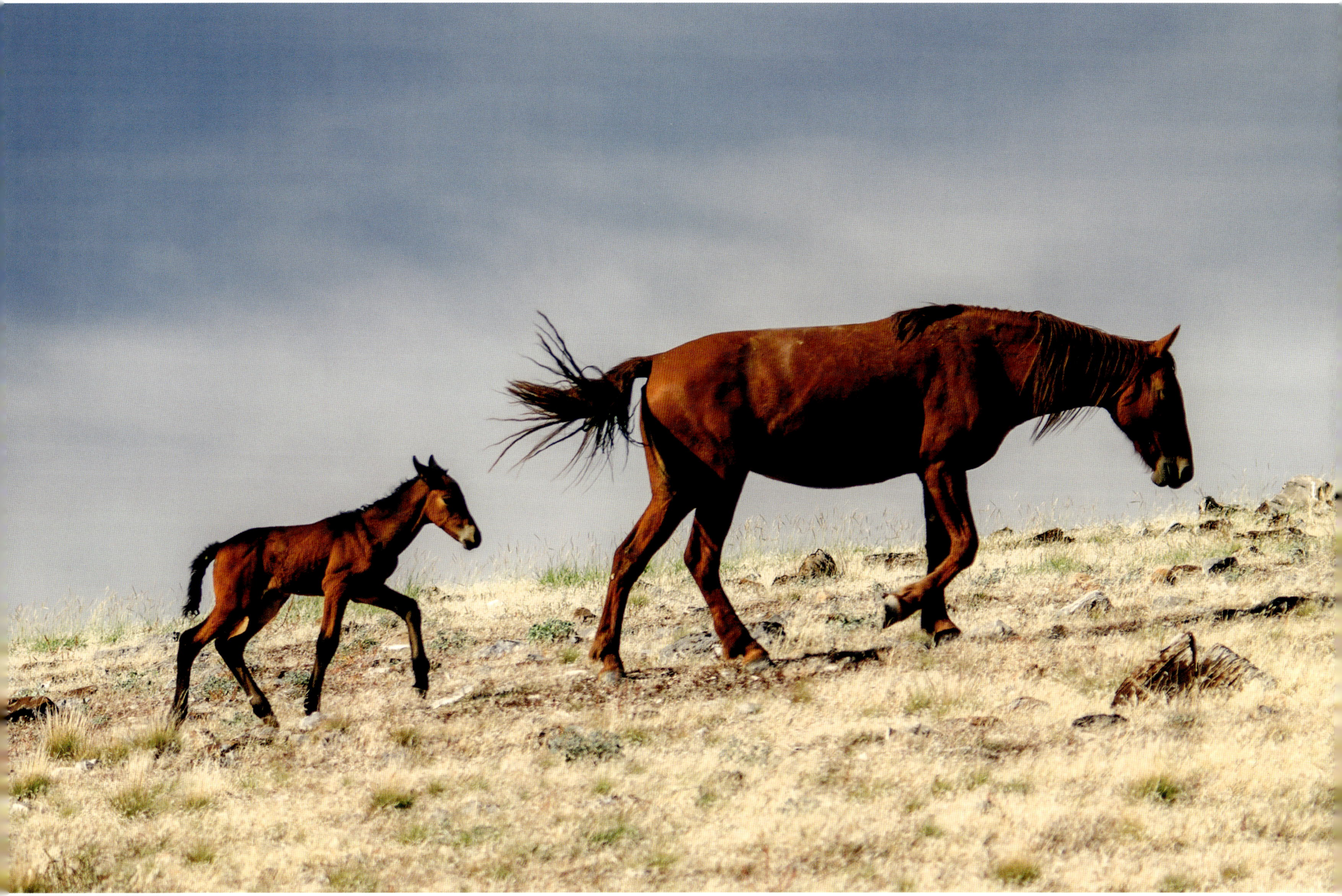

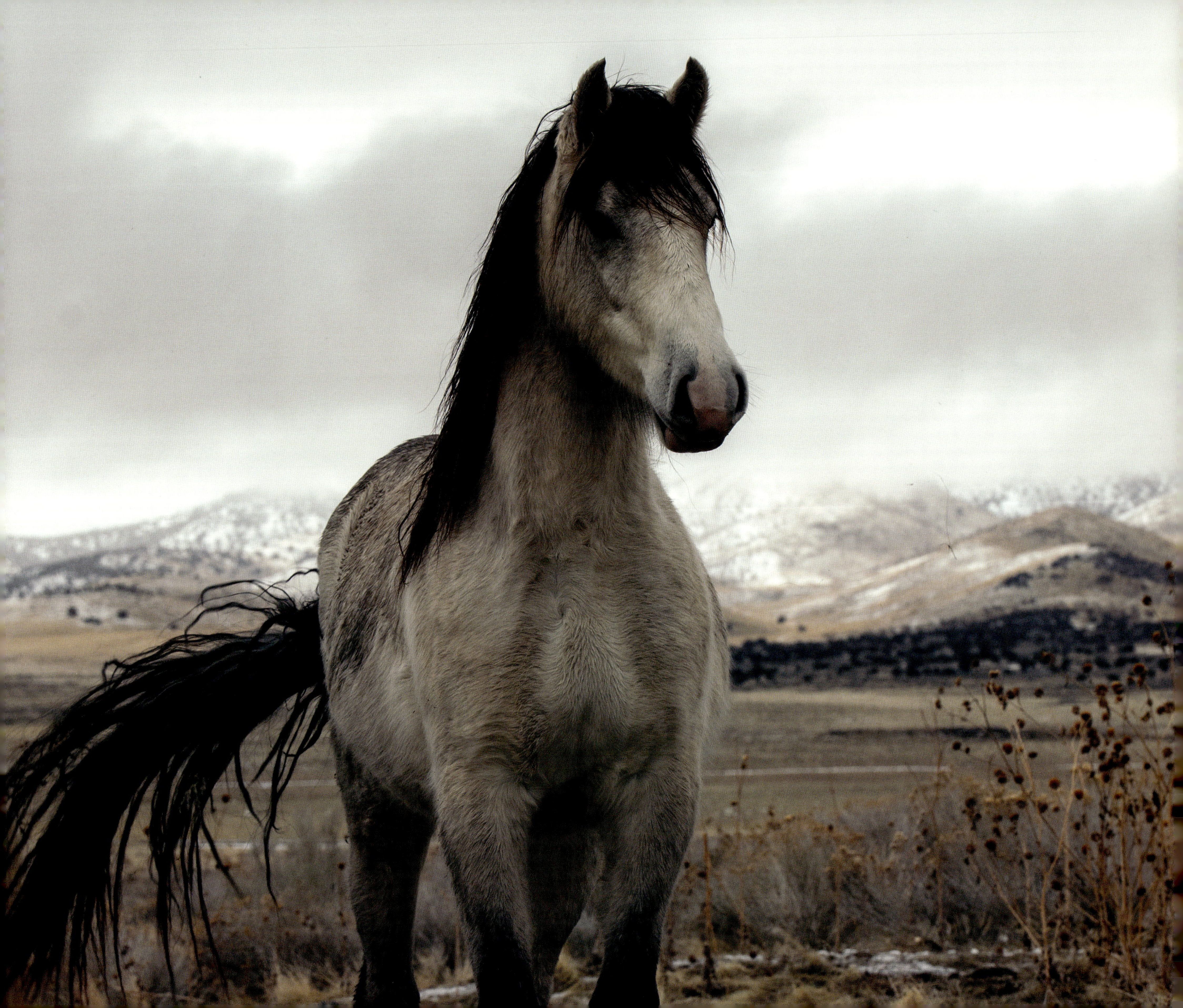

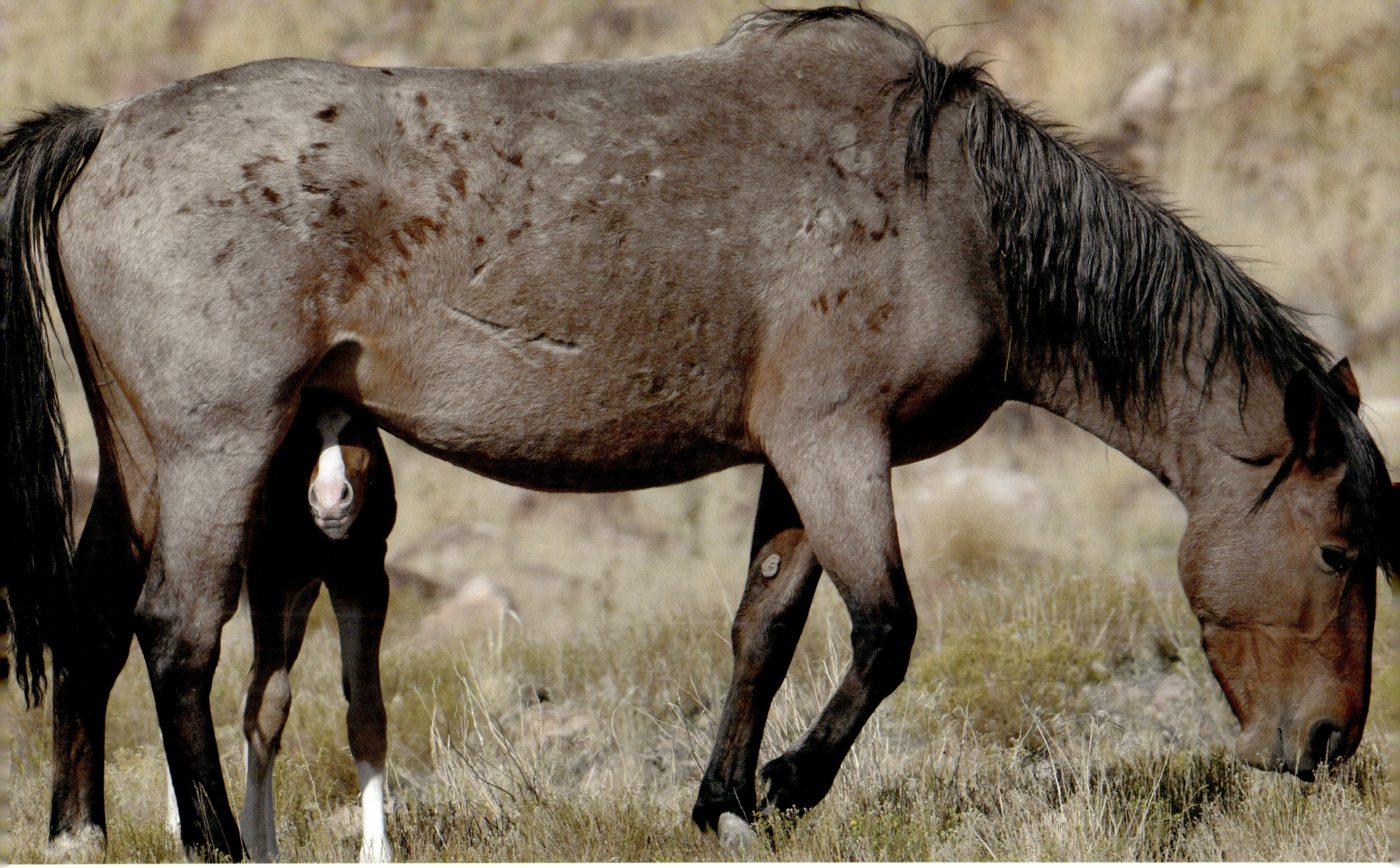

Opposite: The body language of this wild horse indicates that she is on alert: ears forward and head held high.

Above: Peek-a-boo! This mare is a color called roan.

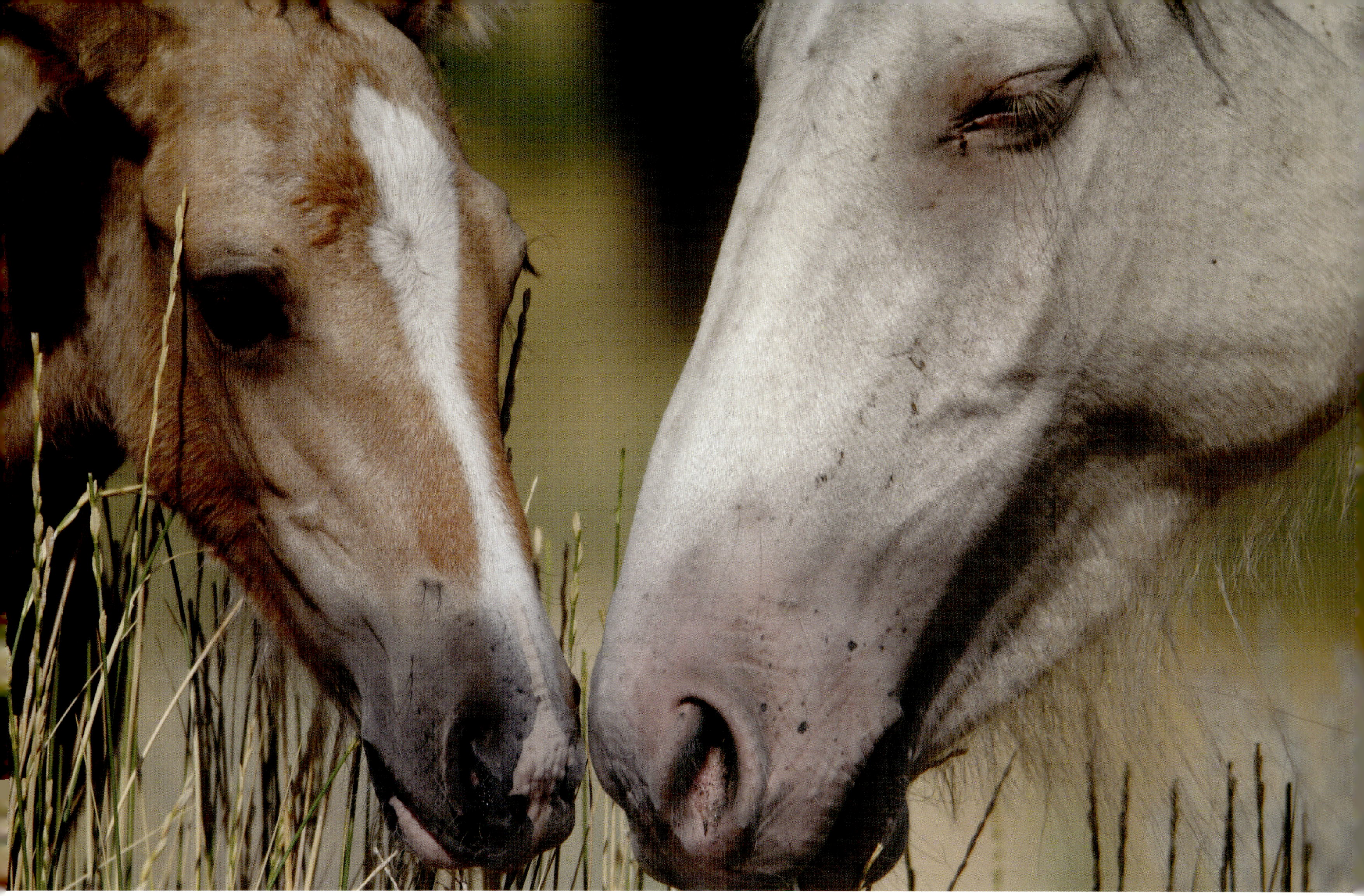

ABOVE: A cremello mare and her palomino foal enjoy some grass together.

OPPOSITE: A buckskin mare with her newborn black foal.

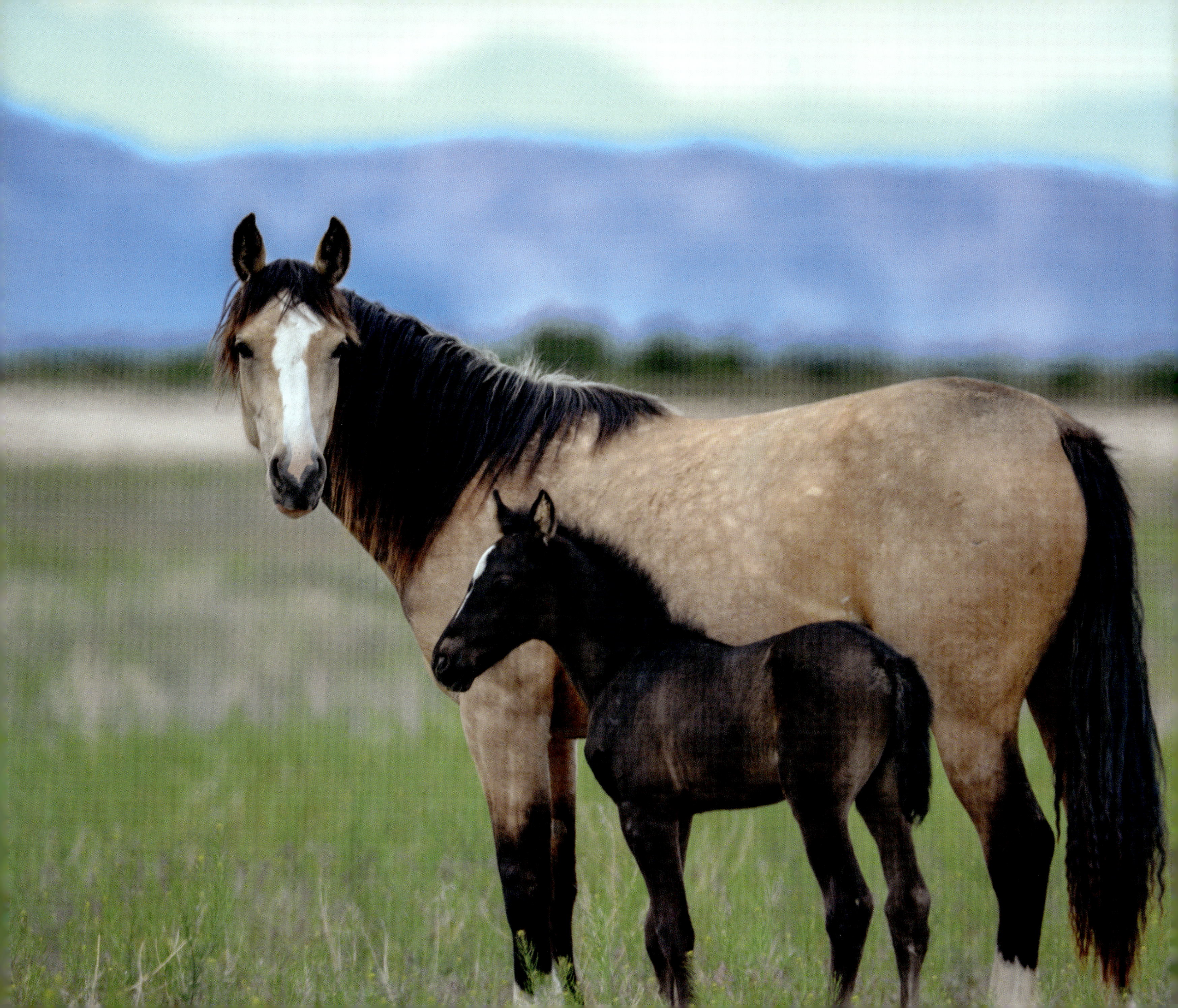

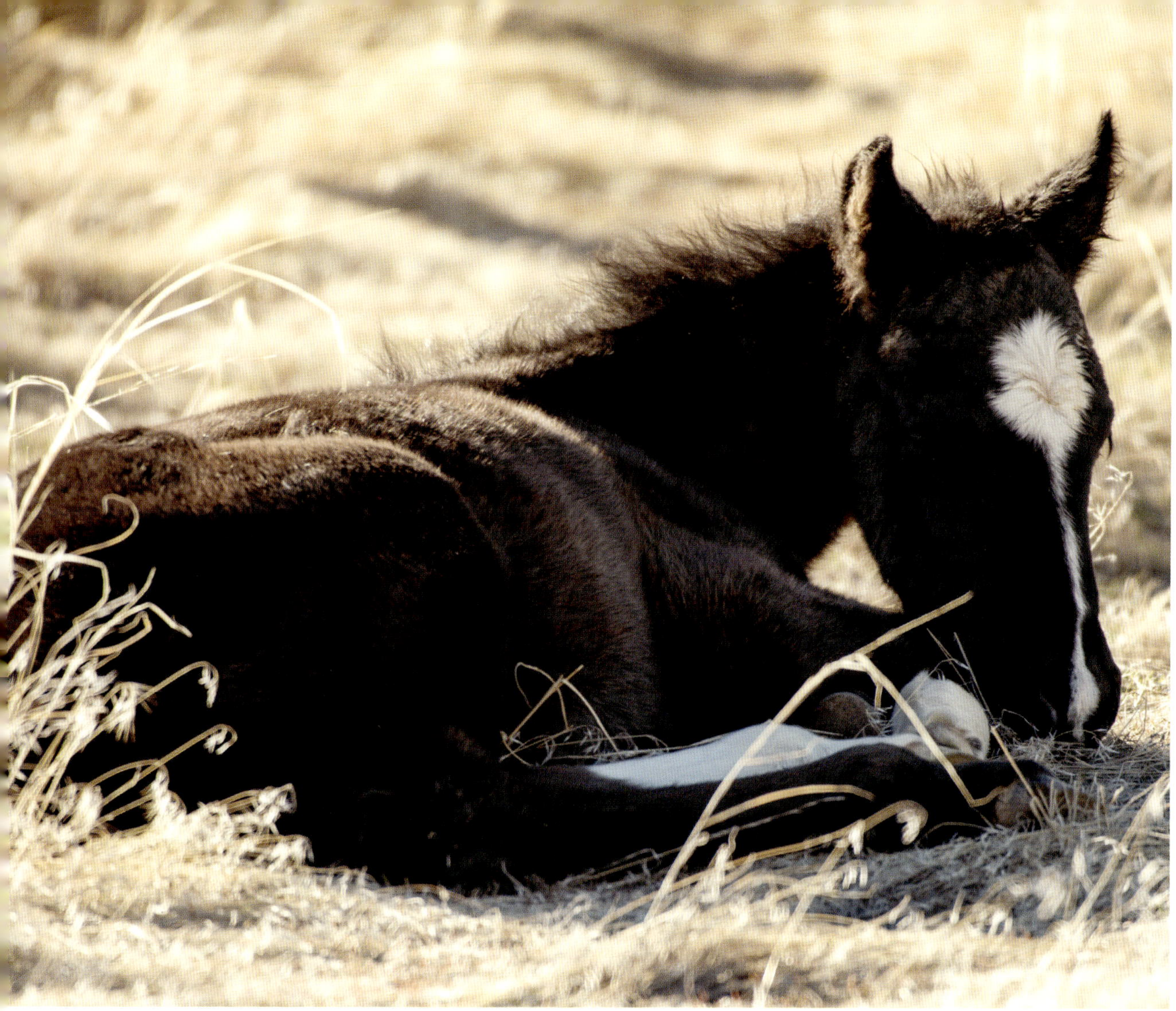

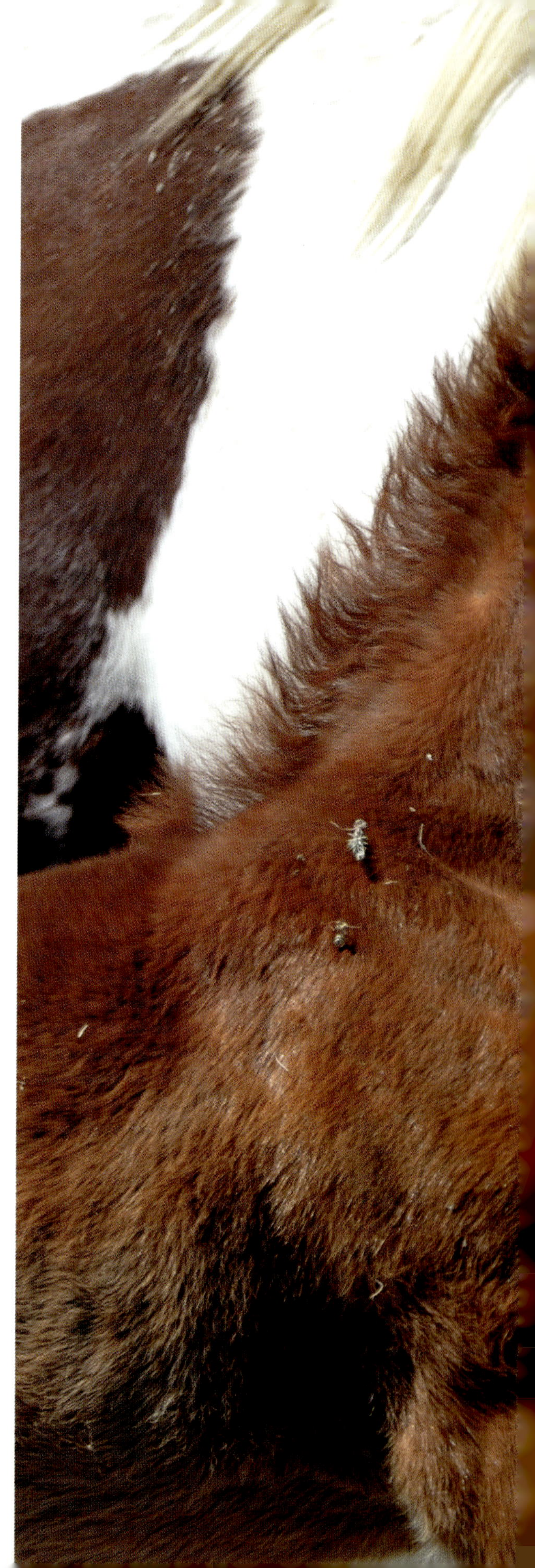

Above: A newborn colt takes a much-needed nap while the rest of his band grazes nearby.

Right: A pinto mare communicates with her foal—or it could just be that she's yawning.

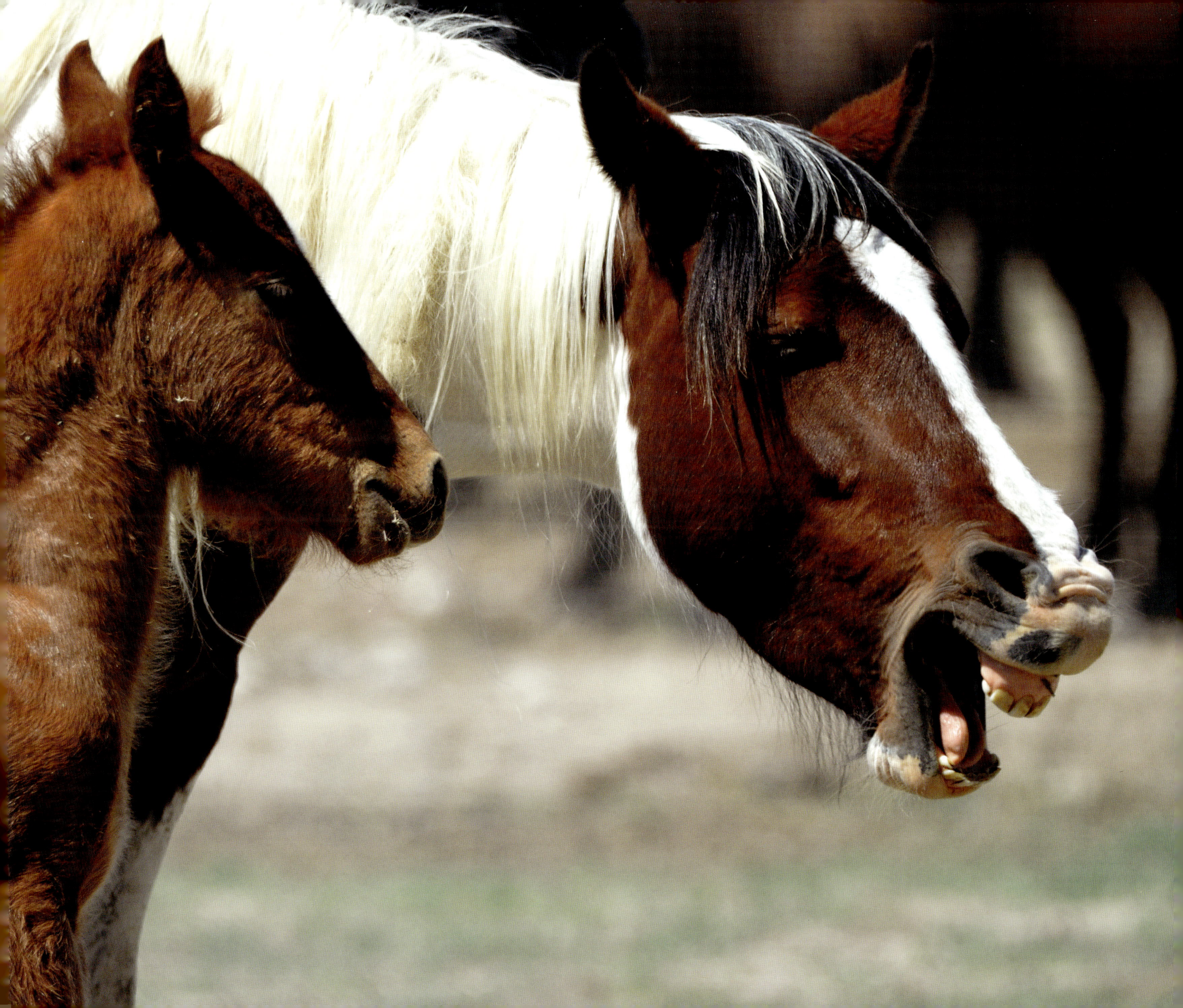

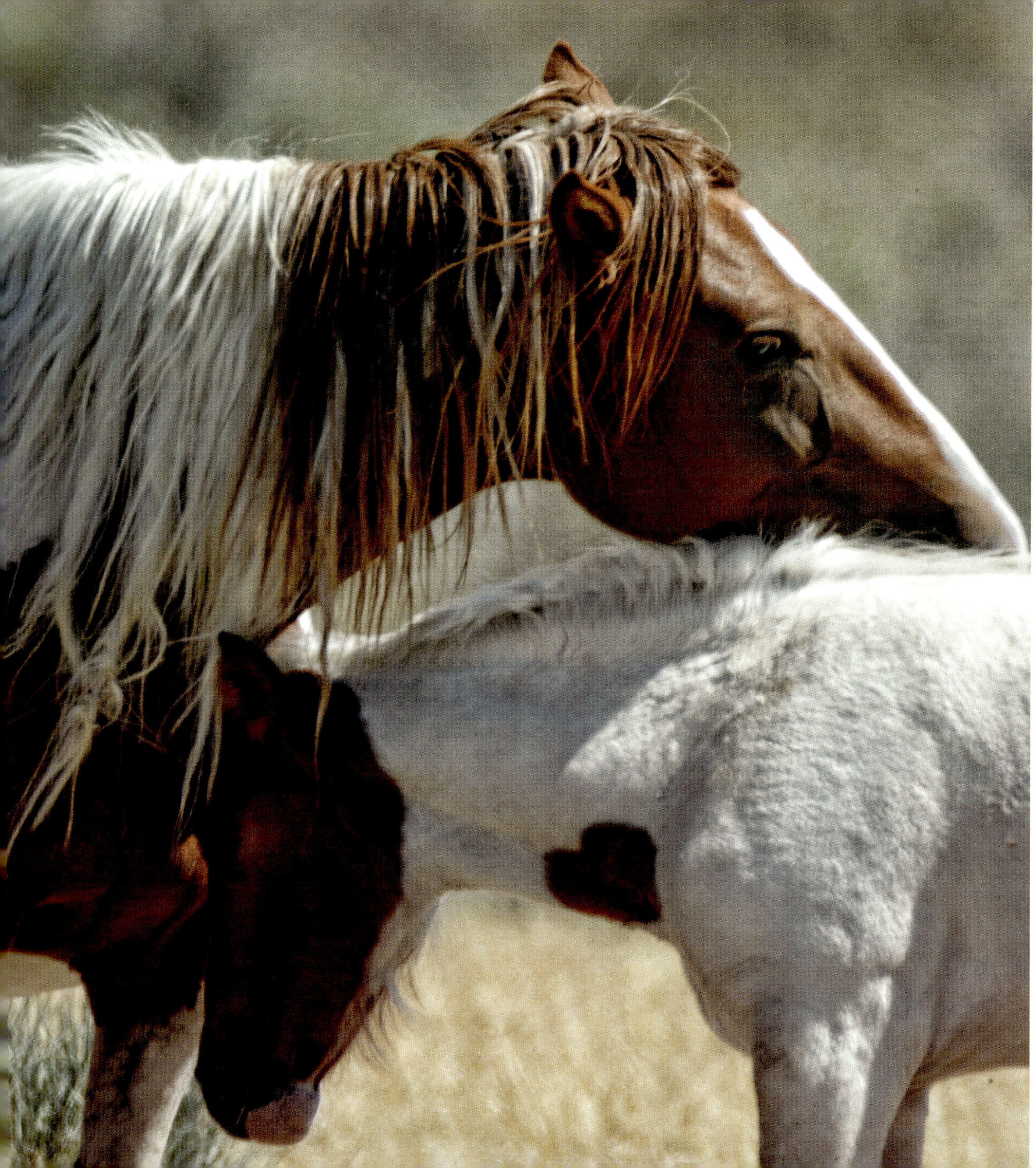

Left: The bond between a mare and her newborn foal is extremely close during the first few weeks.

Opposite: A newborn foal will seek out a drink of milk any chance it can as the band moves about grazing.

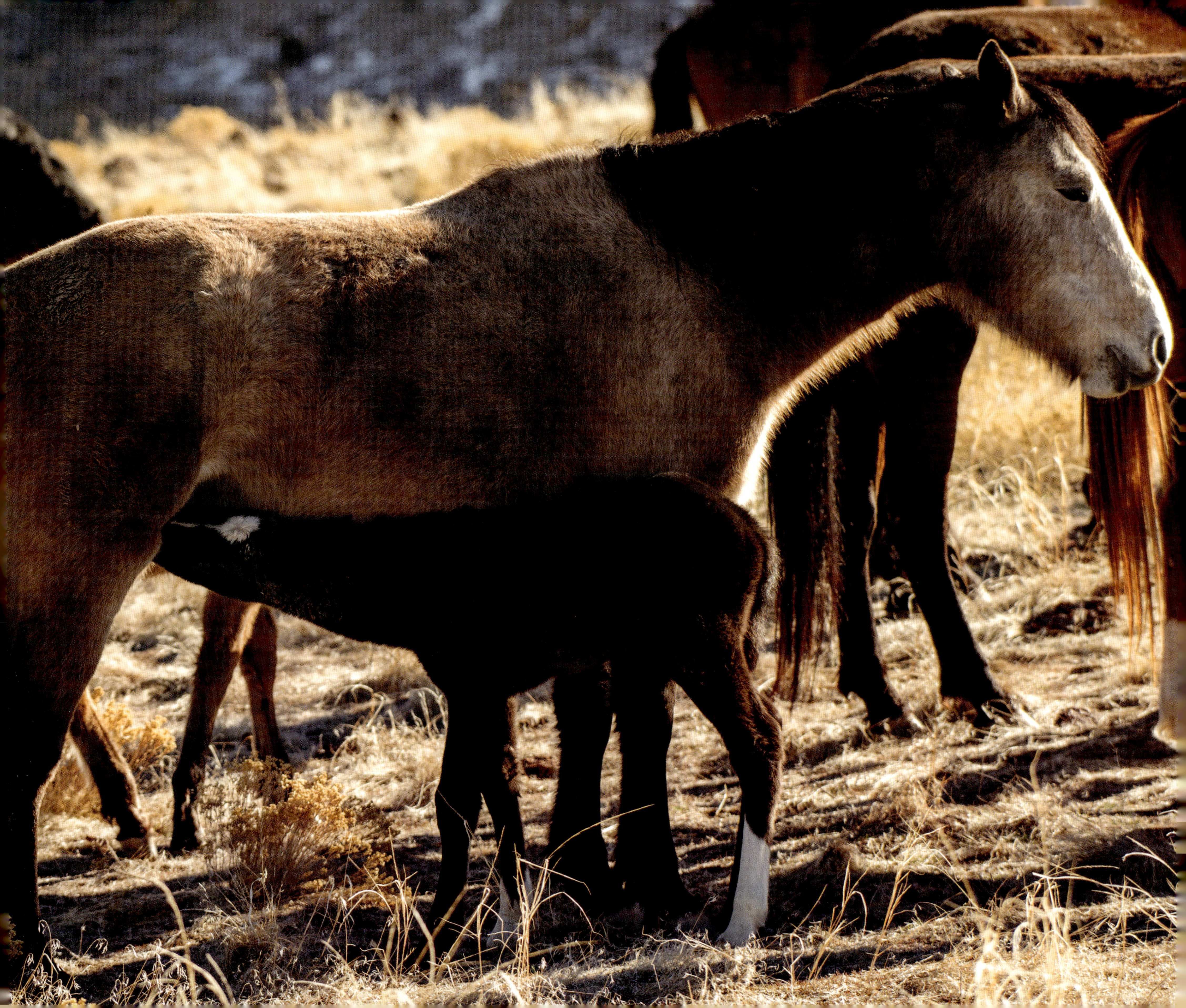

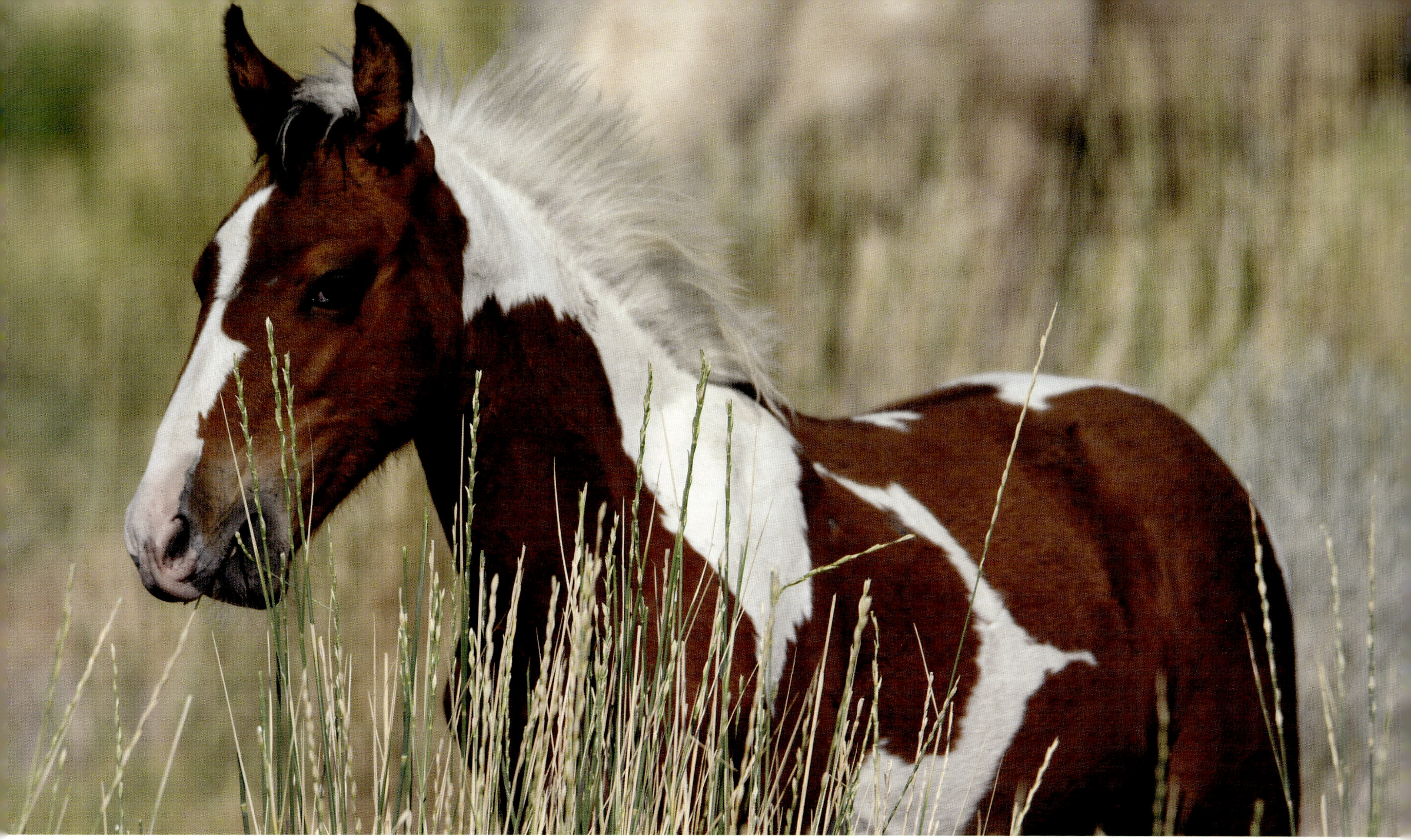

ABOVE: This pinto wild horse has a coat pattern called a tobiano (Toe-bee-ah'-no). The tobiano horse appears to be white with large spots of color overlapping the white.

OPPOSITE: If you watch a newborn colt for a while, he will always provide one adorable photo as he interacts with his mom.

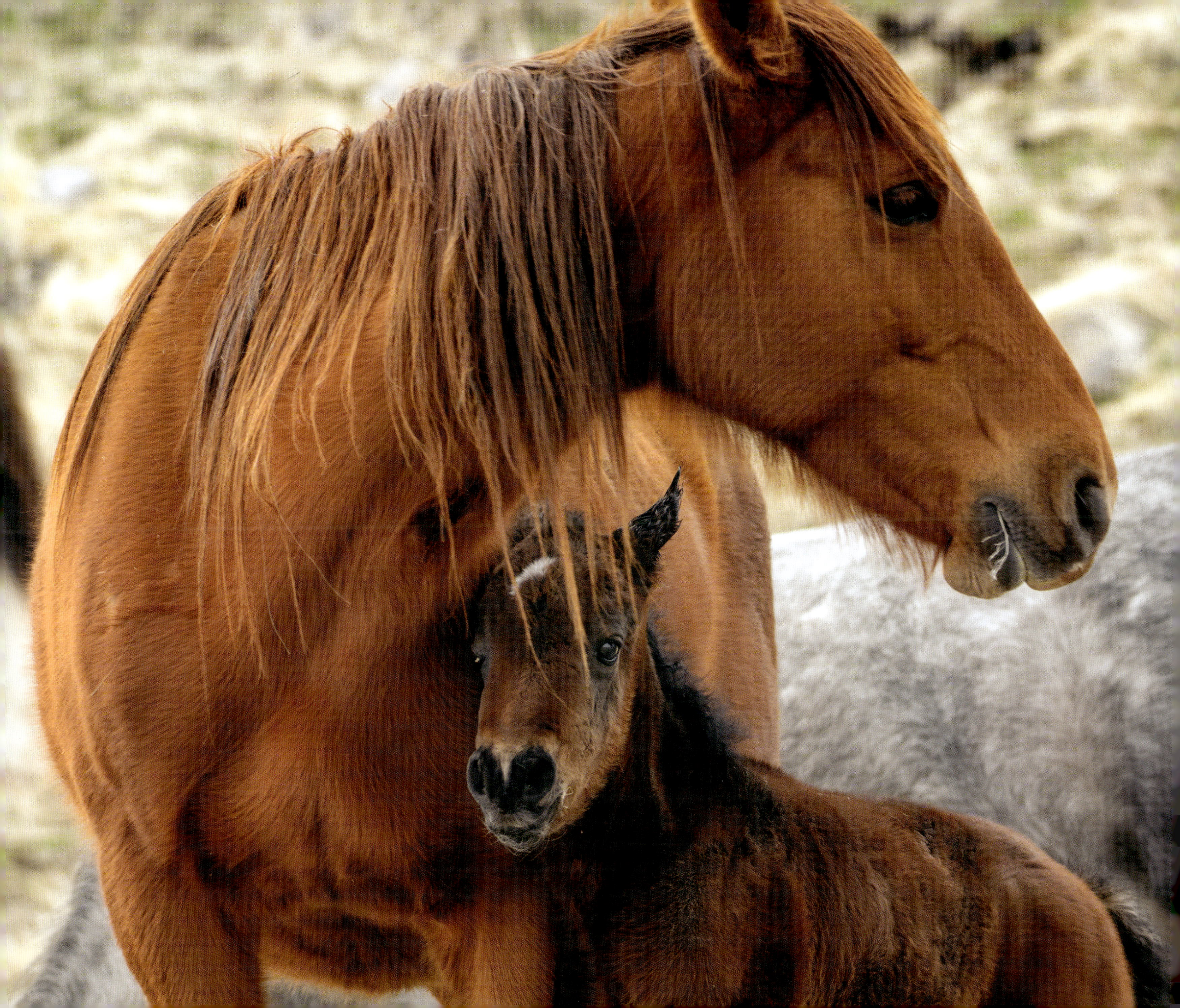

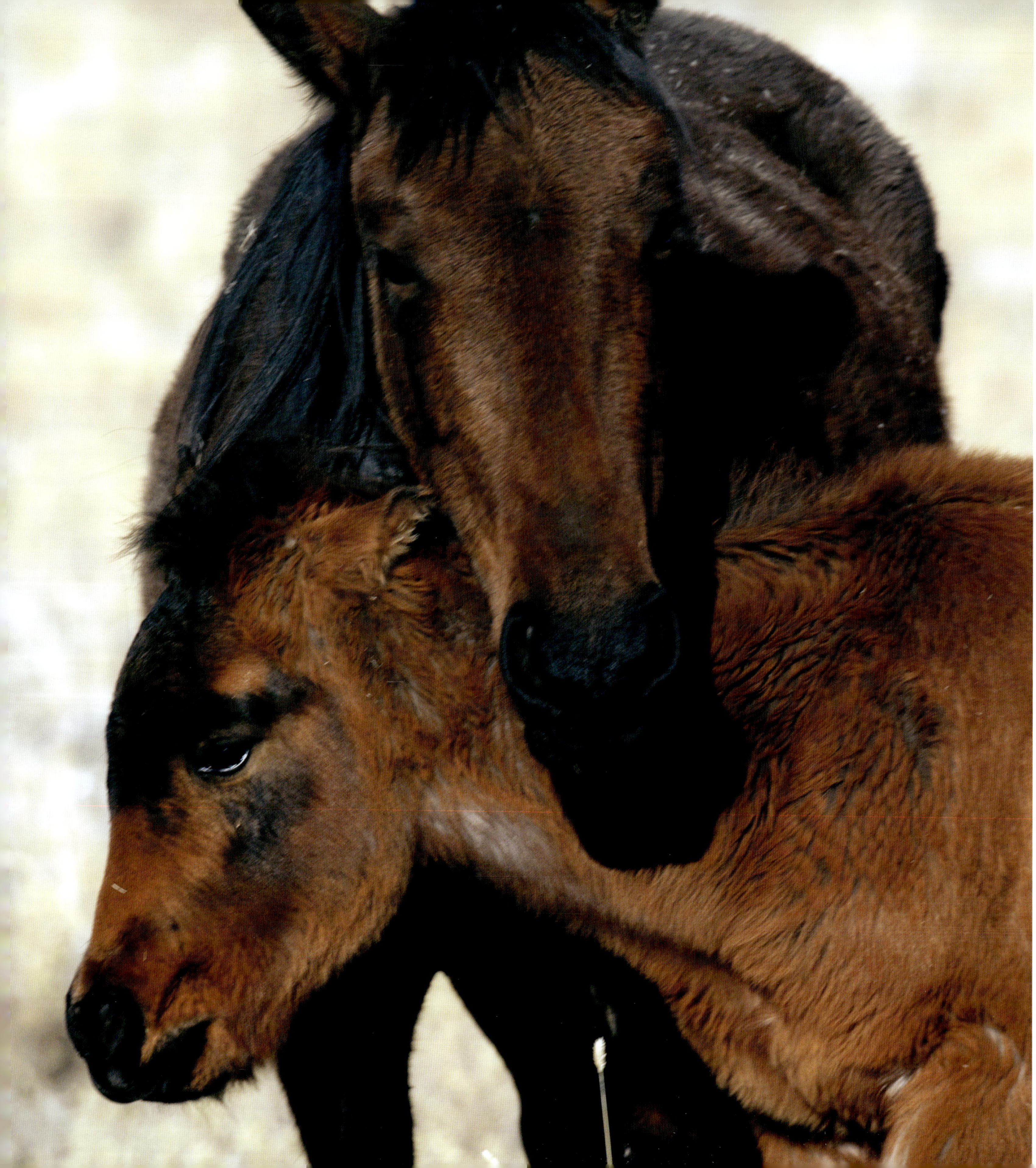

Left and opposite: This newborn foal has a coat color called chestnut, but you can see darker patches of hair coming in and the black points on its nose and mane. This horse will eventually have a bay coat color like its mom.

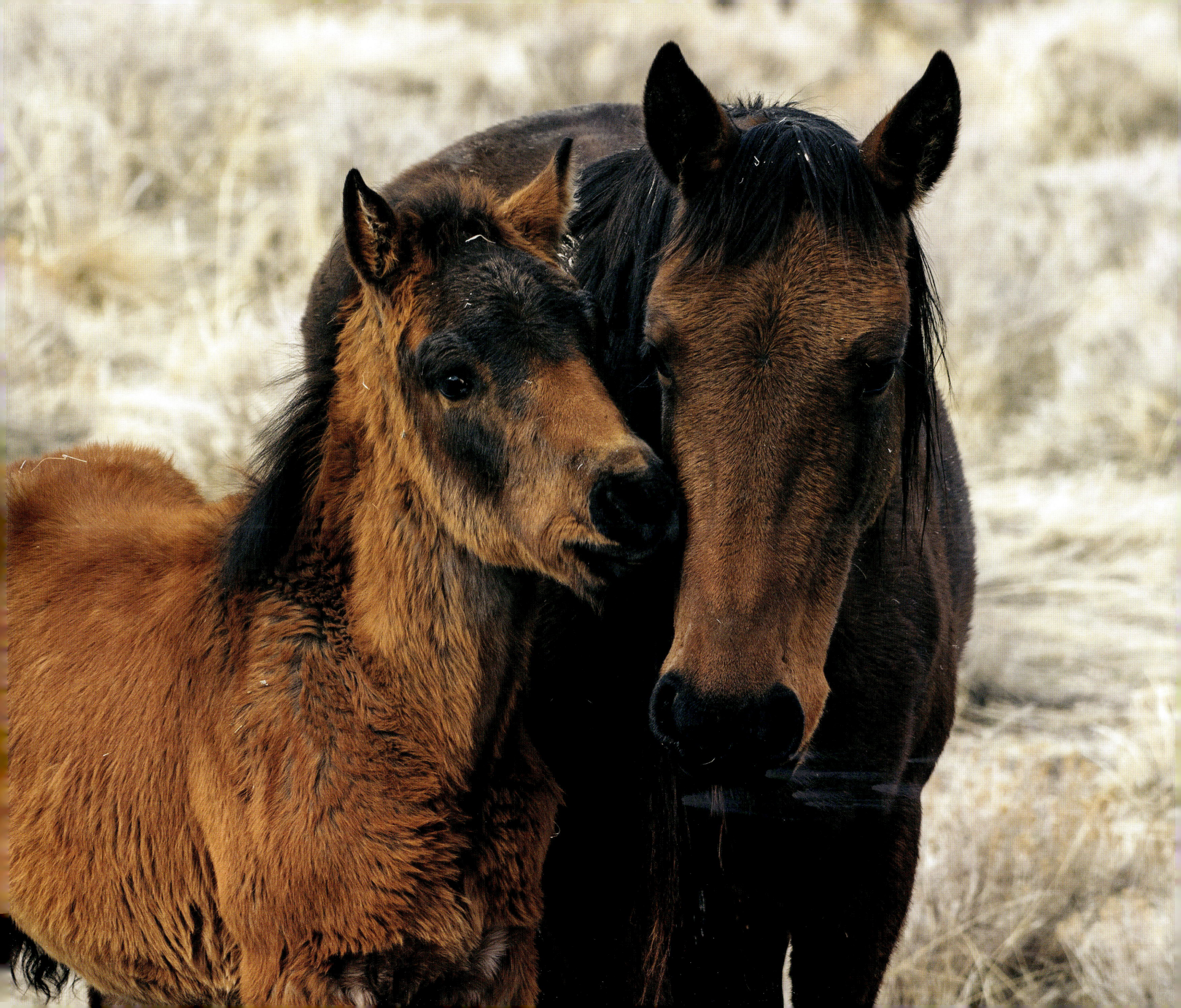

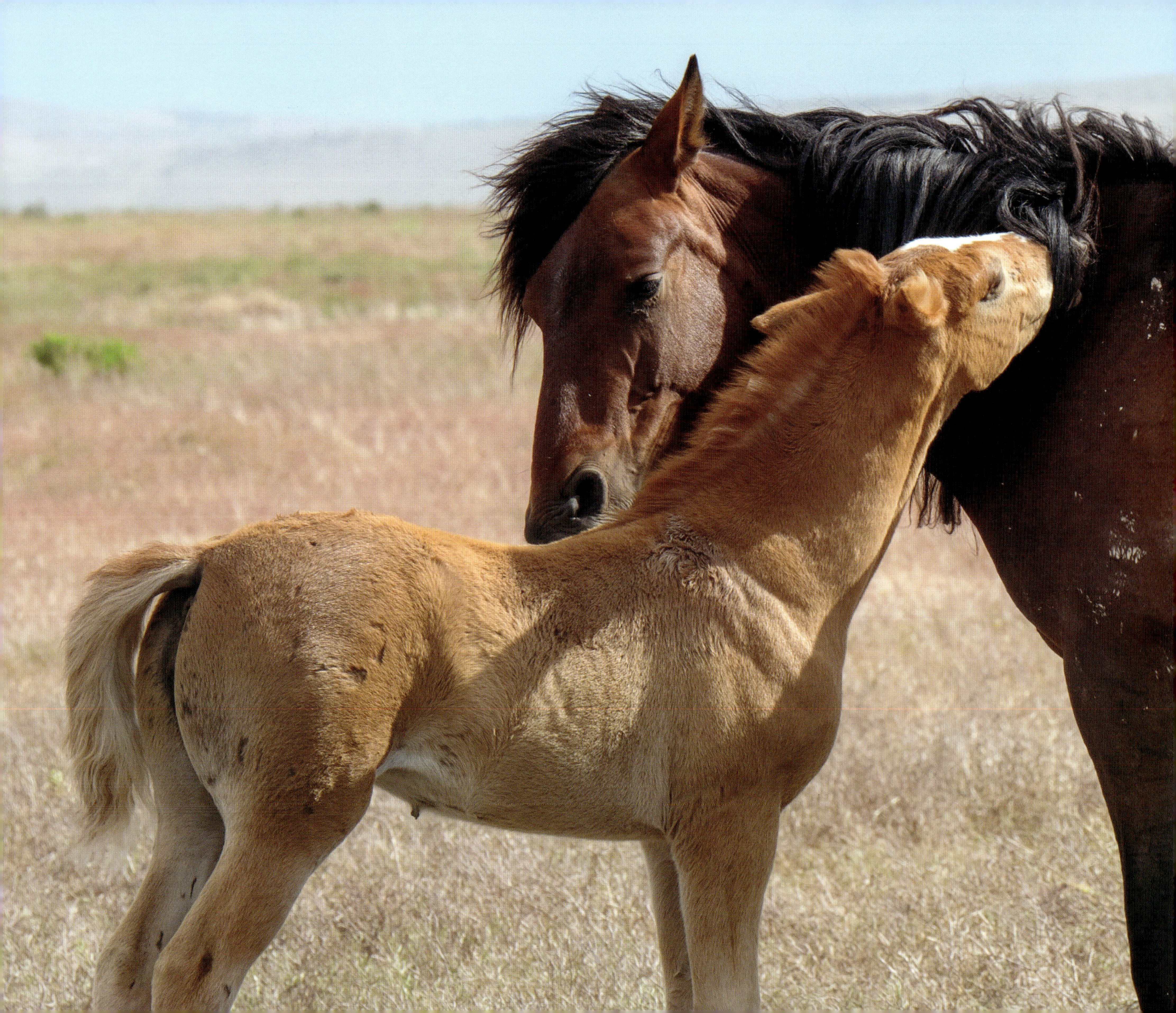

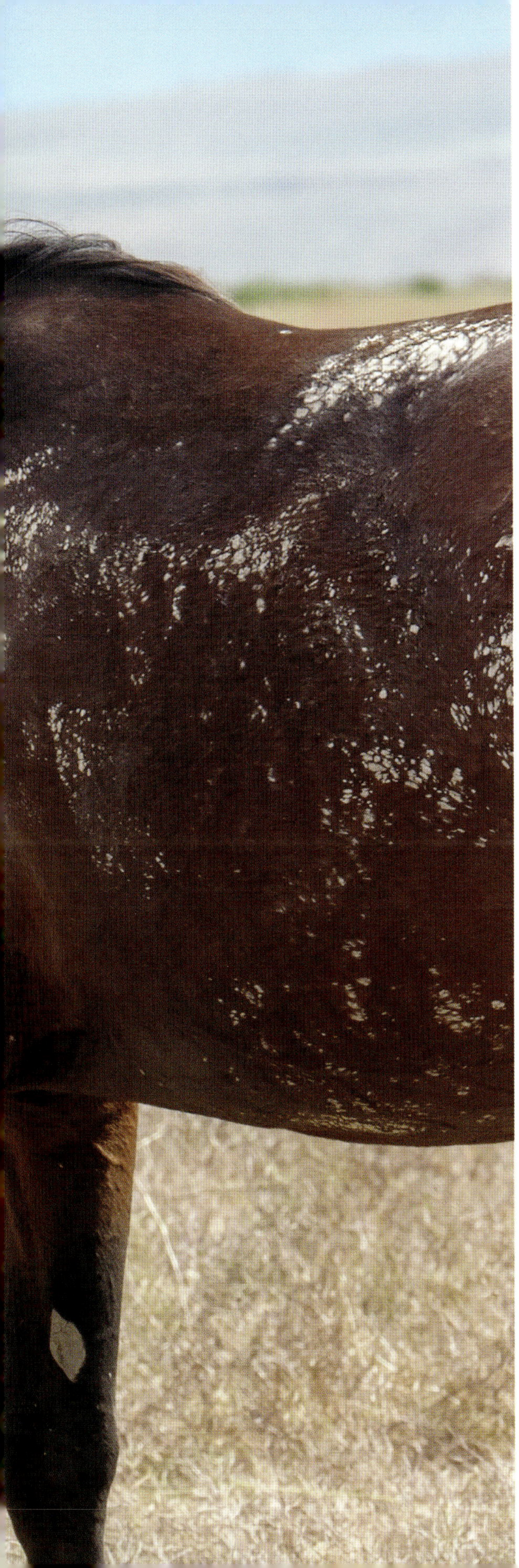

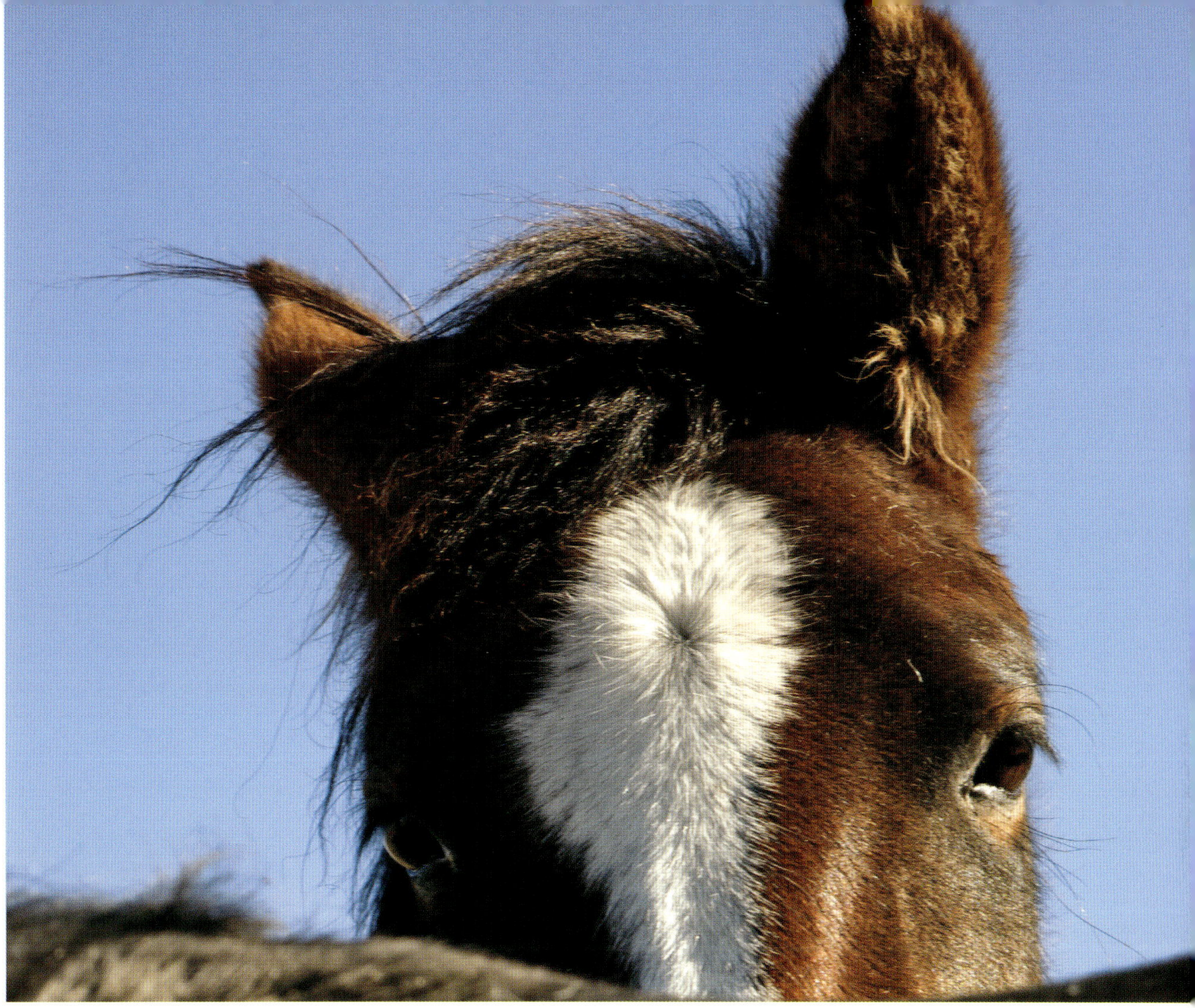

LEFT: A mare and foal groom one another.

ABOVE: A wild horse's ears can tell you a lot about what they are thinking. This horse has its left ear toward me (listening to what I am doing); the right ear is turned toward the rest of the herd, maintaining awareness of their location and movements.

NEXT PAGE: The white of a horse's face is referred to as markings; the star and strip patterns are shown here.

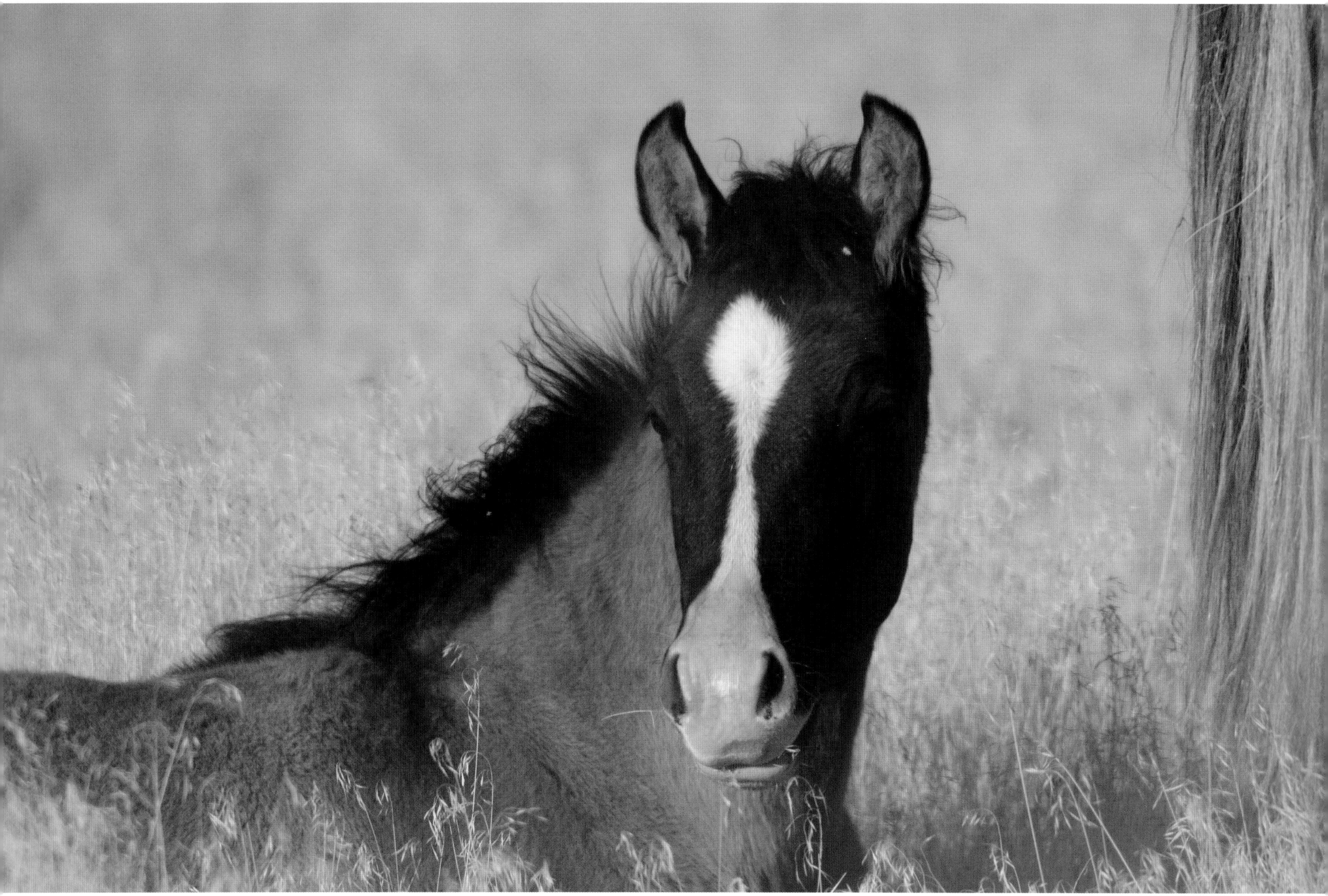

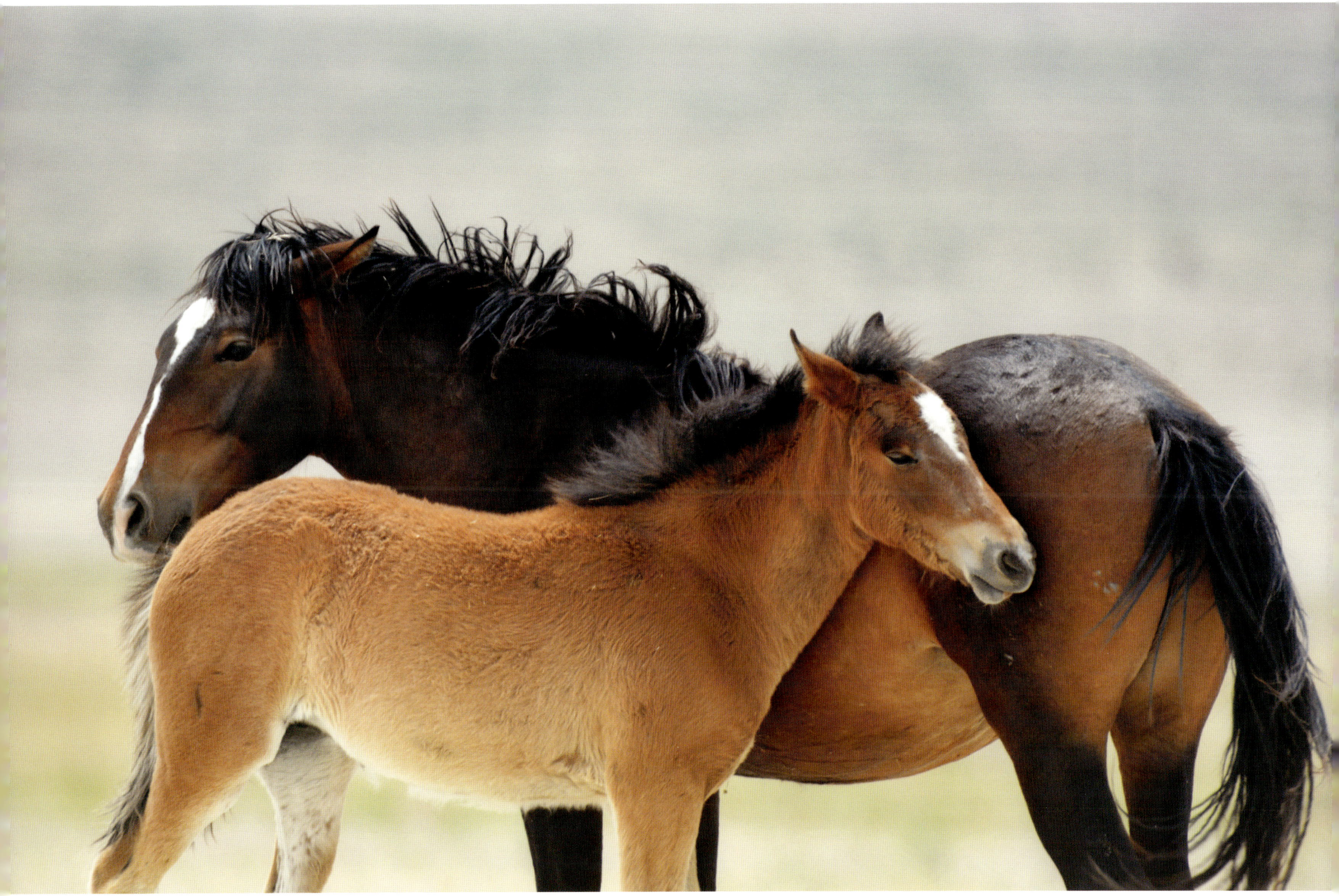

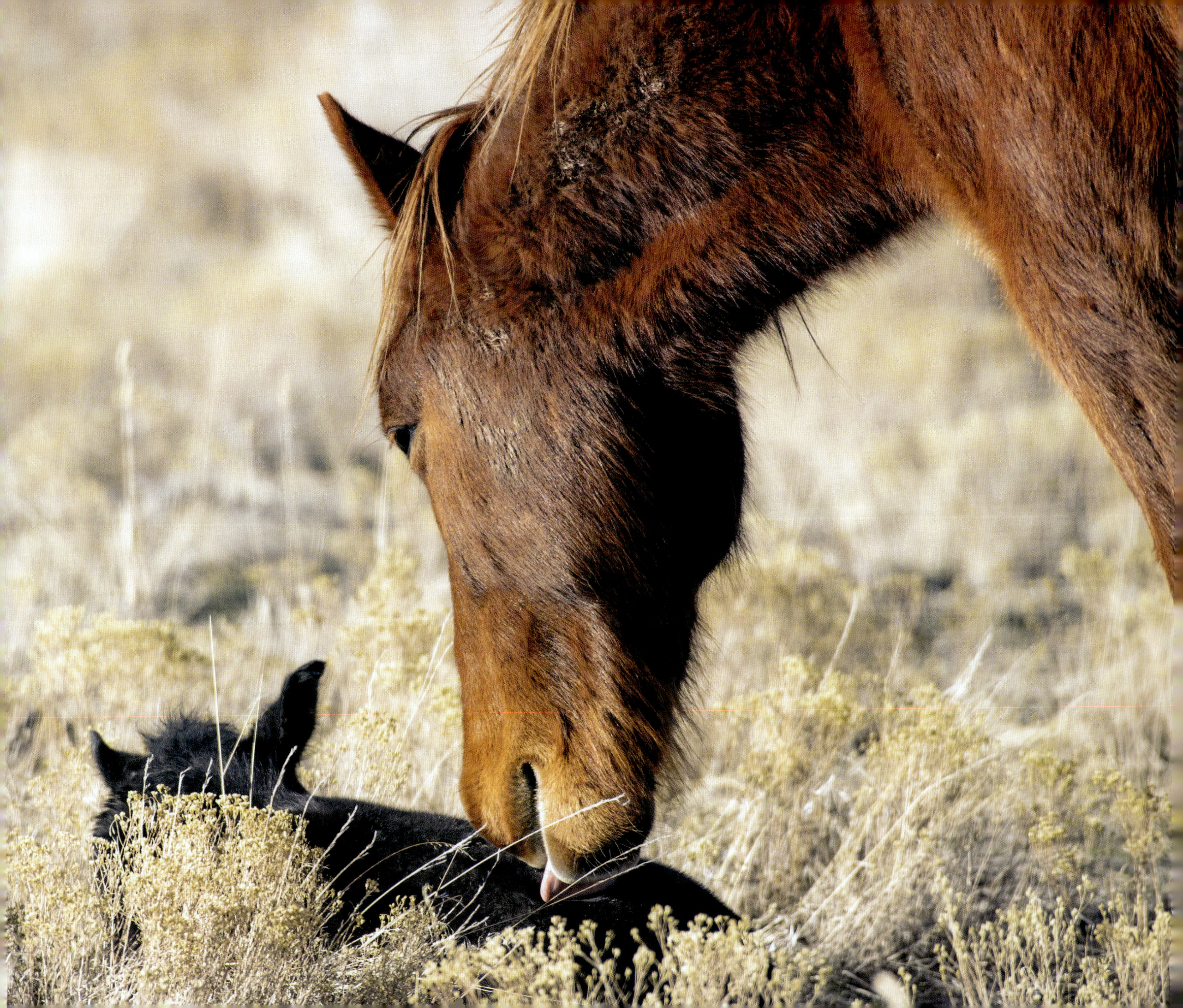

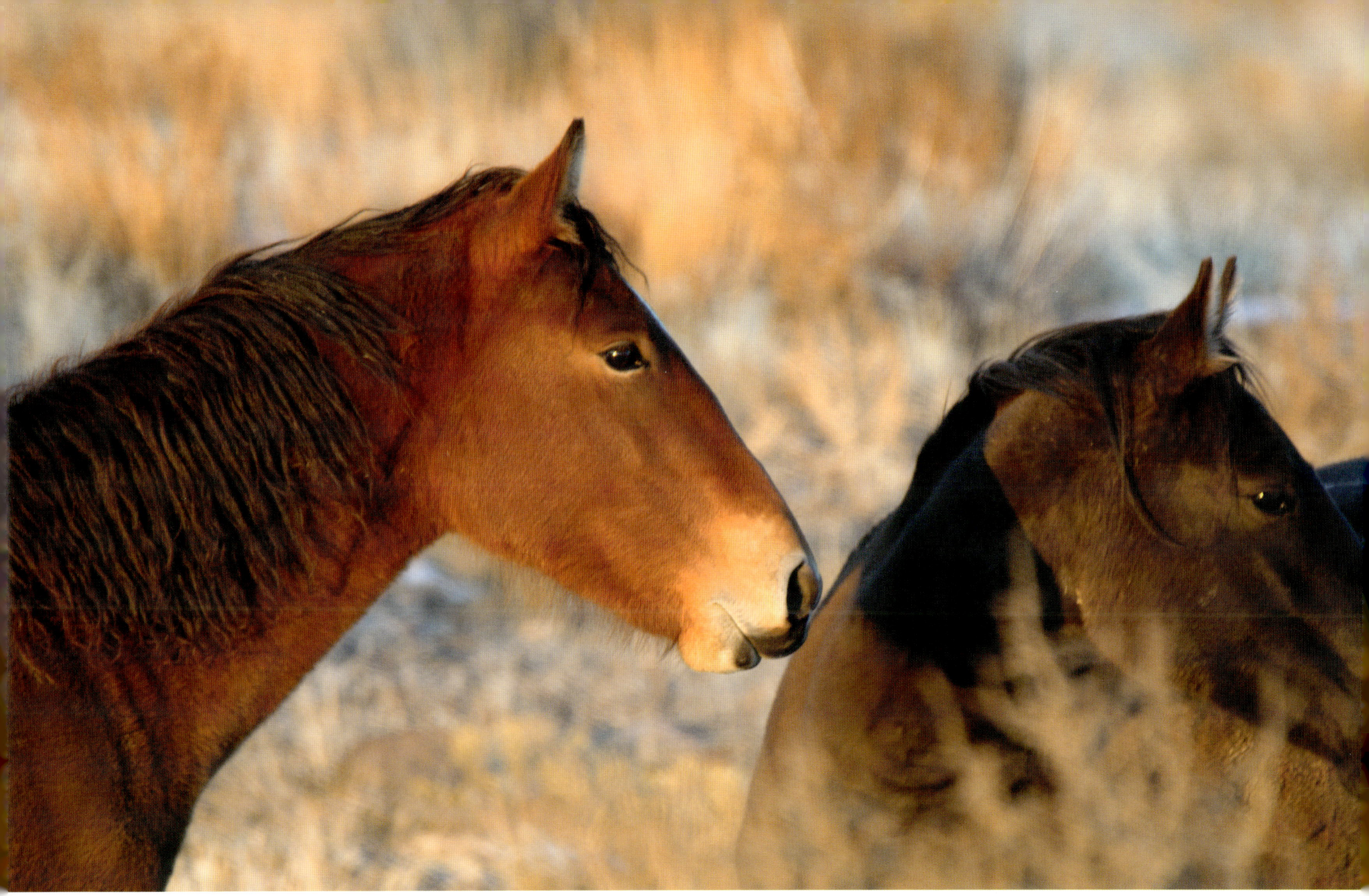

OPPOSITE AND ABOVE: The winter's evening sunlight makes for stunning photographs of the wild horses.

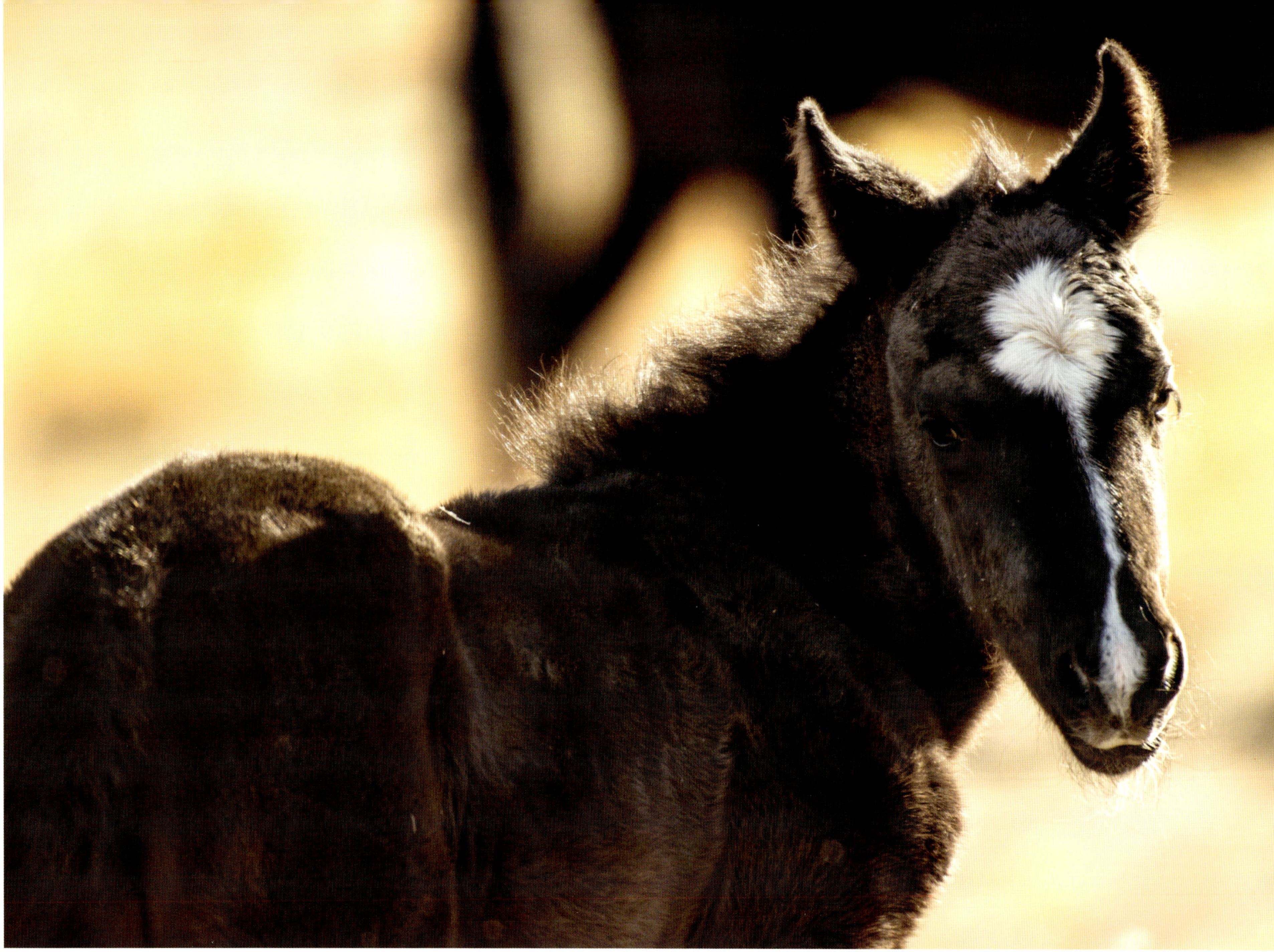

ABOVE: Newborn foals have longer and more whiskers on their noses than more mature horses. It is believed that they help guide the newborn to their mother's teats.

OPPOSITE: Something has caught the attention of these two young colts.

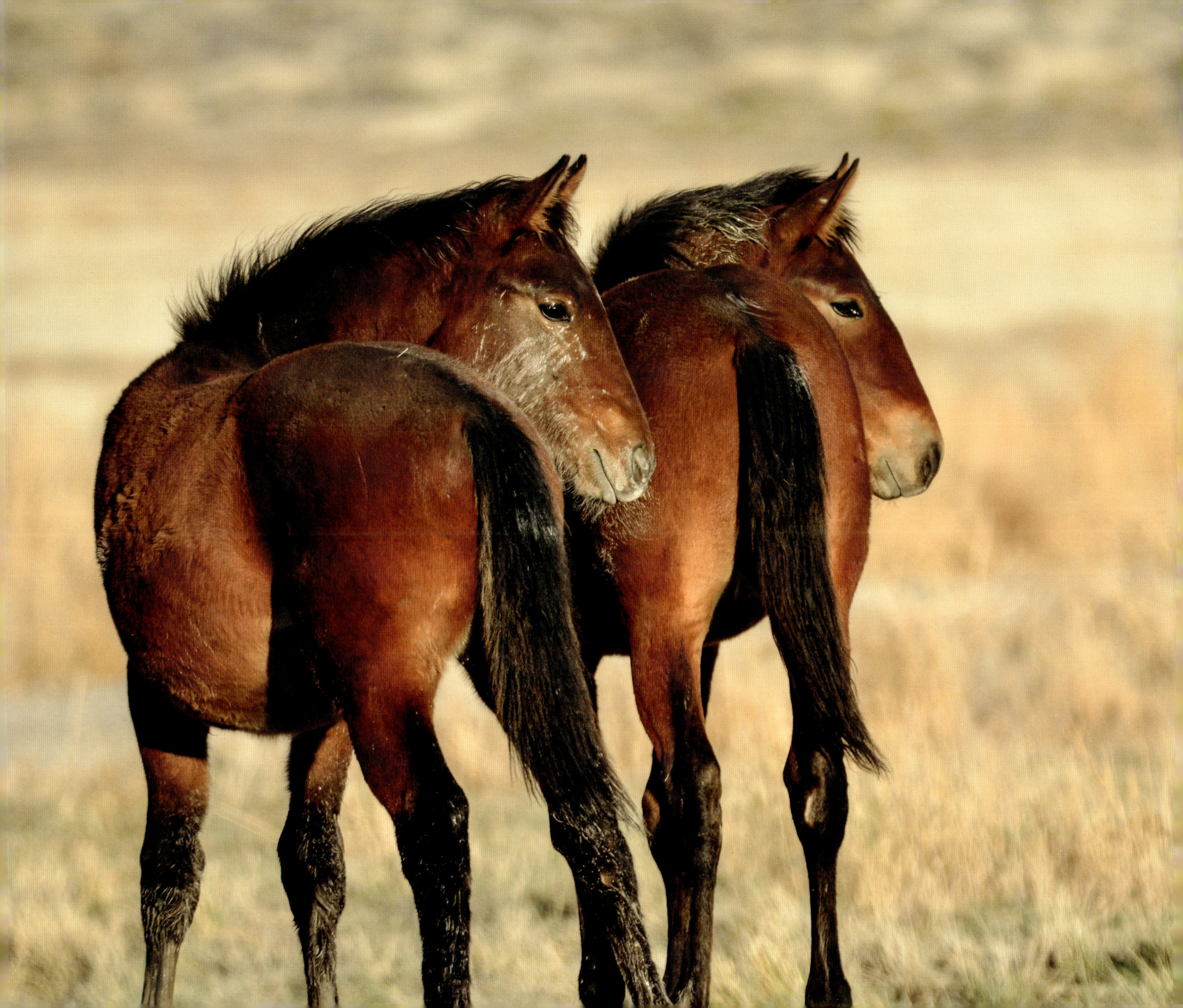

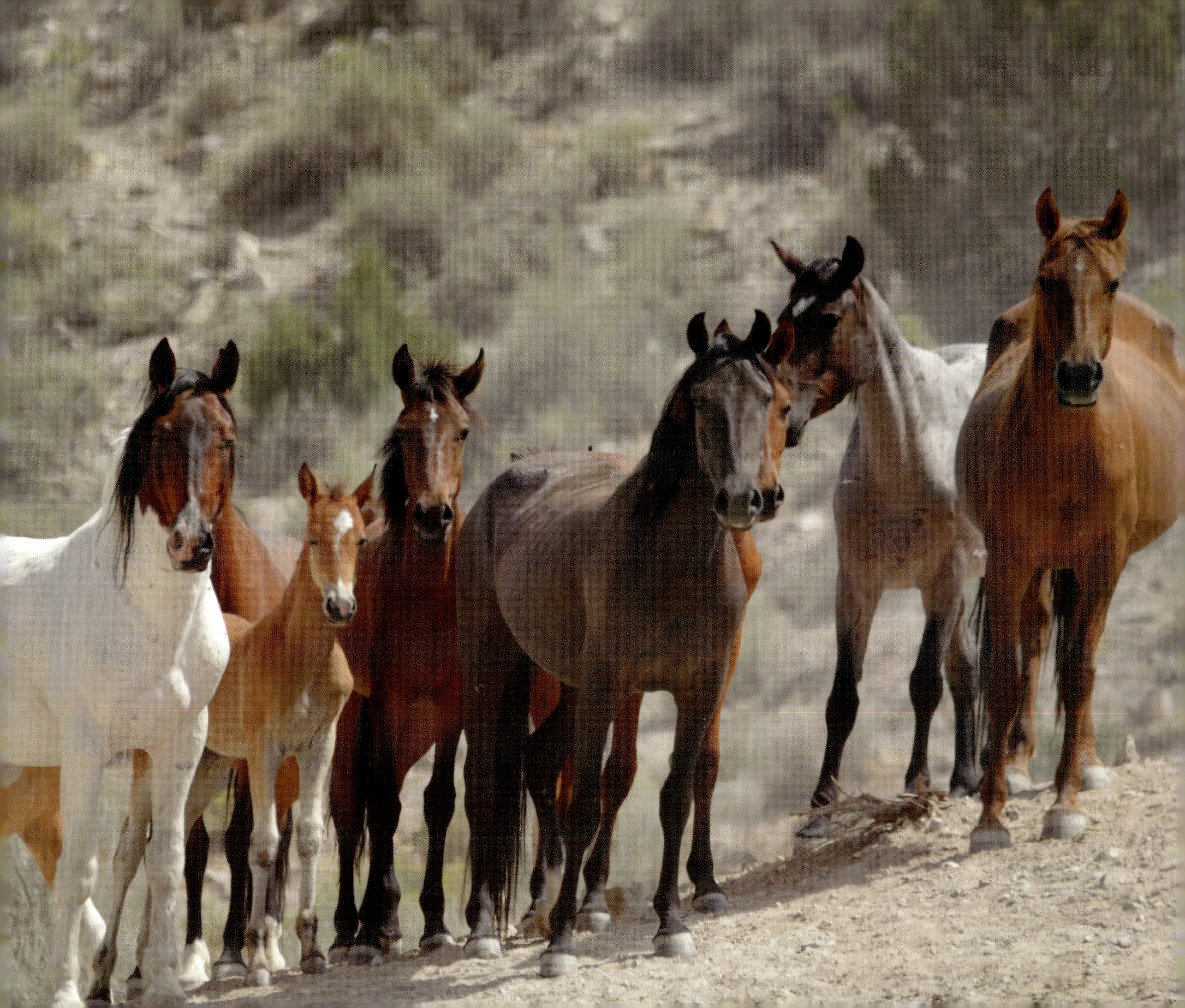

CEDAR MOUNTAIN MUSTANGS

♦ ♦ ♦

The Cedar Mountain range in Utah has been home to the Cedar Mountain herd since the 1800s. Like most wild horse herds, these roaming horses descended from domestic stock: remounts and horses from ranchers, pioneers crossing the plains, and the Salt Lake Valley station of the US Army were turned out onto the range, eventually becoming the herd that graces these lands today. Photographing these majestic horses can be a challenge—if they see a human or a vehicle before you catch a glimpse, they disappear. Years of following them and learning their habits of foraging, a sum of patience, and a whole lot of luck have let me come away with some breathtaking photographs. The Cedar Mountain herd is the most colorful herd of horses in the West. Watching this herd thunder across the plains in a range of roans, pintos, palominos, grays, sorrels, and bays is a humbling reminder of nature's paintbrush and the beauty of wild steeds.

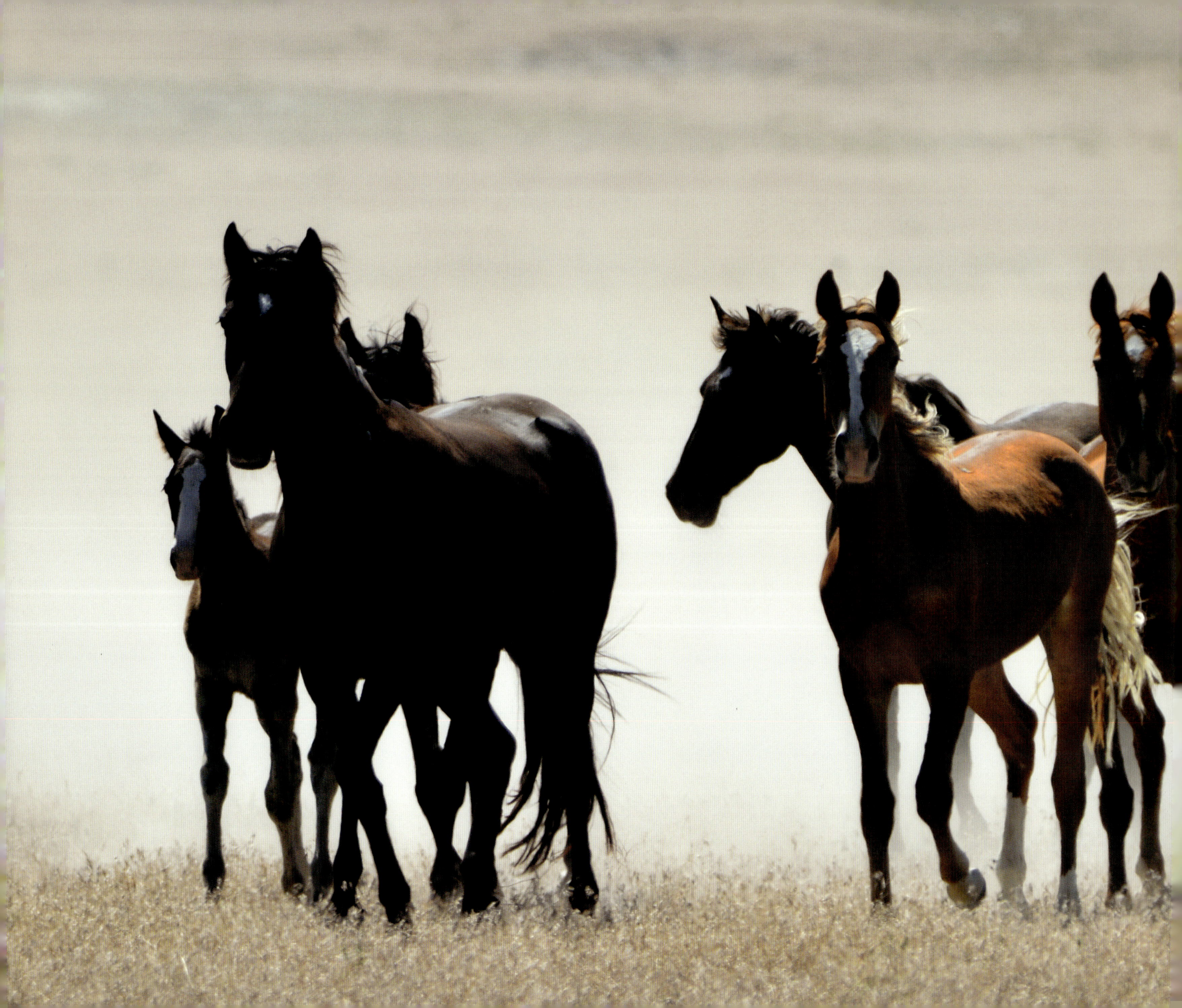

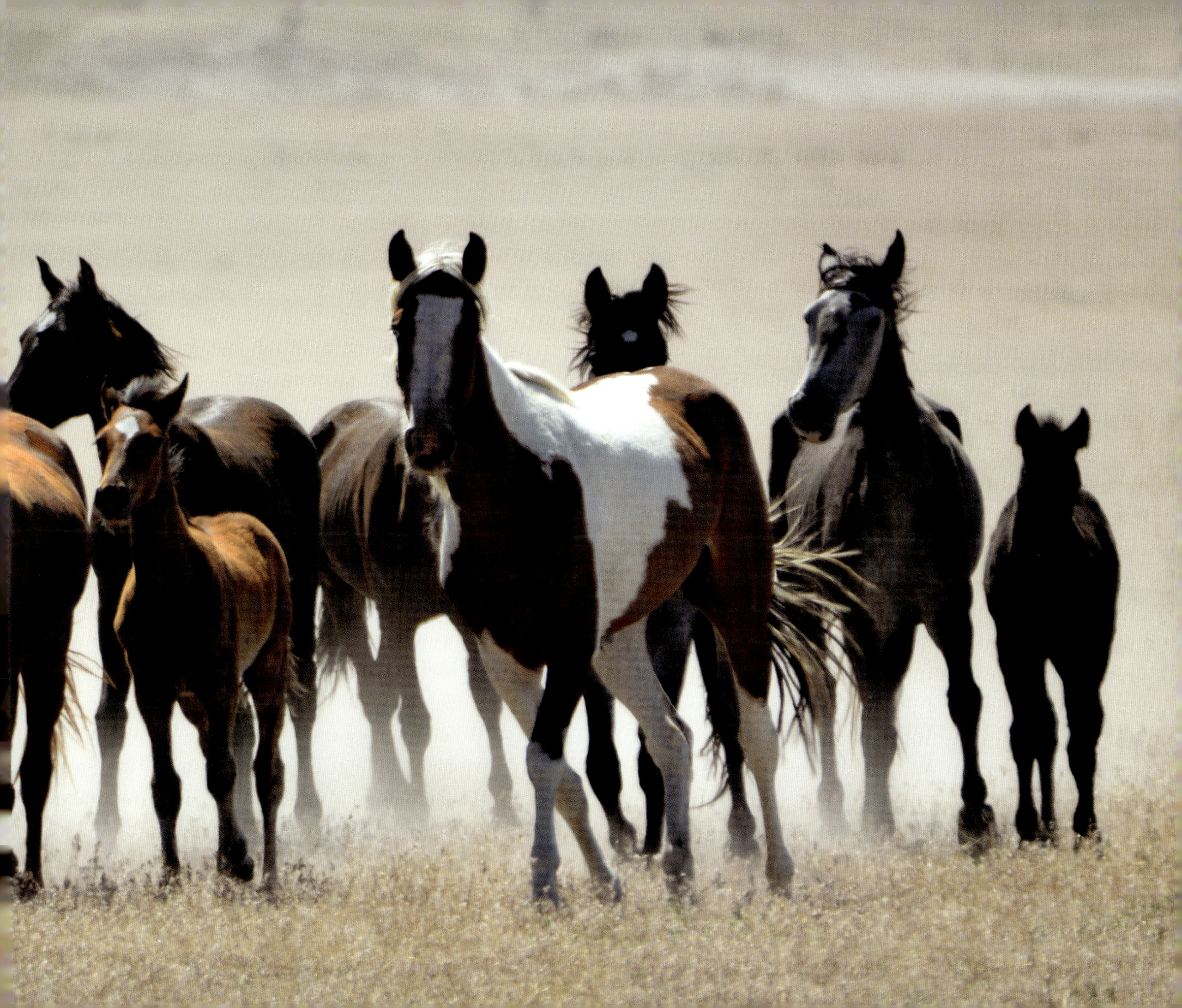

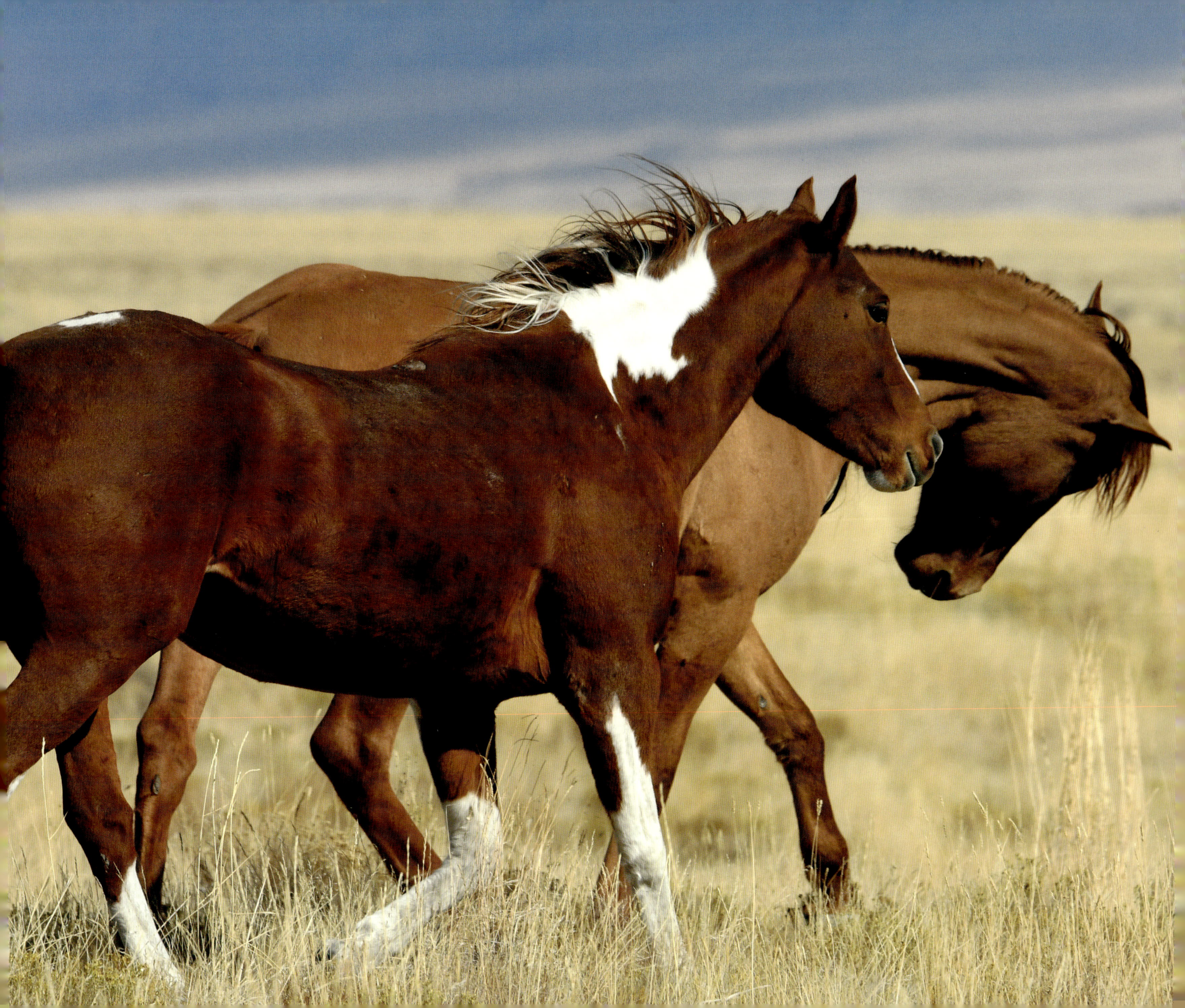

PREVIOUS PAGE: Cedar Mountain horses run out across the desert to investigate what's coming toward them.

OPPOSITE: Some pinto horses only have a few splashes of white on their coat; a leg marking of white that extends more than halfway up their leg is appropriately called a stocking.

RIGHT: Some wild horses of the West have a more refined and delicate look, not typical of mustangs. Taking into consideration the horses that were turned out years ago on the Cedar Mountain range, this mare probably has some thoroughbred blood in her DNA.

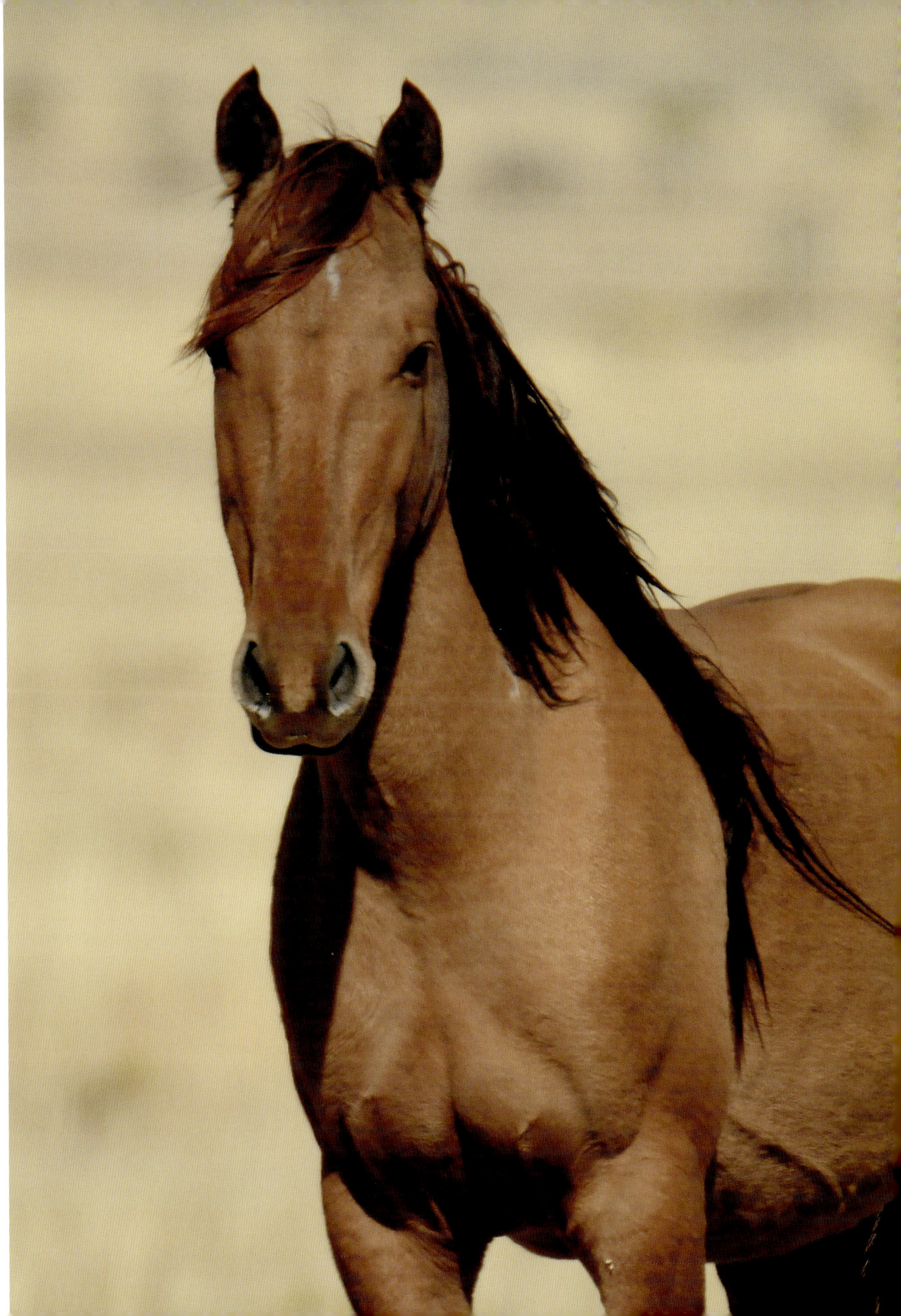

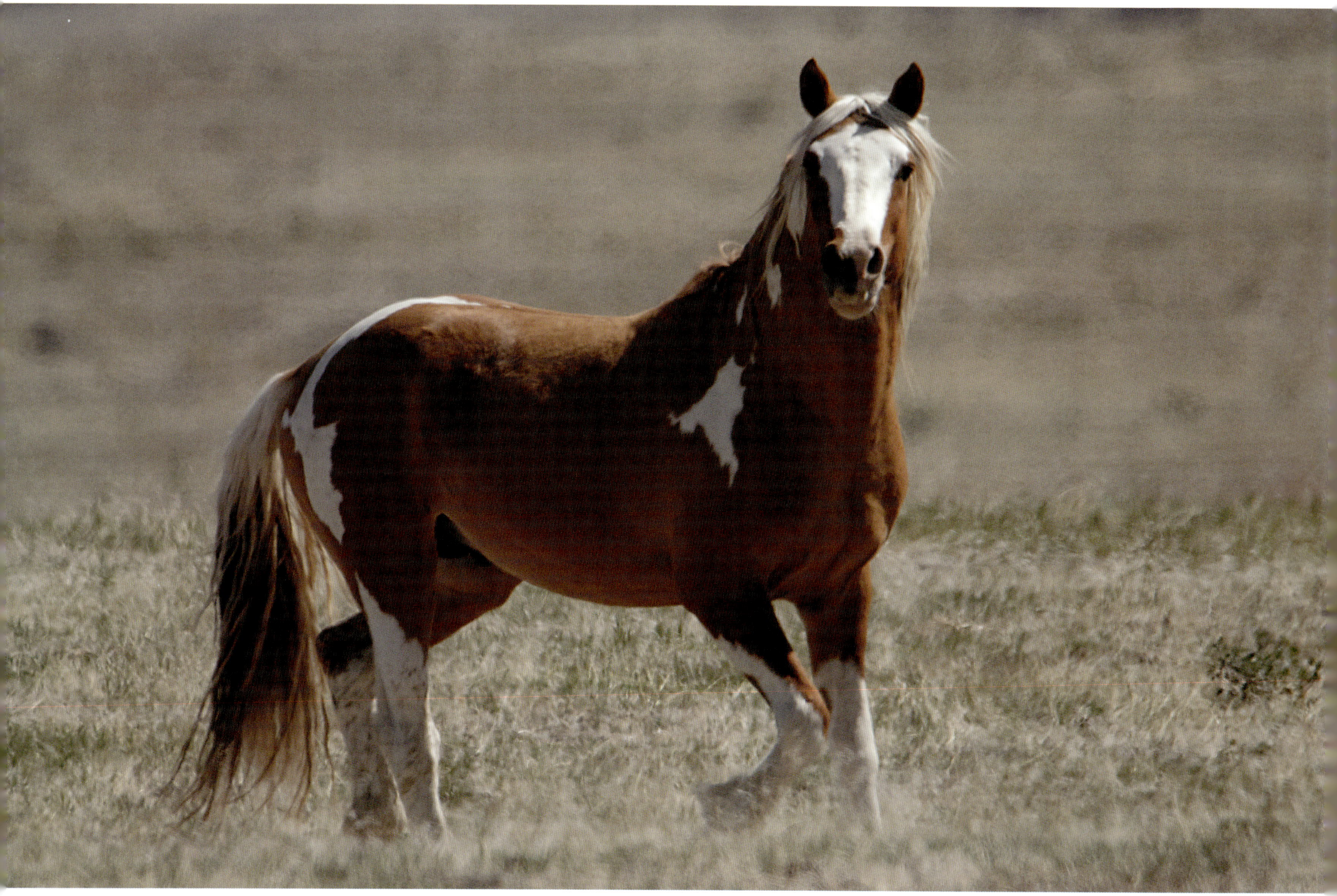

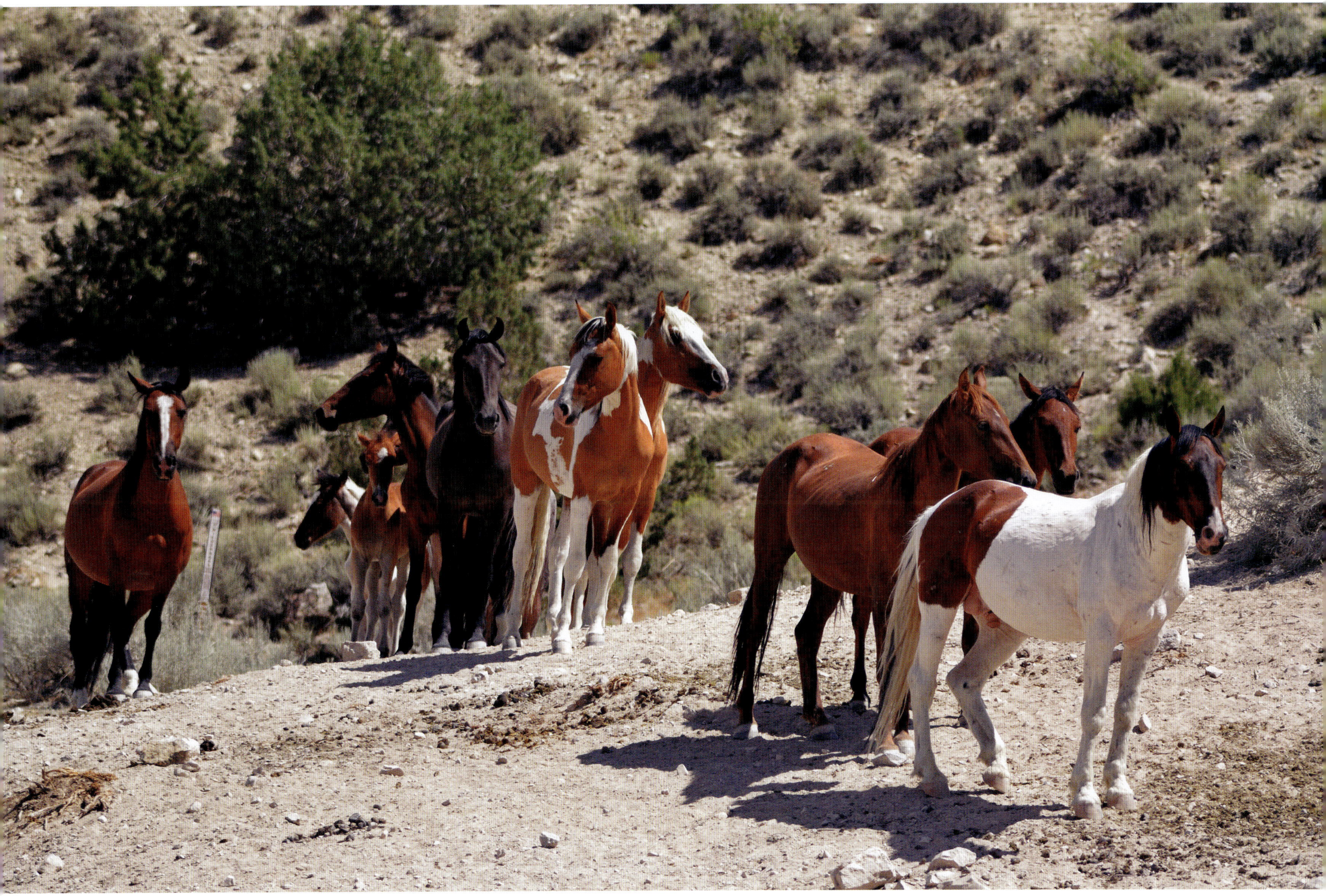

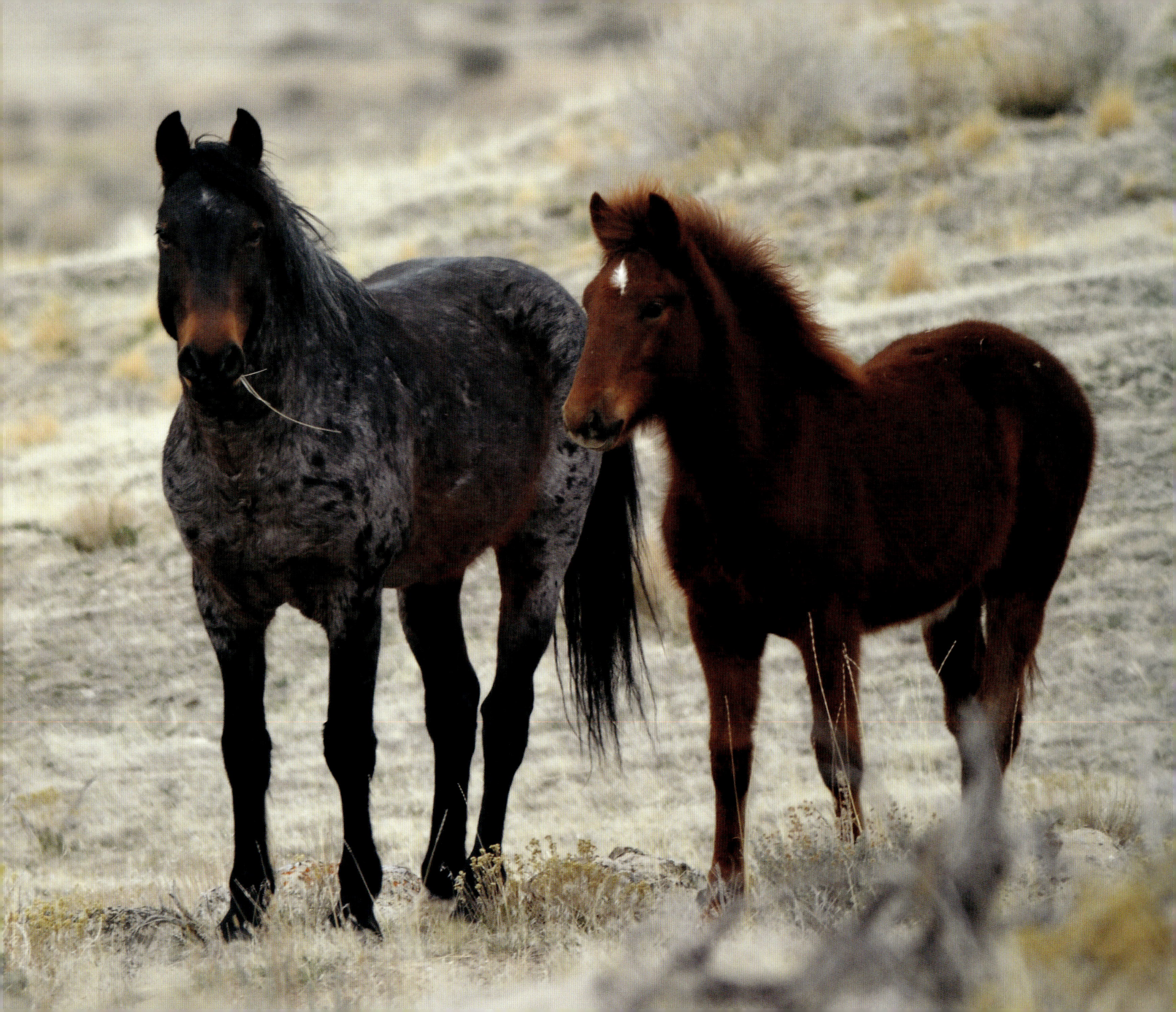

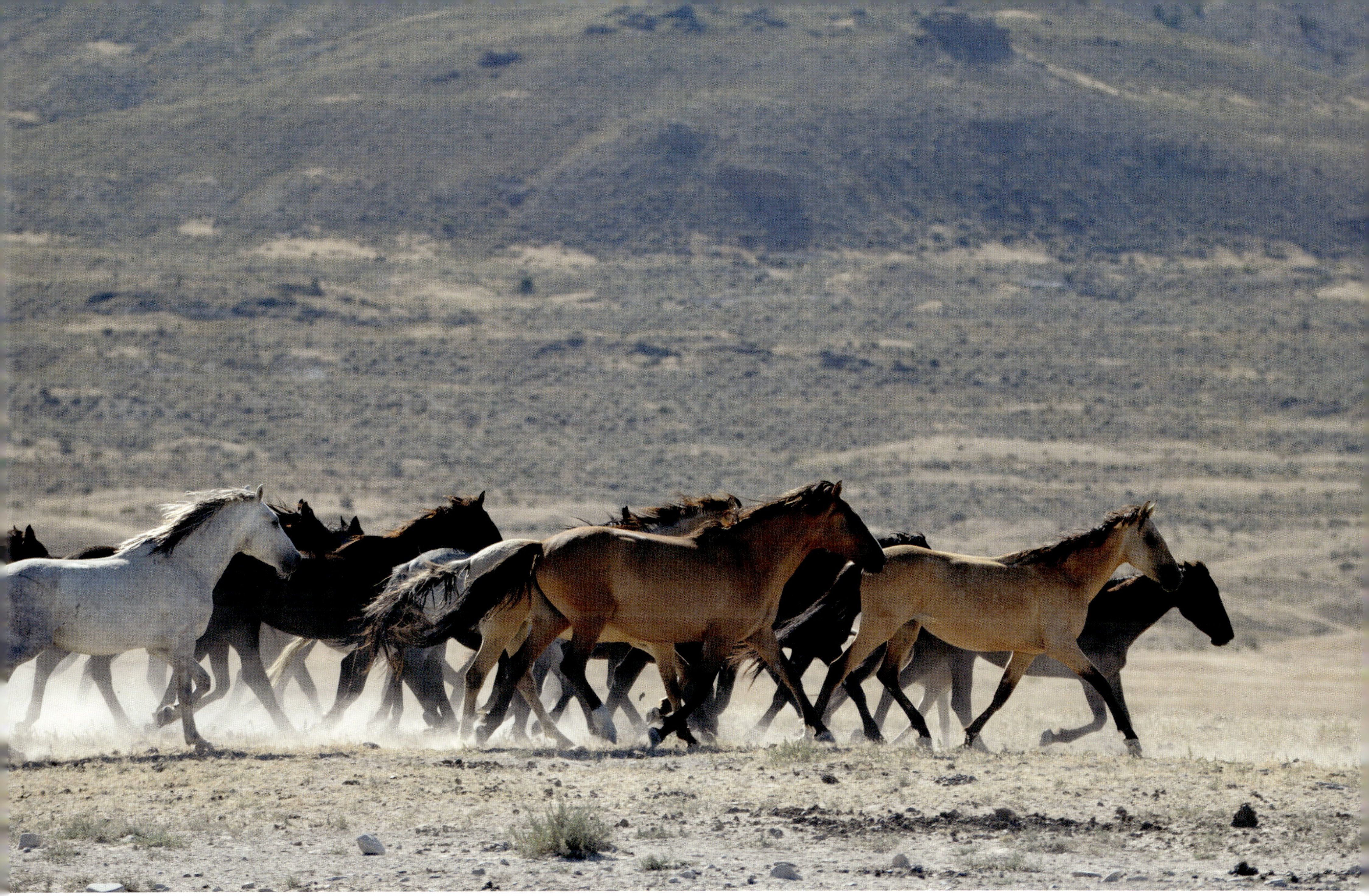

Previous page left: The unique coat pattern of this Cedar Mountain stallion is what makes the adoption of these horses popular.

Previous page right: A family band on high alert as a lone bachelor stallion approaches the waterhole.

Opposite: A blue roan stud and his colt. The blue roan coat has a base color of black. It is one of the rarest colors to breed for in the domestic horse. In the wild, there are several found in many of the herds.

Above: Typical Cedar Mountain horses—if they see you first, they'll run away, making them a challenge to photograph.

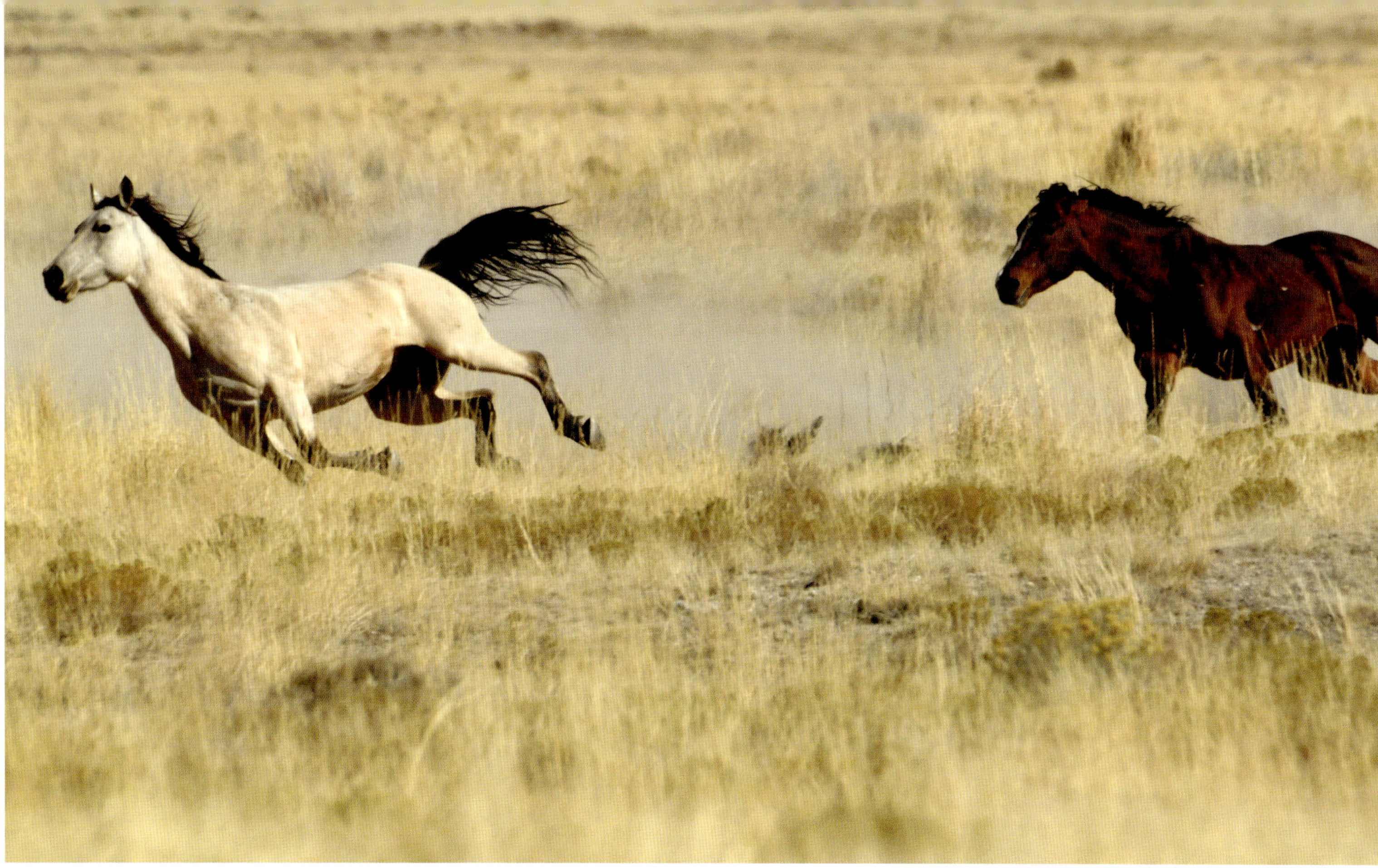

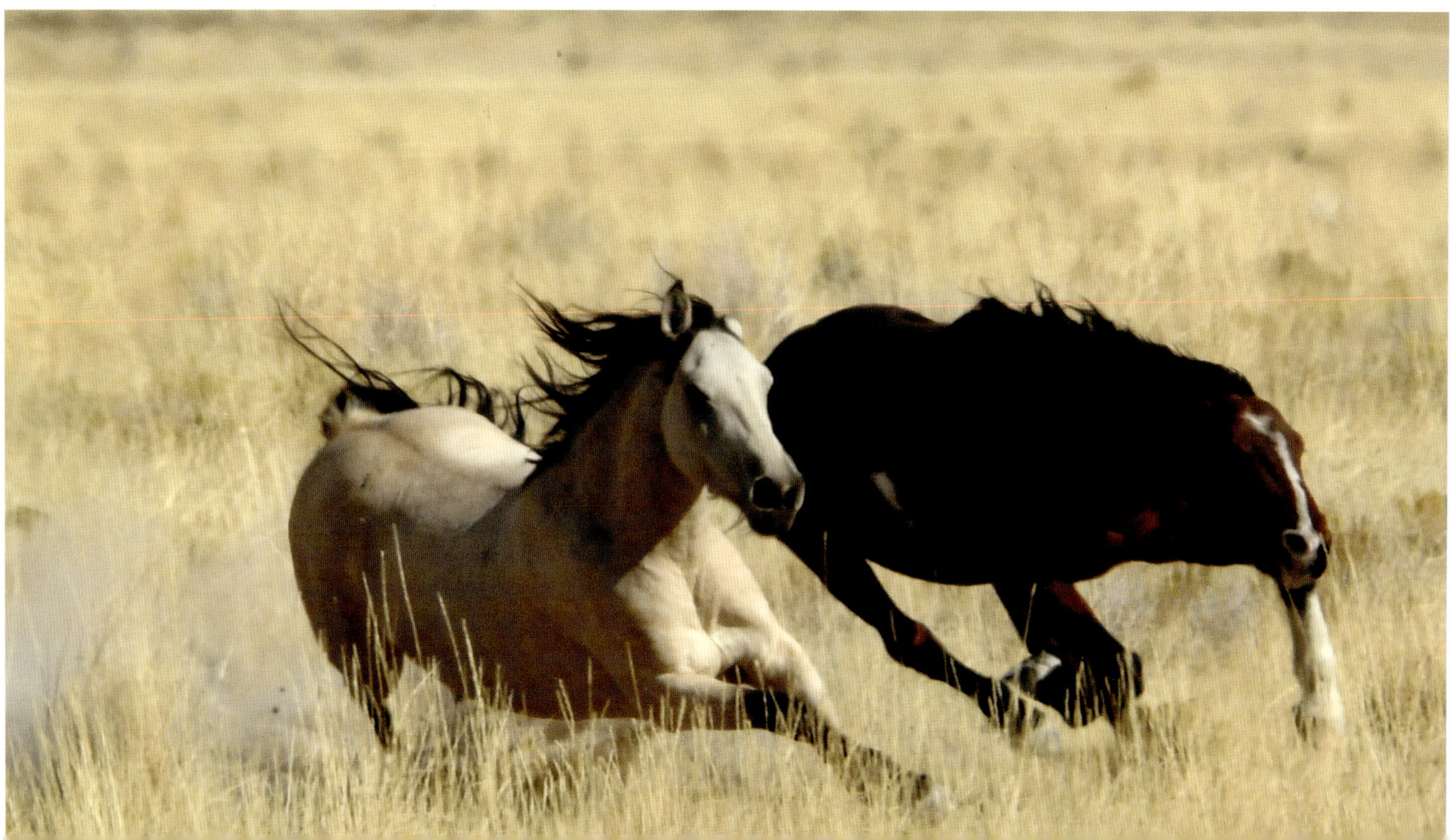

Clockwise, from left: This band stallion has to really work to get this mare back into his band. An aerial shot of a large band of horses running through the Utah desert. This feisty mare keeps the band stallion running after her for about ten minutes.

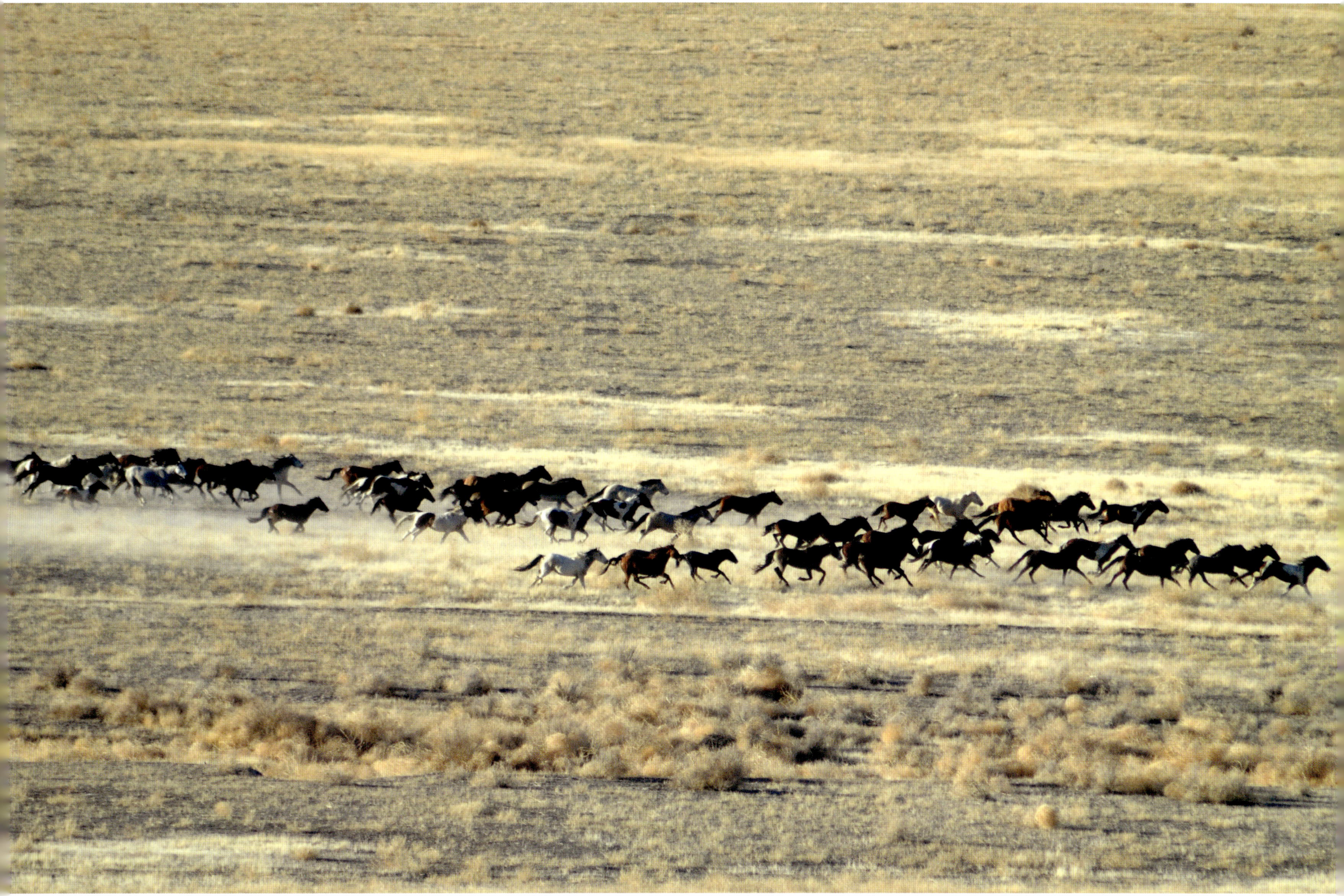

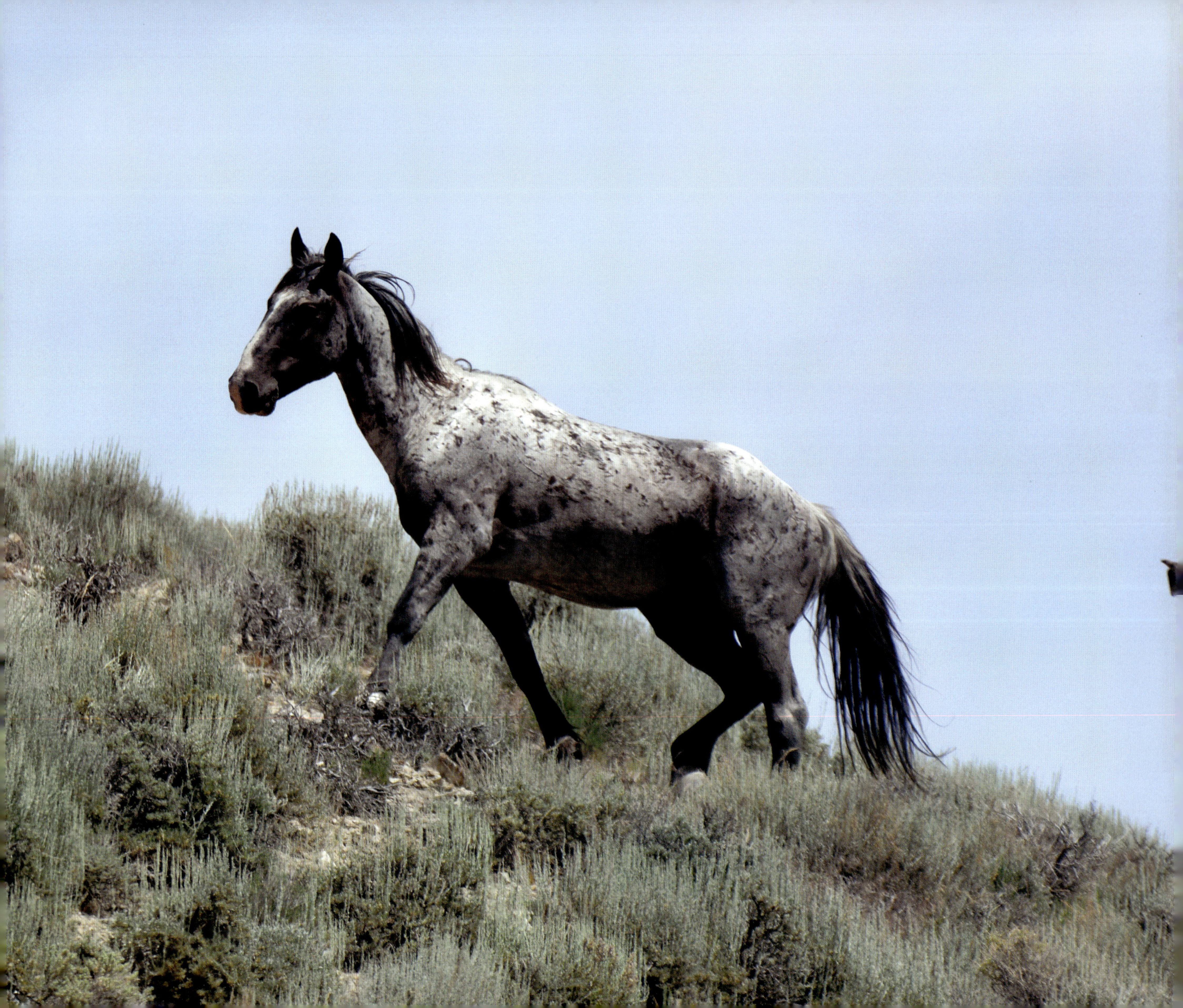

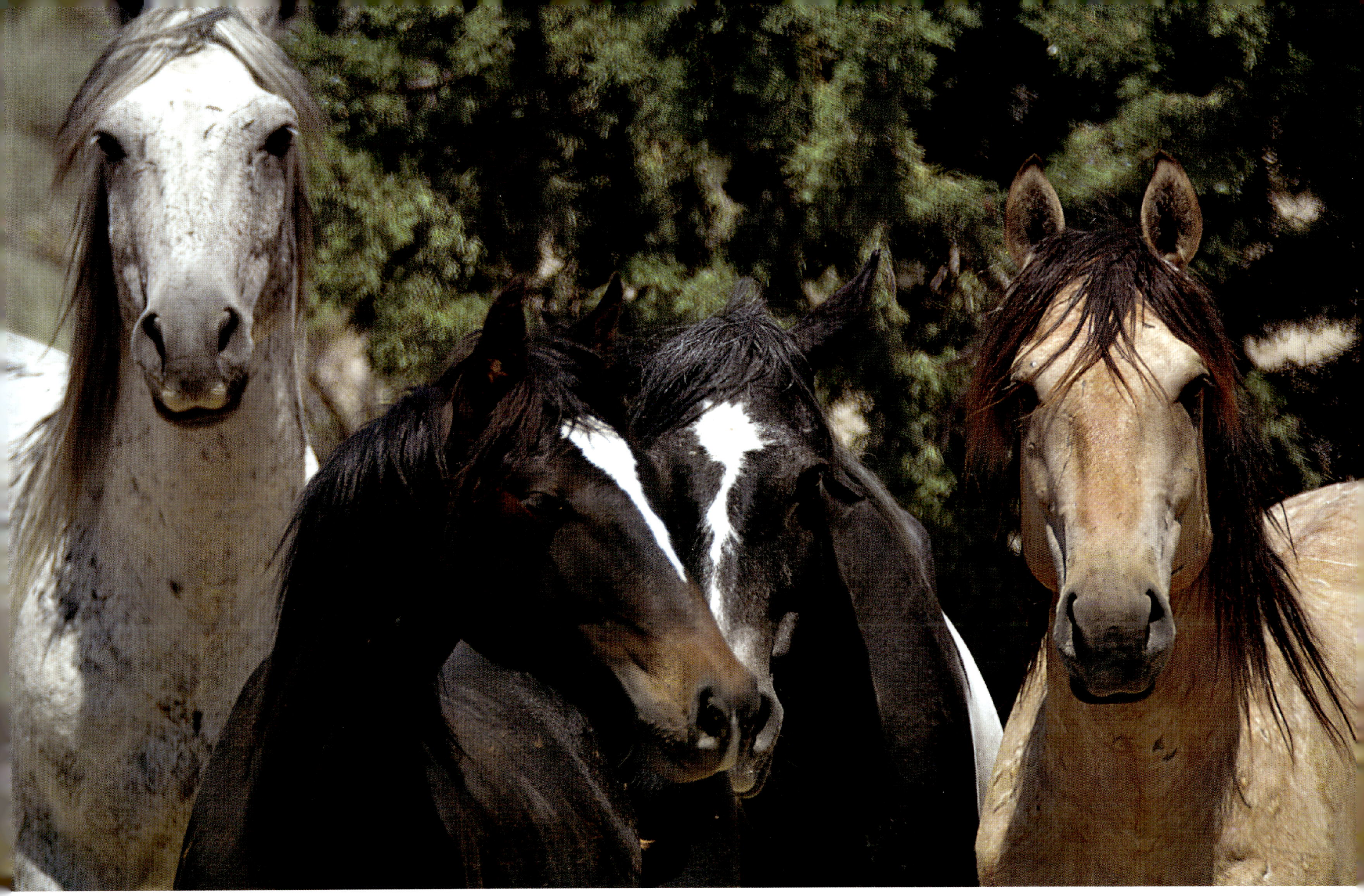

Opposite: Cedar Mountain horses are known for being strong mountain and trail horses, as most of their travel is in the mountains.

Above: A small but curious group of bachelor stallions at the Cedar Spring area.

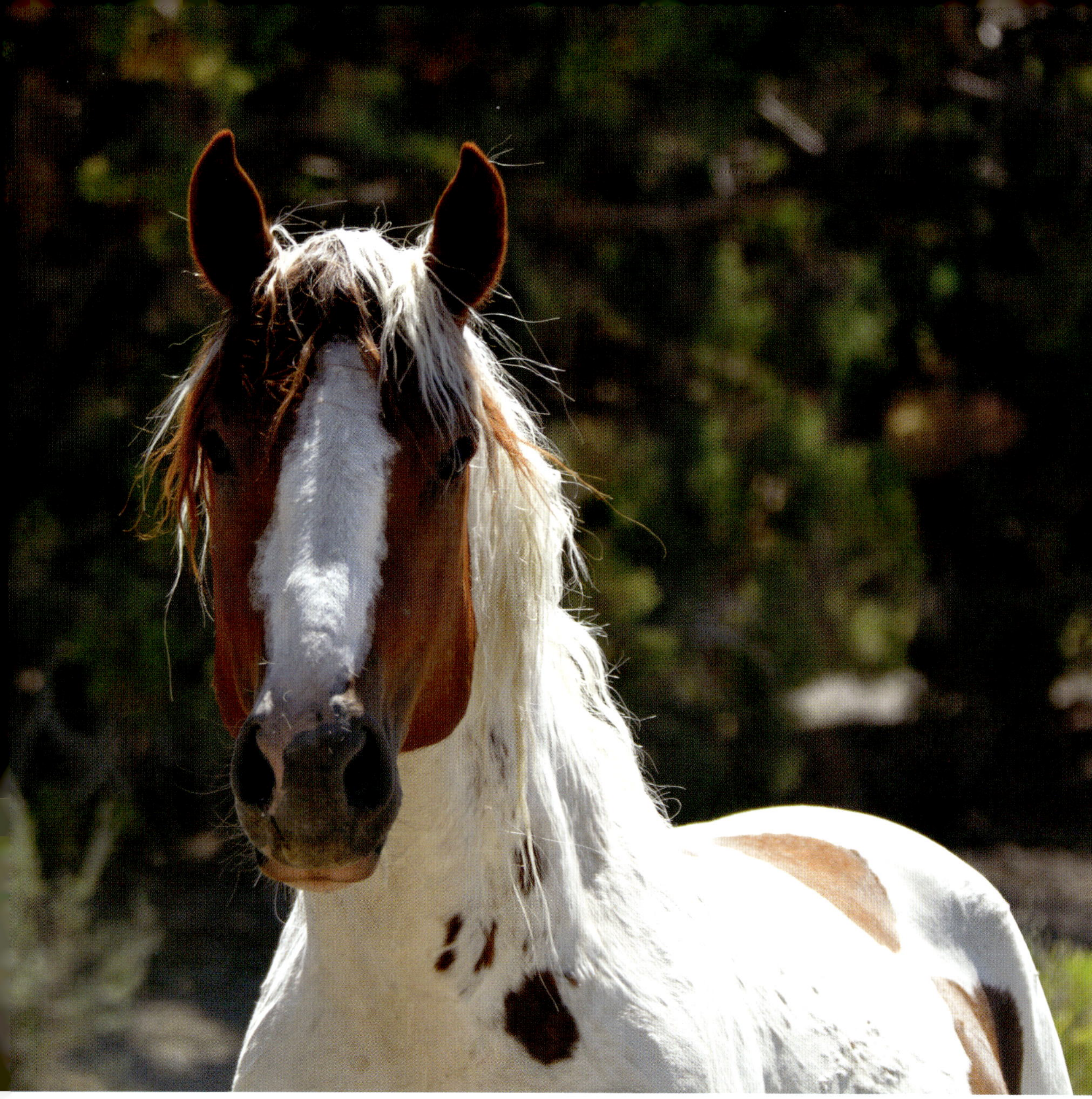

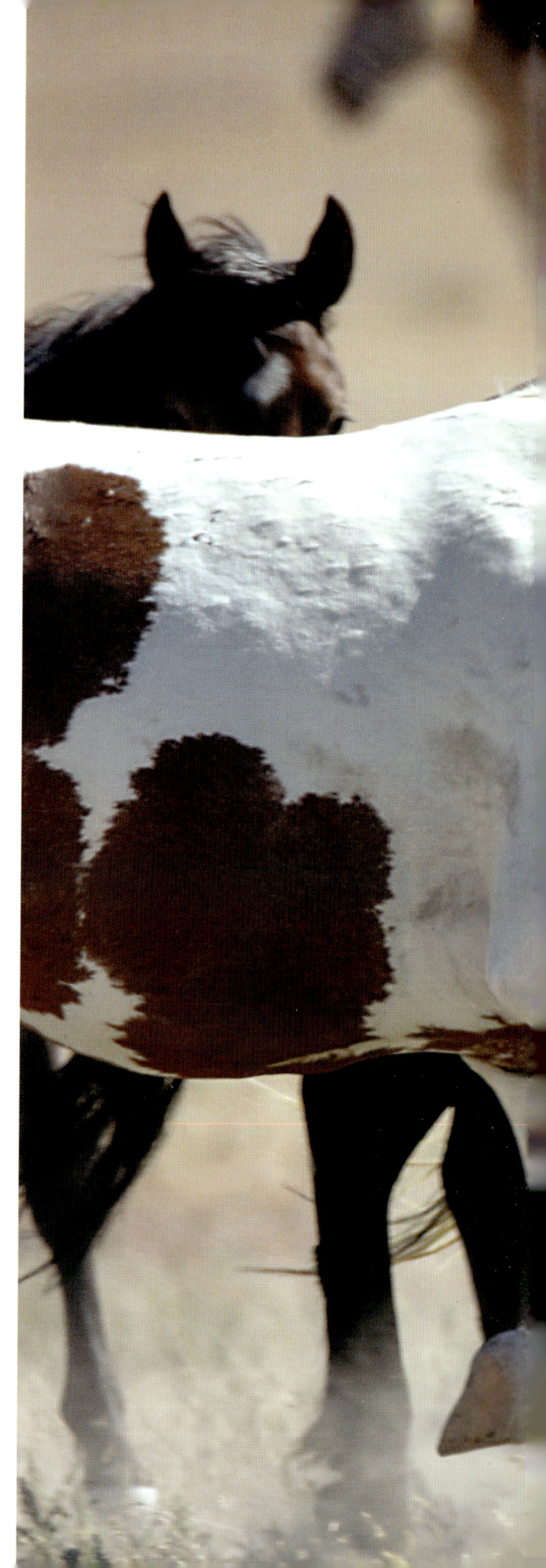

Above: This pinto bachelor stallion has a face marking called a blaze (a large solid patch of white); his coat color is mostly white with just a few spots.

Right: A pinto band stallion snakes a group of his mares back into the band.

Next page: A curious family band stands on alert.

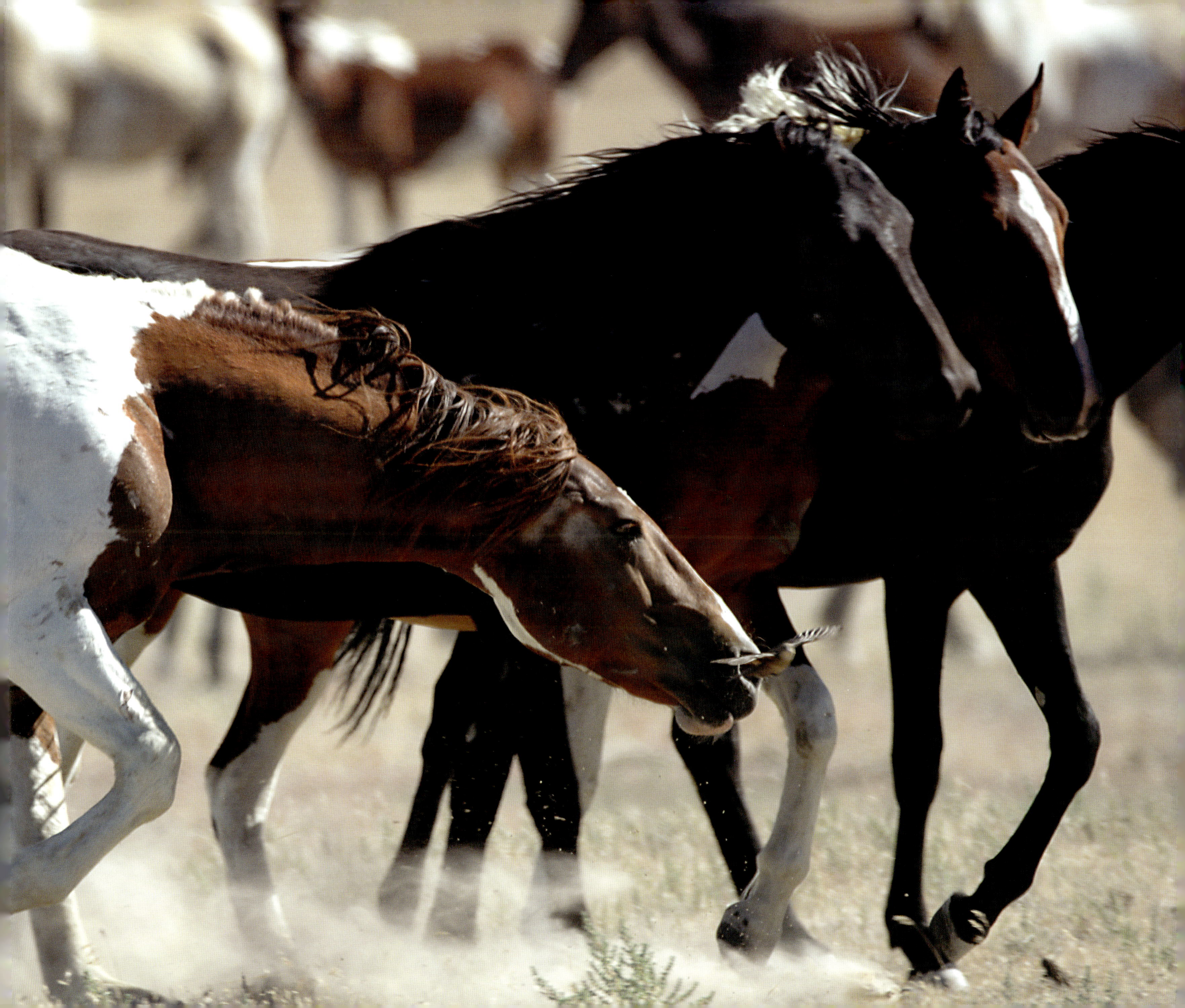

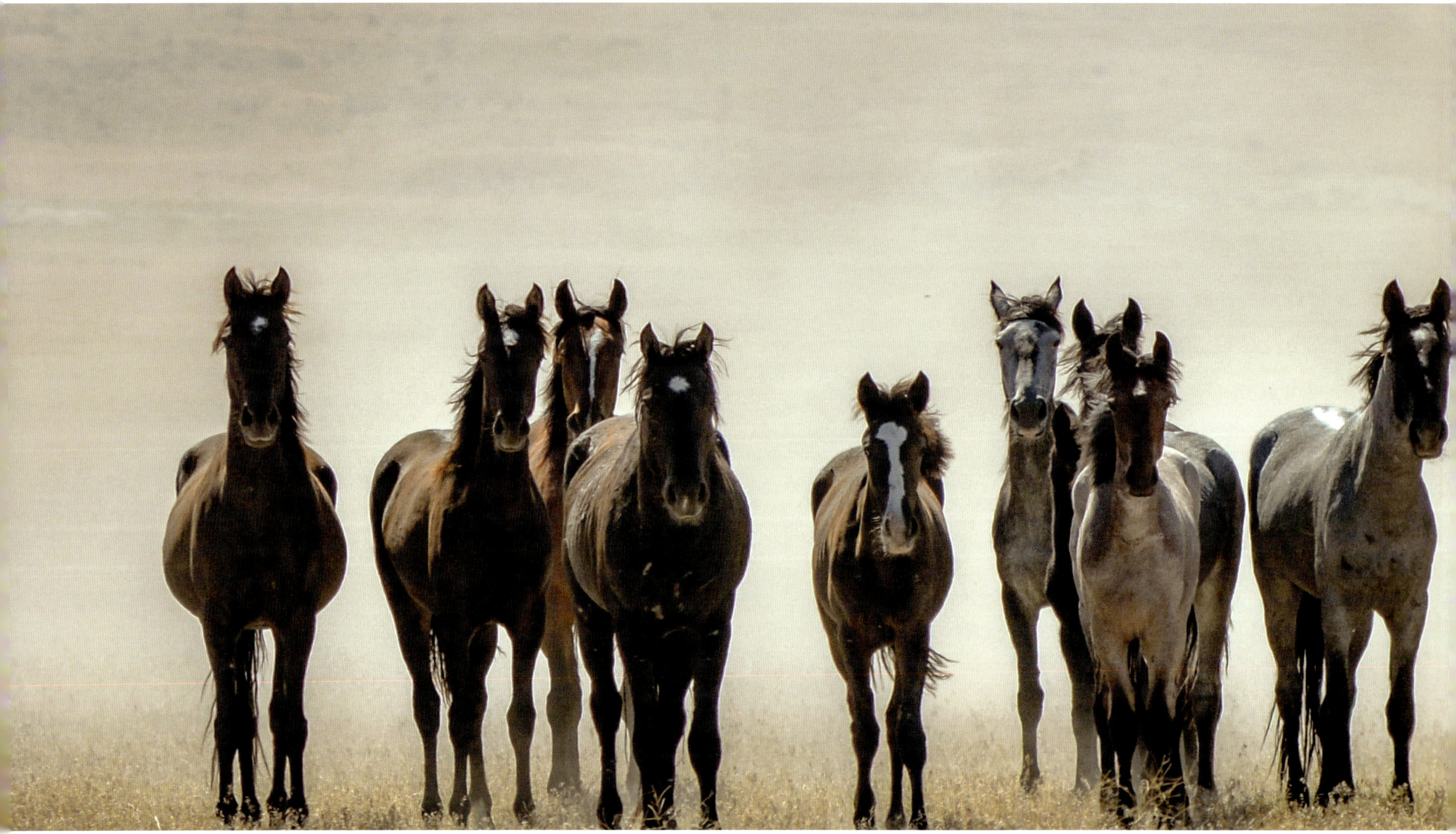

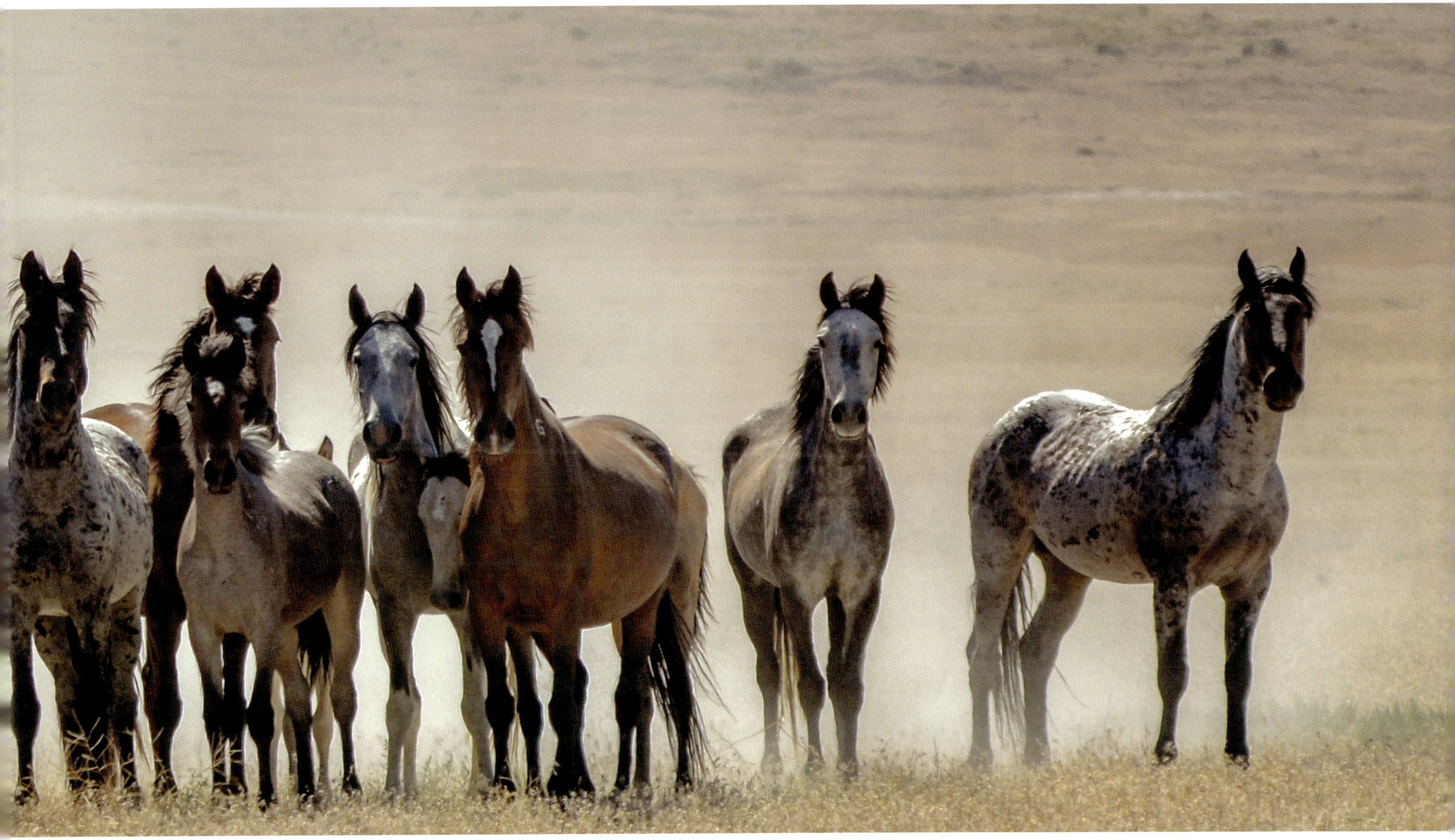

ACKNOWLEDGMENTS

I would like to thank and acknowledge the following people who helped me along my photographic journey of the wild horses: Carey McClellan, Tami Howell, Gus Warr, and Lisa Reid with the Bureau of Land Management's Wild Horse and Burro program. Without their willingness to share their knowledge of the wild horses and their habits I would not have been able to spend the past fourteen years photographing the horses and learning the stories they have to tell. I would also like to thank Cliff and Janet Tipton: I would not have been successful with my own mustangs without their sharing the skills it takes to gentle a wild horse. And thank you to Buzz Peterson who taught me much about service and giving back to our community, and the importance of what a wild horse can mean to someone who struggles.

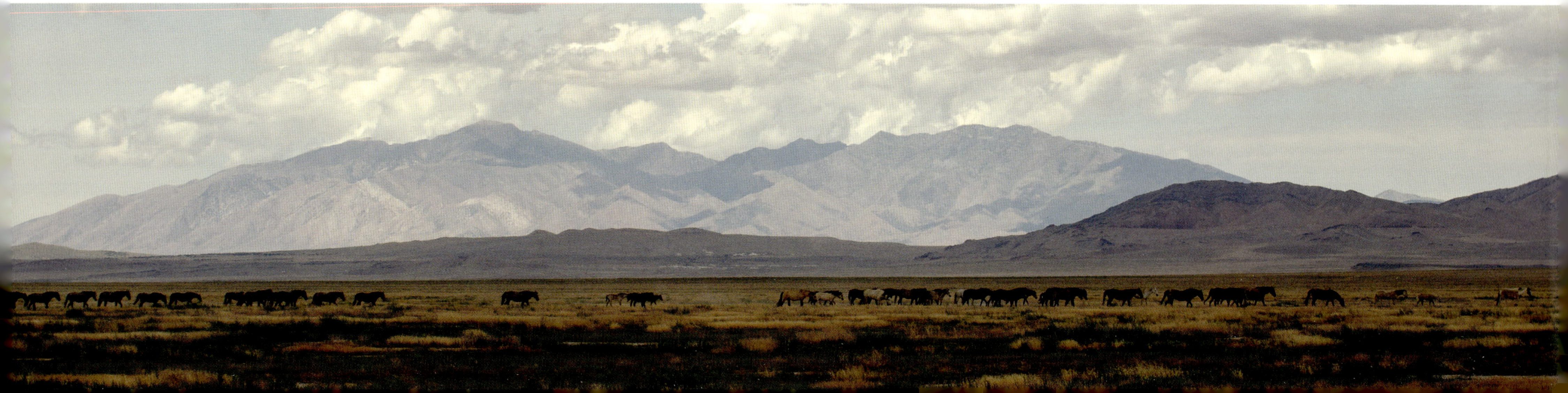

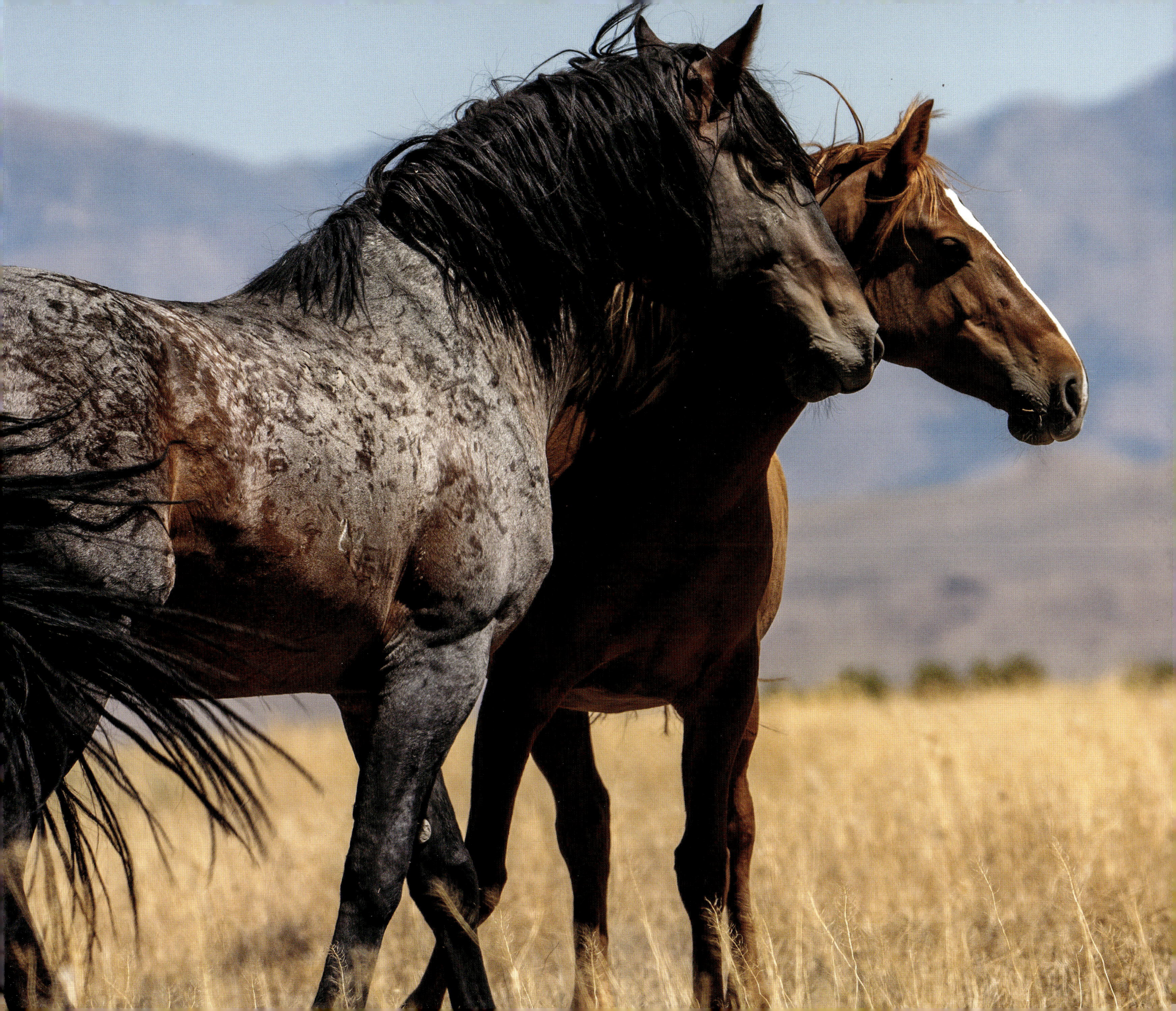

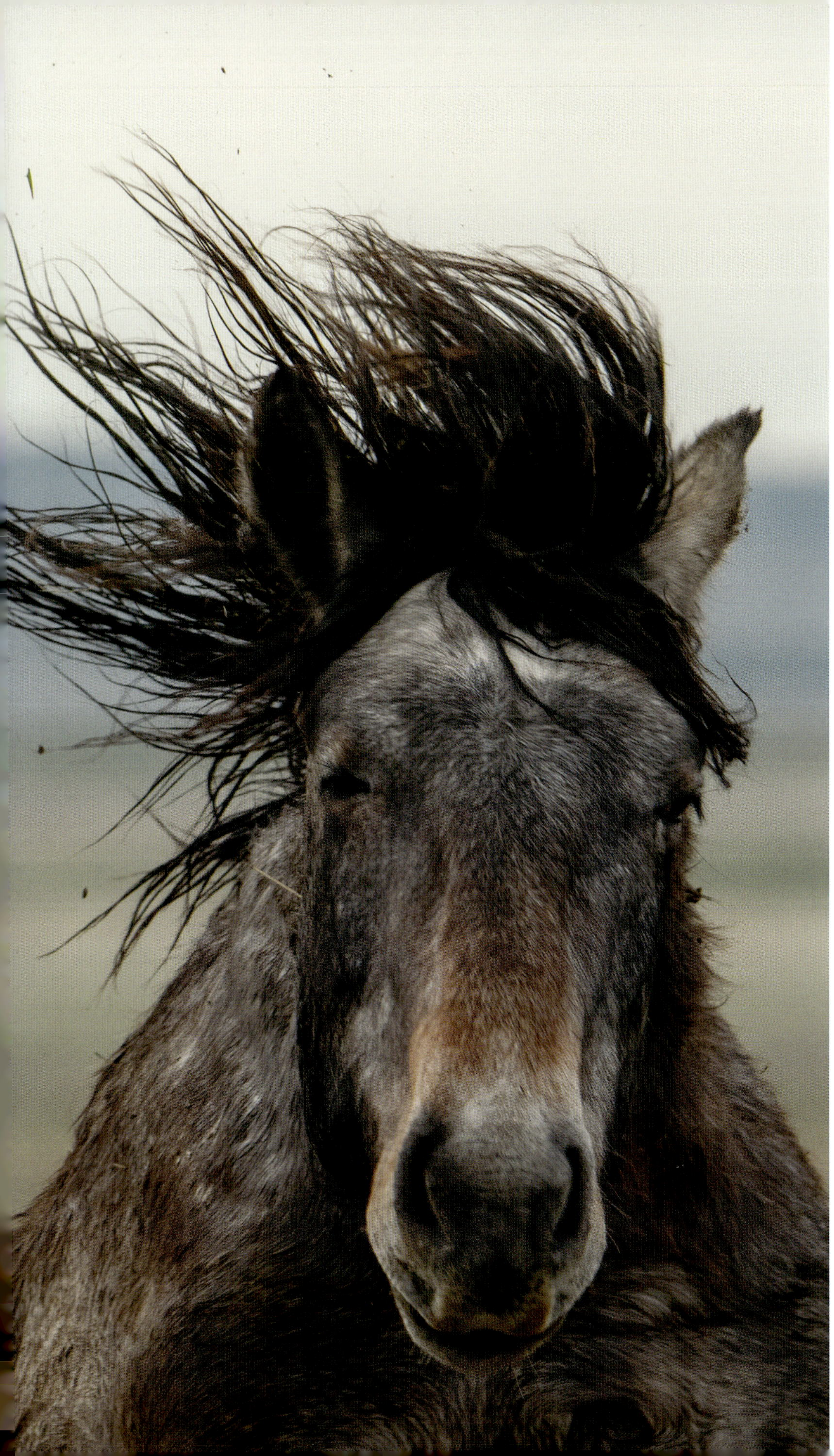

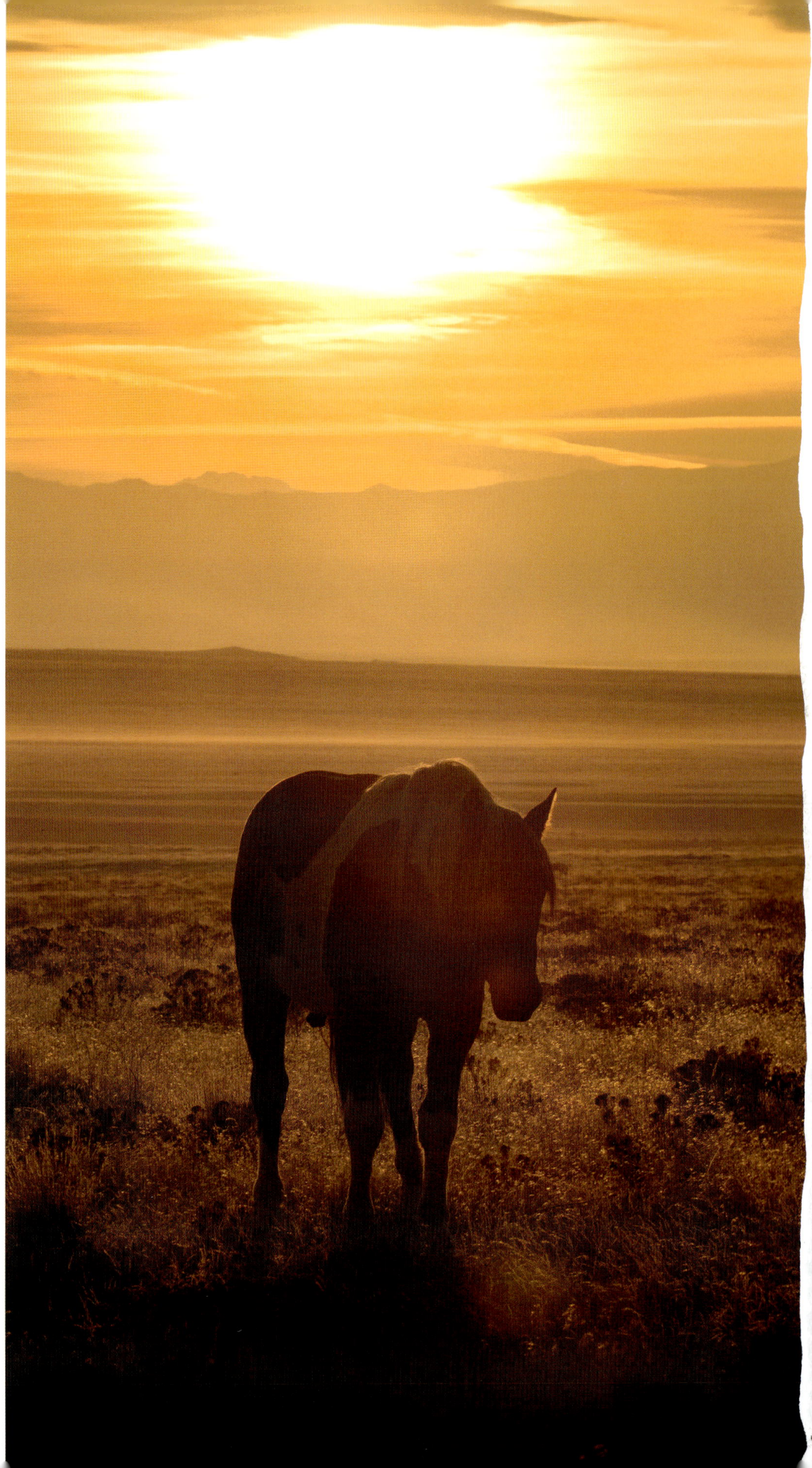

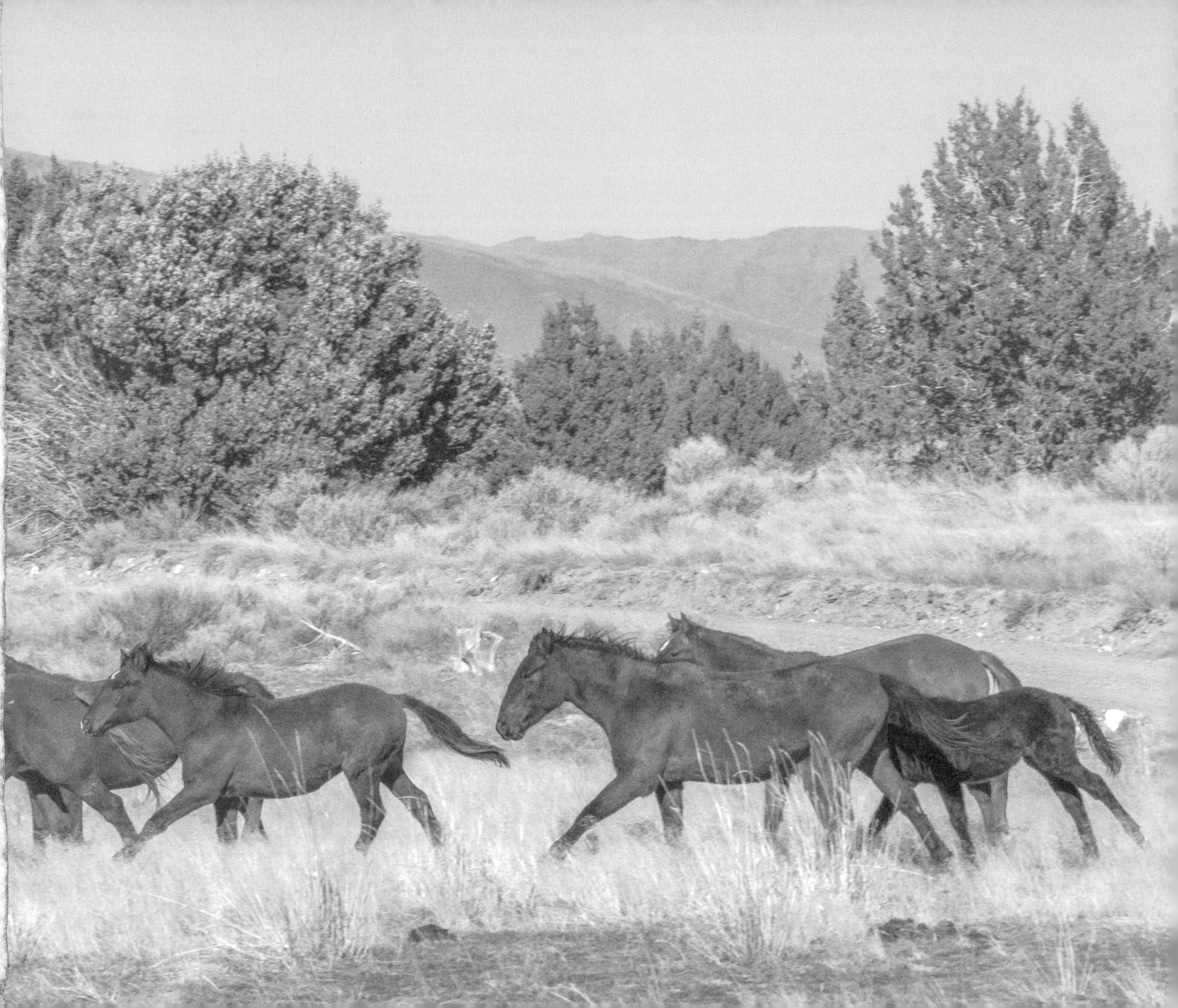

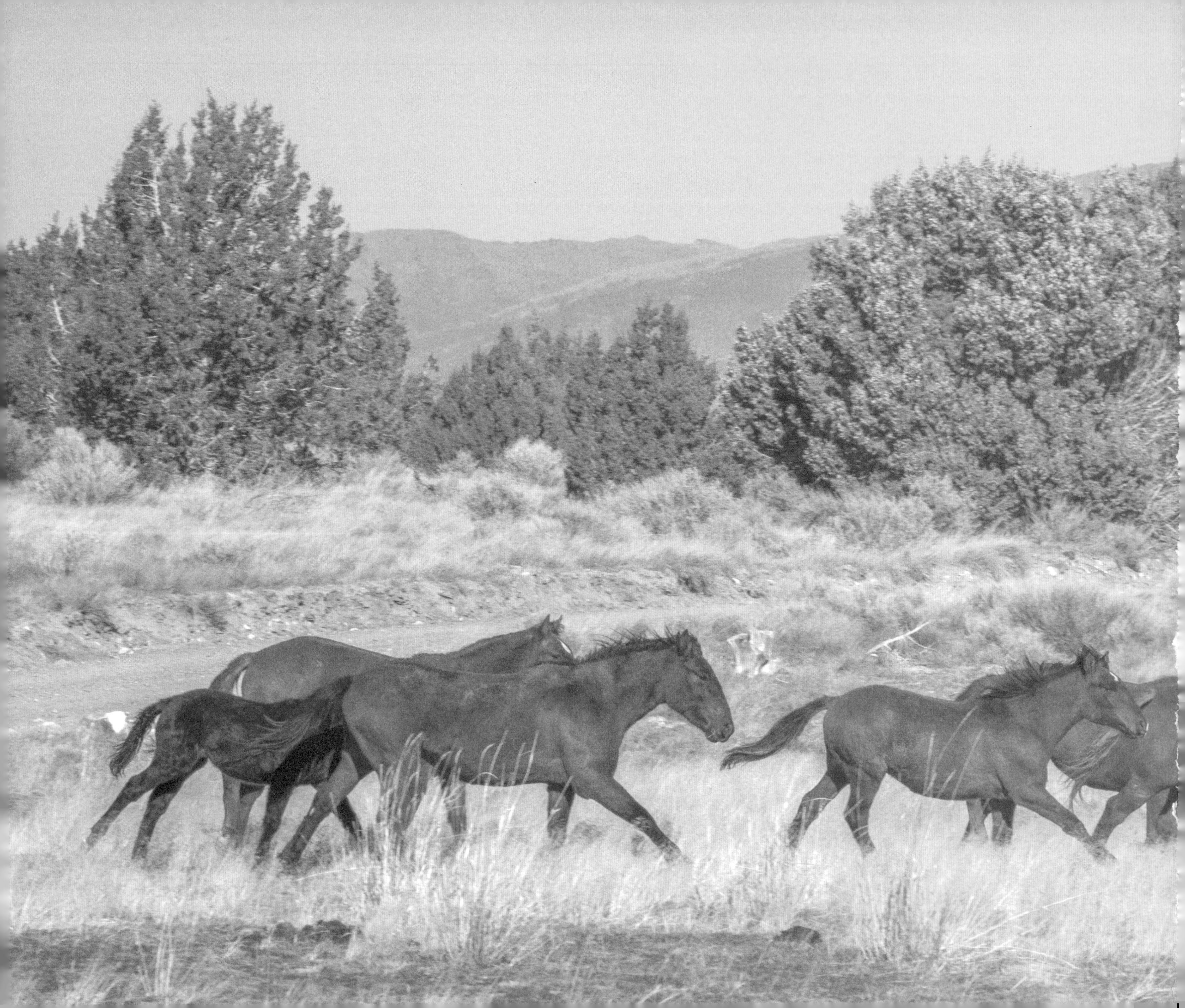